THE CAMBRIDGE COMPANI

QUR'ĀN

As the living scriptural heritage of ı
speaks with a powerful voice in our
dictions of sociological theorists that secularity would inexorably eradicate the social and political influences of religious belief, the effective force of faith-based rhetoric continues to expand. Nowhere is that more evident than with the religious tradition of Islam. Like its sibling faiths, Judaism and Christianity, Islam professes a belief in divine–human communication as expressed and encoded in written form and has canonised a core set of documents as the repository of this revelation. Just as other scriptural religions, Islam has also developed a centuries-long tradition of interpretation or exegesis of its holy writings. Generations of exegetes, shaped by their particular contexts and confessional orientations, have moulded meaning from the words of the Qur'ān, tying traditional understandings to the ever-evolving task of reinterpretation.

Nevertheless, efforts to introduce the Qur'ān and its intellectual heritage to English-speaking audiences have been hampered by the lack of accessible and available resources. Scholarship in qur'ānic studies, a field that has flourished in the last few decades, remains sequestered in specialised monographs and journals. *The Cambridge Companion to the Qur'ān* promises to remedy that situation. Jane McAuliffe, a distinguished scholar of the Islamic tradition, has brought together some of the best and most knowledgeable scholars in the field to explain the complexities of this world-changing text. The *Companion* comprises fourteen chapters, each devoted to a single topic of central importance to the study of the Qur'ān. While rich in historical, linguistic and literary detail, chapters also reflect the influence of other disciplines as the field of qur'ānic studies increasingly draws on the work of anthropologists, sociologists, philosophers, art historians and cultural critics. For both the university student and the general reader, *The Cambridge Companion to the Qur'ān* provides a clear, compact and comprehensive entrée to a text that for centuries has guided and shaped the lives of millions.

JANE DAMMEN MCAULIFFE is Professor in the Departments of History and Arabic and Dean of Arts and Sciences at Georgetown University. Her numerous publications have focused primarily on the Qur'ān, on early Islamic history and on the multiple relations between Islam and Christianity. Her books include *Qur'ānic Christians: An analysis of classical and modern exegesis* (1991), *'Abbāsid authority affirmed* (1995) and *With reverence for the Word: Medieval scriptural exegesis in Judaism, Christianity and Islam* (2003), and she has edited the five-volume *Encyclopaedia of the Qur'ān* (2001–6).

CAMBRIDGE COMPANIONS TO RELIGION

A series of companions to major topics and key figures in theology and religious studies. Each volume contains specially commissioned chapters by international scholars which provide an accessible and stimulating introduction to the subject for new readers and non-specialists.

Other titles in the series

THE CAMBRIDGE COMPANION TO CHRISTIAN DOCTRINE
edited by Colin Gunton (1997)

THE CAMBRIDGE COMPANION TO BIBLICAL INTERPRETATION
edited by John Barton (1998)

THE CAMBRIDGE COMPANION TO DIETRICH BONHOEFFER
edited by John de Gruchy (1999)

THE CAMBRIDGE COMPANION TO LIBERATION THEOLOGY
edited by Chris Rowland (1999)

THE CAMBRIDGE COMPANION TO KARL BARTH
edited by John Webster (2000)

THE CAMBRIDGE COMPANION TO CHRISTIAN ETHICS
edited by Robin Gill (2001)

THE CAMBRIDGE COMPANION TO JESUS
edited by Markus Bockmuehl (2001)

THE CAMBRIDGE COMPANION TO FEMINIST THEOLOGY
edited by Susan Frank Parsons (2002)

THE CAMBRIDGE COMPANION TO MARTIN LUTHER
edited by Donald K. McKim (2003)

THE CAMBRIDGE COMPANION TO ST PAUL
edited by James D. G. Dunn (2003)

THE CAMBRIDGE COMPANION TO POSTMODERN THEOLOGY
edited by Kevin J. Vanhoozer (2003)

THE CAMBRIDGE COMPANION TO MEDIEVAL JEWISH PHILOSOPHY
edited by Daniel H. Frank and Oliver Leaman (2003)

THE CAMBRIDGE COMPANION TO JOHN CALVIN
edited by Donald K. McKim (2004)

THE CAMBRIDGE COMPANION TO URS VON BALTHASAR
edited by Edward T. Oakes, SJ and David Moss (2004)

THE CAMBRIDGE COMPANION TO REFORMATION THEOLOGY
edited by David Bagchi and David Steinmetz (2004)

THE CAMBRIDGE COMPANION TO AMERICAN JUDAISM
edited by Dana Evan Kaplan (2005)

THE CAMBRIDGE COMPANION TO KARL RAHNER
edited by Declan Marmion and Mary E. Hines (2005)

THE CAMBRIDGE COMPANION TO FRIEDRICH SCHLEIERMACHER
edited by Jacqueline Mariña (2005)

THE CAMBRIDGE COMPANION TO THE GOSPELS
edited by Stephen C. Barton (2006)

Forthcoming

THE CAMBRIDGE COMPANION TO ISLAMIC THEOLOGY
edited by Tim Winter

THE CAMBRIDGE COMPANION TO EVANGELICAL THEOLOGY
edited by Timothy Larsen and Daniel J. Treier

THE CAMBRIDGE COMPANION TO THE

QUR'ĀN

Edited by Jane Dammen McAuliffe
Georgetown University

CAMBRIDGE
UNIVERSITY PRESS

CAMBRIDGE UNIVERSITY PRESS
Cambridge, New York, Melbourne, Madrid, Cape Town, Singapore, São Paulo

Cambridge University Press
The Edinburgh Building, Cambridge CB2 2RU, UK

Published in the United States of America by Cambridge University Press, New York

www.cambridge.org
Information on this title: www.cambridge.org/9780521539340

First published 2006

Printed in the United Kingdom at the University Press, Cambridge

A catalogue record for this publication is available from the British Library

ISBN-13 978-0-521-83160-4 hardback
ISBN-10 0-521-83160-1 hardback

ISBN-13 978-0-521-53934-0 paperback
ISBN-10 0-521-53934-x paperback

This book is dedicated
to
Sister Mary Roy McDonald
12 October 1917–27 March 2006
and
George Michael Wickens
7 August 1918–26 January 2006

Contents

Figures

Notes on contributors

ASMA BARLAS is Professor of Politics at Ithaca College, New York, where she is the founding director of the Center for the Study of Culture, Race and Ethnicity. She has also been on the board of directors for the Center for the Study of Islam and Democracy in Washington, DC. Her recent publications include *'Believing women' in Islam: Unreading patriarchal interpretations of the Qur'ān* (2002) and *Islam, Muslims and the US: Essays in religion and politics* (2004).

SHEILA BLAIR shares the Norma Jean Calderwood University Professorship of Islamic and Asian Art at Boston College. Her publications include *A compendium of chronicles: Rashid al-Din's illustrated History of the world* (1995) and *Islamic inscriptions* (1998), as well as numerous works co-authored with Jonathan Bloom, such as *The art and architecture of Islam: 1250–1800* (1994) and *Islamic arts* (1997). Her tenth book, *Islamic calligraphy*, is due out in 2006.

JONATHAN BLOOM is joint Norma Jean Calderwood Professor of Islamic and Asian Art at Boston College. His publications include *Minaret: Symbol of Islam* (1989), *Paper before print: The history and impact of paper in the Islamic world* (2001) and *Early Islamic art and architecture* (2002), as well as many works on Islamic art and architecture, several co-authored with Sheila Blair, the most recent of which is *Islam: A thousand years of faith and power* (2000, repr. 2001 and 2002).

FRED M. DONNER is Professor of Near Eastern History in the Department of Near Eastern Languages and Civilizations and the Oriental Institute at the University of Chicago and editor of *al-Uṣūr al-Wusṭa, the Bulletin of Middle East Medievalists.* His publications on the early period of Islamic history include *The early Islamic conquests* (1981), *The conquest of Arabia* (1993), a volume in the *History of al-Ṭabarī* project, and his more recent *Narratives of Islamic origins: The beginnings of Islamic historical writing* (1998), as well as numerous articles.

CLAUDE GILLIOT is Professor in Arabic and Islamic Studies at the University of Aix-en-Provence, and is on the editorial board of *Arabica: Journal of Arabic and Islamic Studies/Revue d'études arabes et islamiques.* His publications include *Exégèse, langue et théologie en islam: L'exégèse coranique de Tabari* (1990) and numerous articles, especially on noteworthy figures from the classical exegetical tradition on the Qur'ān.

WILLIAM A. GRAHAM is Murray A. Albertson Professor of Middle Eastern Studies in the Faculty of Arts and Sciences and John Lord O'Brian Professor and Dean of the Faculty of Divinity at Harvard University. A specialist in the early religious history of Islam, he is author of *Divine word and prophetic word in early Islam* (1977) and his *Beyond the written word: Oral aspects of scripture in the history of religion* (1986) has won critical acclaim.

NAVID KERMANI is presently working as a freelance writer in Cologne, Germany. As a long-term fellow at the Institute for Advanced Study in Berlin (Wissenschaftskolleg), he collaborated on numerous projects relating to the comparative study of religions. His interest in performative aesthetics is seen in his *Gott ist schön: Das ästhetische Erleben des Koran* (2000). His latest book, *Der Schrecken Gottes: Attar, Hiob und die metaphysische Revolte* (2005), deals with the Job-motif in the Middle East and Europe. For his literary and academic work, he has received several prizes, the latest being the 'Europe-Prize' 2004 of the Heinz Schwarzkopf-Foundation.

ALEXANDER KNYSH is Professor of Islamic Studies at the University of Michigan at Ann Arbor. He has published extensively (in English, Russian and Arabic) on local manifestations of Islam, from manuscript traditions to saint cults. Recent English publications include *Ibn al-Arabi in the later Islamic tradition: The making of a polemical image in medieval Islam* (1998) and *Islamic mysticism: A short history* (2000).

FRED LEEMHUIS is Professor of Islamic Studies at the Department of Theology and Religious Studies at the University of Gröningen, The Netherlands. His interests encompass both textual-linguistic issues and modern socio-religious trends in the Arab world. Among his publications are *The D and H stems in koranic Arabic: A comparative study of the function and meaning of the faʿʿala and ʾafʿala forms in koranic usage* (1977), a Dutch translation of the Qur'ān and field reports on his work on the Qur'ān manuscripts found in recent excavations at the Dakhla Oasis in Egypt.

JANE DAMMEN McAULIFFE is Professor in the Departments of Arabic and of History and Dean of Arts and Sciences at Georgetown University in Washington, DC. In addition to many articles and book chapters, she has published *Qurʾānic Christians: An analysis of classical and modern exegesis* (1991), *ʿAbbāsid authority affirmed* (1995) and *With reverence for the word: Medieval scriptural exegesis in Judaism, Christianity and Islam* (2003). More recently, she has been the general editor of Brill's five-volume *Encyclopaedia of the Qurʾān.*

DANIEL A. MADIGAN is Professor of Islamic Studies and Muslim–Christian Relations at the Pontifical Gregorian University in Rome, where he is also Director of the Institute for the Study of Religions and Cultures. Specialising in the Abrahamic scriptural heritage, he has published a volume entitled *The Qurʾān's self-image: Writing and authority in Islam's scripture* (2001).

HARALD MOTZKI is Professor of Islamic Studies at the University of Nijmegen, The Netherlands. His extensive publications on Islamic social, legal and religious history include *Die Anfänge der islamischen Jurisprudenz: Ihre Entwicklung in*

Mekka bis zur Mitte des 2./8. Jahrhunderts (1991; Eng. trans. *The origins of Islamic jurisprudence: Meccan fiqh before the classical schools* (2002)), *The biography of Muhammad: The issue of the sources* (2000) and *Ḥadīth: Origins and developments* (2004).

ANGELIKA NEUWIRTH holds the Chair of Arabic Studies at the Freie Universität of Berlin, where she directs the Seminar für Semitistik und Arabistik. She has published extensively on the text of the Qur'ān, especially on its formal qualities and its source criticism, particularly as regards its liturgical uses. Her numerous publications on the Qur'ān – among which are both German and English articles and book chapters, such as 'Vom Rezitationstext über die Liturgie zum Kanon: Zu Entstehung und Wiederauflösung der Surenkomposition im Verlauf der Entwicklung eines islamischen Kultus' (1996) and 'Mekkan texts – Medinan additions? Politics and the re-reading of liturgical communications' (2004) – were initiated with her critically acclaimed Habilitation work, *Studien zur Komposition der mekkanischen Suren* (1981).

ANDREW RIPPIN is Professor of History and Dean of the Faculty of Humanities at the University of Victoria, Canada. His research into the formative period of Islamic civilisation in the Arab world, as well as the history of the Qur'ān and its interpretation, has resulted in numerous publications, a selection of which are collected in his *The Qur'ān and its interpretative tradition* (2001). He is also the author of *Muslims, their religious beliefs and practices* (two volumes, 1990 and 1993; 2001², 2005³, as a single volume).

ABDULAZIZ SACHEDINA is Francis Ball Professor of Religious Studies at the University of Virginia. A core member of various initiatives such as the Preventive Diplomacy project of the Center for Strategic and International Studies (CSIS), his recent publications include *The just ruler* (al-sulṭān al-ʿādil) *in Shīʿite Islam: The comprehensive authority of the jurist in Imamite jurisprudence* (1998) and *Islamic roots of democratic pluralism* (2001).

STEFAN WILD is emeritus Professor of Semitic Philology and Islamic Studies at the University of Bonn, Germany. In addition to the political aspects of Islamic history, his research interests include classical Arabic literature and lexicography, as well as modern Arabic literature. Editor of *Die Welt des Islams*, his recent publications include *The Qur'ān as text* (1996) and *Mensch, Prophet und Gott im Koran* (2001).

Introduction

JANE DAMMEN McAULIFFE

According to a thirteenth-century compilation of qur'ānic knowledge – a medieval 'companion to the Qur'ān' – the Arabic Qur'ān contains 323,015 letters, 77,439 words, more than 6,000 verses and 114 chapters or sūras.[1] This makes it a rather modestly sized text when contrasted with the Upanishads, the Mahabharata and the Pali canon of Buddhist writings. But why would these titles come immediately to mind as the point of comparison? The quick answer to that question lies in their classification as 'scripture' or 'sacred text' or 'holy writ' or 'divine word' or even 'classics'. These works, and many others that could be added, found their place in the late nineteenth-century publishing project known as *The sacred books of the East.*[2] That project itself marked an important moment in the conceptual expansion of such categorisation. For centuries, the English term 'scripture', and its equivalents in European languages, had been virtually synonymous with the Bible. While it was recognised, particularly by Christian apologists and missionaries, that other texts were revered by their respective religious communities, that recognition was usually negative and antagonistic.

THE PECULIAR CATEGORY OF SCRIPTURE

It is only rather recently that the term 'scripture' has itself become a contested category, a subject of scholarly interest and debate. An obvious, but not unique, reason is its etymology and derivation from the Latin word for 'writing', *scriptura* (pl. *scripturae*). Not all texts that have achieved a normative status within particular religious communities are written texts and, for others, writing is not the primary form of their dissemination. Scholars of comparative religion have discovered that this category, a category conceived within a Jewish and Christian framework, does not translate easily and accurately to other religious traditions. Neither content nor form suffices to define and delimit this concept. But 'scripture' does describe a connection between a particular community and a particular text. It names a relationship. Rather than designating a quality that inheres in a text, the term marks an affiliation between a text and those who accord it special status. People who do not acknowledge or share that affiliation will study and treat such texts differently from those who do. As commonly classified, the Qur'ān falls into this category of 'scripture' and that categorisation shapes the way in which it has been read, by both Muslims and non-Muslims, and the way in which scholars have treated it.

THE SELF-CONSCIOUSLY SCRIPTURAL SCRIPTURE

Within the past decade increasing attention has been paid to what I would call the 'self-declarative' quality of the Qur'ān. In the words of one scholar, the Qur'ān 'describes itself by various generic terms, comments, explains, distinguishes, puts itself into perspective vis-à-vis other revelations, denies hostile interpretations, and so on'.[3] An earlier essay made an even more categorical declaration: 'the Qur'an is the most meta-textual, most self-referential holy text known in the history of world religions'.[4] Another astute reader of the Qur'ān remarks that the 'abiding enigma of the text is that, along with verses that are to be construed as timeless divine pronouncements, it also contains a large amount of commentary upon and analysis of the processes of its own revelation and the vicissitudes of its own reception in time'.[5] The Qur'ān's 'self-declarative' or 'self-referential' nature expresses itself in various forms but one important expression is found in the qur'ānic term *kitāb*, a common Arabic word that is frequently, but insufficiently, rendered as 'book'. A careful collection and analysis of the 261 appearances of this word in the Qur'ān – to say nothing of the many more occurrences of its cognates – reveal multiple significations that range from the divine inventory of all creation to the eschatological record of every human deed. The Qur'ān's representation of itself as '*kitāb*' – its self-declaration or self-characterisation as such – is linked to these documentations of divine knowledge but in a fluid and open-ended fashion.

This very ambiguity has exercised Western scholarship on the Qur'ān for well over a century. Successive scholars have asked whether the Prophet was consciously occupied with the production of a written corpus, a calque on such earlier codices as the Hebrew Bible and the New Testament, and whether he saw this as a defining mark of his prophethood. While numerous, and competing, responses to this historical puzzle have been proposed, none has secured sustained consensus. Consequently, the Qur'ān's many self-declarations continue to tantalise: 'That is the *kitāb* about which there is no doubt, guidance for those who fear God' (Q 2:2); 'indeed, we revealed it as an Arabic *qur'ān* so that you may understand' (Q 12:2); 'these are the verses of the *kitāb* and a *qur'ān* that makes clear' (Q 15:1); 'a *kitāb* that we have revealed to you, full of blessing so that you may reflect upon its verses' (Q 37:29); 'rather, it is a glorious *qur'ān*' (Q 85:21). I have used the Arabic words *kitāb* and *qur'ān*, rather than giving their English equivalents, in order to capture the polysemous quality of these terms. Verses such as these represent but a small fraction of the Qur'ān's textual self-referencing; equally prominent are frequently found self-descriptives like 'glorious', 'truthful', 'flawless', 'wise'.

Among the most perplexing of these self-declarative verses is one that begins: 'He is the one who revealed to you the *kitāb* in which there are clear verses – they are the 'mother' of the book – and others which are ambiguous.' Q 3:7 continues with several more statements but for now I want to highlight the contrast drawn between the terms that I have translated as 'clear' and 'ambiguous'. My rendering of these terms represents but one of several interpretive traditions on this verse but it suffices to invoke the decisive classification. By dividing its contents into two hermeneutical categories, the 'clear' or 'defined' and the 'ambiguous' or 'undefined', the Qur'ān creates – to borrow a phrase from biblical studies – its own 'canon within the canon'. It adduces an additional form of self-description and self-characterisation, one oriented to the interpretative parameters of different kinds of verses.

In its self-conscious scripturality, the Qur'ān does not simply define and describe itself. It also situates itself in relation to other 'books', to other 'scriptures'. It clearly expresses an awareness of divine revelation as a chronological sequence, a series of time-specific disclosures intended for particular peoples. Q 2:136 marks the milestones in that chronology: 'Say, "We believe in God and what has been revealed to us and in what was revealed to Abraham and Ishmael, and Isaac, and Jacob, and the tribes, in what Moses and Jesus were given and in what the prophets were given from their lord."' Q 4:136 urges belief in the '*kitāb* that he [God] revealed before' and promises perdition for those who do not believe in 'God and his angels and his *kutub* [plural of *kitāb*] and his messengers and the last day'. Being more explicit about these '*kutub*', in yet other passages the Qur'ān designates 'what Moses and Jesus were given' as the Torah (*Tawrāt*) and the Gospel (*Injīl*), recognising their respective positions in the continuity of revelation.

The notion that each successive scripture confirms its predecessor wins repeated affirmation in the Qur'ān (Q 2:42, 3:3, 12:111 and 46:12, among many other instances) with the Gospel's confirmation of the Torah (Q 5:46) used as the primary example. But recognition and confirmation do not equal perpetual validation. Among its strongest self-declaratives are the Qur'ān's assertions of its overriding pre-eminence, its utter finality. With this revelation, God has completed his salvific sequencing of prophets and messengers. The words spoken to Muḥammad, the 'seal of the prophets', constitute God's full and final guidance for humankind.

Assertions of pre-eminence are but one of the ways in which another essential quality of the Qur'ān manifests itself. The Qur'ān is an argumentative text. Even the most casual reader cannot help but be struck by the omnipresence of debate and disputation, of apologetic and polemic, of postulation and refutation. As I have remarked in an earlier essay, 'the operative voice in any given pericope, whether it be that of God, of Muḥammad or of another protagonist, regularly addresses actual or implicit antagonists'.[6] A recent study of this phenomenon finds in the qur'ānic text 'full arguments with premises and conclusions, antecedents and consequents, constructions *a fortiori*, commands supported by justification, conclusions produced by rule-based reasoning, comparisons, contrasts, and many other patterns'.[7] Viewed from the perspective of historical analysis, the Qur'ān quite clearly represents a *Sitz im Leben* of religious contestation. Continued claims to its own supremacy play out both retrospectively and prospectively. The qur'ānic abrogation of previous scriptures argues that differences between the Qur'ān and such earlier revelations as the Torah and the Gospel are a consequence of deliberate or inadvertent corruption in the transmission of these prior texts. Looking forward in time, Q 2:23 challenges any would-be future prophet to 'produce a sūra like' those of the Qur'ān and Q 17:88 declares that even the combined efforts of humans and jinn could create nothing equal to it. This human incapacity to meet the qur'ānic challenge serves as the principal justification for the doctrine of the Qur'ān's inimitability. These dual concepts – the corruption of earlier canonical texts and the human incapacity to match its excellence – buttress theological testimonies to the unique stature of this scripture.

READERS AND THEIR DISCONTENTS

For the unprepared reader, however, affirmations of inimitability and avowals that the Qur'ān is the 'miracle' that substantiates Muḥammad's claim to prophethood, can be hard to square with an initial exposure to the text. The Qur'ān is not an easy read. If the comments of colleagues and friends over the years are any indication, I suspect that few who tackle the text cold, who simply pluck a paperback translation from a bookshop shelf, persevere to the concluding sūras. Expectations of how a 'scripture' or a 'classic' should be structured – how it should 'read' – contribute to the frequently experienced frustrations. European and North American readers almost inevitably bring to the reading of the Qur'ān biblically formed assumptions that 'scripture' will behave in a certain way, will have a narrative structure, will move forward in time, will assemble its genres into distinct sections. Even so sophisticated a student of Islamic literature as Theodor Nöldeke (d. 1930), a renowned German scholar of the Qur'ān, fell prey to such presumptions:

> On the whole, while many parts of the Koran undoubtedly have considerable rhetorical power, even over an unbelieving reader, the book, aesthetically considered, is by no means a first-rate performance. To begin with what we are most competent to criticise, let us look at some of the more extended narratives. It has already been noticed how vehement and abrupt they are where they ought to be characterized by epic repose. Indispensable links, both in expression and in the sequence of events, are often omitted, so that to understand these histories is sometimes far easier for us than for those who heard them first, because we know most of them from better sources. Along with this, there is a great deal of superfluous verbiage; and nowhere do we find a steady advance in the narration.[8]

Nöldeke goes on to render a negative judgement on the Joseph account in the Qur'ān (Q 12) as compared 'with the story in Genesis, so admirably conceived and so admirably executed in spite of some slight discrepancies'. His criticism addresses not only the narrative elements of the Qur'ān but the non-narrative, as well, where 'the connection of ideas is extremely loose, and even the syntax betrays great awkwardness'.[9]

For most Western readers, the Bible operates as the literary template against which other sacred books are assessed. Even those who have had no direct exposure to the biblical text absorb this presumption because the Bible's echoes and archetypes have informed so much of subsequent Western literature. In an interesting turn, the world of biblical scholarship itself has felt the force of these popular preconceptions. The atomistic focus of much historical-critical exegesis has been challenged by recent calls for more integrated readings. These challenges make the further claim that such holistic readings can minimise the distance between the ancient and contemporary interpreter, can recapture – albeit at a more sophisticated level – the perspective of pre-critical reading.

The biblical scholars who make these assertions must argue that current literary expectations of what constitutes a 'book' are no different than those of the biblical expositors. In other words, they must contend that both contemporary readers and scholars and ancient readers and scholars are equally concerned with matters of internal coherence and consistency and of narrative development and closure. Against such claims, however, must be placed the views of those who assert that preoccupations of this sort were frequently absent in the production process of many biblical books: 'The compilers of the biblical books were not trying to produce "works" in the literary sense, with a clear theme or plot and a high degree of closure, but rather anthologies of material which could be dipped into at any point.'[10]

To shift such expectations and to ease the frustrations of unprepared readers it may help if we return to the limitations of the term 'scripture' with its etymological roots sunk in the soil of the written word. Notions of genre discrimination, narrative development and chronological coherence recede in importance when the focus shifts from reading to recitation. As experienced by Muslims over the past fourteen centuries, the majority of whom could neither speak nor read Arabic, the Qur'ān is primarily sound, not script. The earliest instruction in the Qur'ān, that given to small children in elementary recitation classes, ignores the sequence of the sūras. These students start with the shortest sūras, those at the end of the written text, and they learn to vocalise them by repeating the sounds that emerge from their teacher's mouth. The children chant in Arabic but as most do not know that language, they have no idea what they are chanting and the meaning of their chant must be explained to them. Yet for these children and for their elders, the sounds themselves are powerful, whether immediately intelligible or not. Understood to be God's own words divinely dictated to his final prophet, they are full of sacred blessing.

For those who do speak Arabic, the aural and textual beauty of the Qur'ān has been avowed for centuries. The sheer majesty of the language, its rhetorical force and the vitality of its rhythmical cadences produce a powerful impact on people who can appreciate its linguistic and literary qualities. Classical treatises even collect the stories of those who have been 'slain by the Qur'ān', mortally overwhelmed by its sublime sounds.[11] Whether apocryphal or not, accounts of fainting, falling unconscious or even expiring portray a form of textual reception that is utterly foreign to contemporary expectations of linear narrative function.

READERS AND THEIR REASONS

Yet from the time of the Qur'ān's appearance on the global literary stage, many non-Muslim readers have persevered. They have come to the text by different paths, drawn to it for diverse reasons. For some, in both medieval and modern times, the purpose has been apologetics and polemics. The Qur'ān is a window into the mind of the enemy and must be read to find arguments with which to refute that adversary. In its most virulent forms, such reading becomes an act of geopolitical aggression. A less antagonistic version would engage the text as a prelude to proselytisation, seeking an entrée for religious or ideological conversion. Whether the conviction sought be a conversion to evangelical Christianity or to democratic pluralism, the textual approach is the same. Both the belligerent and the benign versions of this approach manifest themselves in our electronic world of blogs and chat rooms.

Other readers cultivate the Qur'ān with an attitude of cultural curiosity. They are attracted by the literary status of the text, by its position in the pantheon of world literature. Their interest may be formed and honed within a scholarly discipline like history or philology or comparative literature. If their textual investigations are to be rigorous and academically fruitful, such readers must be well versed in qur'ānic Arabic and in the literature and culture of the classical Islamic world as well as its historical contexts.

Finally, there are the readers who come to the Qur'ān for religious reasons, seeking spiritual enlightenment and personal transformation. These, of course, share the motivations of devout Muslims and many eventually make the profession of faith that marks entrance into the community of believers. For such readers, the Qur'ān takes on the fully relational quality of 'scripture' or 'sacred book', the ultimate source of guidance and insight. 'It is a treasure-house, an ocean, a mine: the deeper religious readers dig, the more ardently they fish, the more single-mindedly they seek gold, the greater will be their reward.'[12]

Three fascinating figures can serve to exemplify these approaches. None was born Muslim or nurtured from infancy in the rhythms and tonalities of the recited text. Neither did any of these three anticipate the impact this sacred book would have on his life. In different historical periods and from different perspectives, Peter the Venerable, Ignaz Goldziher and Muhammad Asad turned their attention to the Qur'ān. It is no overstatement to say that each in his own fashion changed the course of qur'ānic studies. For our present purposes, however, I am more interested in introducing them as embodiments of particular forms of reading, of different ways of approaching the text of the Qur'ān.

Safely lodged in a Parisian library lie the results of a remarkable vision, a fateful journey and a successful scholarly collaboration. At the age of twenty-eight, Pierre Maurice de Montboissier was elected abbot of Cluny, centre of a monastic empire so vast that it encompassed hundreds of monasteries and thousands of monks.[13] The son of a Burgundian nobleman, this monk, who was to become known as Peter the Venerable (d. 1156), entered the Cluniac order while still a teenager but within a few decades became one of the most prominent churchmen of his generation. High among the many accomplishments for which history remembers Peter was his role in the production of the first complete Latin translation of the Qur'ān. Why would a French abbot have commissioned such a translation? Fortunately for us, Peter left a record of his reasons, one that can be culled from both his correspondence and his polemical writings.[14] Peter's motivations for supporting qur'ānic scholarship were clear and straightforward. They can be succinctly captured in the phrase 'know the enemy'. In the eyes of Peter and others of his era, Islam was a grievous heresy and a false religion, one which should be denounced and combated at every turn. Yet such a formidable adversary could only be adequately refuted if it were properly understood. Peter recognised that central to such understanding was a knowledge of the Qur'ān, a knowledge in the service of refutation.

In 1142, Peter set out for Spain, intent upon visitations to the Cluniac monasteries there and prompted by an invitation from Emperor Alfonso VII, whose grandfather had been a benefactor to Cluny.[15] He spent a prolonged period in Spain but whether he conceived his plan of translating key Islamic texts at this point or earlier is unknown. What is known, however, is that during his sojourn he met and commissioned a group of translators and informants to produce Latin versions of the Qur'ān,[16] as well as of other Arabic works dealing with ḥadīth, the life of the Prophet and Islamic theology.[17] The Qur'ān's translator was an English cleric and archdeacon of the church of Pamplona, Robert of Ketton.[18]

Peter's translation project was no disinterested scholarly exercise. His substantial subventions – and his letters mention that the translators were well remunerated – underwrote the foundational work for a polemical attack. While there is evidence that Peter the Venerable tried to interest others in writing this polemic, his efforts were unsuccessful and he eventually decided to do it himself. He was certainly no novice to such endeavours, having already written several works addressed to the correction of various Christian heresies. Nevertheless, his *Liber contra sectam sive haeresim Saracenorum*, along with a similar treatise directed at the Jews, have achieved particular importance because 'they represent the first European books dealing with these faiths in which talmudic and koranic sources are cited verbatim within a carefully structured Christian argument'.[19]

More than seven centuries separate Peter from the Hungarian scholar Ignaz Goldziher (d. 1921) but an even greater gulf spans the distance between their reasons for attending to the Qur'ān. Despite Goldziher having died more than seventy-five years ago, his work remains vital for the field of qur'ānic studies. Scholars continue to mine his published corpus and to build their own arguments on the basis of, or in disagreement with, some of his fundamental insights. Goldziher was born in the Hungarian town of Székesfehérvár and educated in both his native country and in Germany, studying in Berlin and Leipzig – where he received his Ph.D. in 1869 – and then doing postdoctoral work in Leiden and Vienna. His doctoral work prepared him in Hebrew, Arabic and Syriac and culminated in a thesis on a medieval Arabic commentary on the Bible.[20] Quite a lot can be known about the intellectual development of this extraordinary scholar and the past few decades have seen the steady increase of books and articles on various aspects of Goldziher's biography and bibliography.

In a fashion that our email age may never be able to replicate, the study of his life and scholarly maturation is facilitated by a wealth of personal data. Goldziher kept a diary and was a prolific correspondent, leaving a rich written record from which much can be gleaned. He also kept an account of the profoundly formative trip of several months that he took to the Middle East at the age of twenty-three. Already a philological prodigy, he used this journey to learn Arabic dialects, to buy books and to become the 'first European allowed to attend the Theological lectures of the Al-Azhar'.[21]

Goldziher is generally recognised as a key figure in the foundation of the modern field of Arabic and Islamic studies. He drew upon the work of such important predecessors as Theodor Nöldeke and his own teacher H. L. Fleischer (d. 1888) and was deeply informed by currents of biblical studies that had emerged with the Haskala and its modernising and rationalising ideals. As a Hungarian Jew, he was attracted to the promise of religious reform, seeing it as both an important end in itself and as a means of achieving the full assimilation of Jews into the social fabric of their respective countries.

It is clear from a review of Goldziher's education that he, like most 'Orientalists' in the nineteenth century, was deeply influenced by the new insights and methodologies being explored by biblical scholars and, like many others of his generation, suffered the backlash that such scholarship generated. Both he and his contemporary Julius Wellhausen (d. 1918) were shaped by the perspective of Abraham Geiger (d. 1874) who insisted that all religious texts were human productions, decisively determined by the historical contexts that generated them. Goldziher took this insight into Islamic studies: 'The method he espoused, and which he was the first to apply systematically to the study of Islam on such a broad-ranging scale, viewed texts not as depositories of mere facts that research should ferret out and line up one after another, but as sources in which one could discern the stages of transformation through which a community based on a common religious vision had passed as it struggled to come to terms with a host of new situations and problems. By careful and critical analysis of these sources, one could extrapolate important new insights on such processes of development not only in religious thought, but in literature, social perceptions, and politics as well.'[22]

Goldziher's publications command a topical breadth that few contemporary scholars could hope to equal. He wrote on Bedouin life, the culture of Muslim Spain, the development of ḥadīth, the literary history and theory of early Arabic poetry, and many other matters. None of his works, however, has had more lasting value than his lectures on the history and varieties of qur'ānic interpretation.[23] Contemporary work on this subject continues to cite this seminal study and it remains an active part of the scholarly conversation. For breadth and acuity it has yet to be superseded. Certainly there have been efforts to update Goldziher's *Richtungen* and to draw upon the much larger number of Qur'ān commentaries that have been edited and published in the past century. Nevertheless, Goldziher's volume remains vital to the scholarly conversation about the Qur'ān and its interpretation. He still stands as one of the most astute readers of this tradition.

Goldziher read the Qur'ān and its centuries of interpretive literature from the perspective of the academically informed outsider. Our final figure in this typological triptych shared that stance initially but eventually abandoned it for the full embrace of religious conversion. About fifty years ago, a journalist by the name of Muhammad Asad published a memoir that captured the attention of reviewers and the reading public alike. Entitled *The road to Mecca*, it spun a tale of travel and religious reflection, a spiritual pilgrimage that took one man from his roots in eastern European Jewry through a conversion to Islam to a significant contribution to Muslim scholarship on the Qur'ān. Leopold Weiss (d. 1992), Asad's birth name, was born in the first year of the twentieth century and lived until its last decade.[24] His family insisted on an intensive education in Hebrew and the major Jewish texts. Weiss did not continue such studies at the University of Vienna, however, and after completing his degree pursued a career in film writing and journalism. A trip to Jerusalem in the earlier 1920s offered Weiss his first exposure to the Muslim world. More prolonged periods followed and included contact with some of the Egyptian intellectuals who were leading a Muslim modernist movement.[25] Asad himself, after his conversion, was to write extensively in support of such modernist ideals.[26]

The turning point in Weiss' spiritual journey occurred in his mid-twenties. As he recounts the moment of his conversion to Islam, the echo of that much earlier conversion narrative to be found in the *Confessions* of Saint Augustine is unmistakable. For Augustine it was an unseen child's voice from across a garden wall that prompted him to pick up the Bible and read the first passage (Romans 13:13) upon which his eyes fell. For Asad it was a moment of spiritual insight during a Berlin subway ride that turned him towards a deeper engagement with the Qur'ān. He speaks of the moments after he returned to his house and spotted his Qur'ān lying open on his study desk: 'Mechanically, I picked up the book to put it away, but just as I was about to close it, my eye fell on the open page before me, and I read.'[27] Q 102 jumped out at him as a direct response to the sense of human despair that had overwhelmed him on his ride home and convinced him that the Qur'ān 'was a God-inspired book'.[28] His profession of faith (*shahāda*) before the leader of a Muslim community followed shortly, and within the year, Leopold Weiss – now Muhammad Asad – left on his first pilgrimage to Mecca.

Years in Saudi Arabia followed and were succeeded by those in India where his stature as a Muslim intellectual continued to increase. In 1936, he was offered the editorship of *Islamic Culture*, a journal published in Hyderabad whose previous editor had been the British convert and Qur'ān translator, Marmaduke Pickthall (d. 1936).[29] Asad was interned during World War II but in its aftermath he assumed increasingly important political and diplomatic posts in the newly created state of Pakistan. In 1952, he moved to New York as, for a brief period, Pakistan's representative to the United Nations.

Asad's most extended immersion in qur'ānic studies did not begin until he was almost sixty years old. After moving to first Geneva and then Tangiers, he began to work on a new English translation of the Qur'ān. He was prompted to this by dissatisfaction with existing translations and by a desire to enshrine an avowedly modernist hermeneutic. The reasons for his dissatisfaction are interesting. Largely linguistic, they apply to both Muslim and non-Muslim efforts to render the Qur'ān into a western language. Asad contends that no non-Arab, whether a Muslim or not, can capture the true 'spirit' of the language through academic study, even when supplemented by conversation with contemporary, urban Arabs. Only someone who has spent time with the desert Bedouin of the Arabian peninsula – as Asad himself did – can 'achieve an intimate understanding of the diction of the Qur'ān'.[30] He also takes full account of precisely that stylistic element of the Qur'ān that Nöldeke found so troubling. Classical rhetorical analysis of the Qur'ān uses the technical term *ījāz* to designate instances of concision or brevity in the text. In Asad's assessment this is lauded as 'that inimitable ellipticism which often deliberately omits intermediate thought-clauses in order to express the final stage of an idea as pithily and concisely as is possible within the limitations of human language. This method of *ījāz* is, as I have explained, a peculiar, integral aspect of the Arabic language, and has reached its utmost perfection in the Qur'ān. In order to render its meaning into a language which does not function in a similarly elliptical manner, the thought-links which are missing – that is, *deliberately omitted* – in the original must be supplied by the translator.'[31] While the reception of Asad's rendering, like that of many others, has not been uncontroversial, there are 'many English-speaking Muslims who will attest to the appeal of this translation, and who rely upon it daily'.[32]

Peter the Venerable, Ignaz Goldziher and Muhammad Asad represent three different reasons for reading the Qur'ān. While the polemicist, the scholar and the convert need not be separate and independent entities – overlap is obviously possible – they often are. For our purposes, they can operate as heuristic devices, ways to identify the diverse perspectives from which the Qur'ān is approached, studied and analysed.

FOR THE READERS OF THIS BOOK

The present volume seeks to assist readers of the second sort, those who bring to their reading of the Qur'ān a preliminary perception of its literary, historical and anthropological potential. Some of these readers may undertake its intellectual examination with a religiously informed appreciation of the text but with little or no understanding of the scholarship that surrounds the Qur'ān. Other readers may have never even opened the Qur'ān but are curious about a book that has guided the lives of millions both present and past. Yet others may have an informed perception of another significant scripture, such as the Bible, and will likely pose a set of questions to the Qur'ān that are based on that perspective.

The story of the Qur'ān as told through these chapters moves from context to text and from text to textual history and impact. **Part I** provides the basic historical background and then raises the most contested issue in contemporary scholarship on the Qur'ān, the question of its very origins. **Part II** turns to the text itself with a thematic, literary and experiential analysis. In **Part III**, the history of the Qur'ān's transmission deals with such diverse modes of textual replication as the human voice, the production of manuscripts and printed copies, and calligraphic inscription on buildings and other objects. **Part IV** examines another form of textual history, the ways in which the Qur'ān has generated an enormous literature of interpretation, has influenced every area of Muslim intellectual life and has evoked extensive scholarly investigation in European and American academic circles. The final section, **Part V**, looks more closely at issues within the interpretive tradition that are of particular interest to today's readers.

The colleagues whom I invited to write these chapters responded quickly and positively to my request. Each holds a university appointment and each recognised the need for a volume that could offer to a new generation of students both essential information about the Qur'ān and a summation of current scholarship in the field of qur'ānic studies. As will be clear from the chapter notes and bibliographies, these colleagues have made important contributions to the scholarly investigation of the topics on which they have written. With this volume, however, they have agreed to write for a broader audience than that of specialists in Islamic studies. While such specialists will undoubtedly find much of interest in these pages, my hope is that they will prove equally engaging to those who have had little or no exposure to the Qur'ān as a subject of scholarly attention. A few words about each of the following fourteen chapters should help readers orient themselves to this book's overall sequence but also permit them to pick and choose those chapters that are of immediate interest.

In Chapter 1, *Fred Donner* presents a sketch of Muḥammad's life and of the Qur'ān's revelation, as based on the standard biographical accounts of the Prophet, and raises issues about the historiography of those accounts. The qur'ānic text itself takes centre stage in Chapter 2 as *Claude Gilliot*, drawing upon traditional narratives but also questioning their reliability, describes how the oral revelations became the written and codified text. This part of the story continues in Chapter 3 with *Harold Motzki*'s exposition of forms of contemporary scholarship that pose a challenge to the classical accounts of these collection and redaction stories. Textual content takes the foreground with *Daniel Madigan*'s presentation in Chapter 4 of qur'ānic theology and its principal postulations. Chapter 5 switches the lens from theological to literary examination as *Angelika Neuwirth* describes the text and offers a succinct structural analysis. In Chapter 6, co-authors

William Graham and *Navid Kermani* explain the oral conveyance of the Qur'ān in both its technical developments and its functional reception. *Fred Leemhuis* presents information in Chapter 7 on the Qur'ān's multiple forms of transmission, both ancient and modern. With the second co-authored chapter in this volume, *Sheila Blair* and *Jonathan Bloom* turn our attention in Chapter 8 to the visual and to the omnipresence of qur'ānic inscription in the material culture of the Muslim world. In Chapter 9, I introduce the interpretation of the Qur'ān by offering a concise case study and presenting some of the principal foci and major figures in the history of qur'ānic commentary. *Alexander Knysh*'s discussion in Chapter 10 of significant areas of intellectual endeavour in the classical Muslim world concentrates upon philology, jurisprudence and ethics, theology and philosophy, as well as literature and rhetoric. In Chapter 11, *Andrew Rippin* charts the emergence of a 'scholarly' or academic approach to the Qur'ān, especially as this develops in the nineteenth and twentieth centuries. With Chapter 12, *Asma Barlas* raises the first of three contemporary readings of the Qur'ān by attending to recent exegesis by Muslim women. Chapter 13 continues this concentration on contemporary readings with *Stefan Wild*'s presentation of modern political interpretation and of the politics of interpretation itself. Finally, in Chapter 14, *Abdulaziz Sachedina* brings forward the question of interreligious relations as these can be comprehended from a qur'ānic perspective.

While the organisation and arrangement of these chapters should make a continuous reading beneficial, I have also asked each author to treat his or her particular topic in a manner that would allow the resultant chapter to be read independently of the others. For this reason, several chapters deal – in diverse ways – with the crucial question of the origin of the qur'ānic text. In the past three decades, no single issue in the field of qur'ānic studies has generated more controversy than this one.[33] Entire bodies of scholarship hinge on the question of whether the traditional narratives of the Qur'ān's collection, codification and written dissemination can be considered historically reliable or not. The process of textual formation and inscription in the aftermath of the Prophet's death has been the subject of intense scrutiny. Coupled with this concentration on textual stabilisation stands an equally close examination of what can be called the 'pre-history' of the text. Scholars of both Arabic and cognate languages have sought to identify themes and narratives found in earlier near eastern literature, perhaps filtered through intermediate recapitulations such as liturgies and lectionaries, and 'recaptured' in Muḥammad's public message as this found expression in the codified text of the Qur'ān. Consequently, several authors in this collection have alluded to, or expanded upon, these contentious topics as an inextricable part of their larger project. The resulting multiplicity of scholarly perspectives offers readers of this volume a good glimpse of a lively and current scholarly exchange.

The authors who have collaborated in the creation of this volume have successfully balanced the twin demands of accuracy and accessibility. They have made an effort to keep the technical apparatus of scholarship, such as endnotes and extensive bibliographies, to a minimum but without sacrificing the needs of those readers who will want to use this book as a launching pad for more detailed investigations of specific subtopics. The transliteration of Arabic and other terms follows the now standard American format used, with small variations, by the Library of Congress, leading academic journals and the *Encyclopaedia of the Qur'ān*.[34] The word 'Qur'ān', which more closely represents the Arabic original, is preferred to the now-outdated rendering of 'Koran'. In analogous fashion, its adjectival form is given as 'qur'ānic' and is lower-cased to follow the English-language conventions of 'Bible' and 'biblical', respectively. For the earlier periods of Islamic history, the death dates of prominent figures are provided in both Muslim and western versions (i.e., *hijrī* and *mīlādī*).

To enhance the reader's visual enjoyment and to introduce some of the diversity and beauty of qur'ānic manuscripts, I have included fourteen photographs, placing one at the beginning of each chapter. While, with one exception, there is no direct relation between the textual calligraphy and the contents of the chapter that it precedes, taken together this set of manuscript pages exemplifies one form of the dissemination of the Qur'ān to which several chapters refer. The single exception is Chapter 2 which makes illustrative reference to a few of the photographs. These examples have also been selected to offer readers a sense of the geography and chronology of that dissemination.

Assuming that most readers will use this *Companion* in conjunction with an English translation of the Qur'ān, I should say a word about some of these translations. Most large bookstores will stock copies of the ones that I will mention and they are readily available from online booksellers. I should also note, however, that while the authors of this book's chapters may have drawn upon one or more of these English translations, I made no attempt to impose a single version as mandatory. Many scholars of the Qur'ān, such as those who have contributed to the present volume, prefer to make their own verse renderings directly from the qur'ānic text.

For the past generation, the most widely recommended translation of the Qur'ān for academic purposes has been that of A. J. Arberry. Arberry attempted 'to produce something which might be accepted as echoing however faintly the sublime rhetoric of the Arabic Koran'.[35] In the eyes – and ears – of most readers he did so successfully. Consequently, his version has often been reprinted in various paperback editions. Another frequently found translation, and one that has long been popular with Muslim readers, is that of the British convert to Islam Mohammed Marmaduke Pickthall.[36] Pickthall's intent was to provide a close and faithful rendering of the Arabic text and to do so in a language that would sound like 'scripture' to English-speaking ears. To this end, he used a form of archaic expression reminiscent of the King James Bible, with liberal use of 'thee', 'thy' and 'thou' as well as of verbal forms such as 'giveth' and 'thinketh'. While Pickthall reliably conveys the meaning of the Arabic, its antique form of expression strikes most contemporary readers as odd and outdated. Probably the most popular version of the Qur'ān among Muslims in the English-speaking world is that of Abdullah Yusuf Ali which was originally issued in Lahore as consecutive fascicles. Yusuf Ali sought 'to make English an Islamic language'.[37] He embellished his work with a free-verse, running commentary and extensive textual notation.

A more recent publication, and one to which I have already referred, is Muhammad Asad's *The message of the Qur'ān*.[38] While Asad's translation reflects a decidedly modernist agenda, it also manifests a skilful use of language and is enriched with excellent annotations. For 'an American version in contemporary English', readers can turn to *The Qur'an: The noble reading* by T. B. Irving, also a Muslim convert.[39] Even newer are the translations by two prominent scholars, M. Fakhry and M. A. S. Abdel Haleem, that have appeared in the past decade and have garnered good reviews.[40] Two older, but still widely available translations are those of J. M. Rodwell,[41] which was first published in 1861, and of N. J. Dawood,[42] initially issued in 1956, a year after Arberry's version appeared. Less frequently found, at least in contemporary bookstores, is Edward Henry Palmer's translation which was published as volumes six and nine of Max Müller's *Sacred books of the East*.[43] An important translation project, but one of interest primarily to scholars, is Richard Bell's effort to refine the chronological analysis of qur'ānic material and to represent the extensive redaction that he was convinced the text had undergone.[44]

For those interested in the history of the English translation of the Qur'ān, the work of George Sale is indispensable – and still available, at least from second-hand dealers. Sale's version first appeared in 1734 with the lengthy title: *Koran: Commonly called the Alkoran of Mohammed. Translated into English immediately from the original Arabic; with explanatory notes, taken from the most approved commentators. To which is prefixed a preliminary discourse.*[45] The 'preliminary discourse' itself is 145 pages and marks an important point in the dissemination of information about Islam to the English-speaking world.[46]

Note should also be made of some partial translations that provide selected excerpts from the qur'ānic text, often in particularly fine renditions. Two of special value are K. Cragg, *Readings in the Qur'ān* and M. Sells, *Approaching the Qur'ān*.[47] Readers may also wish to consult the English-language concordance for the Qur'ān that has been built on the basis of Arberry's translation.[48]

Finally, I would like to draw attention to the ever-increasing proliferation of Qur'ān translations on the Internet. I do so, however, with the now-common caveat that the integrity of Internet texts cannot always be trusted. Some of these translations are searchable text files while others can be downloaded or purchased as compact disks. Since URLs change frequently (or disappear altogether) the best way to find these websites is by experimenting with keyword combinations. Sites and compact disks that feature the Arabic text of the Qur'ān often include recitation as an additional feature, providing instant access to the aesthetic experience described in Chapter 6. Even for those with no knowledge of Arabic, hearing the Qur'ān recited by world-renowned masters offers an invaluable entrée into the Muslim experience of the holy book.

In selecting an English edition of the Qur'ān, I always counsel students and colleagues to choose at least two versions, if possible. Combining a paperback copy with an online reproduction makes this easy to do. Reading two translations simultaneously quickly reminds us that every translation is an act of interpretation. The divergent renderings of many words and phrases will also alert readers to those areas of the text that have been the subject of particular scrutiny by both commentators and scholars alike.

I close this introduction with an expression of gratitude to all those who have contributed to the completion of this volume. My editor at Cambridge University Press, Marigold Acland, has offered excellent and timely guidance. My research assistant, Clare Wilde, has laboured long hours to produce consistency in the final manuscript. Most especially, I thank my collaborating colleagues: Fred Donner, Claude Gilliot, Harald Motzki, Daniel Madigan, Angelika Neuwirth, William Graham, Navid Kermani, Fred Leemhuis, Jonathan Bloom, Sheila Blair, Alexander Knysh, Andrew Rippin, Asma Barlas, Stefan Wild and Abdulaziz Sachedina. They have honoured me with their enthusiasm for this project, their prompt submission of promised chapters and their unfailing interest and support.

Notes

1. Badr al-Dīn al-Zarkashī, *al-Burhān fī ʿulūm al-Qurʾān*, ed. M. A. al-F. Ibrāhīm, 4 vols. (Cairo: Maktabat Dār al-Turāth, 1985), vol. I, p. 249. The verse totals cited by al-Zarkashī vary from 6,104 to 6,236.
2. F. Max Müller, *The sacred books of the East*, 50 vols. (Oxford: Clarendon Press, 1879–1910). For Müller, the study of comparative religion was closely tied to that of comparative philology and he formulated a developmental theory of religious evolution that was heavily influenced by Darwinism. F. Max Müller, *Lectures on the origin and growth of religion* (New York: Charles Scribner's Sons, 1899).
3. S. Wild, 'The self-referentiality of the Qurʾān: Sura 3:7 as an exegetical challenge', in J. D. McAuliffe, B. D. Walfish and J. W. Goering (eds.), *With reverence for the word: Medieval scriptural exegesis in Judaism, Christianity, and Islam* (New York: Oxford University Press, 2003), p. 422.
4. S. Wild, '"We have sent down to thee the book with the truth . . .": Spatial and temporal implications of the qurʾanic concepts of nuzūl, tanzīl and ʾinzāl', in S. Wild (ed.), *The Qurʾān as text* (Leiden: Brill, 1996), p. 140.
5. D. Madigan, 'Book', in J. D. McAuliffe (ed.), *Encyclopaedia of the Qurʾān*, 5 vols. (Leiden: Brill, 2001–6), vol. I, pp. 249–50. Compare this with the recent remark of a biblical scholar who observes that 'as a document' the Hebrew Bible 'displays an astonishing lack of textual self-consciousness'. J. Berlinerblau, *The secular Bible: Why nonbelievers must take religion seriously* (Cambridge: Cambridge University Press, 2005), p. 28.
6. J. D. McAuliffe, '"Debate with them in the better way": The construction of a qurʾānic commonplace', in A. Neuwirth et al. (eds.) *Myths, historical archetypes and symbolic figures in Arabic literature: Towards a new hermeneutic approach* (Stuttgart: Steiner, 1999), pp. 163–88.
7. R. Gwynne, *Logic, rhetoric, and legal reasoning in the Qurʾān: God's arguments* (London: RoutledgeCurzon, 2004), p. x.
8. T. Nöldeke, *Sketches from eastern history*, trans. J. S. Black (Beirut: Khayats, 1963), pp. 34–5.
9. Ibid., p. 35.
10. J. Barton, 'What is a book? Modern exegesis and the literary conventions of ancient Israel', in J. C. De Moor (ed.), *Intertextuality in Ugarit and Israel* (Leiden: Brill, 1998), p. 6.
11. N. Kermani, *Gott ist schön: Das ästhetische Erleben des Koran* (Munich: C. H. Beck, 2000), pp. 376–85.
12. P. J. Griffiths, *Religious reading: The place of reading in the practice of religion* (New York: Oxford University Press, 1999), p. 41.
13. J. Kritzeck, *Peter the Venerable and Islam* (Princeton: Princeton University Press, 1964).
14. Ibid., pp. 27–8 for a list of these sources.
15. Ibid., pp. 10–11.
16. For a study of the annotations to this translation that demonstrates their reliance upon qurʾānic commentaries, see T. Burman, *Religious polemic and the intellectual history of the Mozarabs, c. 1050–1200* (Leiden: Brill, 1994), pp. 84–9 and passim.

17. This collection survives as MS lat. 1162 of the Bibliothèque de l'Arsenal in Paris. For a manuscript description of the Qur'ān translation, see M.-Th. D'Alverny, 'Deux traductions latines du Coran au moyen âge', *Archives d'histoire doctrinale et littéraire du Moyen Age* 22–3 (1947–8), 69–131.
18. For more detailed identification see J. Kritzeck, 'Peter the Venerable and the Toledan collection', in G. Constable and J. Kritzeck (eds.), *Petrus Venerabilis, 1156–1956: Studies and texts commemorating the eighth centenary of his death* (Rome: Herder, 1956), pp. 176–201.
19. Kritzeck, *Peter*, p. 25.
20. L. Conrad, 'The pilgrim from Pest: Goldziher's study tour to the Near East (1873–1874)', in I. R. Netton (ed.), *Golden roads: Migration, pilgrimage and travel in mediaeval and modern Islam* (Richmond, Surrey: Curzon Press, 1993), p. 122.
21. R. Simon, *Ignác Goldziher: His life and scholarship as reflected in his works and correspondence* (Leiden: Brill, 1986), p. 44.
22. L. Conrad, 'Ignaz Goldziher on Ernest Renan: From Orientalist philology to the study of Islam', in M. Kramer (ed.), *The Jewish discovery of Islam: Studies in honor of Bernard Lewis* (Tel Aviv: The Moshe Dayan Center for Middle Eastern and African Studies, 1999), p. 162.
23. I. Goldziher, *Die Richtungen der islamischen Koranauslegung* (Leiden: Brill, 1920).
24. For a summary biography, but one that is quite critical of Asad, especially his anti-Zionism, see M. Kramer, 'The road from Mecca: Muhammad Asad (born Leopold Weiss)', in Kramer (ed.), *Jewish discovery*, pp. 225–47.
25. For his acquaintance with Muṣṭafā al-Marāghī (d. 1945) who eventually became Shaykh al-Azhar, see M. Asad, *The road to Mecca* (New York: Simon and Schuster, 1954), p. 188.
26. His first and perhaps best-known work on this subject is *Islam at the crossroads* (Delhi: Arafat, 1934). It was eventually published in Arabic as *al-Islām ʿalā muftaraq al-ṭuruq*.
27. Asad, *Road to Mecca*, p. 309.
28. Ibid., p. 310.
29. Kramer, 'Road from Mecca', p. 235.
30. M. Asad, *The message of the Qur'ān* (Gibraltar: Dar Al-Andalus, 1980), p. v.
31. Ibid., pp. v–vi. Emphasis in original.
32. Kramer, 'Road from Mecca', p. 242.
33. Two of many recent examples: K.-H. Ohlig and G.-R. Puin (eds.), *Die dunklen Anfänge: Neue Forschungen zur Entstehung und frühen Geschichte des Islams* (Berlin: Verlag Hans Schiler, 2005); H. Berg (ed.), *Method and theory in the study of Islamic origins* (Leiden: Brill, 2003).
34. J. D. McAuliffe (ed.), *Encyclopaedia of the Qur'ān*, 5 vols. (Leiden: Brill, 2001–6).
35. A. J. Arberry, *The Koran interpreted* (New York: Macmillan, 1955), p. x.
36. M. M. Pickthall, *The meaning of the glorious Koran: An explanatory translation* (New York: New American Library, 1930).
37. A. Y. Ali, *The holy Qur'ān: English translation and commentary (with Arabic text)* (Lahore: Shaikh Muhammad Ashraf, 1934), p. iv.
38. See note 30 above for full bibliographic information.

39. T. B. Irving, *The Qur'an: The noble reading* (Cedar Rapids, IA: The Mother Mosque Foundation, 1993), p. xxi.
40. M. Fakhry, *The Qur'an: A modern English version* (Reading, UK: Garnet, 1997); M. A. S. Abdel Haleem, *The Qur'an: A new translation* (Oxford: Oxford University Press, 2004).
41. J. M. Rodwell, *The Koran: Translated from the Arabic, the suras arranged in chronological order; with notes and index* (London: Hertford, 1861). This has been reissued with the sūras in canonical order and a new introduction by Alan Jones. *The Koran* (London: J. M. Dent, 1994).
42. N. J. Dawood, *The Koran: A new translation* (Harmondsworth, Middlesex: Penguin, 1956).
43. E. H. Palmer, *The Qur'ân* (Oxford: Clarendon Press, 1880).
44. R. Bell, *The Qur'ān translated, with a critical re-arrangement of the surahs*, 2 vols. (Edinburgh: T. and T. Clark, 1937–9).
45. Published London: C. Ackers (for J. Wilcox), 1934.
46. On the history of qur'ānic translation see H. Bobzin, 'Translation of the Qur'ān', in McAuliffe (ed.), *Encyclopaedia*, vol. V, pp. 340–58. For the most comprehensive bibliographies of translations of the Qur'ān, see: I. Binark and H. Eren, *World bibliography of translations of the meanings of the holy Qur'an: Printed translations 1515–1980*, ed. Ekmeleddin Ihsanoglu (Istanbul: Research Centre for Islamic History, Art and Culture, 1986), esp. pp. 65–175 for English translations; N. Sefercioglu, *World bibliography of translations of the holy Qur'an in manuscript form: Turkish, Persian and Urdu translations excluded*, ed. Ekmeleddin Ihsanoglu (Istanbul: Research Centre for Islamic History, Art and Culture, 2000).
47. K. Cragg, *Readings in the Qur'ān* (London: Collins, 1988); M. Sells, *Approaching the Qur'ān: The early revelations* (Ashland, OR: White Cloud Press, 1999).
48. H. Kassis, *A concordance of the Qur'an* (Berkeley: University of California Press, 1983).

Part I

Formation of the qur'ānic text

Fig. 1 Fragment of right half of frontispiece of early eighth-century Qur'ān manuscript (Ṣan'ā', Dār al-Makhṭūṭāt, Inv. No. 20–33.1). Photograph courtesy of Hans Casper Graf von Bothmer, Saarbrucken

1 The historical context

FRED M. DONNER

The Qur'ān, considered by believing Muslims to be a literal transcript of God's word as revealed to the prophet Muḥammad (*c.* 570–632 CE), poses a number of interesting, and sometimes vexing, questions when we attempt to discuss its historical context. In one sense, the Qur'ān's theological status as divine word negates the very idea of it having a historical context at all, for it implies that the text is of eternal and unchanging validity. Muslim tradition even asserts that it had been revealed on several other occasions, to earlier communities via their prophets. This being so, the historical context in which a particular passage was revealed to Muḥammad can be understood only as an accident, and has no real bearing on the meaning of a passage at all, which is immutable and intrinsic.

Despite the Qur'ān's theological status, Muslims over the centuries elaborated highly detailed traditions about the Qur'ān's historical context. This took the form of a vast biographical literature on the Prophet and his time which, loosely following traditional usage, we can call the *sīra* literature.[1] The *sīra* literature was compiled by Muslim sages during the several hundred years following Muḥammad's death in 11/632, and offers a richly detailed account of Muḥammad's life, of his receipt of the revelations that are enshrined in the qur'ānic text, and (although less fully) of the codification of the revelation in the years following his death to produce the text of the Qur'ān as we have it today. Most Western scholarship on the Qur'ān and its context has drawn heavily on the *sīra* literature for its basic documentation.

TRADITIONAL NARRATIVE OF ISLAMIC ORIGINS

According to the traditional Islamic origins narrative, Muḥammad belonged to the tribe of Quraysh, which dominated the town of Mecca in western Arabia, where he was born sometime in the third quarter of the sixth century. Mecca had only meagre agricultural potential – the spring of Zamzam provided sufficient water, but the town was situated in a rocky valley that was not suitable for extensive farming, only household garden plots. (In this, Mecca differed from some other west Arabian settlements, like the oases at Yathrib, later Medina, and Khaybar, which had open land with fields of barley, vegetables and, above all, vast plantations of date-palms.) Instead, Quraysh prospered on a combination of regional caravan trade and stewardship of a large shrine centred on a cubical stone building, the Kaʿba. This combination of commercial and cultic activity put Quraysh in touch with people of many tribes from diverse corners of Arabia.

The *sīra* literature presents Mecca's cult as a pagan one to the god Hubal, and depicts the Arabian religious environment in which Muḥammad grew up as overwhelmingly pagan – the final vestiges of the ancient near eastern religious tradition. The shrine itself was surrounded by a sacred area or *ḥaram*, delimited by boundary stones, which included the whole town of Mecca. Quraysh, as guardians of the shrine, imposed regulations on all who entered the town, including forbidding them from engaging in violence; and they enforced these regulations with the help of various other tribes who lived outside Mecca but honoured its religious cult (and utilised its markets). This ban on violence meant that Mecca's *ḥaram* was safe ground where merchants could market their goods without fear of being plundered, and where representatives of hostile tribes could meet to resolve their feuds without fear of ambush.

Muḥammad belonged to the clan of Hāshim within Quraysh; his father died before he was born, and when he was a young boy, his mother also died, so that he was raised to adulthood by his paternal uncle, Abū Ṭālib, who was head of the Hāshim clan at the time. Some clans of Quraysh had become wealthy through their trading activities, and were assigned responsibility for key rituals in the Kaʿba cult. Other clans, however, were of more modest means; Hāshim was one of these. Despite his relatively humble origins, however, Muḥammad is portrayed by the *sīra* as participating actively in the commercial life of Mecca in his youth and adolescence – for example, he is said to have accompanied his uncle and guardian Abū Ṭālib on caravans to southern Syria. He also participated in the cultic activities of Mecca in his early years. As a result of these experiences, he acquired as a young man a reputation for skill, tactfulness, honesty and fairness. These qualities attracted the attention of a well-to-do widow, Khadīja, who hired him to manage her caravan trade; later, she proposed marriage to him, which Muḥammad accepted.

Around 610 CE, when Muḥammad was perhaps forty years old or so, he began to withdraw occasionally to the desolate outskirts of Mecca to engage in meditation. During one of these retreats, he started to have visions and hear voices informing him that God had chosen him to receive the divine word – that, in other words, he was a prophet. Initially terrified by this experience and reluctant to take on this charge, he was comforted and reassured by Khadīja – who is thus honoured by Muslims as the first person to recognise his prophecy – and eventually accepted his new role as bearer of God's message to humankind, particularly to his fellow-Quraysh of Mecca. After this initial experience, revelations came to him on a regular basis; in each instance, he was physically overwhelmed by the revelatory experience and emerged from it with the new passages burned indelibly into his memory. It was these passages that, memorised or written down by his followers, were edited together some years after his death in 11/632 to form the Qur'ān.

Muḥammad's message

The basic doctrines that Muḥammad taught were that God was one, the creator of humankind and the natural world, and that the recognition of a plethora of pagan deities was an affront to God and his unity. Closely tied to this was the notion that the world would end at the last judgement, when all souls would be brought before God and judged by him on the basis of how they had lived their lives. Those who had believed in the one God and lived righteously would be rewarded after death by enjoying eternal bliss in heaven, whereas unbelievers and the impious would suffer everlasting torment in hell.

Muḥammad began preaching the message embedded in these revelations to his fellow Meccans, and won some early adherents, but many members of Quraysh were deeply suspicious of his preaching. To judge from the testimony of the Qur'ān itself, some were sceptical of Muḥammad's claims that there was an afterlife in which they would be reborn. Others were incensed by Muḥammad's claim that unbelievers could not enter heaven, which implied that their Quraysh ancestors, who had died pagans, were burning in hellfire – a shocking insult in a society whose members identified themselves mainly by their lineage. Whatever the reasons, Muḥammad and his followers faced increasing opposition and, as time went on, harassment by Quraysh. Some of his followers took refuge with the Christian king of Abyssinia (an episode about which we know, unfortunately, very little). His uncle Abū Ṭālib, as head of the clan of Hāshim, protected him and refused to hand him over to the other clans of Quraysh, who organised a boycott of Hāshim. With the death of Abū Ṭālib, however, and, at around the same time, of his wife Khadīja, Muḥammad was deprived of his most important sources of practical and emotional support. As his situation deteriorated further, Muḥammad began to search for support outside Mecca, with little success until he encountered a group from the oasis of Yathrib, some 350 kilometres north of Mecca, at a trade fair near Mecca. Impressed with his teachings and thinking that he could serve as arbiter for Yathrib's own bitter internal feuds, they returned the following year and made an agreement to welcome and support Muḥammad in Yathrib. Some time thereafter, in 622 CE, Muḥammad and his supporters in Mecca emigrated to Yathrib – henceforth to be known as Medina – and established themselves there. The *hijra*, as this emigration is called, marked the beginning of the Muslim community as an autonomous political community, and the year in which it took place – 622 CE – was subsequently adopted by Muslims as the year 1 of the Islamic calendar (AH 1).

The move to Medina

Muḥammad faced numerous challenges in his years in Medina, but succeeded gradually in establishing his mastery over the town both as its religious leader and in practical terms. Medina's inhabitants included the indigenous Aws and Khazraj tribes, formerly pagan but now following Muḥammad's religious teachings. They were styled collectively the *anṣār* or 'Helpers' because of their assistance to Muḥammad and his followers at a crucial time, but despite this common appellation, the Aws and Khazraj still retained some of their traditional antipathy for one another. Another important element of the population were the numerous Jews of Medina. Traditional sources speak especially of three large Jewish clans – the Qaynuqāʿ, Naḍīr and Qurayẓa – but there were as well smaller groups of Jews affiliated with various clans of the Aws or Khazraj. Muḥammad's followers from Mecca formed yet another population group, called *muhājirūn* ('those who had made the *hijra*'). All these groups are mentioned in the text of an agreement between Muḥammad and the people of Medina (sometimes called, rather misleadingly, 'the constitution of Medina'), which has survived in the *sīra* literature. It lays out the idea that all these groups are to form a single *umma* or community for mutual defence, of which Muḥammad was to be the head.

Forging a unified community in Medina from this mixed population was, however, a difficult assignment. Some people (mostly from Aws or Khazraj) were outwardly counted among Muḥammad's supporters but worked against him and his religious ideas behind the scenes; they are called *munāfiqūn* or 'hypocrites', and Muḥammad had to contend with their machinations for much of his career in Medina. More serious still was the opposition of Medina's Jews to Muḥammad's leadership. It appears that Muḥammad hoped at first to win the Jews of Medina not only to his political leadership but also to his claim that he was a prophet continuing the line of prophets known from the Hebrew Bible, such as Abraham, Moses and Joseph. It is not clear exactly how or why his relationship with the Jews went awry; the *sīra* literature offers numerous tales of the Jews' opposition (without clarifying whether that opposition was fundamentally political or was basically a rejection of Muḥammad's prophetic claims), but also hints that desire to seize lands held by the Jews, perhaps to relieve the distress of the *muhājirūn*, may have been one of Muḥammad's motivations. In any case, the *sīra* accounts describe how each of the three major Jewish clans in turn was either exiled from Medina (with loss of their lands) or, in the case of the Qurayẓa, liquidated – the men executed, the women and children seized as slaves. After the Qurayẓa were eliminated late in 5/627, Muḥammad's leadership in Medina was no longer seriously contested.

The *sīra* literature also details certain episodes in Muḥammad's personal life that apparently became matters of public controversy or had important implications for the community in some way. It notes his marriages, some of which had political significance, such as his union with Zaynab, who belonged to the powerful Umayya clan of Quraysh; and it relates the scandalous rumours that circulated when his favourite wife, ʿĀʾisha, caught up with and rejoined the caravan that had inadvertently left her behind in the company of a young man who had given her transport.

Expeditions and battles

Another central theme in Muḥammad's career in Medina as recounted in the *sīra* literature was his struggle against Quraysh and his home town of Mecca. Muḥammad's ambition to subdue Mecca sprang partly, perhaps, from a desire to settle scores with Quraysh, who had in effect expelled him from the city; and it may also have been to provide plunder to support the poor *muhājirūn*. But his desire to overcome Mecca also had a religious dimension, for Muḥammad came to see the Kaʿba in Mecca as a formerly monotheist shrine first established by Abraham, so that restoration of pure monotheist worship there became an important issue for him. This attitude was reflected in Muḥammad's decision that his believers should no longer pray towards Jerusalem, as they had previously, but towards the Kaʿba in Mecca – a change that may have been related to his deteriorating relationship with Medina's Jews. Closely connected to his struggle for supremacy with Quraysh were Muḥammad's many efforts to win over the nomadic groups of western Arabia, whose support often determined the political balance between the two towns of Mecca and Medina.

Whatever his motivations may have been, Muḥammad began to organise raiding parties to attack Meccan caravans shortly after arriving in Medina. After several minor raids, Muḥammad ambushed a large Meccan caravan at Badr in 2/624, which resulted in the death of a number of leaders of Quraysh, seizure of much booty and the taking of numerous prisoners for ransom. Quraysh responded a year later by organising an expedition against Medina. Battle was joined at a place called Uḥud just outside Medina, and while it was a setback for Muḥammad's forces, with quite a few of his men killed, the Meccans did not press their advantage and occupy Medina or kill Muḥammad, whose men in subsequent years continued to harass Meccan caravans. Then, in 5/627, the Meccans assembled a large coalition of local tribes and again marched against Medina, intending presumably to finish Muḥammad off. Medina was besieged for roughly a month, during which some skirmishing took place, but partly because Muḥammad and his followers built a trench to defend one vulnerable flank, the city was not taken and the Meccan alliance began to unravel. The so-called 'Battle of the Trench' had demonstrated Mecca's overwhelming military superiority, but had once again left Muḥammad and his followers standing, though presumably somewhat humiliated.

Muḥammad launched further raids in the months after the Battle of the Trench (a period that also included the liquidation of the Qurayẓa Jews, who were said to have been in treasonous contact with the Meccans during the siege). Then, in 6/628, Muḥammad organised his followers to march to Mecca unarmed, in order to perform the *ʿumra* (lesser pilgrimage rites) at the Kaʿba. The Quraysh were stupefied by this move, since barely a year before they had chastised Muḥammad by besieging Medina itself, and doubtless thought they had 'taught him a lesson'. They blocked his entry to the town with armed forces at a place called al-Ḥudaybiya, just at the border of the Meccan *ḥaram*. Here Muḥammad engaged in negotiations with the Meccans in which he agreed to respect a ten-year armistice and to return to Medina, but secured permission to enter Mecca the following year to do the pilgrimage.

Some of Muḥammad's followers thought that he had given away too much in the al-Ḥudaybiya agreement – for example he had abjured raiding the caravans of the Meccans – but in the year and a half following this negotiation, Muḥammad steadily consolidated his political position in the Ḥijāz and increasingly isolated Mecca politically and militarily. A key stroke was Muḥammad's campaign against the oasis of Khaybar, 150 kilometres north of Medina, undertaken just a few months after al-Ḥudaybiya. Khaybar had a primarily Jewish population, including many of the Medinan Jews who had been exiled by Muḥammad, and had long been allied with Quraysh against Muḥammad, who thus had to contend with hostile forces on two sides. By conquering Khaybar and requiring its inhabitants to pay tax, Muḥammad greatly improved his strategic (and financial) situation in relation to Mecca. Muḥammad and his followers made further raids on various communities not aligned with Mecca, and then successfully completed their first pilgrimage since the *hijra* at the end of 7/early 629. Following it, clashes between allies of Mecca and those of Muḥammad, and the latter's increasingly dominant position, created conditions in which Muḥammad could consider subduing Mecca directly, on the grounds that the Meccans had broken their treaty obligations. Late in 8/early 630, he assembled a large force of Medinans and a variety of tribal allies from the Ḥijāz, marched on Mecca, and secured the capitulation of its leaders, notably Abū Sufyān of the Umayya clan. Only a few of his most bitter opponents were executed; the majority, who recognised his claim to be prophet and renounced polytheism, he welcomed into his new movement – even giving some of the leaders of Quraysh important assignments as a way of cementing their loyalty. He proceeded to purify the Kaʿba and its environs of remnants of polytheist worship and dedicated it henceforth to the worship of the one God.

During the last several years of his life, then, Muḥammad became the unchallenged political leader of western Arabia, as well as fulfilling the role of a monotheist prophet. Shortly following his occupation of Mecca his forces defeated a large alliance of tribesmen at the Battle of Ḥunayn. After giving them fairly lenient terms, he then enlisted their aid in subduing the remaining large town of the Ḥijāz, al-Ṭāʾif. He then returned to Medina, from where he ruled and where he remained except for another two visits to Mecca to perform the pilgrimage (end of 9/631 and 10/632). During the final two years of Muḥammad's life he dispatched raiding parties to secure the submission of many smaller towns or tribal groups, and delegations from many groups, sometimes from distant areas of Arabia, arrived in Medina to tender their submission or conclude an alliance with the man who was now clearly the leading figure in western Arabia. In the year 11/632, after a short illness, Muḥammad died in Medina in the lap of his favourite wife, ʿĀʾisha.

SETTING THE QUR'ĀN IN CONTEXT

Throughout the life just sketched on the basis of the traditional *sīra* literature, Muḥammad is said to have continued to receive revelations. In the centuries following Muḥammad's life, Muslims developed a whole science, called *asbāb al-nuzūl* or 'occasions of the revelation', whose goal was to identify the historical context of qur'ānic passages. In general terms, Muslim scholars categorised each sūra as being either 'Meccan' or 'Medinan', depending on when they thought it was revealed. They also strove to define much more precisely the exact moment in Muḥammad's life during which each qur'ānic verse or passage had been revealed. The underlying implication of such an exercise, of course, is that knowing the context in which a verse was revealed will tell us something important about how to understand the verse, or about its potential legal force. What specific situation in the Prophet's life was it revealed to address? So, for example, Q 8 (Sūrat al-Anfāl, 'The Spoils') was said by exegetes to have been revealed immediately after the Battle of Badr, to deal with the questions raised by the booty seized in that battle. The famous verse 3 in Q 4 (Sūrat al-Nisā', 'The Women'), which allows Muslims to take up to four wives, is related to the aftermath of the Battle of Uḥud, when the heavy losses among the believers left many women orphaned or widowed. Q 2 (Sūrat al-Baqara, 'The Cow'), verses 142–5, comment on the change of the *qibla* and verses 11–20 of Q 24 (Sūrat al-Nūr, 'Light') are said to address the scandalous rumours circulated by some of the 'hypocrites' against Muḥammad's wife ʿĀ'isha. The biographical information provided by the *sīra* literature is thus intimately tied to the text of the Qur'ān itself. It should be noted, however, that in many instances the qur'ānic passage that the exegetes link to a particular episode is quite general in its tone, and lacks any specific indication that the episode is in fact connected with the event. Q 8, for example, does not mention Badr explicitly, and the place name Uḥud never occurs in the Qur'ān at all.

Codification of the text

After Muḥammad's death in 11/632, the revelations of course ceased, and the community was faced with the vexing question of how to order its affairs (including its political and religious leadership) in the absence of their prophet. This crucial subject is beyond the limits of the present essay, but it is important to say a few words about how Muslim tradition views the process by which the revelations Muḥammad received were ultimately codified to form the text of the Qur'ān as it exists today.

Muslim sources offer contradictory, or perhaps merely divergent, information on this process. On the one hand, there is a strong tendency in the sources to emphasise the oral nature of transmission of the Qur'ān text; the revelations were first received by Muḥammad in oral form, and were then recited by him to his followers, who in turn then learned them, or parts of them, by heart. The very word *qur'ān* seems to mean 'recitation', particularly recitation for liturgical purposes. Later Muslim tradition advanced the view that the Qur'ān's characterisation of Muḥammad (in Q 7:157–8) as *al-nabī l-ummī* meant 'the prophet who did not know how to write'. On the other hand, the Qur'ān also frequently refers to the revelations as *al-kitāb*, 'the book' (although in some cases this may be an allusion to a heavenly written archetype, not the earthly text). Muslim tradition speaks of several people who served as Muḥammad's scribes and were responsible for writing down the revelations for him. It also tells of various people in Muḥammad's community, such as his wife 'Ā'isha, who possessed written transcripts or copies of at least part of the revelations at the time of his death. It seems very likely, therefore, that upon Muḥammad's death, sections of the revelation were known by heart by some members of the community, and other segments were preserved in written form.

The history of the text in the years immediately after Muḥammad's death is not clear.[2] Muslim tradition reports that an early collection may have been prepared in the caliphate of Abū Bakr (r. 11–13/632–4), which was later kept by the caliph 'Umar (r. 13–23/634–44) and then by the latter's daughter Ḥafṣa, widow of the Prophet. It is not clear, however, whether this written collection was complete or not, nor whether it had any official status. There are also vague reports of other collections held by various parties, about which we know virtually nothing, assuming the reports have any validity at all. More specific are the accounts that ascribe the preparation of an official written copy to the time of the third caliph, 'Uthmān (r. 23–35/644–55). 'Uthmān asked Zayd b. Thābit – who had been one of Muḥammad's scribes and who is said to have been involved in the collection supposedly prepared under Abū Bakr – to lead an editorial team to prepare a complete, official text of the Qur'ān. To do so, he was to examine all known written collections and to interview all persons who had memorised parts of the text, and on this basis to prepare the complete written copy. This official ''Uthmānic text' is generally considered to be the archetype for the Qur'ān text as we have it today, but many questions remain regarding the relationship of the 'Uthmānic text to both the revelations of Muḥammad's time and to the Qur'ān of today.

The relationship of the ʿUthmānic text to the revelations received by Muḥammad is clouded by the existence of numerous collections of variant readings that have survived, attributed to a number of early scholars who were widely known for their excellence in reading and reciting the Qurʾān, and who claimed to base their readings on pre-ʿUthmānic traditions.[3] The existence of these variants implies that the recitation of the text was far from uniform. Most variants are minor, but some are significant and involve not just vocalisation but completely different words. The 1924 Cairo edition of the Qurʾān, which is the most widely used version today, follows one of these readings, that of the Kūfan ʿĀṣim b. Bahdala (d. 127 or 128/745), as transmitted by his student Ḥafṣ b. Sulaymān, while the other readings are mainly ignored by lay readers and even by most scholars. The full import, however, of these variants for our understanding of the ʿUthmānic text and its relationship to the revelations as they existed in Muḥammad's time is still not clear.

Another problem is that the ʿUthmānic text, from what we know of it, was written in a highly defective script – essentially providing only a rough consonantal 'skeleton', without vowels and without diacritical marks to distinguish two or more consonants that were written with the same shape. It was only after the passage of several centuries that fully vocalised, unequivocal texts were prepared of the different variant versions. This means that in its original form, the ʿUthmānic text could only have been 'read' easily by people who already knew it. On the one hand, this suggests that for much of the text, at least, a strong tradition of oral recitation may have existed, and that the ʿUthmānic text served mainly as a mnemonic device to aid in recitation. On the other hand, it opens the possibility that the fully vocalised texts that were eventually prepared could have contained erroneous vocalisations, further clouding our perception of the relationship of today's vocalised text to the revelations of Muḥammad's time – that is, of the relationship to the Qurʾān, as we have it today, to its presumed historical context.

Western scholars have also tended to accept, until recently, the broad context provided by the *sīra* literature: the consensus was for many years that Muḥammad did, in fact, live in Mecca and Medina and that his career followed roughly the path outlined in the *sīra* and summarised above.[4] A milestone in Western analysis of the Qurʾān's contents in light of the *sīra* was the appearance of the first edition of Theodor Nöldeke's *Geschichte des Qorans* in 1860.[5] Nöldeke, following the lead of Muslim scholars, divided the Qurʾān into Meccan and Medinan sūras, but he also used criteria of style and content to subdivide further the Meccan passages into early, middle and late. His reconstruction of the chronology of the revelations has continued to exert a powerful influence on most Western Qur'ān scholars, even until today.[6] A few subsequent scholars, such as Richard Bell and Régis Blachère, have attempted alternative chronological reconstructions which differ in some measure from Nöldeke's, but most Western students of the text have until recently remained largely beholden to Nöldeke's reconstruction.

The real question facing qur'ānic scholarship at the beginning of the twenty-first century is whether the Arabian setting described by the *sīra* literature is the actual historical context in which the Qur'ān emerged. The rise in recent decades of a highly sceptical school of historical analysis regarding the origins of Islam – including particularly the *sīra* literature – has cast grave doubt on much of the earlier work that took the framework provided by the *sīra* for granted. The roots of this sceptical attitude towards the traditional Muslim sources go back to the pioneering work of nineteenth-century scholars such as M. J. de Goeje and Ignaz Goldziher and were developed in the twentieth century by scholars such as Joseph Schacht, but the approach really came to the fore in the 1970s. John Wansbrough asserted that the Qur'ān was not a stable canon of sacred text until at least two centuries or more after the death of Muḥammad in 11/632 – contrary to the traditional view, which considers the ʿUthmānic text to be quite firmly established a mere two decades after Muḥammad's death.[7] He also believed that the actual context in which the Qur'ān emerged was not Arabia, but what he termed the 'sectarian milieu' of monotheistic debate in places with long-established monotheist communities, particularly Iraq and Palestine.[8] Recent work suggests that Wansbrough's hypothesis of a very late crystallisation of the Qur'ān text outside Arabia is not in accord with the internal evidence of the text itself, which implies a very early crystallisation (before the first civil war, 36–41/656–61) and, for at least parts of the text, an origin in western Arabia.[9]

Sīra as exegesis?

Wansbrough and some other writers, partly following earlier writers such as Henri Lammens, also argued that the traditional *sīra* materials do not represent an independent body of information that might be used to understand the text of the Qur'ān, but rather were fabricated precisely to explain various verses of the Qur'ān.[10] Patricia Crone and Michael Cook, whose book *Hagarism* unleashed an avalanche of work on Islam's origins, were far less radical than Wansbrough in their view of the date of the Qur'ān, which they thought was probably codified in the late seventh century, but they took a similarly critical view of much of what was contained in the *sīra* literature.[11]

The issues raised by these recent sceptical writers and their critical predecessors have yet to be definitively resolved by scholars of the Qur'ān. There is evidence to support the contention that some reports in the *sīra* literature are of dubious validity and may, in fact, have originated in the need to invent a supposed historical context for exegetical readings of particular verses. This evidence includes such things as inner contradictions in the *sīra* narratives, the presence of numerological symbolism, structural hints that some of the *sīra* stories originated in exegesis of the Qur'ān. There is also evidence of a desire to generate an idealised view of Muḥammad or to elaborate on biblical tropes. On the other hand, there is evidence to support the contention that the *sīra* narratives originated independently of the Qur'ān and were linked to the exegetical process only at a secondary stage.[12] Scholars differ greatly in their judgements about the degree to which these characteristics undermine the historical reliability of the *sīra* literature, some rejecting its testimony almost completely, others feeling that the main outlines of the *sīra* are probably authentic.[13] But even if one contends that the problematic elements are only a small part of the *sīra*, one's ability to rely on it is undermined because there is as yet no generally accepted and foolproof method for distinguishing what might be true from what might be false.

Taken together, these two facts – that the Qur'ān text crystallised at an early date, and that the *sīra* reports are sometimes exegetical – suggest that we must consider the relationship of the Qur'ān to its context in a manner that reverses the procedure normally adopted when studying the relationship of a text to its context. Rather than relying on the *sīra* reports about a presumed historical context to illuminate the meaning of the Qur'ān text, we must attempt to infer from the qur'ānic text what its true historical context might have been, and in this way check on the historicity of various reports in the *sīra*.[14] Efforts to do this are still in their infancy, but several hypotheses about the Qur'ān's nature and context seem to be emerging as possibilities that bear further investigation. One is that the traditional *sīra* literature may greatly overstate the significance of paganism as the context or background against which the Qur'ān emerged. Gerald Hawting has recently made a strong case for the proposition that the Qur'ān's references to *mushrikūn*, 'polytheists', are in fact hyperbolic products of intra-monotheist polemics and not evidence of an actual pagan background at all.[15] Similarly, the *sīra* literature may downplay the significance of Christianity or Judaism in the formation of Islam and the Qur'ān. The relationship of the Qur'ān to Judaism and Christianity has long been an important focus of attention for Western scholars, going back as far as the work of Abraham Geiger in the mid-nineteenth century and Tor Andrae, Richard Bell and Charles Torrey (among others) in the early twentieth. Some of this earlier work was crassly reductionist, but more recent work, particularly by Günter Lüling and Christoph Luxenberg, as well as by Wansbrough, has reopened these issues in a more sophisticated way, although the interpretations offered differ significantly from one another, and have been roundly criticised by some. This work generally suggests, however, that scholars need to look at the broader context of near eastern religion in late antiquity to find the Qur'ān's historical and intellectual setting, and not just the Arabian context. And, if we do so, we must consider seriously the importance of religious phenomena that were widespread in the late antique near east, such as ascetic piety (especially strong in Syrian Christianity) and apocalypticism, echoes of both of which can be found in early Islam and in the Qur'ān.

Another emerging issue for scholars is the way the Qur'ān text was transmitted, which has a bearing on our understanding of its actual nature as a text and, consequently, its historical context. The aforementioned works by Lüling and Luxenberg, as well as articles by James Bellamy, have suggested that, contrary to the traditional view of an unbroken oral tradition, parts of the Qur'ān text must, at some stage, have been transmitted in written form without a controlling tradition of oral recitation, at least for those passages. This does not yet tell us exactly when or how this written transmission occurred, but it means that we must be willing to entertain a variety of possibilities, and wait until future research on the Qur'ān either confirms or refutes them. Among these possible hypotheses are some close to the traditional view, according to which the Qur'ān emerged from the career of Muḥammad but was transmitted partly in written form before the production of the ʿUthmānic text. Alternatively, it may turn out that parts of the Qur'ān go back to older written texts (of Christian or Jewish or other origin?) that pre-date Muḥammad's career, and were incorporated into the revelations in some form. Yet another possibility is that the qur'ānic text, with all its diversity of style and content, is a collation of originally independent textual corpora hailing from different communities of believers in Arabia, whose relations with Muḥammad and his prophetic activities remain to be determined. Only when further research has more fully clarified some of these issues will we be able to know with any certainty just what the Qur'ān's historical context truly was.

Notes

1. On the *sīra* literature generally, see M. Hinds, 'Maghāzī', in *Encyclopaedia of Islam*, new ed., 11 vols. (Leiden: Brill, 1979–2002), vol. V, pp. 1,161–4, and W. Raven, 'Sīra', in *Encyclopaedia of Islam*, new ed., vol. IX, pp. 660–3. See also J. Horovitz, *The earliest biographies of the Prophet and their authors*, ed. L. I. Conrad (Princeton: Darwin Press, 2002), particularly Conrad's introduction.
2. The classic treatment of the issues discussed in the next several paragraphs is found in Th. Nöldeke, *Geschichte des Qorāns* (Göttingen: Dieterich, 1860); second ed., revised by F. Schwally, G. Bergsträsser and O. Pretzl, 3 vols. (Leipzig: Dieterich, 1919–38); a convenient summary in English is provided in W. M. Watt, *Bell's Introduction to the Qur'ān* (Edinburgh: Edinburgh University Press, 1970), pp. 40–56.
3. On variant readings, see R. Paret, 'Ḳirā'a', in *Encyclopaedia of Islam*, new ed., vol. V, pp. 127–9, and A. T. Welch, 'al-Ḳur'ān. 3. History of the Ḳur'ān after 632', in *Encyclopaedia of Islam*, new ed., vol. V, pp. 404–9. The variants are tabulated in A. Jeffery, *Materials for the history of the text of the Qur'ān* (Leiden: Brill, 1937).
4. Readable Western accounts based closely on the traditional *sīra* literature include W. M. Watt, *Muḥammad at Mecca* (Oxford: Oxford University Press, 1953), as well as his *Muḥammad at Medina* (Oxford: Oxford University Press, 1956) and his *Muḥammad, prophet and statesman* (Oxford: Clarendon Press, 1961); F. E. Peters, *Muḥammad and the origins of Islam* (Albany: SUNY Press, 1994); and M. Gaudefroy-Demombynes, *Mahomet* (Paris: Albin Michel, 1957).
5. The greatly expanded revised edition prepared by F. Schwally, G. Bergsträsser and O. Pretzl (1909–38) is usually referred to today.
6. E.g., A. Neuwirth, *Studien zur Komposition der mekkanischen Suren* (Berlin: DeGruyter, 1981); T. Nagel, *Medinensische Einschübe in Mekkanischen Suren* (Göttingen: Vandenhoeck and Ruprecht, 1995).
7. J. Wansbrough, *Quranic studies: Sources and methods of scriptural interpretation* (Oxford: Oxford University Press, 1977).
8. J. Wansbrough, *The sectarian milieu: Content and composition of Islamic salvation history* (Oxford: Oxford University Press, 1978).
9. F. M. Donner, *Narratives of Islamic origins: The beginnings of Islamic historical writing* (Princeton: Darwin Press, 1998), ch. 1.
10. Besides Wansbrough's *Quranic studies*, see A. Rippin, 'The function of *asbāb al-nuzūl* in qur'ānic exegesis', *Bulletin of the School of Oriental and African Studies* 51 (1988), 1–20; M. Schöller, *Exegetisches Denken und Prophetenbiographie: Eine quellenkritische Analyse der Sīra-Überlieferung zu Muḥammads Konflikt mit den Juden* (Wiesbaden: Otto Harrassowitz, 1998).
11. P. Crone and M. Cook, *Hagarism: The making of the Islamic world* (Cambridge: Cambridge University Press, 1977).
12. Among the works addressing these issues are P. Crone, *Meccan trade and the rise of Islam* (Princeton: Princeton University Press, 1987); U. Rubin, *The eye of the beholder: The life of Muḥammad as viewed by the early Muslims* (Princeton: Darwin Press, 1995) and his *Between Bible and Qur'ān: The Children of Israel and the Islamic self-image* (Princeton: Darwin Press, 1999); Schöller, *Exegetisches*

Denken; M. J. Kister, *Studies in Jāhiliyya and early Islam* (London: Variorum, 1980).

13. Relatively few critical scholars have adopted a 'bunker mentality' and chosen to defend the *sīra* in all its details as accurate; it can be questioned, in light of the overwhelming evidence that the *sīra* does contain interpolations of later attitudes and needs, whether such scholars can be considered critically minded at all.
14. This is the procedure adopted in W. M. Watt, *Muḥammad's Mecca: History in the Qur'ān* (Edinburgh: Edinburgh University Press, 1988).
15. G. Hawting, *The idea of idolatry and the emergence of Islam* (Cambridge: Cambridge University Press, 1999); however, his adoption of Wansbrough's contention that the locus of this activity was not Arabia, but Iraq and Syria, is less convincing. See F. M. Donner, 'Review of G. Hawting, *The idea of idolatry and the emergence of Islam*', *Journal of the American Oriental Society* 121 (2001), 336–8.

Further reading

Andrae, T., 'Der Ursprung des Islams und das Christentum', *Kyrkshistorisk årsskrift* 23 (1923), 149–206; 24 (1924), 213–92; 25 (1925), 45–112.

Bell, R., *The origin of Islam in its Christian environment*, London: Macmillan, 1926.

The Qur'an translated, 2 vols., Edinburgh: T. and T. Clark, 1937.

Bellamy, J., 'More proposed emendations to the text of the Qur'ān', *Journal of the American Oriental Society* 116 (1996), 196–204.

'Some proposed emendations to the text of the Koran', *Journal of the American Oriental Society* 113 (1993), 562–73.

Blachère, R., *Le Coran, traduction nouvelle*, 2 vols., Paris: G.-P. Maisonneuve, 1949–50.

Conrad, L. I., 'Editor's introduction', in J. Horovitz, *The earliest biographies of the Prophet and their authors*, ed. L. I. Conrad, Princeton: Darwin Press, 2002, pp. ix–xxxviii.

Crone, P., *Meccan trade and the rise of Islam*, Princeton: Princeton University Press, 1987.

Crone, P. and M. Cook, *Hagarism: The making of the Islamic world*, Cambridge: Cambridge University Press, 1977.

De Goeje, M., *Mémoire sur la conquête de la Syrie*, second ed., Leiden: Brill, 1900.

Donner, F. M., 'Muḥammad's political consolidation up to the conquest of Mecca: A reassessment', *Muslim World* 69 (1979), 229–47.

Narratives of Islamic origins: The beginnings of Islamic historical writing, Princeton: Darwin Press, 1998.

'Review of G. Hawting, *The idea of idolatry and the emergence of Islam*', *Journal of the American Oriental Society* 121 (2001), 336–8.

Gaudefroy-Demombynes, M., *Mahomet*, Paris: Albin Michel, 1957.

Geiger, A., *Was hat Mohammed aus dem Judenthume aufgenommen?*, Bonn: F. Baaden, 1833.

Goldziher, I., *Muhammadanische Studien*, 2 vols., Halle: Max Niemeyer, 1889–90, Eng. trans. C. R. Barber and S. M. Stern, *Muslim studies*, 2 vols., London: George Allen and Unwin, 1967–71.

Hawting, G., *The idea of idolatry and the emergence of Islam*, Cambridge: Cambridge University Press, 1999.

Hinds, M., 'Maghāzī', in *Encyclopaedia of Islam*, new ed., 11 vols., Leiden: Brill, 1979–2002, vol. V, pp. 1,161–4.

Horovitz, J., *The earliest biographies of the Prophet and their authors*, ed. L. I. Conrad, Princeton: Darwin Press, 2002 (Originally published in *Islamic Culture* 1 (1927) and 2 (1928).)

Jeffery, A., *Materials for the history of the text of the Qur'ān*, Leiden: Brill, 1937.

Kister, M. J., *Studies in Jāhiliyya and early Islam*, London: Variorum, 1980.

Lammens, H., 'Qoran et tradition: Comment fut composée la vie de Mahomet', *Révue des sciences religieuses* 1 (1910), 27–51.

Lüling, G., *A challenge to Islam for reformation: The rediscovery and reliable reconstruction of a comprehensive pre-Islamic Christian hymnal hidden in the Koran under earliest Islamic reinterpretations*, Delhi: Motilal Banarsidass Publishers, 2003.

Über den Ur-Koran, Erlangen: Verlag H. Lüling, 1974.

Luxenberg, Ch. (pseud.), *Die Syro-Aramäische Lesart des Koran*, Berlin: Das Arabische Buch, 2000.

Nagel, T., *Medinensische Einschübe in Mekkanischen Suren*, Göttingen: Vandenhoeck and Ruprecht, 1995.

Neuwirth, A., *Studien zur Komposition der mekkanischen Suren*, Berlin: DeGruyter, 1981.

Nöldeke, Th., *Geschichte des Qorāns*, Göttingen: Dieterich, 1860; second ed., revised by F. Schwally, G. Bergsträsser and O. Pretzl, 3 vols., Leipzig: Dieterich, 1919–38.

Paret, R., 'Ḳirā'a', in *Encyclopaedia of Islam*, new ed., 11 vols., Leiden: Brill, 1979–2002, vol. V, pp. 127–9.

Peters, F. E., *Muḥammad and the origins of Islam*, Albany: SUNY Press, 1994.

Raven, W., 'Sīra', in *Encyclopaedia of Islam*, new ed., 11 vols., Leiden: Brill, 1979–2002, vol. X, pp. 660–3.

Rippin, A., 'The function of *asbāb al-nuzūl* in qur'ānic exegesis', *Bulletin of the School of Oriental and African Studies* 51 (1988), 1–20.

Rubin, U., *Between Bible and Qur'ān: The Children of Israel and the Islamic self-image*, Princeton: Darwin Press, 1999.

The eye of the beholder: The life of Muḥammad as viewed by the early Muslims, Princeton: Darwin Press, 1995.

Schacht, J., 'A revaluation of Islamic traditions', *Journal of the Royal Asiatic Society* (1949), 143–54.

Schöller, M., *Exegetisches Denken und Prophetenbiographie: Eine quellenkritische Analyse der Sīra-Überlieferung zu Muḥammads Konflikt mit den Juden*, Wiesbaden: Otto Harrassowitz, 1998.

Torrey, Ch., *The Jewish foundations of Islam*, New York: Jewish Institute of Religion, 1933.

Wansbrough, J., *Quranic studies: Sources and methods of scriptural interpretation*, Oxford: Oxford University Press, 1977.

The sectarian milieu: Content and composition of Islamic salvation history, Oxford: Oxford University Press, 1978.

Watt, W. M., *Bell's Introduction to the Qur'ān*, Edinburgh: Edinburgh University Press, 1970.
Muḥammad at Mecca, Oxford: Oxford University Press, 1953.
Muḥammad at Medina, Oxford: Oxford University Press, 1956.
Muḥammad, prophet and statesman, Oxford: Clarendon Press, 1961.
Muḥammad's Mecca: History in the Qur'ān, Edinburgh: Edinburgh University Press, 1988.
Welch, A. T., 'al-Ḳur'ān. 3. History of the Ḳur'ān after 632', in *Encyclopaedia of Islam*, new ed., 11 vols., Leiden: Brill, 1979–2002, vol. V, pp. 404–9.

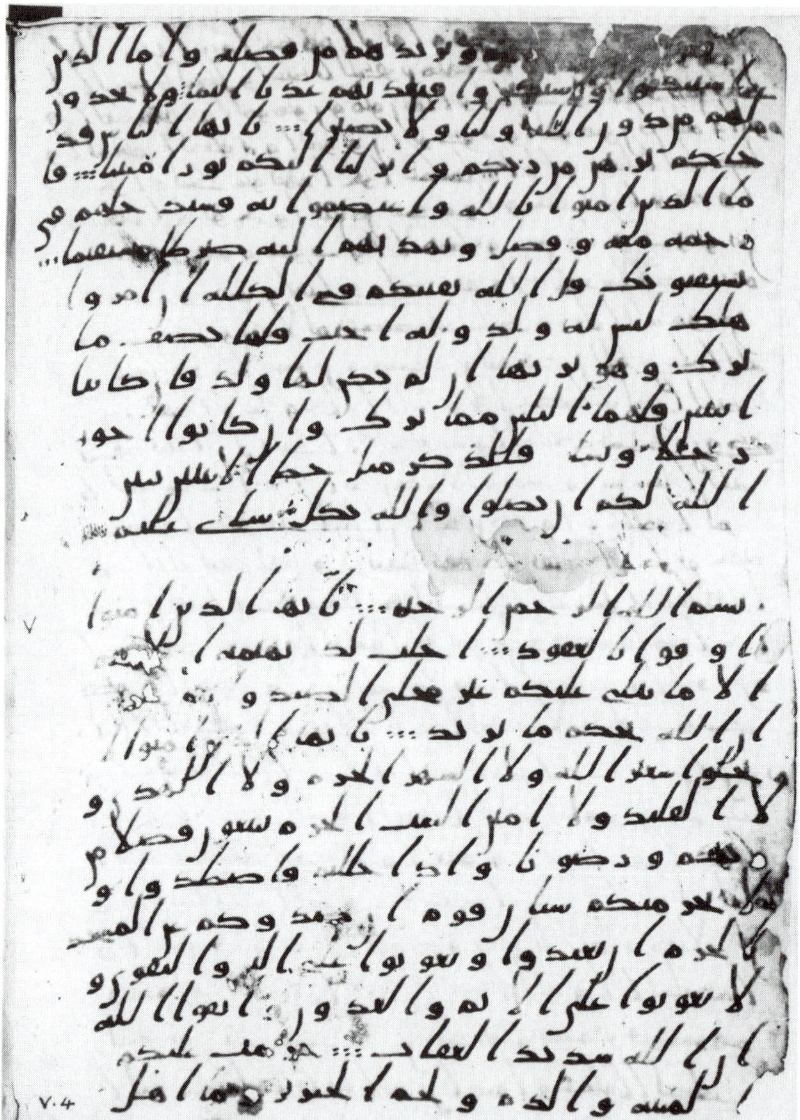

Fig. 2 Parchment folio from the end of a seventh- or early eighth-century Qur'ān manuscript in *ḥijāzī* script in vertical format, containing the final verses of Q 4 (Sūrat al-Nisā', 'The Women') and the beginning of Q 5 (Sūrat al-Mā'ida, 'The Table'). Note that there is a space left between the sūras, but no title (BNF Arabe 328a, fol. 20v). Courtesy of the Bibliothèque nationale de France, Paris

2 Creation of a fixed text

CLAUDE GILLIOT

In the Islamic representation, the Qur'ān is the scripture containing the revelations 'recited' by Muḥammad and preserved in a fixed, written form. The majority view among Muslim authorities is that *qur'ān*, an Arabic verbal noun, comes from *qara'a*, 'to recite', 'to declaim', 'to read aloud'. Some Western scholars, however, think that it is derived from the Syriac *qeryānā* (reading, scripture, lectionary). That the origin of the word is not Arabic seems to be confirmed by the interpretation given by an ancient exegete of Jewish origin, Abū 'Ubayda (d. 209/824–5), who understands what could have been the first revelation delivered by Muḥammad: *iqra' bi-smi rabbika* (Q 96:1; which the majority of the exegetes understand as 'Read/recite: in the name of your lord'), as 'Proclaim/Call upon the name of your lord' (cf. Hebrew: *qra bshem adonai*; Syriac: *qrā b-shem māryā*).

THE STATUS OF THE QUR'ĀN DURING MUḤAMMAD'S LIFETIME

The Qur'ān and Muḥammad's prophetic experience are very closely linked. Often the text responds explicitly to Muḥammad's historical situation and even sometimes to his domestic problems. The Muslim theological position is that God is the speaker throughout the Qur'ān, Muḥammad the recipient, and the angel Gabriel the intermediary agent of the qur'ānic revelations. But in what seem to be the oldest parts of the Qur'ān, the speaker and the sources of revelation are not mentioned (Q 91:1–10); in some passages there is no indication referring to a deity as a source of the message (Q 103:1–3) and in others Muḥammad seems to be the speaker (Q 81:15–21). In the earliest passages where Muḥammad's God is mentioned, he is spoken of in the third person, usually as 'my lord' or 'your lord' (Q 43:64; 96:1–8, etc.). According to some verses, Muḥammad himself had the vision of God (Q 53:11; 81:23). In the earliest passages that indicate the source of their revelation, God is the speaker (Q 73:5; 87:6). A number of late Meccan and

Medinan passages present God as reciting the verses, the Qur'ān and the book (*kitāb*) to Muḥammad (e.g., Q 2:252; 3:108; 45:6).

But at the same period some passages have the effect of raising God from the action of direct revelation (Q 42:51–2); rather the revelation is 'brought down' by 'the true spirit' (26:192–3), or by 'the spirit of holiness' (Q 16:102). Because in an early Medinan verse (Q 2:97) the agent of revelation is said (for the first and only time) to be the angel Gabriel, Muslim exegetes have identified, on this basis and on that of traditions attributed to Muḥammad, the 'spirit' in the earlier passages as Gabriel.[1]

Different chronologies of the sūras and of passages of the Qur'ān have been proposed by Muslim and Western scholars but both groups use the classification of Meccan and Medinan periods.[2] The different chronologies of Western scholarship are based on the style, vocabulary and content of the sūras and passages: first or early Meccan period, second or middle Meccan period, third or late Meccan period. As for the Medinan revelations, their chronological order is determined by the subject matter which reflects Muḥammad's growing political power and the development of events in Medina.

There is a general consensus that either Q 96:1–5 or 74:1–7 represents the first proclamation of verses uttered by Muḥammad. As would be expected, the final passages were sought among Medinan sūras; for Muslim scholars these are Q 5, 9 or 110. Some pointed to other verses of the same period. It is probable that for a period, perhaps for years, Muḥammad and the first Muslims retained the passages delivered to him only in their memories. It also seems, however, that over time much of the Qur'ān was written down in some form during his lifetime.

But the problems involved in this matter are of great complexity. The later apologists of Islam, who were challenged by Christians and others to credit Muḥammad with a miracle that could authenticate his claim to prophethood, asserted that the Qur'ān itself was a miracle.[3] One of the points they made was that Muḥammad could neither read nor write. Not all Western scholars agree with this assessment.[4] Mecca was in regular communication with regions where writing was commonly used, particularly with the town of al-Ḥīra, and it is said that Meccans had learned writing from al-Ḥīra and al-Anbār. Companions, informants or close relations of Muḥammad, like Waraqa b. Nawfal, the cousin of his first wife, Khadīja, could read and/or write. For instance, the secretary of Muḥammad, Zayd b. Thābit, had been a pupil in the Jewish school of Medina.

Both memory and writing have been the modes of conservation of the revelations delivered by Muḥammad. After Muḥammad went to Medina, his employment of secretaries is attested. Among the names which are mentioned in this office are: ʿUthmān, Muʿāwiya b. Abī Sufyān (d. 60/680), Ubayy b. Kaʿb, (the Jew) Zayd b. Thābit and ʿAbdallāh b. Abī Sarḥ. The problem is that these revelations were not always invariant. After having been revealed, some of them were 'raised', that is 'suppressed' or 'abrogated' (by God, according to Muslim reports), probably as a consequence of the evolution of Muḥammad's ideas and needs. So it is difficult to speak of a 'fixed text' during his lifetime.

The fact that the Qur'ān contains words which are not of Arabic origin provides an indication that Jewish and Christian scriptures, the latter probably in Syriac, were known in both Mecca and Medina. Some of the technical terms found in connection with the word *qur'ān* (itself of non-Arabic origin) do not derive from Arabic. Among these are *āya* (sign, miracle, verse), related to Hebrew *ōth* and Syriac *āthā* (sign), and *sūra* (chapter of the Qur'ān), which seems to be derived from the Syriac *sūrṭā*. All these matters and others argue for the pre-history of the Qur'ān – what I have elsewhere called 'the reconstruction of the Qur'ān uphill' – which can be deduced from a critical reading of the Muslim reports themselves.

Another problem is that of the language and style of the Qur'ān. In the qur'ānic text, collocation of the term '*qur'ān*' with the adjective *ʿarabī* ('Arabic', Q 12:2; 20:113; 39:28, etc.) as well as other elements, such as the doctrine of the 'inimitability' of the Qur'ān involving a special interpretation of the 'challenge verses' (Q 2:23; 10:38; 11:13, etc.),[5] have led to the Islamic conceptualisation of a *lingua sacra*.[6] Briefly put, this is the belief that Arabic is the best of tongues and that the Arabic of the Qur'ān is flawless and unmatchable. It seems that when the Quraysh heard some utterances of Muḥammad delivered as Qur'ān, they were not particularly impressed. Some of them accused him of using human informants before delivering his 'divine' message. The answer of the Qur'ān was: 'And we know that they say: Only a man teaches him. The speech (*lisān*) of whom they falsely hint is outlandish, and this is clear (*mubīn*) Arabic speech' (Q 16:103). But this usual translation is misleading, because *mubīn* is the active participle of a causative-factitive, meaning 'making clear'. It was interpreted, however, by the Islamic theologians and philologists as 'clear Arabic', and, by extension, 'pure' and 'best', 'the best of all languages', that of the Quraysh, Muḥammad's tribe. This then led to mythical narratives about the superiority of Arabic,[7] all in support of the idea that the Arabic of the Qur'ān is an exalted language, a *lingua sacra*.

Some Western scholars have drawn attention to the importance of the Aramaic or Syriac substratum in the formation of the Qur'ān,[8] and recently notice has been taken of the relation of some passages of the Qur'ān to the Diatessaron of Tatian.[9] This has given new impulse to the study of the possible informants of Muḥammad and to investigation of peculiarities and oddities in the language and style of the Qur'ān.[10]

THE COLLECTIONS, REDACTION AND TEXTUAL HISTORY OF THE QUR'ĀN AFTER THE DEATH OF MUḤAMMAD

The collection(s) of the Qur'ān

The consensus of the Islamic tradition asserts that the Qur'ān was not collected during the life of the Prophet, although it is said that copies of various sūras were available during his lifetime. According to a widespread report with many variants, at the time of Muḥammad's death, the Qur'ān was written only upon leafless palm-branches and stumps of palm-branches, or other material support such as the shoulder-blades of camels, ribs of animals, white or flat stones, pieces of cloth or of skin, or papyrus, or wooden boards, etc. Numerous narratives relate that the text was collected from these materials as well as 'from the hearts of men'.[11] But the scenario faces at least two problems: one of them has to do with terminology, the other with the collection of the text.

For classical Muslim scholars, the Arabic verb *jamaʿa*, a term commonly found in these narratives, means not only to collect, but also to know by heart or 'to remember the whole of the Qur'ān'. For example, it is said that 'Six persons memorised (*jamaʿa*) the Qur'ān during the life of the messenger of God: Ubayy b. Kaʿb, Abū l-Dardā', Zayd b. Thābit, Saʿd b. ʿUbayd and Abū Zayd', but occasionally some names on the list are different, people do not know with certainty who Abū Zayd really was, and the name of the sixth one has been forgotten!

The Baghdādī Muʿtazilī Abū l-Qāsim al-Balkhī (al-Kaʿbī, d. 319/931) noted a contradiction between this report and another one: 'Nobody has collected (or memorised, *jamaʿa*) the Qur'ān during the life of the Prophet.' So great was the embarrassment of the Muslim scholars in the face of such traditions that the Ashʿarī theologian al-Bāqillānī (d. 403/1013) was compelled to distinguish among seven meanings of the verb *jamaʿa* in order to remove the ambiguity and find a solution that could accord with the thesis of the collection of the Qur'ān by Abū Bakr and ʿUthmān.[12]

These two names signal the collection stories to be found in traditional Muslim sources. Two collections are usually mentioned, sometimes three.

A 'first' collection is said to have taken place under the reign of the first caliph, Abū Bakr (r. 11–13/632–4). 'Umar b. al-Khaṭṭāb (who was to succeed him as caliph in 13/634) became anxious when many of the reciters/readers of the Qur'ān were killed during the Battle of Yamāma in 12/633. Fearing that large portions of it would be irretrievably lost, he counselled Abū Bakr to make a collection of the text. At first Abū Bakr hesitated to do something that had not been done under the authority of Muḥammad. But in the end he accepted this responsibility and commissioned Zayd b. Thābit, who had been one of the secretaries of Muḥammad in Medina. The latter then proceeded to collect the Qur'ān from the materials mentioned above and he wrote it on sheets. He gave these to Abū Bakr; after the latter's death they passed to 'Umar, and on 'Umar's death to his daughter Ḥafṣa, one of the widows of Muḥammad.

Another collection occurred some twenty years later, during the caliphate of 'Uthmān, when dissensions among followers of other 'collections' induced the caliph to make an official collection of the Qur'ān. We are told, among other things, that during expeditions against Armenia and Azerbaijan, disputes concerning the reading of the Qur'ān arose among the troops, and the general Ḥudhayfa b. al-Yamān laid the matter before the caliph and urged him to take steps to put an end to the differences. After having taken counsel with senior Companions of Muḥammad, ʿUthmān commissioned the Medinan Zayd b. Thābit to collect the Qur'ān, associating with him three members of noble Meccan families: ʿAbdallāh b. al-Zubayr, Saʿīd b. al-ʿĀṣ and 'Abd al-Raḥmān b. Thābit. Saʿīd b. al-ʿĀṣ was regarded as an expert in the Arabic language; he and the two other Meccan redactors were chosen because they belonged to the Quraysh tribe of Mecca, which was the tribe of Muḥammad. ʿUthmān borrowed from Ḥafṣa the copy made under the direction of Abū Bakr, and on its basis requested that a standard codex be written out in the 'pure' dialect of Quraysh. He wanted the standardised Qur'ān to be preserved in the Quraysh dialect in which it was supposed to have been delivered to Muḥammad. According to some reports, if these three Meccan collaborators were to differ with Zayd's reading or choice at any point, the disputed passage had to be corrected and rewritten in the 'original' dialect.

ʿUthmān ordered that the other codices should be burned or destroyed and that the 'codex of Zayd' ('ʿUthmānic codex') alone should be preserved (in Medina) and copies made to be sent to each of the main centres of the empire: Mecca, Baṣra, Kūfa and Damascus. The order of 'Uthmān was executed everywhere, save in Kūfa where the great Companion of Muḥammad, 'Abdallāh b. Masʿūd and his partisans, refused it.

The problem for later scholars was to assure Muslims that there was an absolute continuity between what had been delivered to Muḥammad and this 'ʿUthmānic codex'. The expression 'ʿUthmānic codex' or 'codex of ʿUthmān' that is being used here can be considered a convention, for two reasons. First of all, because the misadventures detailed about the transmission and codification of the Qur'ān – as both orally delivered and transmitted in writing – are so great, the ancient Muslim narratives on these subjects offer no real clarity about what 'ʿUthmānic codex' means. Secondly, even if Muslims believe that the Qur'ān we have now is the 'ʿUthmānic codex', our analysis of Muslim narratives on the matter does not leave us with the same certainty.[13]

Some Muslim scholars, like al-Ḥākim al-Naysābūrī (d. 405/1014), suggest that the Qur'ān was collected three times. The first time was by Muḥammad, basing this interpretation on the report of Zayd b. Thābit that stated, 'We used to compose (*nu'allif*) the Qur'ān from the leaves . . .', in the following way: 'Muḥammad used to say that this verse should be put in this sūra.' The second time was under Abū Bakr, but not in a definitive codex. The third time was under ʿUthmān in a 'definitive single' codex.

Occasionally other collections of the Qur'ān are also mentioned, for instance that of Sālim, an emancipated slave of the Companion Abū Ḥudhayfa, who was 'the first one to collect the Qur'ān in a codex', that is (in Arabic) a *muṣḥaf*, a word he had learnt from the Ethiopians. Eventually, also ʿAlī b. Abī Ṭālib, the Prophet's son-in-law and the fourth caliph, is sometimes credited with having collected it.

The codices of the Companions and the variant readings

ʿUthmān's effort to obtain uniformity in the qur'ānic texts may, on the whole, have been successful, but in practice other readings were by no means forgotten. Most of the larger qur'ānic commentaries, such as those of al-Ṭabarī (d. 310/923),[14] Ibn al-Jawzī (d. 597/1200) and Abū Ḥayyān al-Andalūsī (d. 745/1344), refer to such 'non-canonical' readings, and a great number of special books were written on that subject. The presumption is that at an early period Companions or other Muslims began to write down as much as they could of the Qur'ān, but in a society where people were accustomed to the dominance of oral tradition some of them feared that these codices might be 'incomplete'. It is perhaps the reason why the phrase used by some Companions, 'to collect the Qur'ān', was interpreted by various commentators as 'to memorise the Qur'ān'.

On the basis of the *Book of the codices* of Ibn Abī Dāwūd al-Sijistānī (d. 316/929), which he edited, and on other sources Arthur Jeffery has distinguished between two categories of codices: fifteen 'primary codices' of the Companions and thirteen 'secondary codices' attributed to Muslims of the second generation. In the course of time, however, some of the written collections pertaining to the 'primary codices' secured special authority in various centres of the Islamic world: that of one of the close Companions of Muḥammad, ʿAbdallāh b. Masʿūd (d. 33/653) in Kūfa, that of Ubayy b. Kaʿb (d. 18/639, or 29/649) in Syria, and that of Abū Mūsā l-Ashʿarī (d. 42/662 or later) in Baṣra. There exist no copies of these early codices, either primary or secondary, but some of their features and variants are known through later sources like qurʾānic commentaries, as noted above, and special works. The codex of Ibn Masʿūd seems to have been different from that of ʿUthmān in several points: it did not include the first sūra, and appears to have contained many 'synonymic variants', etc. The codex of Ubayy seems to have been less important. Its best-known peculiarity is that it contained two short sūras which are not in the codex of ʿUthmān, nor in that of Ibn Masʿūd.

The process of the establishment of a canonical text did not end with the supposed ʿUthmānic codex. First, the copies of the ʿUthmānic model-codex (*al-imām*) that were sent to the metropolitan centres of Islam appear not to have been identical.[15] Some of them may have contained mistakes, as the following tradition suggests: 'When the codices were written, they were submitted to ʿUthmān, who noted several incorrect words (or passages), and he said: "Do not change them, the Arabs will change them", in other versions, "They will change them with their tongues", or "The Arabs will pronounce them correctly".'

There was also another big problem, the deficiencies of the Arabic script. In the first century and even later, Arabic was written in a *scriptio defectiva*, i.e., without vowels or diacritical points, these last permitting the suppression of the ambiguity of most Arabic consonants (of the twenty-eight consonants of the Arabic alphabet, only six are not ambiguous). So, for example, there was one shape to express *b*, *t*, *th*, and in the beginning and middle of words *n*, *y* (or *ī*); then *d* and *dh* (interdental spirant); emphatic *t* and emphatic *z*; ʿ(laryngeal fricative) and *gh* (uvular *r*, or *r* of the Parisians); *f* and *q* (glottal occlusive). Additionally, the short vowels were not marked, nor were the long ones consistently indicated. Although the reader who was familiar with the language would, in most cases, have no difficulty ascertaining which pronunciation was intended, there were so many words which permitted quite different vocalisations that instances of dubious pronunciation were not infrequent. There was also a permissible variance in grammatical forms which had not, as yet, been greatly restricted.

It is hardly possible that the *scriptio plena* would have been introduced all at once by the grammarian Abū l-Aswad al-Du'alī (d. 69/688), as is sometimes suggested. But it is possible that the impetus came from scholars of Baṣra with a method apparently copied from that used in Syriac texts: dots or strokes were used to mark readings. Al-Ḥajjāj b. Yūsuf (d. 95/714) is generally credited with having improved the orthography of 'Uthmān's codex during the reign of the Umayyad caliph 'Abd al-Malik (r. 65–86/685–705), probably during the period of al-Ḥajjāj's governorship of Iraq (75–95/694–714). The process probably continued to evolve even after the time of al-Ḥajjāj, considering the range of issues that had to be dealt with: distinguishing between consonants with a similar shape, marking of long vowels, marking of short vowels, as well as certain other matters, such as the doubling of consonants, etc.

The evidence of early copies of the Qur'ān that have survived, such as the Arabic manuscript 328 (a) (Fig. 2) of the National Library in Paris (end of the seventh century CE; in which a space was left between the sūras but the titles do not appear), or the manuscript Or. 2165 (Fig. 3) of the British Library (probably second/eighth century; in which the titles of the sūras were added later with a deliberately different calligraphic style),[16] show that for some considerable time the new system was used sparingly and mainly in connection with variants.

Chronologically, several periods can be distinguished in the acceptance of the qur'ānic readings/variants, as discussed below.[17]

Before the general acceptance of the 'Uthmānic codex

The introduction of the 'Uthmānic ductus, with unmarked consonantal structure, does not seem to have had an immediate and decisive effect on the limitation of variant readings. On the whole, it appears that in the second/eighth century *variae lectiones* with a different ductus, especially from Ibn Mas'ūd's codex, were still freely discussed and were called *qirā'āt* (readings), and sometimes *ḥurūf* (manners of speaking/writing). Both words were apparently used interchangeably for 'Uthmānic and non-'Uthmānic readings, as F. Leemhuis has shown in his study of the qur'ānic commentaries of the Kūfans Sufyān al-Thawrī (d. 161/778) and al-Farrā' (d. 207/822), and the Yemeni 'Abd al-Razzāq (d. 211/827).[18] Particularly the treatment by al-Farrā' of the variant readings from Ibn Mas'ūd shows that in his time they could be discussed in equal terms with the 'Uthmānic text. The guiding principle was that these readings should be well known, either from a codex or from a well-established tradition. Another criterion for accepting a variant reading was that it should be in accordance with the rules of the Arabic language.

The ʿUthmānic codex itself still left room for different readings. As seen above, the codices of Medina, Mecca, Damascus, Kūfa and Baṣra are said to have presented slight differences in some places. At this time, however, the discussion of which was the primary text, the codified or the recited, also played a major role in the evolution of the history of the gradual acceptance of the ʿUthmānic codex as the exclusive authority.

This appears in a different treatment of the *variae lectiones* in the works identically entitled *The good significations of the Qurʾān* (*Maʿānī l-Qurʾān*) by al-Akhfash al-Awsaṭ (d. 215/830) and by al-Farrāʾ. The latter, reflecting the grammatical tradition of Kūfa (home to Ibn Masʿūd's codex!) treats more *variae lectiones* that presuppose a different shape or ductus than the former. Unlike al-Farrāʾ, al-Akhfash's criterion is that such readings, which must be in good Arabic, should also be in accordance with the ʿUthmānic codex to be accepted.

After the general acceptance of the ʿUthmānic codex

Two generations later, the principle expressed by the traditionist, theologian and literary figure Ibn Qutayba (d. 276/889), was the following: 'All of them [qurʾānic readings] which are in accordance with our codex [i.e., the ʿUthmānic codex], not departing from its writing, we are allowed to use in the recitation.' It should be noted that this period is characterised by a codification in nearly all fields: grammar, poetry, literature, criteria for accepting the prophetic traditions, exegesis, jurisprudence, theology, etc. A shift towards the consolidation, standardisation and canonisation of concepts and doctrines was manifest. The same Ibn Qutayba, for instance, wrote a book entitled *On poetry and poets*, in the introduction to which he stipulated the rules of the Arabic poem (*qaṣīda*), another one on *The interpretation of the differences in ḥadīth* (prophetic traditions) and a third on the *Interpretation of difficult qurʾānic passages*, codifying in both of these latter works the principles of interpretation for their respective subject fields. This evolution corresponds politically with the 'imperial period' (Fr. *moment impérial*).

At the end of the third/ninth century, for the exegete al-Ṭabarī (d. 310/923) the criterion for accepting a reading was whether it was in accordance with the codices of the five cities to which copies of the ʿUthmānic codex, i.e., their consonantal ductus, had been sent.[19] Of course, he also has other criteria: linguistic, 'sound transmission', reading accepted by the 'majority' of the great readers, etc., but the definitive criterion is that of accordance with the ductus of the 'codices of the Muslims'.

This evolution corresponds to a time in which only readings based on the ʿUthmānic codex were accepted for liturgical use, a development illustrated by the activities of a traditionist (specialist in the transmission of the traditions of the Prophet and of the first generations of Muslims) and qurʾānic reader Ibn Mujāhid (d. 324/936). A reader of Baghdād, Ibn Shanabūdh (d. 328/939), who in public worship had recited readings of Ibn Masʿūd, Ubayy and others, was brought to trial and flogged in 323/935 for reciting qurʾānic words or passages 'in irregular readings at variance with the consensus'. Clearly, there was a shift in the meaning of *qirāʾa* (reading) from 'manner of reciting the Qurʾān' to 'manner of reciting the established written text in accordance with the ʿUthmānic ductus of the Qurʾān'. Another Baghdādī reader, also a traditionist and grammarian, Ibn Miqsam (d. 354/965), is credited with three versions of a book on the seven readings. Like Ibn Mujāhid, he seems to have accepted the principle of limiting variants. But unlike him, he advocated complete freedom to vowel the received consonantal ductus in any fashion consistent with Kūfan grammar. This was seen as 'submitting the Qurʾān to grammar'. At the instigation of Ibn Mujāhid, he was tried before judges and witnesses (notaries), and made to recant on threat of chastisement.[20]

Before Ibn Mujāhid, others had tried to 'restrain' (this is the interpretation of most Orientalists nowadays) the number of accepted reading 'systems' – as, for example, did Aḥmad b. Jubayr al-Kūfī (d. 258/871) who had composed a book on five acceptable readings, one for each city to which ʿUthmān had remanded a codex. This is the reason why some modern scholars see the enterprise of Ibn Mujāhid less as an attempt to arrest the proliferation of readings, than as a struggle against too much independence for the grammarians who were expected to limit themselves to materials 'which had enjoyed a high level of recognition and successive transmission (*tawātur*)'.[21]

In any event, Ibn Mujāhid's work had an enormous influence, and in the course of time a general consensus emerged that recognised the recensions of two transmitters of each of the seven readings as authoritative. Medina: (1) Nāfiʿ (d. 169/785), in the transmissions of Warsh (d. 197/813) and Qālūn (d. 220/835). Mecca: (2) Ibn Kathīr (d. 120/738), in the transmissions of al-Bazzī (d. 250/864) and Qunbul (d. 291/904). Damascus: (3) Ibn ʿĀmir (d. 118/736), in the transmissions of Hishām b. ʿAmmār (d. 245/859) and Ibn Dhakwān (Abū ʿAmr, d. 242/857). Baṣra: (4) Abū ʿAmr b. al-ʿAlāʾ (d. 154/771), in the transmissions of al-Dūrī (Ḥafṣ b. ʿUmar, d. 246/860) and al-Sūsī (Ṣāliḥ b. Ziyād, d. 261/874). Kūfa, with three authorities: (5) ʿĀṣim (d. end 127 or early 128/745) in the transmissions of Ḥafṣ b. Sulaymān (d. 180/796) and

Ibn ʿAyyāsh (d. 193/809); (6) Ḥamza b. Ḥabīb (d. 156/773 or 158/775), in the transmissions of Khalaf (b. Hishām al-Bazzār, d. 229/844) and Khallād (d. 220/835); (7) al-Kisāʾī (d. 189/805), in the transmissions of al-Dūrī and Abū l-Ḥārith al-Layth (d. 240/854). The reason why Ibn Mujāhid chose seven readers is not clear. It may be because they met the criterion of broad authentication. But it is also possible that this number suggested that these were the 'seven *aḥruf*' (manners of reciting?) in which, according to a tradition attributed to Muḥammad,[22] the Qur'ān is said to have been revealed. This equivalency, however, was never universally accepted by the Muslim scholars.

Muslim scholars found that other famous readers met the same criterion of acceptance. Three became known as 'the three after the seven', and books were composed on the 'ten readers', for instance that by the grammarian of Nishapur, Ibn Mihrān (Abū Bakr Aḥmad b. al-Ḥusayn, d. 381/991), who wrote three books on the ten readings: *The outmost, The comprehensive* and *The extensive* (a commentary on *The comprehensive*). The most frequently cited nowadays is *The unfolding on the ten readings* of Ibn al-Jazarī (d. 833/1429) which can be found on the curricular syllabi of most Islamic faculties, along with its commentaries. These three readings, also with two transmitters each, are the readings of: (8) Abū Jaʿfar Yazīd b. al-Qaʿqāʿ (d. 130/747, Medina), (9) Yaʿqūb al-Ḥaḍramī (d. 205/821, Baṣra) and (10) Khalāf (the same as Ḥamza's first transmitter; Kūfa).

Further developments on this topic produced three kinds of readings distinguished by the Andalusian grammarian and reader Makkī b. Abī Ṭālib al-Qaysī (d. 437/1045):

(1) The readings which are 'recited nowadays in which three characteristics are united': (a) transmission from Muḥammad according to reliable authorities; (b) accordance with the Arabic in which the Qur'ān was revealed; (c) conformity with the ductus of the codex. Readings which join these three features are accepted and their reciting is allowed.
(2) Those which meet the two first criteria, but lack the third. They are acceptable, but cannot be used in recitation, although a minority held the view that it was permissible to recite them in the prayer.
(3) Those which lack either one or both of the two first criteria. They are unacceptable, even if they are in accordance with the ductus of the codex.

From this evolution in the formulation of criteria, it became clear for certain Islamic scholars that conformity with the ʿUthmānic ductus was in itself sufficient for a consensus on the acceptability of readings, and this made room for the acceptance of yet other readings, i.e., 'the four after the ten', or the system of the fourteen readings. Its adherents based their judgements on the opinions of Makkī b. Abī Ṭālib al-Qaysī and Ibn al-Jazarī, but the majority of the authorities considered these four readings to be anomalous (*shādhdha*). These four readers are (also with two transmitters each, who are not given here): (11) Ibn Muḥayṣin (d. 123/740, Mecca), (12) al-Yazīdī (Yaḥyā, d. 202/817, Baṣra), (13) al-Ḥasan al-Baṣrī (d. 110/728, Baṣra), (14) al-Aʿmash (Sulaymān b. Mihrān, d. 148/765, Kūfa).[23]

For the Muslim scholars, the variants which are not accepted in the recitation and in the prayer can be used in exegesis, i.e., to make some interpretations of the text clearer. In order to achieve some theoretical clarity on the question of variant readings, the following categorisation has been proposed recently: (1) 'the small variation' (various readings of the same ductus); and (2) 'the great variation' (variations of the ductus, i.e., non-ʿUthmānic' codex), on the one hand; and (3) 'a greater variation' (an Arabic/Aramaic transliteration of the ductus; in some cases a quasi-palimpsest[24]), on the other hand.[25]

With the passing of time, and because of a pressure for uniformity and/or because of political evolutions, the majority of the different transmissions of variants dropped into disuse for the recitation. Only some remain, e.g.: al-Dūrī's transmission of Abū ʿAmr's reading (Sudan), Warsh's transmission of the reading of Nāfiʿ (now confined to the Maghrib or some African regions under the influence of the Mālikī school of law), and Ḥafṣ' transmission of ʿĀṣim's reading. This latter has been the basis of the standard Egyptian text of the Qur'ān, first published in 1923, which greatly advantaged the spread of this reading. But the study of all the other readings is still pursued in special studies on grammar and on the Qur'ān, and dedicated works and commentaries devoted, in particular, to the seven, but also to the ten or fourteen readings, are part of the curricula of many faculties of Islamic law and theology. Two dictionaries of the qur'ānic readings which are taken from the numerous special books on readings and from the qur'ānic commentaries have been recently published.[26]

QUESTIONS AND PERSPECTIVES

No critical edition of the Qur'ān which could be a basis for its scholarly reconstruction has ever been produced. Two types of reconstruction of this text or 'lectionary' (*qur'ān*) are conceivable: deductive and inductive. The deductive reconstruction would resemble the German project led by G. Bergsträsser (d. 1933) and O. Pretzl (d. 1941). After some initial hesitations, they decided that the ʿUthmānic codex should be the basis of such a critical edition but only the consonantal skeleton of that codex. But since this codex had been edited in Cairo in 1923 (with the points on or under the ambiguous consonants and with the vocalisation), Bergsträsser finally thought that such a new edition was no longer necessary, and that it would be sufficient to establish an *apparatus criticus* (based on the Islamic literature on variant readings, and in accordance with the ʿUthmānic consonantal ductus) for the Cairo edition. After the death of O. Pretzl, however, this project was never realised.

At the same time, the American scholar Arthur Jeffery had another project. For him, the task of preparing a critical edition of the Qurʾān was twofold: 'First that of presenting some form of tradition as for the text itself, and secondly that of collecting and arranging all the information scattered over the whole domain of Arabic literature, concerning the variant readings both canonical and uncanonical.'[27] Jeffery published the variant readings he had collected in his *Materials for the history of the text of the Qurʾān.* He also began to collaborate with the German project, but this enterprise, as mentioned above, did not result in a critical edition of the Qurʾān. Although it has been stated that the material collected by the two German scholars (*c.* 15,000 photographs of ancient manuscripts[28] of the Qurʾān and material on variant readings) perished in the bomb attacks on Munich in the last months of World War II, it is also possible that it still exists somewhere in Munich or more probably in Berlin.[29]

As for the inductive reconstruction, many Islamic traditions on the history of the Qurʾān have been interpreted by some Western scholars as hints of a 'concealed' history of the text before and during the revelations delivered to Muḥammad. Examples are the reports on the informants of Muḥammad to whom the Qurʾān alludes (Q 25:4–5; 16:103). The possibility should not be excluded that whole sections of the Meccan Qurʾān could contain elements originally established by, or within, a group of 'God-seekers' who possessed either biblical or post-biblical or other information.[30] This possibility was reinforced recently by the study of Christoph Luxenberg on the Syro-Aramaic reading of the Qurʾān and by the article of Jan van Reeth, both mentioned above. On this basis, the hypothesis has been expressed recently that the Qurʾān could be partly the product of a group.[31]

Notes

1. A. T. Welch, 'al-Ḳurʾān', in *Encyclopaedia of Islam*, new ed., 11 vols. (Leiden: Brill, 1979–2002), vol. V, p. 403.
2. Th. Nöldeke, *Geschichte des Qorāns*, ed. F. Schwally, G. Bergsträsser and O. Pretzl, 3 vols. in 1 (repr. Hildesheim: G. Olms, 1970), vol. I, pp. 58–261; R. Blachère, *Introduction au Coran* (Paris: G. P. Maisonneuve, 1947), pp. 240–63; Welch, 'al-Ḳurʾān', pp. 414–17.

3. Cl. Gilliot, *Exégèse, langue et théologie en islam: L'exégèse coranique de Ṭabarī* (Paris: J. Vrin, 1990), pp. 73–110; R. C. Martin, 'Inimitability', in J. D. McAuliffe (ed.), *Encyclopaedia of the Qur'ān*, 5 vols. (Leiden: Brill, 2001–6), vol. II, pp. 526–36.
4. W. M. Watt, *Bell's Introduction to the Qur'ān*, rev. and enl. (Edinburgh: Edinburgh University Press, 1970), p. 30.
5. J. Wansbrough, *Quranic studies: Sources and methods of scriptural interpretation* (Oxford: Oxford University Press, 1977), pp. 79–82.
6. Wansbrough, *Quranic studies*, pp. 85–118.
7. Cl. Gilliot and P. Larcher, 'Language and style of the Qur'ān', in McAuliffe (ed.), *Encyclopaedia of the Qur'ān*, vol. III, pp. 118–21.
8. A. Mingana, 'Syriac influence on the style of the Ḳur'ān', *Bulletin of the John Rylands Library* 11 (1927), 77–98, repr. in Ibn Warraq (pseud.), *What the Koran really says: Language, text and commentary* (Amherst, NY: Prometheus Books, 2002), pp. 171–92; Ch. Luxenberg (pseud.), *Die syro-aramäische Lesart des Koran: Ein Beitrag zur Entschlüsselung der Koransprache* (Berlin: Das Arabische Buch, 2000 (Berlin: Hans Schiler, 2004[2])).
9. J. M. F. van Reeth, 'L'évangile du prophète', in D. De Smet et al. (eds.), al–Kitāb: *La sacralité du texte dans le monde de l'Islam, Actes du Symposium international tenu à Leuven et Louvain-la-Neuve du 29 mai au 1 juin 2002* (Leuven: Belgian Society of Oriental Studies, 2004), pp. 155–74.
10. See the seminal study of Th. Nöldeke, 'Zur Sprache des Korans', in Th. Nöldeke, *Neue Beiträge zur semitischen Sprachwissenschaft* (Strassburg: K. J. Trübner, 1910), pp. 1–30; Fr. trans. G.-H. Bousquet, *Remarques critiques sur le style et la syntaxe du Coran* (Paris: A. Maisonneuve, 1953).
11. Abū Bakr b. Abī Dāwūd al-Sijistānī, *Kitāb al-Maṣāḥif*, ed. A. Jeffery, *Materials for the history of the text of the Qur'ān: The Kitāb al-Maṣāḥif of Ibn Abī Dāwūd together with a collection of the variant readings from the codices of Ibn Mas'ūd, etc.* (Leiden: Brill, 1937), pp. 7–9; Nöldeke, *Geschichte des Qorāns*, vol. II, pp. 12–15; Watt, *Bell's Introduction*, p. 40.
12. Claude Gilliot, 'Collecte ou mémorisation du Coran: Essai d'analyse d'un vocabulaire ambigu', forthcoming in *Journal asiatique.*
13. Cl. Gilliot, 'Le Coran, fruit d'un travail collectif?', in De Smet et al. (eds.), al-Kitāb: *La sacralité du texte*, pp. 199–209, 222–3.
14. On the treatment of variant readings by al–Ṭabarī, see Gilliot, *Exégèse*, pp. 135–64.
15. Nöldeke, *Geschichte des Qorāns*, vol. III, pp. 6–19.
16. F. Déroche and S. Noja Noseda, *Sources de la transmission du texte coranique*, 2 vols. (Lesa: Fondazione Ferni Noja Noseda, 1998–2001).
17. F. Leemhuis, 'Readings of the Qur'ān', in McAuliffe (ed.), *Encyclopaedia of the Qur'ān*, vol. IV, pp. 353–63.
18. Ibid., pp. 354–5, and F. Leemhuis 'Ursprünge des Koran als Textus Receptus', in S. Wild and H. Schild (eds.), *Akten des 27. Deutschen Orientalistentages (Bonn – 28. September bis 2. Oktober 1998): Norm und Abweichung* (Würzburg: Ergon, 2001), pp. 301–8.
19. Gilliot, *Exégèse*, pp. 135–48.
20. Ch. Melchert, 'Ibn Mujāhid and the establishment of seven qur'ānic readings', *Studia Islamica* 91 (2000), 20.

21. M. Shah, 'The early Arabic grammarians' contributions to the collection and authentication of qur'ānic readings: The prelude to Ibn Mujāhid's *Kitāb al-Sab'a*', *Journal of Qur'anic Studies* 6 (2004), 94.
22. Gilliot, *Exégèse*, pp. 111–33.
23. For the list of the readers and their transmitters, see Nöldeke, *Geschichte des Qorāns*, vol. III, pp. 186–9; Leemhuis, 'Readings', pp. 359–60.
24. Cl. Gilliot, 'L'embarras d'un exégète musulman face à un palimpseste: Māturīdī et la sourate de l'Abondance (*al-Kawthar*, sourate 108), avec une note savante sur le commentaire coranique d'Ibn al-Naqīb', in R. Arnzen and J. Thielmann (eds.), *Words, texts and concepts crossing the Mediterranean sea: Studies in the sources, contents and influences of Islamic civilization and Arabic philosophy and science, dedicated to Gerhard Endress on his sixty-fifth birthday* (Leuven-Paris-Dudly, MA: Peeters, 2004), pp. 33–69 (on the basis of Ch. Luxenberg, but also of two ancient Muslim exegetes).
25. Gilliot and Larcher, 'Language and style', p. 131.
26. For list and editions (*c.* 60), see Cl. Gilliot, 'Une reconstruction critique du Coran ou comment en finir avec les merveilles de la lampe d'Aladin?', forthcoming in M. Kropp (ed.), *Results of contemporary research on the Qur'ān: The question of a historico-critical text* (Beirut: Orient-Institut der Deutschen Morgenländischen Gesellschaft, 2006), § 12.
27. A. Jeffery, 'Progress in the study of the Qur'ān text', *Muslim World* 25 (1935), 11.
28. On the manuscripts of the Qur'ān, see F. Déroche, 'Manuscripts of the Qur'ān', in McAuliffe (ed.), *Encyclopaedia of the Qur'ān*, vol. III, pp. 255–73, and Déroche and Noja Noseda, *Sources de la transmission.*
29. G. Lüling, *A challenge to Islam for reformation: The rediscovery and reliable reconstruction of a comprehensive pre-Islamic Christian hymnal hidden in the Koran under earliest Islamic reinterpretations* (Delhi: Motilal Banarsidass Publishers, 2003), p. xxi n. 4.
30. Cl. Gilliot, 'Informants', in McAuliffe (ed.), *Encyclopaedia of the Qur'ān*, vol. II, p. 517.
31. Gilliot, 'Le Coran, fruit d'un travail collectif?'

Further reading

Bergsträsser, G., 'Plan eines Apparatus criticus zum Koran', *Sitzungsberichte der Bayerischen Akademie der Wissenschaften, Philosophisch-historische Abteilung* 7 (1930); repr. in R. Paret (ed.), *Der Koran*, Darmstadt: Wissenschaftliche Buchgesellschaft, 1975, pp. 389–97.

Blachère, R., *Introduction au Coran*, Paris: G. P. Maisonneuve, 1947.

Burton, J., 'Collection of the Qur'ān', in J. D. McAuliffe (ed.), *Encyclopaedia of the Qur'ān*, 5 vols., Leiden: Brill, 2001–6, vol. I, pp. 351–61.

Caetani, L., ''Uthmān and the recension of the Koran', *Muslim World* 5 (1915), 380–90.

Déroche, F., 'Manuscripts of the Qur'ān', in J. D. McAuliffe (ed.), *Encyclopaedia of the Qur'ān*, 5 vols., Leiden: Brill, 2001–6, vol. III, pp. 255–73.

Déroche, F. and S. Noja Noseda, *Sources de la transmission manuscrite du texte coranique, I, Les manuscrits de style ḥiǧāzī*, 2 vols., Lesa: Fondazione Ferni Noja Noseda, 1998–2001 (vol. I, *Le manuscrit arabe 328 (a) de la Bibliothèque nationale de France*, 1998; vol. II, *Le manuscrit Or. 2165 de la British Library*, 2001).

De Smet, D., G. de Callatay and J. M. F. van Reeth (eds.), al-Kitāb: *La sacralité du texte dans le monde de l'Islam, Actes du Symposium international tenu à Leuven et Louvain-la-Neuve du 29 mai au 1 juin 2002*, Leuven: Belgian Society of Oriental Studies, 2004.

Gilliot, Cl., 'Collecte ou mémorisation du Coran: Essai d'analyse d'un vocabulaire ambigu', forthcoming in *Journal asiatique*.

'Le Coran, fruit d'un travail collectif?', in D. De Smet, G. de Callatay and J. M. F. van Reeth (eds.), al-Kitāb: *La sacralité du texte dans le monde de l'Islam, Actes du Symposium international tenu à Leuven et Louvain-la-Neuve du 29 mai au 1 juin 2002*, Leuven: Belgian Society of Oriental Studies, 2004, pp. 185–231.

'L'embarras d'un exégète musulman face à un palimpseste: Māturīdī et la sourate de l'Abondance (*al-Kawthar*, sourate 108), avec une note savante sur le commentaire coranique d'Ibn al-Naqīb', in R. Arnzen and J. Thielmann (eds.), *Words, texts and concepts crossing the Mediterranean sea: Studies in the sources, contents and influences of Islamic civilization and Arabic philosophy and science, dedicated to Gerhard Endress on his sixty-fifth birthday*, Leuven-Paris-Dudly, MA: Peeters, 2004, pp. 33–69.

Exégèse, langue et théologie en islam: L'exégèse coranique de Ṭabarī, Paris: J. Vrin, 1990.

'Informants', in J. D. McAuliffe (ed.), *Encyclopaedia of the Qur'ān*, 5 vols., Leiden: Brill, 2001–6, vol. II, pp. 512–18.

'Langue et Coran: Une lecture syro-araméenne du Coran', *Arabica* 50 (2003), 381–93.

'Une reconstruction critique du Coran ou comment en finir avec les merveilles de la lampe d'Aladin?', forthcoming in M. Kropp (ed.), *Results of contemporary research on the Qur'ān: The question of a historico-critical text*, Beirut: Orient-Institut der Deutschen Morgenländischen Gesellschaft (2006).

'Les traditions sur la mémorisation et la composition/coordination du Coran (*ǧam'* et *ta'lîf*) et leur ambiguïté', in Cl. Gilliot and T. Nagel (eds.), *Das Prophetenḥadīṯ: Dimensionen einer islamischen Literaturgattung* (Proceedings of the *Göttinger Kolloquium über das ḥadīt*, Göttingen, Seminar für Arabistik, 3.–4. November 2000), Göttingen: Vandenhoeck and Ruprecht, 2005, pp. 14–39.

Gilliot, Cl. and P. Larcher, 'Language and style of the Qur'ān', in J. D. McAuliffe (ed.), *Encyclopaedia of the Qur'ān*, 5 vols., Leiden: Brill, 2001–6, vol. III, pp. 109–35.

Ibn Warraq (pseud.) (ed. and trans.), *What the Koran really says: Language, text, and commentary*, Amherst, NY: Prometheus Books, 2002.

Jeffery, A., *Materials for the history of the text of the Qur'ān*, Leiden: Brill, 1937.

'Progress in the study of the Qur'ān text', *Muslim World* 25 (1935), 4–16.

Leemhuis, F., 'Readings of the Qur'ān', in J. D. McAuliffe (ed.), *Encyclopaedia of the Qur'ān*, 5 vols., Leiden: Brill, 2001–6, vol. IV, pp. 353–63.

'Ursprünge des Koran als Textus Receptus', in S. Wild and H. Schild (eds.), *Akten des 27. Deutschen Orientalistentages (Bonn – 28. September bis 2. Oktober 1998): Norm und Abweichung*, Würzburg: Ergon, 2001, pp. 301–8.

Lüling, G., *A challenge to Islam for reformation: The rediscovery and reliable reconstruction of a comprehensive pre-Islamic Christian hymnal hidden in the Koran under earliest Islamic reinterpretations*, Delhi: Motilal Banarsidass Publishers, 2003 (first German ed. Erlängen: H. Lüling, 1974; see review by Cl. Gilliot, 'Deux études sur le Coran', *Arabica* 30 (1983), 16–37).

Luxenberg, Ch. (pseud.), *Die syro-aramäische Lesart des Koran: Ein Beitrag zur Entschlüsselung der Koransprache*, Berlin: Das Arabische Buch, 2000; Berlin: Hans Schiler, 2004^2.

Madigan, D. A., *The Qur'ân's self-image: Writing and authority in Islam's scripture*, Princeton: Princeton University Press, 2001 (esp. pp. 13–43).

Martin, R. C., 'Inimitability', in J. D. McAuliffe (ed.), *Encyclopaedia of the Qur'ān*, 5 vols., Leiden: Brill, 2001–6, vol. II, pp. 526–36.

Melchert, Ch., 'Ibn Mujāhid and the establishment of seven qur'ānic readings', *Studia Islamica* 91 (2000), 5–22.

Mingana, A., 'Syriac influence on the style of the Ḳur'ān', *Bulletin of the John Rylands Library* 11 (1927), 77–98; repr. in Ibn Warraq (pseud.) (ed. and trans.), *What the Koran really says: Language, text and commentary*, Amherst, NY: Prometheus Books, 2002, pp. 171–92.

Motzki, H., 'The collection of the Qur'ān: A reconsideration of western views in light of recent methodological developments', *Der Islam* 78 (2001), 1–34.

Nöldeke, Th., *Geschichte des Qorāns*, Göttingen: Dieterich, 1860; vol. II, *Die Sammlung des Qorāns*, ed. F. Schwally, 1919^2; vol. III, *Die Geschichte des Korantexts*, ed. G. Bergsträsser and O. Pretzl, Leipzig: T. Weicher, $1909–38^2$; repr. Hildesheim: G. Olms, 1970, 3 vols. in 1.

'The Koran', in Th. Nöldeke, *Sketches from eastern history*, trans. J. S. Black, London: Adam and Charles Black, 1892, pp. 21–59 (originally published in *Encyclopædia Britannica*, ninth ed., 1883, vol. XVI, pp. 597–606).

'Zur Sprache des Korans', in Th. Nöldeke, *Neue Beiträge zur semitischen Sprachwissenschaft*, Strassburg: K. J. Trübner, 1910, pp. 1–30; Fr. trans. G.-H. Bousquet, *Remarques critiques sur le style et la syntaxe du Coran*, Paris: A. Maisonneuve, 1953.

van Reeth, J. M. F., 'L'évangile du prophète', in D. De Smet, G. de Callatay and J. M. F. van Reeth (eds.), al-Kitāb: *La sacralité du texte dans le monde de l'Islam, Actes du Symposium international tenu à Leuven et Louvain-la-Neuve du 29 mai au 1 juin 2002*, Leuven: Belgian Society of Oriental Studies, 2004, pp. 155–74.

Shah, M., 'The early Arabic grammarians' contributions to the collection and authentication of qur'ānic readings: The prelude to Ibn Mujāhid's *Kitāb al-Sab'a*', *Journal of Qur'anic Studies* 6 (2004), 72–102.

Wansbrough, J., *Quranic studies: Sources and methods of scriptural interpretation*, Oxford: Oxford University Press, 1977.

Watt, W. M., *Bell's Introduction to the Qur'ān*, completely revised and enlarged, Edinburgh: Edinburgh University Press, 1970.

Welch, A. T., 'al-Ḳur'ān', in *Encyclopaedia of Islam*, new ed., 11 vols., Leiden: Brill, 1979–2002, vol. V, pp. 400–28.

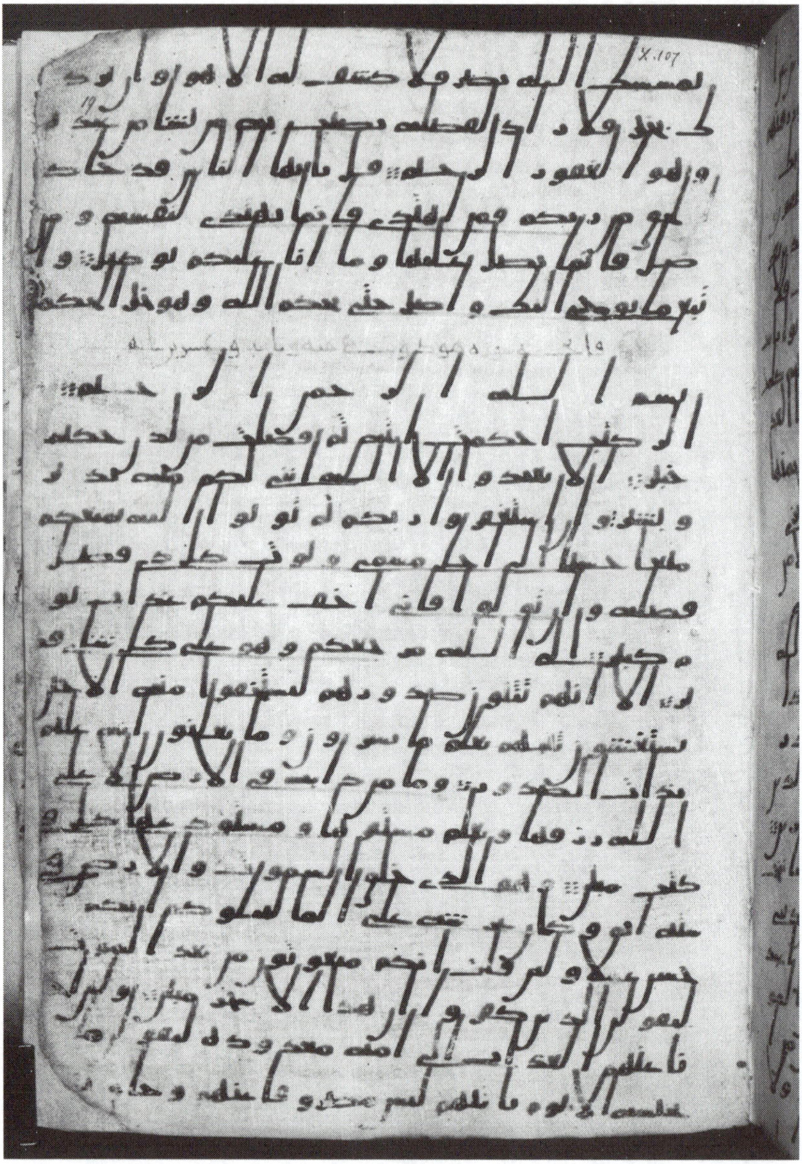

Fig. 3 Folio from an eighth-century Qur'ān manuscript, to which the sūra titles were added later in a deliberately different calligraphic style. Depicted here is the end of Q 10 (Sūrat Yūnus, 'Jonah') and the beginning of Q 11 (Sūrat Hūd) (BL MS Or. 2165, fol. 19a). Courtesy of the British Library, London

3 Alternative accounts of the Qur'ān's formation

HARALD MOTZKI

Friedrich Schwally's revision of Theodor Nöldeke's *Geschichte des Qorāns*, parts one and two, published in 1909 and 1919 respectively, presented the current status of Western scholarship on the Qur'ān's formation at the beginning of the twentieth century. W. Montgomery Watt's revised edition of Richard Bell's *Introduction to the Qur'ān*, published in 1970, provided a new stock-taking of the then widely accepted wisdom on the topic. A comparison of the two works, however, reveals little development in the intervening half century as far as their main topics are concerned. Yet this interlude of relative scholarly calm contrasts sharply with the turbulent decades that followed. From the 1970s onwards several assertions about the origin and formation of the Qur'ān have been the object of detailed revision and the results of these studies more often than not have challenged the accepted wisdom. The year 1970 can thus be considered a watershed in the scholarly history of this research, and Watt's book can serve as a suitable point of reference for a sketch of the more recent developments. In the following, some of these alternative accounts will be introduced taking the primary issue which each of them tackles as a starting-point. The portrayal of each account focuses on its premises, methods and results.

AUTHORSHIP, FORMATION AND CANONISATION

According to the prevailing consensus, the Qur'ān originated in the first third of the seventh century CE in the towns of Mecca and Medina. Its author (in Muslim eyes, its transmitter) was Muḥammad who 'published' his revelations in segments which he later rearranged and edited, in large measure himself. Yet he did not leave a complete and definitive recension. The canonical text such as it has been known for centuries was not achieved until twenty years after the Prophet's death. The qur'ānic material which had been preserved in written and oral forms was then carefully collected at the behest of the third caliph, ʿUthmān, who published it as the only officially authorised version of the Qur'ān. The stylistic uniformity of the whole proves its genuineness. This historical account is based on evidence found in the Qur'ān itself as interpreted in the light of the Muslim tradition, i.e., the biography (*sīra*) of the Prophet and traditions on the collection of the Qur'ān after his death.[1]

All the elements of this account have been challenged by John Wansbrough in his *Quranic studies: Sources and methods of scriptural interpretation* (1977) and *The sectarian milieu: Content and composition of Islamic salvation history* (1978). Wansbrough doubts the value of source analysis that seeks to detect historical facts and to reconstruct 'what really happened'. He begins from the premise that the Muslim sources about the origin of Islam, including Qur'ān, *sīra*, the traditions from the Prophet (*ḥadīth*), qur'ānic exegesis (*tafsīr*) and historiography, are the product of literary activity, i.e., fictional literature, which reflects 'salvation history'. The sources need to be analysed, therefore, as literature, i.e., by using literary-critical methods. Factual historical conclusions can be at best a by-product of such literary analysis.[2] The method of analysis that Wansbrough adopted, form criticism, is drawn from biblical studies.

Wansbrough points to 'the fragmentary character' of the Qur'ān and to the frequent occurrence of 'variants' in both the Qur'ān and other genres of early literature, i.e., texts or narratives that are similar in content but different in structure or wording. These phenomena do not support the idea of a primitive text (*Urtext*), originating from or compiled by an individual author or a text carefully edited by a committee, but are better explained by assuming that the Qur'ān has been created by choosing texts from a much larger pool of originally independent traditions. Wansbrough labels these essential qur'ānic forms 'pericopes' or, because of their content, 'prophetical *logia*'. The latter term does not mean, however, that they derive from the historical Muḥammad. The different *logia* can be reconstructed by form-critical analysis which distinguishes between: (1) the forms through which the themes of revelation are expressed (i.e., the prophetical *logia*); (2) rhetorical conventions by which the *logia* are linked and in which they are clothed; (3) variant traditions in which they have been preserved and (4) exegetical glosses and linguistic or conceptual assimilation.[3]

The content of the prophetical *logia* is characterised by four main themes: retribution, sign, exile and covenant. They display a 'monotheist' imagery known from the Bible and this suggests that the qur'ānic forms of prophetical expression continue already established literary forms. The fact that most texts which articulate the monotheist themes are introduced, sometimes even concluded, by formulas and literary conventions indicates for Wansbrough that these pericopes were originally independent traditions. The formulas function to make the texts suitable for a '*Sitz im Leben*', i.e., a special use such as prayer or preaching. The rhetorical conventions of the Qur'ān are also derived from Jewish and Christian literature. This and the polemical style of the texts suggest an origin in a sectarian milieu, i.e., in communities which distanced themselves from mainstream Judaism and Christianity. Such a milieu can be better imagined in Mesopotamia than in Mecca and Medina.

Analysis of qur'ānic narratives with a similar content ('variant traditions') also leads Wansbrough to the conclusion that they reflect different stages of literary elaboration and that they were originally 'independent, possibly regional, traditions incorporated more or less intact', or sometimes slightly edited, into the canonical compilation of the Qur'ān. Variants of the qur'ānic pericopes are also found in other literary genres, e.g., in the *sīra*. A comparison between qur'ānic and extra-qur'ānic variant traditions shows their commonality and the more expansive narrative formulation of the latter may even suggest an earlier date for them than for the qur'ānic versions. Wansbrough argues, therefore, that the extra-qur'ānic narratives used by Muslim exegetes to explain and illustrate the shorter qur'ānic texts cannot be taken to provide the historical background for the latter.

His form-critical analysis leads Wansbrough to the conclusion that the traditional account of the Qur'ān's formation, that which considers Muḥammad to be its main conduit and the canonical version to be the result of a collection and redaction shortly after his death – an account based essentially on Muslim traditions – cannot be true. For him, these reports are fictions which, perhaps following the Jewish model, aimed at dating the canon back to the early period of Islam. The hypothesis of a much longer development, one lasting many generations, seems more likely. The corpus of the prophetical *logia* that served as source for the compilation of the canon probably developed through oral composition, whereas the emergence of the canonical text itself was a mainly literary undertaking.[4]

Wansbrough dates the canonical version of the Qur'ān to no earlier than the third/ninth century. He sees such a late date for the canonisation of the Qur'ān corroborated by the development of the qur'ānic exegetical literature. In the last part of his *Quranic studies* he dates the beginnings of the juridical ('halakhic') exegesis, which refers to the Qur'ān as a source, to about the same time as the canonisation of the Qur'ān. Joseph Schacht's findings concerning the development of Islamic jurisprudence and the role of the Qur'ān therein are also thought to favour such a late date. That does not mean, however, that there were not any texts labelled *qur'ān* before that date, but only that a canonical, and thus authoritative, collection of them did not yet exist.[5]

If Wansbrough's theory is accepted, there is no way to establish anything of the revelation or the life of the historical Muḥammad from Qur'ān, *sīra, tafsīr* or ḥadīth. To look for historical facts in this sort of literature would be a meaningless research exercise.

COLLECTION, ʿUTHMĀNIC CODEX AND COMPANION CODICES

Most Western Islamicists reject Muslim traditions about a first collection of the Qur'ān made on behalf of the caliph Abū Bakr shortly after the demise of the Prophet as unlikely because the details in these accounts are unconvincing. They accept, however, the traditions about the official collection during the caliphate of ʿUthmān, although these reports also contain problematic details. The text achieved under ʿUthmān is the Qur'ān as we now have it as far as the consonantal text and its structure is concerned. Variant readings of earlier collections made by other Companions and suppressed by ʿUthmān are transmitted that suggest that 'there was no great variation in the actual contents of the Qur'ān in the period immediately after the Prophet's death', only the order of the sūras was not fixed and there were slight variations in reading.[6]

As mentioned above, Wansbrough rejected this account without further study of the relevant sources because it was incompatible with his theory about the formation of the Qur'ān. An alternative account, based on a detailed study of the traditions in question, has been given by John Burton in his book *The collection of the Qur'ān* (1977). Burton starts from the premise, adopted from Ignaz Goldziher and Joseph Schacht, that traditions (*ḥadīths*) do not pass on historical facts about the time and persons they purport to report on, but reflect the opinions of later Muslim scholars who used the traditions to substantiate their own views. His hypothesis is that Islamic source theory (*uṣūl al-fiqh*) 'has fashioned' the traditions which recount the history of the collection of the Qur'ān. In his study Burton argues that these traditions derive from the discussions among the *uṣūl* scholars about the authority of the two main sources of Islamic jurisprudence, the Qur'ān and the *sunna* of the Prophet, as well as about the issue of abrogation (*naskh*) of qur'ānic verses. All the traditions that report collections of the Qur'ān after the death of Muḥammad are, therefore, fictitious hypothetical constructs that were invented to back their legal views. According to Burton, neither a collection on Abū Bakr's behalf nor an official edition made by order of the caliph ʿUthmān ever happened.

Why did the legal scholars invent different collections and claim that the Qur'ān as it exists is the result of an incomplete redaction of the revelations made during ʿUthmān's caliphate? Burton thinks that Muslim legal scholars needed an incomplete qur'ānic text because there were established legal practices which had no basis in the Qur'ān and which had been disputed for that reason. To save these practices scholars claimed that they were based on revelations which did not find their way into the Qur'ān as it was. Such a view presupposed that the Prophet had left no definitive collection of his revelations. To substantiate this supposition, the legal scholars invented reports about the existence of different precanonical collections and then, in order to explain that there was actually only one Qur'ān, they promoted the idea of an incomplete official edition made on ʿUthmān's behalf. If all the traditions about different qur'ānic collections and codices are spurious, the only historically reliable fact that remains is the Qur'ān as it was and is. Yet when and by whom was that Qur'ān compiled? Burton assumes that the Qur'ān as we now have it was that left by Muḥammad himself.[7] Yet this last conclusion does not derive ineluctably from Burton's investigation; other scenarios can be imagined as well.

COMPOSITION OF SŪRAS AND EMERGENCE OF A CANON

The prevalent opinion in qur'ānic scholarship views the original units of revelation to have been short passages. Several such passages were afterwards 'collected' by Muḥammad himself to form the longer sūras. After his death those who compiled the canonical version added to the 'embryonic sūras' all the material circulating as qur'ānic revelations and not yet included somewhere. The change of rhyme indicates where heterogeneous passages have been secondarily assembled.[8] The sūras are thus considered to be textual units in which bits of revelation have been lumped together in some way or other, rather than being unities in themselves.

This view has been challenged by Angelika Neuwirth in her *Studien zur Komposition der mekkanischen Suren* (1981). Her premise is that the individual sūra is the formal unit which Muḥammad chose for his prophecy. Therefore, the individual sūra must be the heuristic basis of a literary study of the Qur'ān, not the Qur'ān as a whole as favoured by others, such as Wansbrough.[9] In her study, Neuwirth analyses the Meccan sūras with the aim of detecting structures within them which the Prophet himself gave to them. Since the verse is an important structural element of the sūra, the first step of an investigation which aims at analysing the composition of sūras is an examination of the traditional systems of separating the verses. Using the rhyme and structure of the verses as criteria, Neuwirth is able to suggest several corrections of the Kūfan division of the verses displayed in the Muslim standard edition.

The qur'ānic verses are marked by end rhymes so the rhyme may have a function in the composition. Since the qur'ānic rhymes and their literary function had not been studied properly before, Neuwirth, in a second step, analyses and describes the different types of rhymes, their occurrence and their development in the three layers of Meccan sūras that Nöldeke had distinguished. She argues that in almost all these sūras change or modification of rhyme functions to organise formally the development of ideas. This function is particularly crucial in the sūras of the earliest Meccan period that are characterised by short verses.

The length of the verses in the Qur'ān varies. They are short in the early sūras and become longer and longer in the second and third Meccan period, respectively. The structure of the verses and the relation between verse and sentence can also be determined by rules of composition. Neuwirth therefore studies the verses and distinguishes different types of verses according to their length. She shows that the use of certain types of verses has consequences for the composition of larger groupings of verses and she emphasises the important role of the '*clausula* phrase' in sūras when the structure of verses becomes more complex.

The next question is: are the verses grouped together in a systematic manner to form larger units, each of them containing a particular content or topic which distinguishes them from one another (termed *Gesätze*)? Secondly, are these larger units of content only arbitrarily or loosely put together to form a sūra or are they combined in a carefully considered way? Here, too, her study detects different types of *Gesätze* and even different types of sūras, each type displaying a similar structure.

Neuwirth's study comes to the conclusion that the sūras, as well as the numerous literary forms found in them, are, from the beginning, composed of clearly proportioned elements. The composition becomes more complex and less varied in the course of time but nevertheless reveals, in most cases, an intentional design. Neuwirth concludes that it must have been the Prophet himself who composed the bulk of the Meccan sūras in the form which they have now, occasional cases of later revision notwithstanding. Whether this can also be proven for the Medinan sūras remains to be examined. The historical context (*Sitz im Leben*) of the Meccan sūras, which can be characterised as texts intended for liturgical recitation, was most probably the early forms of the Islamic worship service. The more composite middle and late Meccan sūras with their ceremonial introductions suggest that they were used as 'lessons' in the liturgical services of the growing Muslim community, comparable to the lessons and recitations of the Jewish and Christian services.[10]

If this evaluation of the Meccan sūras is accepted, a comparison of the structural changes which the sūras underwent in the course of time (reflected in their rough classification into three periods) allows for theories about the first stages of the qur'ānic canon's emergence mirrored in the Qur'ān itself. Neuwirth herself pursued this issue of the 'canonical process' in several later publications.[11] In a study of Q 15 (Sūrat al-Ḥijr), for instance, she argues that the composition and content of this sūra indicate not only that it is a coherent text but also one that presupposes a stock or corpus of several sūras 'published' earlier, among them Q 1 (Sūrat al-Fātiḥa) as an earlier liturgical text. At the same time Q 15 reflects a crucial stage in the emergence of the Islamic community: the introduction of a new form of liturgical service, one which resembles the pattern of the Jewish and Christian services, and emancipates the Islamic cult from the pre-Islamic cultic ceremonies at the Kaʿba.[12]

PRE-ISLAMIC HISTORY

Until the third decade of the twentieth century the issue of Jewish and Christian influences and sources contained in the Qur'ān was a prominent research topic in Western scholarship but then it went out of fashion. Watt mentions the issue only at the end of his *Introduction* in the chapter on 'The Qur'ān and occidental scholarship' and remarks that 'the study of sources and influences, besides being a proper one, has a moderate degree of interest'.[13] He suggests that such a study does not contribute much to the appreciation of the new scriptural synthesis created in the Qur'ān on the basis of earlier ideas.

This view is questioned by Günter Lüling in his study *Über den Ur-Qur'ān: Ansätze zur Rekonstruktion vorislamischer christlicher Strophenlieder im Qur'ān* (1974). His approach is motivated by theories about the development of Jewish and Christian religious ideas, more precisely by the idea that both religions have forgotten or abandoned their primitive dogmas. These dogmas can be rediscovered and reconstructed by re-reading the sources without the distorting lens of the later orthodoxy of the two religions. By manipulating and reinterpreting the sources, this orthodoxy has fostered a development detrimental to the religions and cultures in question.[14] Lüling assumes that the same dynamic has operated in Islam. Another premise of his study is that pre-Islamic Arabia had been flooded with Christian, particularly Judaeo-Christian, ideas, that Christian communities existed all over the peninsula, even in Mecca, and that a large part of pre-Islamic Arabic poetry has a Christian background.

Lüling analyses several sūras (or parts of them) traditionally considered to be early Meccan by asking whether there may be Christian sources behind them that are hidden by the traditional reading and interpretation. He looks for other possible meanings of words and verses, especially in cases where the traditional meaning is opaque, by going back to the primitive significations of words or their meaning in other Semitic languages which may have influenced pre-Islamic Arabic. If this does not yield the expected result, the bare consonantal text (*rasm*) of the Qur'ān, i.e., the script without the dots which distinguish the Arabic letters of the same form, is checked in order to discern whether another reading is possible, one that gives the words or the grammatical construction of the verse the presupposed archaic Judaeo-Christian understanding and fits into the literary form of an assumed Christian text. Sometimes he even suggests that the consonantal text be slightly changed or passages added or deleted. Such emendations of the qur'ānic text are then justified by lexical, grammatical, stylistic and religious-historical arguments.

The results of Lüling's study are the following: The text of the Qur'ān as it is transmitted through the ages contains a pre-Islamic Christian text as a primitive layer. Parts or fragments of this Christian liturgical recitation (*qur'ān*) are scattered throughout the entire Qur'ān. They can be reconstructed and their original meaning recovered. The new reading of such passages provides a grammatically and lexically more convincing text than the traditional reading. The texts belonging to the primitive Christian '*qur'ān*' were written by Christian theologians at least a century before Muḥammad. They are poetic, i.e., have a rhyme, and are structured in strophes of three lines. The language of the primitive Christian texts in the Qur'ān is an elevated literary language which differs from the language of pre-Islamic Arabic poetry and shows grammatical correspondences to early Christian Arabic. According to Lüling the methods which the early Muslims used to recast the primitive texts were largely the same as those he used to recover them.

According to this theory, the Qur'ān as we now have it consists of two types of texts: (1) passages with a double meaning because they were originally Christian texts which had been given a new Islamic meaning, and (2) original Islamic passages which had been added to the Christian ones.

The content of both types of texts is shaped by the ideas of pre-Islamic Arab paganism that were adopted by the Muslims. Since, however, the primitive Christian texts were hostile to the pagan religious concepts, the Muslim Qur'ān has an anti-Christian undertone. A formal characteristic of the Muslim Qur'ān is its composition in rhyme-prose whereas the hidden Christian texts in it were originally written in poetic strophes. Further, the language of the Muslim Qur'ān is not homogeneous and can be classified into four different types of language: (1) the highly literary language of the primitive Christian *qur'ān*; (2) the chaotic 'language' which resulted from the Muslim reinterpretation of the Christian hymns; (3) the language of the early editorial glosses and comments added to the revised primitive Christian texts – these additions were in a colloquial language and may reflect Muḥammad's way of speaking – and (4) the language of the larger, Muslim-originated passages that is literary, perhaps an early form of classical standard Arabic. This language may have been produced by the educated scribes who recorded the Qur'ān at Muḥammad's request.

The Muslim Qur'ān is then, according to Lüling, the result of several stages of textual revision. The first stage was the refashioning of the content and style of the primitive 'Christian *qur'ān*' to fit this document, probably an archaic Christology, confessed by the so-called *ḥunafā'*(sing. *ḥanīf*), into a national pagan Arab framework. This revision was motivated by the wish to create a monotheistic Arab orientation independent of the competing Christian factions of Mecca and their political patrons outside Arabia. This period of revision may have already started two generations before Muḥammad and was continued by him. The second stage of revision of the Qur'ān as it existed then started after the victory of the Muslims over the Meccan Christian (!) *mushrikūn* (according to Lüling, these were people who made Jesus a 'partner' of God). This revision was motivated by a desire to mitigate the anti-Christian tenor of the first revision in order to win these Meccan Christians for the Muslim cause and to hide the real origins of Islam as an anti-Christian movement with pagan and national Arab inclinations. The last stage consisted in a revision of the entire Qur'ān to align it as closely as possible with the standard literary Arabic, the language of the poetry. This editing may have already started during the life of the Prophet but was perhaps finished only after his death.

LANGUAGE AND READING

In the Qur'ān the language used is called 'Arabic' (*'arabī*).[15] There was a lively discussion at the beginning of the twentieth century as to precisely what that means. In what type of Arabic did Muḥammad recite the

Qur'ān? In 1906 Karl Vollers argued that it was originally in the Meccan dialect and that later Muslim scholars redacted the text to make it accord, as far as possible, with the artificial literary language of Arabic poetry. Prominent Islamicists have rejected Voller's theory and hold the view that the language of the Qur'ān is not a dialect but essentially the literary language of the Arab tribes with some Meccan dialectical peculiarities, reflected, for instance, in the orthography of the Qur'ān. The consensus is thus that the Qur'ān has been recited and written in 'a Meccan variant of the literary language'.[16]

That does not mean, however, that all words contained in the Qur'ān are 'pure Arabic', i.e., derived from the reservoir of Arabic roots. Western scholars have identified many loanwords from other languages, most of them belonging to the Aramaic-Syriac group of Semitic languages. The list published by Arthur Jeffery in 1938 contains about 322 loanwords[17] that amount to 0.4 per cent of the complete qur'ānic vocabulary (proper names included). A large portion of these loanwords are already found in pre-Islamic Arabic texts and can be considered part of the Arabic language before the Qur'ān.[18] That means that the loanwords found in the Qur'ān do not contradict the common assumption that its language is essentially a literary Arabic close to that of the pre- and early Islamic poetry and to the classical Arabic of prose texts written in the Islamic period.

The first codices of the Qur'ān were written in a *scriptio defectiva,* i.e., without short vowels, even without some long vowels, and without distinguishing between consonants of a similar shape. (The Arabic term for this skeletal form of qur'ānic script is *rasm.*) This script was very difficult to read and, therefore, theoretically a potential source of variant readings and interpretations. In practice, however, substantial differences of reading remained minimal because 'knowledge of the Qur'ān among the Muslims was based far more on memory than on writing', the script being 'little more than an elaborate mnemonic device'.[19] The correct reading of the Qur'ān was transmitted from the Prophet's time onwards by Qur'ān-reciters (*qurrā'*) who knew the text by heart. On the basis of the oral reading tradition the defective script of the early codices was gradually improved during the first Islamic centuries and so the written qur'ānic text emerged as we know it today.[20]

This view was challenged by Lüling as mentioned above. He not only rejects the view that the Qur'ān is a text which derives almost completely from one 'author' (Muḥammad), but also disputes the idea that the language of the Qur'ān is homogeneous. Only the original Muslim parts are close to classical Arabic. In his attempt to retrace a primitive Christian liturgical text in the Qur'ān he sometimes suggests that Arabic words have a meaning closer to their Aramaic or Hebrew counterparts than the meaning current in classical Arabic, assuming that the pre-Islamic Arabic *koine* (standard language) was influenced by Aramaic, then the *lingua franca* of the near east.[21] Lüling is also convinced that the primitive *qur'ān* has been consciously changed by Muḥammad and later Muslims.

In a more radical form similar ideas about the original language of the Qur'ān are expounded in a study by Christoph Luxenberg (a pseudonym) entitled *Die syro-aramäische Lesart des Koran* (2000). Its premises are that Syro-Aramaic was the most important literary and cultural language in the region of the vicinity in which the Qur'ān originated. Since Arabic was not yet a literary language, educated Arabs used Syro-Aramaic for literary purposes. This suggests that literary Arabic itself was developed by Arabs educated in the Syro-Aramaic culture. These Arabs were mostly Christianised and brought much of their religious and cultural language into Arabic. These premises lead Luxenberg to the hypotheses that the Qur'ān, as one of the earliest specimens of literary Arabic, must reflect this Syro-Aramaic heritage and that in addition to words already identified as Syro-Aramaic loanwords, many more lexical items and syntactical structures, generally considered to be genuine Arabic by Muslim and Western scholars, may be of Syro-Aramaic origin.

The study focuses on qur'ānic passages that Western scholars consider obscure and on which early Muslim exegetes expressed variant interpretations. Luxenberg's philological method involves several steps. The first is to check al-Ṭabarī's (d. 310/923) large commentary of the Qur'ān and the *Lisān al-'Arab*, the most substantial lexicon of classical Arabic, to see whether the early exegetes preserved a meaning of the unclear words that better fits the context than the meaning assumed by the most prominent Western translations. If this search does not yield a result, he next asks whether there is a homonymous lexical root in Syro-Aramaic that has a meaning other than that of the Arabic word and one clearly better suited to the context. If this exercise proves futile, Luxenberg then returns to the undotted form (*rasm*) of the word to determine whether another reading (dotting) of it produces an Arabic or Aramaic word or root that makes more sense. If this step also fails he tries to translate the alleged Arabic word into Aramaic in order to deduce its meaning from the semantic of the Syro-Aramaic expression. Should this step prove unproductive, he consults the material preserved from Aramaic-Arabic lexica of the fourth/tenth century searching for meanings of Arabic terms unknown in classical and modern Muslim sources of Arabic but recorded by Christian lexicographers. A final step has him reading an Arabic word according to the Syro-Aramaic phonetic system, a process that, as Luxenberg claims, sometimes produces a useful meaning.

Luxenberg doubts that there has existed a continuous tradition of reading and commenting on the Qur'ān from the time of the Prophet onwards because some Muslim traditions contradict that claim. The qur'ānic writing of Aramaic names suggests that they were transliterated from Syro-Aramaic and therefore not originally pronounced according to the traditional reading based on the (later) phonetic rules of classical Arabic, but in the Aramaic way (e.g., not Jibrīl and Mūsā, but Gabriēl and Mōshē). Luxenberg gives examples of qur'ānic expressions which do not smoothly fit the context when read according to the rules of the classical Arabic grammar, but are perfectly translatable if read as Syro-Aramaic terms. He concludes from these cases that grammatical forms of Arabic and Syro-Aramaic occur in the Qur'ān side by side and, therefore, the Qur'ān cannot be understood and explained only on the basis of the grammatical rules fixed for classical Arabic.

Luxenberg discusses several examples of words which seem to suggest that in the earliest written qur'ānic texts the undotted 'tooth letters' were used not only to indicate the letters *b, t, th, n, ī/y* as in classical and modern Arabic, but occasionally the long vowel *ā* which in standard Arabic orthography is rendered by a long vertical stroke.[22] He argues that several words of the Qur'ān had been read and dotted wrongly because later readers and copyists did not know this early function of the 'tooth letter' any more. This and other obviously wrong cases of dotting prove for him that there was no continuous reading tradition after the death of the Prophet. Later Muslim scholars and copyists of the Qur'ān reconstructed its reading and interpretation on the basis of written copies.

In his study Luxenberg reviews the translation and interpretation of several qur'ānic verses and a few short sūras arguing that they have been misunderstood because particular words have been interpreted from the viewpoint of the classical Arabic lexicon and grammar. Reading them, in contrast, as Syro-Aramaic words and taking into account that qur'ānic expressions may also reflect the phenomena of Syro-Aramaic grammar, produces more plausible meanings. In a few cases his reconstruction leads to a Christian content.

The results of his analyses corroborate Luxenberg's premises: the language of the Qur'ān is a mixture of Aramaic and Arabic. This has consequences for the understanding of the historical background. If the Qur'ān was 'published' in the language of the Quraysh, as Muslim tradition states, and if this language was neither an Arabic dialect nor the standard literary language of Arabic poetry, but a mixed language of Syro-Aramaic and Arabic that was understood by Muḥammad's Meccan compatriots, then, Luxenberg presumes, Mecca must originally have been an Aramaic settlement. The many cases of qur'ānic words and passages which remained unclear to Muslim scholars and were misread by them suggest that the knowledge of the Meccan language spoken at the time of Muḥammad had been lost by the period when the punctuation and exegesis of the qur'ānic text began. According to Luxenberg, this must have been in the second half of the second/eighth century because the Muslim reconstruction and interpretation of the Qur'ān is based on the literary Arabic language standardised at that time. He thus assumes a gap of one and a half centuries between the first 'publishing' and recording of the Qur'ān and the final editing by which it received its traditional form. During this period the Qur'ān was preserved only in written form and, so it appears, did not play a significant role in Muslim cult and community. Luxenberg suggests that had the situation been otherwise, the tradition of reading the Qur'ān as it developed in the time of the Prophet would not have been cut off.

CONCLUDING REMARK

The alternative accounts of the Qur'ān's formation presented in this chapter have been described without a concurrent evaluation of them. Each is a sophisticated piece of scholarship that deserves to be carefully studied for the quality of its arguments and methods. The reader interested in the scholarly echo which these alternative accounts provoked will find the relevant literature in 'Further reading'.

Notes

1. W. M. Watt, *Bell's Introduction to the Qur'ān* (Edinburgh: Edinburgh University Press, 1970), chs. 2 and 3.
2. J. Wansbrough, *The sectarian milieu: Content and composition of Islamic salvation history* (Oxford: Oxford University Press, 1978), pp. ix, 118–19, and his '*Res ipsa loquitur:* History and mimesis' (Jerusalem: The Israel Academy of Sciences and Humanities, 1987) (Albert Einstein Memorial Lectures); repr. in H. Berg (ed.), *Method and theory in the study of Islamic origins* (Leiden/Boston: Brill, 2003), pp. 10–19.
3. J. Wansbrough, *Quranic studies: Sources and methods of scriptural interpretation* (Oxford: Oxford University Press, 1977), ch. I.
4. Ibid.
5. Ibid., pp. 44, 170–202.
6. Watt, *Bell's Introduction*, ch. 3.

7. J. Burton, *The collection of the Qur'ān* (Cambridge: Cambridge University Press, 1977), chs. 1, 6–10.
8. Watt, *Bell's Introduction*, pp. 38–9, 90–7, 111, 113.
9. A. Neuwirth, *Studien zur Komposition der mekkanischen Suren* (Berlin/New York: Walter de Gruyter, 1981), pp. 1–2.
10. Ibid., passim.
11. A. Neuwirth, 'Vom Rezitationstext über die Liturgie zum Kanon: Zu Entstehung und Wiederauflösung der Surenkomposition im Verlauf der Entwicklung des islamischen Kultus', in S. Wild (ed.), *The Qur'ān as text* (Leiden: Brill, 1996), pp. 69–105, and her 'Referentiality and textuality in *sūrat al-ḥijr*: Some observations on the qur'ānic "canonical process" and the emergence of a community', in I. J. Boullata (ed.), *Literary structures of religious meaning in the Qur'ān* (Richmond, Surrey: Curzon Press, 2000), pp. 143–72. See also her 'Qur'ān, crisis and memory: The qur'ānic path towards canonization as reflected in the anthropogonic accounts', in A. Neuwirth and A. Pflitsch (eds.), *Crisis and memory in Islamic societies* (Beirut: Orient-Institut der Deutschen Morgenländischen Gesellschaft, 2001), pp. 113–52.
12. Neuwirth, 'Referentiality and textuality'.
13. Watt, *Bell's Introduction*, pp. 184–5.
14. G. Lüling, *Über den Ur-Qur'ān: Ansätze zur Rekonstruktion vorislamischer christlicher Strophenlieder im Qur'ān* (Erlangen: H. Lüling, 1974), pp. 176–85, 401–12.
15. Q 12:2; 20:113; 39:28; 41:3; 42:7; 43:3; cf. 13:37; 16:103; 26:195; 41:44; 46:12.
16. Watt, *Bell's Introduction*, pp. 83–4.
17. A. Jeffery, *The foreign vocabulary of the Qur'ān* (Baroda: Oriental Institute, 1938).
18. Watt, *Bell's Introduction*, pp. 84–5.
19. Ibid., pp. 47–8.
20. Ibid.
21. Lüling, *Über den Ur-Qur'ān*, pp. 30, 51–4, 91, 93, 113, 165, 192, 305, 382–4.
22. This observation is corroborated by the earliest fragments of qur'ānic manuscripts; see G.-R. Puin, 'Über die Bedeutung der ältesten Koranfragmente aus Sanaa (Jemen) für die Orthographiegeschichte des Korans', in H.-C. Graf von Bothmer, K.-H. Ohlig and G.-R. Puin, 'Neue Wege der Koranforschung', *Magazin forschung* (Universität des Saarlandes) 1 (1999), 37–40, on http://www.uni-saarland.de/verwalt/kwt/f-magazin/1-99/Neue_Wege.pdf, esp. 39–40.

Further reading

Adams, C. J., 'Reflections on the work of John Wansbrough', in H. Berg (ed.), *Islamic origins reconsidered: John Wansbrough and the study of early Islam, Special issue of Method and theory in the study of religion* 9 (1997), 75–90.

Berg, H., 'The implications of, and opposition to, the methods and theories of John Wansbrough', in H. Berg (ed.), *Islamic origins reconsidered: John Wansbrough and the study of early Islam, Special issue of Method and theory in the study of religion* 9 (1997), 3–22.

de Blois, F., 'Review of C. Luxenberg, *Die syro-aramäische Lesart des Koran*', *Journal of Qur'anic Studies* 5 (2003), 92–7.

Böwering, G., 'Chronology and the Qur'ān', in J. D. McAuliffe (ed.), *Encyclopaedia of the Qur'ān*, 5 vols., Leiden: Brill, 2001–6, vol. II, pp. 316–35.
Bragué, R., 'Le Coran: Sortir du cercle?' (Review of C. Luxenberg, *Die syro-aramäische Lesart des Koran* and of A.-L. Prémare, *Les fondations de l'islam*), *Critique: Revue générale des publications françaises et étrangères* 671 (2003), 232–51.
Burton, J., 'Collection of the Qur'ān', in J. D. McAuliffe (ed.), *Encyclopaedia of the Qur'ān*, 5 vols., Leiden: Brill, 2001–6, vol. I, pp. 351–61.
The collection of the Qur'ān, Cambridge: Cambridge University Press, 1977.
van Ess, J., 'Review of J. Wansbrough, *Quranic studies*', *Bibliotheca Orientalis* 35 (1978), 353.
Gilliot, Cl., 'Deux études sur le Coran', *Arabica* 30 (1983), 16–37.
'Langue et Coran: Une lecture syro-araméenne du Coran', *Arabica* 50 (2003), 381–93.
Gilliot, Cl. and P. Larcher, 'Language and style of the Qur'ān', in J. D. McAuliffe (ed.), *Encyclopaedia of the Qur'ān*, 5 vols., Leiden: Brill, 2001–6, vol. III, pp. 109–35.
Günther, S., 'Review of G. Lüling, *Über den Ur-Qur'ān*', *al-Qanṭara* 16 (1995), 485–9.
Hopkins, S., 'Review of C. Luxenberg, *Die syro-aramäische Lesart des Koran*', *Jerusalem Studies in Arabic and Islam* 28 (2003), 377–80.
Ibn Rawandi, 'On pre-Islamic Christian strophic poetical texts in the Koran: A critical look on the work of Günther Lüling', in Ibn Warraq (pseud.) (ed. and trans.), *What the Koran really says: Language, text and commentary*, Amherst, NY: Prometheus Books, 2002, pp. 653–710.
Jeffery, A., *The foreign vocabulary of the Qur'ān*, Baroda: Oriental Institute, 1938.
Leemhuis, F., 'Codices of the Qur'ān', in J. D. McAuliffe (ed.), *Encyclopaedia of the Qur'ān*, 5 vols., Leiden: Brill, 2001–6, vol. I, pp. 347–51.
Lüling, G., *Die Wiederentdeckung des Propheten Muhammad: Eine Kritik am 'christlichen' Abendland*, Erlangen: H. Lüling, 1981.
Über den Ur-Qur'ān: Ansätze zur Rekonstruktion vorislamischer christlicher Strophenlieder im Qur'ān, Erlangen: H. Lüling, 1974; Eng. ed., *A challenge to Islam for reformation: The rediscovery and reliable reconstruction of a comprehensive pre-Islamic Christian hymnal hidden in the Koran under earliest Islamic reinterpretations*, Delhi: Motilal Banarsidass Publishers, 2003.
Luxenberg, C., *Die syro-aramäische Lesart des Koran: Ein Betrag zur Entschlüsselung der Koransprache*, Berlin: Das Arabische Buch, 2000; rev. ed. Berlin: Hans Schiler, 2004.
Madigan, D. A., *The Qur'ān's self-image: Writing and authority in Islam's scripture*, Princeton: Princeton University Press, 2001.
Motzki, H., 'The collection of the Qur'ān: A reconsideration of western views in light of recent methodological developments', *Der Islam* 78 (2001), 1–34.
'Muṣḥaf', in J. D. McAuliffe (ed.), *Encyclopaedia of the Qur'ān*, 5 vols., Leiden: Brill, 2001–6, vol. III, pp. 463–6.
Neuwirth, A., 'Einige Bemerkungen zum besonderen sprachlichen und literarischen Charakter des Koran', in W. Voigt (ed.), *XIX Deutscher Orientalistentag vom 28. September bis 4. Oktober 1975 in Freiburg im Breisgau. Vorträge*, Wiesbaden: F. Steiner, 1977, pp. 736–9; Eng. trans. 'Some notes on the distinctive linguistic and literary character of the Qur'ān', in A. Rippin (ed.), *The Qur'ān: Style and contents*, Aldershot, Hampshire: Ashgate, 2001, pp. 253–7.

'Form and structure of the Qur'ān', in J. D. McAuliffe (ed.), *Encyclopaedia of the Qur'ān*, 5 vols., Leiden: Brill, 2001–6, vol. II, pp. 244–65.

'Qur'ān and history – a disputed relationship: Some reflections on qur'ānic history and history in the Qur'ān', *Journal of Qur'anic Studies* 5 (2003), 1–18.

'Qur'ān, crisis and memory: The qur'ānic path towards canonization as reflected in the anthropogonic accounts', in A. Neuwirth and A. Pflitsch (eds.), *Crisis and memory in Islamic societies*, Beirut: Orient-Institut der Deutschen Morgenländischen Gesellschaft, 2001, pp. 113–52.

'Referentiality and textuality in *sūrat al-ḥijr*: Some observations on the qur'ānic "canonical process" and the emergence of a community', in I. J. Boullata (ed.), *Literary structures of religious meaning in the Qur'ān*, Richmond, Surrey: Curzon Press, 2000, pp. 143–72.

'Review of J. Burton, *The collection of the Qur'ān*', *Orientalistische Literaturzeitung* 76 (1981), 372–80.

'Review of J. Wansbrough, *Quranic studies*', *Die Welt des Islams* 23/24 (1984), 539–42.

Studien zur Komposition der mekkanischen Suren, Berlin/New York: Walter de Gruyter, 1981.

'Vom Rezitationstext über die Liturgie zum Kanon: Zu Entstehung und Wiederauflösung der Surenkomposition im Verlauf der Entwicklung des islamischen Kultus', in S. Wild (ed.), *The Qur'ān as text*, Leiden: Brill, 1996, pp. 69–105; Fr. trans. 'Du text de récitation au canon en passant par la liturgie: A propos de la génèse de la composition des sourates et de sa redissolution au cours du développement du culte islamique', *Arabica* 47 (2000), 194–229.

'Zum neueren Stand der Koranforschung', in F. Steppat (ed.), *XXI. Deutscher Orientalistentag vom 24. bis 29. März 1980 in Berlin. Vorträge*, Wiesbaden: Steiner, 1983, pp. 183–9.

Nöldeke, Th., *Geschichte des Qorāns*, rev. by F. Schwally, G. Bersträsser and O. Pretzl, 3 vols. in 2, Leipzig: T. Weicher, 1909–38.

Phenix, R. R./C. B. Horn, 'Review of C. Luxenberg, Die syro-aramäische Lesart', *Hugoye: Journal of Syriac Studies* 6 (January 2003), on http://syrcom.cua.edu/Hugoye.

Puin, G.-R., 'Über die Bedeutung der ältesten Koranfragmente aus Sanaa (Jemen) für die Orthographiegeschichte des Korans', in H.-C. Graf von Bothmer, K.-H. Ohlig and G.-R. Puin, 'Neue Wege der Koranforschung', *Magazin forschung* (Universität des Saarlandes) 1 (1999), 37–40, on http://www.uni-saarland.de/verwalt/kwt/f-magazin/1-99/Neue_Wege.pdf.

Rippin, A., 'Literary analysis of Qur'ān, *tafsīr*, and *sīra*: The methodologies of John Wansbrough', in R. C. Martin (ed.), *Approaches to Islam in religious studies*, Tucson: University of Arizona Press, 1985, pp. 151–63, 227–32.

'Review of A. Neuwirth, *Studien zur Komposition der mekkanischen Suren*', *Bulletin of the School of Oriental and African Studies* 45 (1982), 149–50.

'Foreign vocabulary', in J. D. McAuliffe (ed.), *Encyclopaedia of the Qur'ān*, 5 vols., Leiden: Brill, 2001–6, vol. II, pp. 226–37.

Robinson, N., *Discovering the Qur'ān: A contemporary approach to a veiled text*, London: SCM Press, 1996.

Rodinson, M., '[Fr.] Review of G. Lüling, *Über den Ur-Qur'ān*', *Der Islam* 54 (1977), 321–5.

Wansbrough, J., *Quranic studies: Sources and methods of scriptural interpretation*, Oxford: Oxford University Press, 1977.

'*Res ipsa loquitur*: History and mimesis', Jerusalem: The Israel Academy of Sciences and Humanities, 1987 (Albert Einstein Memorial Lectures); repr. in H. Berg (ed.), *Method and theory in the study of Islamic origins*, Leiden/Boston: Brill, 2003, pp. 3–19.

The sectarian milieu: Content and composition of Islamic salvation history, Oxford: Oxford University Press, 1978.

Watt, W. M., *Bell's Introduction to the Qur'ān*, Edinburgh: Edinburgh University Press, 1970.

Welch, A., 'Ḳur'ān', in *Encyclopaedia of Islam*, new ed., 11 vols., Leiden: Brill, 1979–2002, vol. V, pp. 400–28.

Whelan, E., 'Forgotten witness: Evidence for the early codification of the Qur'ān', *Journal of the American Oriental Society* 118 (1998), 1–14.

Part II

Description and analysis

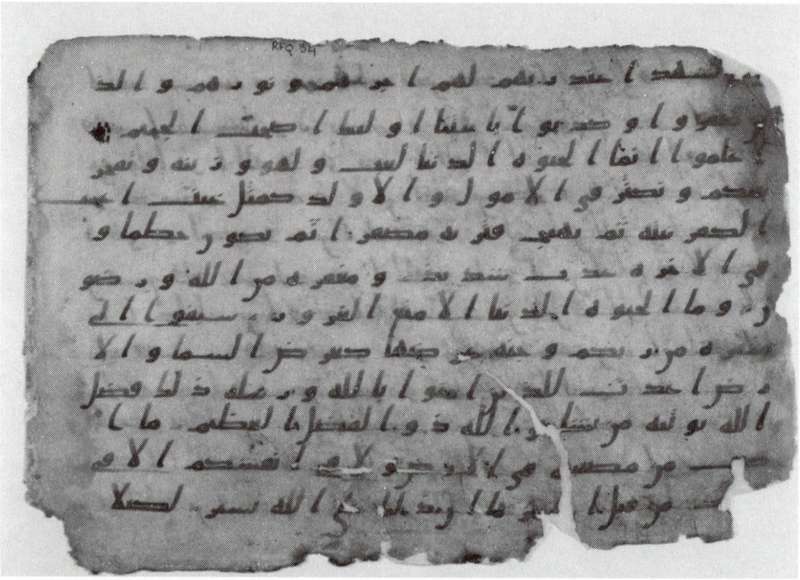

Fig. 4 Qur'ān fragment from an eighth-century *ḥijāzī* parchment in horizontal format, depicting Q 57:19–23 (Khalili Collection KFQ 34). Courtesy of the Nasser D. Khalili Collection of Islamic Art, London

4 Themes and topics

DANIEL A. MADIGAN

It is not uncommon for people to ask what the Qur'ān (or any other scripture for that matter) actually says on a particular issue. Thus it might be useful to preface this chapter with a few comments on the way that question is framed, and what it presumes. That word 'actually' suggests the questioner believes a text has a single, objectively verifiable meaning. Yet when texts speak – and that is a particularly appropriate verb in the Qur'ān's case – they speak to particular people in particular circumstances. The Qur'ān's meaning, as Wilfred Cantwell Smith has pointed out, is the history of its meanings.[1] That is true in both an internal and an external sense. First, the Qur'ān reflects the history of its own development over the more than twenty years of its address to a varied audience. Second, since the time of its canonisation it has been read by a very diverse community of faith in widely different historical contexts.

So what the Qur'ān 'actually' says, is what it says to actual readers, especially believing readers. No community of faith reads its scripture with a detachment that strives for some elusive objectivity: believers read scriptures, often at the same time reading things into them. Nor are scriptures necessarily read as a whole, with the community feeling it has to reconcile and explain every detail of the text. There are in most traditions what have been called 'canons within the canon'. A 'scriptural' approach to any subject does not emerge simply from the sacred text, but rather brings that text into conversation with other elements both from within and from outside the tradition. This chapter, then, will offer one reading of the Qur'ān's main concerns. Though it may be possible to discern historical development in some aspects of the Qur'ān's thought, by and large this will be a reading of the text as it currently stands, fixed as a canon of scripture, and therefore presuming a substantial unity in its thought.

God could be said to be the subject of the Qur'ān in a double sense: first in that God is the speaker – the Qur'ān's 'I' or 'We' – and second that in many respects God is the centre of the text's attention. For this reason it would be inaccurate to speak of God as one theme among the many treated by the revelation; each of its themes revolves around the divine nature and the divine initiative. Therefore, in discussing each area of the Qur'ān's content in this chapter, we will take as the starting point God's attributes and actions as specified in the text itself. Many of these attributes are among what are called the most beautiful names (*al-asmā' al-ḥusnā*), a term used three times in the Qur'ān: 'He is God, the creator, the maker, the shaper. To him belong the most beautiful names. All that is in the heavens and the earth glorifies him. He is the mighty, the wise' (Q 59:24; see also Q 17:110; 20:8).

God's title in the Qur'ān is Allāh, generally taken to be a contraction of the Arabic *al-ilāh* meaning 'the God'. The name seems to have been familiar in pagan pre-Islamic Arabia as the name of a high god, and the way in which the Qur'ān uses it when addressing Jews and Christians suggests that for them too it was a familiar usage. It is close to, though not simply identifiable with, the word for God (*Alāhā*) in the Aramaic used by these two groups of believers at the time, and it is the name still used for God by Arabic-speaking Christians. Another title which seems to have functioned independently as a personal name for God in the earlier parts of the Qur'ān is al-Raḥmān ('the merciful'). It too is attested as the name of a divinity in southern and central Arabia prior to the emergence of Islam. In what are considered to be the later parts of the Qur'ān, however, al-Raḥmān apparently becomes subordinate to the name Allāh, as witness the invocation placed at the beginning of all but one of the sūras: 'In the name of God (Allāh), the merciful (*al-raḥmān*), the compassionate (*al-raḥīm*).'[2]

GOD IS ONE, ABSOLUTE

Without doubt the Qur'ān's most insistent assertion is that God is one, to the exclusion of all others, and this has become the heart of the Muslim profession of faith. Thirty times in the Qur'ān the phrase 'there is no deity but him' is repeated. Several other times the people are reminded of God's unity in words reminiscent of Israel's *shema*; for example 'Your God is one God; there is no God but him, the beneficent, the merciful' (Q 2:163). The listeners are continually told to serve or to put their trust in none but God. In three of these affirmations God speaks in the first person. For example, 'He sends down the angels with the spirit of his command on those of his servants whom he wills, (saying) "Warn people that there is no God but me, so fear me"' (Q 16:2; see also Q 20:14; 21:25). In a striking usage the Qur'ān tells us (Q 3:18) God himself bears witness (*shahida*) that there is no god apart from him. From this comes the divine name *al-shahīd*. Q 17:111 sums up the doctrine: God has no partner (*sharīk*), no patron (*walī*), no offspring (*walad*). Sūrat al-Ikhlāṣ (Q 112) commands the recitation of the creedal statement: 'He, God, is one (*aḥad*). God is the everlasting (*al-ṣamad*). He has neither begotten nor been begotten, and none is his equal (*kufuwan*).'

The insistence on the unicity of God is not simply a concern for numerical unity. The uniqueness extends to many of God's attributes – for example, God alone is eternal (*al-qayyūm*, Q 2:255), glorious (*dhū l-jalāl*, Q 55:27; *al-majīd*, Q 85:15), sufficient unto himself (*al-ghaniyy*, Q 6:133), most high (*al-aʿlā*, Q 87:1), powerful (*al-qādir*, Q 6:65; *al-qadīr*, Q 30:54; *al-qawiyy*, Q 11:66), the first and the last (*al-awwal wa-l-ākhir*, Q 57:3).

GOD IS CREATOR

All of this would be, in a sense, academic were it not for the fact that God is creator (*al-khāliq*, Q 59:24; *al-khallāq*, Q 15:86), initiator (*al-bāriʾ*, Q 59:24), shaper (*al-muṣawwir*, Q 59:24) and originator of the heavens and the earth (*badīʿ al-samāwāti wa-l-arḍi*, Q 2:117). Without creation there would be neither proof of, nor witnesses to, God's unrivalled supremacy.

The Qurʾān presents a decidedly anthropocentric view of God's creativity. God's role in the creation of human beings – both of the first person and of each successive individual born through the normal process of procreation – is rehearsed several times in the Qurʾān. While the angels and jinn are created from fire (e.g., Q 15:27), the human is said to be created by God's hands (Q 38:75–6) from earth (*arḍ*, cf. Q 20:55), dust (*turāb*, Q 3:59; 30:20) and from various forms of clay (*ṭīn*, Q 6:2; *ṣalṣāl*, Q 15:26; 55:14). God breathes his spirit into the creature (Q 15:29; 32:9; 38:72). God forms human beings in stages (*aṭwār*, Q 71:14) in the womb: 'We created the human being from an extract of clay; then made it a drop in a safe lodging; then we made the drop a clot, and then made the clot a little lump. Then we made the little lump bones, then clothed the bones with flesh, and then caused it to grow as another creation. So blessed be God, the best of creators' (Q 23:12–14).

The heavens and the earth are all arranged for humanity: 'God is the one who created the heavens and the earth, and makes water descend from the sky, so bringing forth fruit to nourish you, and who makes ships to serve you, that they may sail the sea at his command, and has made rivers to be of service to you; and puts the sun and the moon, constant in their courses, at your service, and has made serve you also night and day' (Q 14:32–3).[3] Even the stars have been made in order to help people find their way (Q 6:96–7).

Furthermore, it is not only animal and inanimate creation that are thus subjected to the human beings God creates. When God tells the angels of his intention to create a human being, they protest, knowing the trouble that will be wrought on earth by this creature made from 'black mud' (cf. Q 2:30). At the moment of the creation, the angels are ordered by God to bow down to Adam, and so they do, with the exception of Iblīs, who is then condemned for his rebellion and becomes the enemy and tempter of humanity. The story is told seven times in the Qur'ān, each time in a slightly different form.[4]

Many of the divine attributes can be found in created things, though of course God is their origin and perfection. God, who is all-hearing (*al-samī'*, Q 2:127) and all-seeing (*al-baṣīr*, Q 17:1), appoints also for humanity hearing and sight (Q 32:9). While others may be alive, they are so only because the living one (*al-ḥayy*, Q 2:255) is also the giver of life (*al-muḥyī*, Q 41:39). Others may be merciful, wise and judicious, but God is 'the most merciful of those who exercise mercy' (*arḥam al-rāḥimīn*, Q 7:151) and 'the most just of judges' (*aḥkam al-ḥākimīn*, Q 95:8). God alone comprehends all things (*muḥīṭ*, Q 3:120; *wāsi'*, Q 2:115) whereas others comprehend only what God wills (Q 2:255). God alone is omniscient (*al-'alīm*, Q 2:32),[5] and others know only as much as God teaches them. At the moment of his creation, God teaches Adam the names of things – something the angels do not know – and God then humbles the angels by demonstrating their comparative ignorance (Q 2:31–3).

FAITH: THE ACKNOWLEDGEMENT OF GOD AS SOVEREIGN CREATOR

The relationship of humanity to God is predicated on the fact that it is God who has given us life. Indeed we are told that this relationship was already acknowledged by human beings before we were individually created: 'When your lord brought forth from the children of Adam, from their loins, their seed, and made them testify of themselves, saying, "Am I not your lord?" They said, "Indeed yes. We so testify"' (Q 7:172). We are bound to God, then, in a relationship of gratitude, with the obligation to recognise the rich gift that is ours not only in having been created ourselves, but in having the rest of creation constantly shaped around our human needs. Thus there is a profound connection between faith (*īmān*) and gratitude (*shukr*).[6] As creator, God alone is a sure guide (*hādī*, Q 25:31) to life in the world, and human beings must allow themselves to be guided (*al-muhtadūn*, Q 2:157) or they will go astray (*al-ḍāllīn*, Q 1:7). God alone can be advocate (*wakīl*,

Q 73:9), protector (*walī*, Q 2:107; *mawlā*, Q 2:286) and guardian (*ḥāfiẓ*, Q 12:64; *ḥafīẓ*, Q 11:57).

The essence of unbelief, therefore, is ingratitude – the word *kufr* is used for both. It consists in failing to acknowledge God as creator, and so seeking protection, guidance and help from others than God. It is a failure to take seriously what is perfectly evident about God from creation. 'He gives you some of anything you ask him; if you were to count the favours of God, you would not be able to number them. Man (*al-insān*) is truly a wrong-doer, an ingrate [*kaffār* – an intensive form of the more common *kāfir*]' (Q 14:34). 'He has created the heavens and the earth with truth. He makes night succeed day, and day succeed night, and he makes subservient the sun and the moon, each running for an appointed term. Is not he the mighty (*al-ʿazīz*), the forgiving (*al-ghaffār*)? He created you from one soul, then from it he made its mate; and he has provided for you eight pairs of cattle. He created you in your mothers' wombs – creation after creation – in threefold darkness. Such is God, your lord. His is the sovereignty. There is no God but him. How then did you turn away? If you are ungrateful (*in takfirū*), God has no need of you, nor is he pleased with ingratitude (*al-kufra*) from his servants; but if you are grateful (*in tashkurū*), he is pleased with you for that' (Q 39:5–7). 'Lo! your lord is gracious towards humanity, but most of them do not give thanks' (Q 27:73). The sight and hearing that God gave us at our creation turn out to have been useless because we have denied the very evidence of those eyes and ears (Q 46:26).

IN CREATING, GOD REVEALS

God's first revelation, then, is in creation. Just as the creative activity of God is continuous and not merely confined to an initial moment, the Qur'ān insists that God is constantly providing 'signs' (*āyāt* or *āy*, plurals of *āya*) that manifest all we need to know about God and about our rightful place in relationship to God.[7] Natural phenomena pointing to the creator are there to be comprehended by anyone who has the intelligence (*ʿaql*) to reflect on them (*tafakkara*), to acknowledge their truth (*ṣaddaqa*) and to respond with faithful submission (*īmān, islām*). Inanimate creation itself recognises and submits to God's sovereignty: 'Have they not observed all things that God has created, how their shadows bend to right and left, making prostration to God, and how they are humble?' (Q 16:48; see also Q 13:15). Humans, however, pay little attention to these obvious evidences of God's sovereignty. They are heedless (*ghāfil*, Q 7:136) and ignorant (*jāhil*, Q 6:34); they forget (*nasū*, Q 9:67). Though they may turn to God when in danger of their lives, as soon as the threat passes they turn back to other divinities or agencies as partners with or rivals to God (Q 29:65; 39:8).

GOD HAS NO PARTNERS

It is traditionally understood that there are two audiences addressed by the assertion of God's uniqueness: the pagans of Mecca on the one hand, and the People of the Scripture (*ahl al-kitāb*, also translated as People of the Book), the Jews and Christians, on the other. It has been customary to read the Qur'ān's polemic against the Meccans as though they were principally worshippers of idols, and the Islamic historical tradition has elaborated a great deal on the little there is in the text explicitly about idols.[8] As a result of this there may have been too strong a distinction drawn between the two audiences. What unites these two groups is their tendency to associate other powers with God. Though the Christians and Jews are not explicitly accused of the sin of *shirk*, of being polytheists, at least some of these People of the Scripture are to be considered unbelievers (e.g., Q 2:105; 3:186). The Christians deify Christ (Q 5:72; 9:30); they are accused of reducing God to merely 'the third of three' (Q 5:73), and they consider Jesus and his mother 'two gods apart from God' (Q 5:116). The Jews are said to consider ʿUzayr (Ezra) to be the son of God (Q 9:30). Given these criticisms, therefore, commentators on the Qur'ān are not slow to apply the term *mushrik* (associater, polytheist) also to People of the Scripture.

The Qur'ān envisages a network of relationships defined by the notion of protective friendship. It is essential to choose the right *walī* or *mawlā*. Ultimately God alone can be counted on as protector, though the angels also perform this role at God's command (Q 41:31), as do the messenger and the believing community (Q 5:55). The believers are protective friends to one another and should not choose as protectors People of the Scripture (Q 5:51, 57), hypocrites (Q 4:88–9), or unbelievers – even members of their own family (see, for example, Q 4:139; 9:23). Those who choose other than God as protector end up, whether they realise it or not, with the demons (*al-shayāṭīn*) as their patrons (Q 7:27, 30) and it is for those demons that the unbelievers are fighting rather than for God (Q 3:175; 4:76).

GOD'S MESSENGERS

The abundant revelation in nature has by itself mostly failed to elicit the appropriate response from human beings. They scarcely remember their primordially sworn testimony to God's uniqueness and sovereignty, nor do they reflect on the evidence that surrounds them. Even the first human being was found to be lacking in fidelity to the covenant God made with him (Q 20:115). Therefore, God sends messengers to warn of the consequences of such infidelity. Hundreds of times the Qur'ān uses words from the Arabic root *dh-k-r* indicating that messengers are sent to remind (*dhakkara*) human beings of their covenant (*mīthāq, ʿahd*): 'Remember God's graciousness to you and his covenant by which he bound you when you said, "We have heard and obeyed." Revere God. He knows the nature of hearts' (Q 5:7). The messengers remind people of God's blessing (*baraka, niʿma*) and the signs (*āyāt*) all around them. They call their people to faith (Q 40:10), to salvation (Q 40:41) and to guidance (cf. Q 7:148).

The messengers are also charged with relating and with interpreting for their people the history of God's dealing with humanity – the history of prophecy and the fate of the nations that have passed away before them. For example, Q 24:34: 'We have sent down for you revelations that make things clear, and the example of those who passed away before you, as an admonition for the godfearing.'

In the Qur'ān God continually revisits the signs in nature and history with a series of formulaic refrains expressing the desired response: 'Perhaps you/they might . . .' 'Will you/they not . . .?' 'Surely in that there are signs for a people who . . .'. The verbs used in these three refrains are strikingly intellectual – learn, reflect, reason, remember, heed, perceive, think. The *āyāt* of God, woven into nature, manifested in history, rehearsed and detailed by God's messengers, are all intended to reveal to humanity an insight into the nature of things that God alone possesses. They are there to be 'read' and the appropriate conclusions drawn. The signs, however, are not merely for information; they are intended to challenge those who encounter them to reflect and to respond in faith. Once this transforming knowledge has been gained, it is unthinkable that people should return to following their own or others' uninformed ideas (*ahwāʾ*) about how things are: 'Say, "The guidance of God is the guidance. If you were to follow their vain ideas after what has come to you by way of knowledge, then you would have neither protector nor helper against God"'(Q 2:120).

The *āyāt* that constitute God's revelation in nature and in history come to the people repeated, as it were, in the form of verses (also *āyāt*) of scripture to be remembered and recited. The purpose of God's repeatedly choosing messengers and entrusting them with a message is to call people back to the acknowledgement of a truth already evident in the signs around them. It could be said that there is no essential difference between the verses and the natural or historical signs: all are there to remind the forgetful and heedless of the fundamental truth of God's sovereignty and bounteous care.

GOD WRITES

God's knowledge of everything in creation (Q 6:59; 34:3) and of everything people do (both good and bad, Q 36:12; 82:11–12) is often mentioned using the metaphor of writing and records. So also God is said to write rewards (Q 5:21; 7:156; 21:105), entitlements (Q 2:187; 4:127), punishments (Q 22:4; 4:127) and obligations (e.g., Q 2:178, 180, 183, 216, 246) – including obligations God takes on himself (Q 6:12, 54). God determines by writing the course of events (Q 3:154; 7:156; 9:51; 58:22). The Qur'ān's use of the language of writing and recording for God's knowledge and authority is closely linked to its concept of scripture (*kitāb*, literally 'a writing', pl. *kutub*). The scriptures God gives through the prophets are exercises of God's authority and revelations of God's knowledge. Obviously they cannot contain all that God commands and knows: 'If all the trees on earth were pens, and the sea [were ink], with seven more seas to help it, the words of God would not be exhausted. God is mighty, wise' (Q 31:27). A community that is given scripture and continues to recite it and live by it is in a relationship through which God continues to guide it.

Since the truth does not change, it is axiomatic for the Qur'ān that the present revelation contains fundamentally the same message as that given to the earlier messengers. The believers are expected to accept the revelations given before Muḥammad (Q 2:4, 136; 4:60, 162), since God communicated with those messengers as he has done with Muḥammad: 'We communicated to you (*awḥaynā ilayka*) as we communicated to Noah and the prophets after him, as we communicated to Abraham and Ishmael and Isaac and Jacob and the tribes, and Jesus and Job and Jonah and Aaron and Solomon, and as we granted David the Psalms' (Q 4:163); 'Say, "We believe in God and what has been sent down to us and in what was sent down to Abraham, and Ishmael, and Isaac, and Jacob, and the tribes, and in what Moses and Jesus were given, and in what the prophets were given by their lord – we make no distinction between any of them – and to him do we submit"' (Q 2:136). The term that binds together these diverse manifestations of revelation is *kitāb*: 'O you who believe, believe in God and his messenger and the *kitāb* that he has sent down to his messenger, and the *kitāb* that he sent down before. Whoever disbelieves in God and his angels and his *kutub* and his messengers and the last day has already gone far astray' (Q 4:136).[9]

The Qur'ān sees itself as confirming (*muṣaddiq*) the previous revelations[10] in the same way Jesus is said to have come to confirm the Torah given to Moses (Q 3:50; 5:46; 61:6). It pays a great deal of attention to asserting and defending its status as scripture that has been sent down by God – *tanzīl* (e.g., Q 45:2) – rather than the human or demonic word of a poet or soothsayer: 'But no! I swear by what you see and what you cannot see that it is indeed the speech of a noble messenger. It is not poet's speech – how little you believe! Nor is it diviner's speech – how little you remember! Rather it is something being sent down from the lord of the worlds. If he had invented falsehoods against us, we would have taken him by the right hand and severed his life-artery, and none of you could have held us off from him' (Q 69:38–47; see also 52:29).

No other figure in the Qur'ān is treated in such detail and at such length as Moses – recognisably similar to the figure known from the Bible and Jewish haggada. Characteristically for the Qur'ān, all this material is presented not in a single structured narrative, but in myriad references of varying length and complexity – references that take for granted some knowledge of Moses' story. In many respects Moses is the model for Muḥammad, combining as he does a role as liberator of his people with the roles of lawgiver and channel of revelation.

The Qur'ān also appeals to a history of prophecy unknown to the Judaeo-Christian tradition to show that what is taking place in the career of Muḥammad follows a perennial pattern in God's dealings with people. The stories of these messengers, the Midianite Shuʿayb,[11] and the Arabs, Hūd[12] and Ṣāliḥ,[13] follow a schema very similar to that traditionally recounted about Muḥammad during his time in Mecca – the messenger is sent to his own people to call them back to the worship of the one God; he is rejected by most, accused of being possessed or merely a poet, and then is vindicated by the divine punishment brought on the unbelievers. In the case of Muḥammad, of course, it remained to be seen how the divine chastisement would be expressed (cf. Q 46:35).

Apart from emphasising Muḥammad's place in the centuries-long company of God's messengers, the Qur'ān has two other important interests in its recounting of the history of prophecy. The first of these is the figure of Abraham (Ibrāhīm), who is identified in the Qur'ān, no less than in the Bible, as the very model of the believer. Many elements of the Abraham story have parallels in the biblical or in post-biblical Jewish traditions, though the telling is spread out through twenty-five sūras.[14] Other elements, however, are unique to the Qur'ān: Abraham and Ishmael build (or restore) the Kaʿba and institute its associated rituals (Q 2:125–7). Abraham prays to God for the people of the place, that they might always be a nation submissive to God (*umma muslima*), and that a messenger like himself be sent to them (Q 2:128–9). Eight times the Qur'ān refers to him as *ḥanīf*, generally taken to mean a pious monotheist, since the word is contrasted with *mushrik*.[15] In Q 30:30 the religion of Abraham (i.e., of a *ḥanīf*) is described as being that according to which God formed human nature (*fiṭrat Allāh*), and there is no changing what God has created. Muḥammad in his turn is told to say to the Christians and Jews who seek to win him for their religions that he is to prefer this original, natural religion of Abraham (*millat Ibrāhīm*, Q 2:135). They are criticised for arguing about Abraham when he precedes both Moses and Jesus, both Torah and Gospel (Q 3:65). Perhaps each was claiming to be the genuine heirs of the patriarch, whereas in fact 'Abraham was neither a Jew, nor a Christian; rather he was a *ḥanīf* who had submitted himself (*muslim*) to God, and he was not one of those who associate partners with God (*mushrikūn*)' (Q 3:67).

Abraham is of key importance to the Qur'ān's understanding of religion: he is recognised as an essential part of the Jewish and Christian traditions – even to the extent that each of them would fight to claim him – yet at the same time his tradition has firm roots in Arabia, roots that pre-date either of the other traditions that look to him as a foundational figure. Islam, then, is presented as anything but a new religion. It is the return to the source, in two senses: the prophetic source of monotheism, and the real source of Arabian traditional religion. That is why it is in a position both to confirm and to offer a critique of other branches of the Abrahamic tradition: 'O People of the Scripture! Now has our messenger come to you, making clear for you much in the scripture (*al-kitāb*) that you used to hide' (Q 5:15). Accusations of altering the scriptures, common in the tradition, are not easily sustained from the text, which uses derivatives of the verb *ḥarrafa* (Q 2:75; 4:46; 5:13, 41). It probably indicates that what is at issue is misinterpretation, perhaps even deliberate, resulting from taking words out of context or ignoring certain passages.

This critique of existing religious traditions is the second concern underlying the Qur'ān's presentation of the history of prophecy. Jesus (ʿĪsā) is not reduced to a schematic figure like some of the other prophets. He retains many features familiar from either mainstream or heterodox Christian traditions. Yet the Qur'ān is anxious to set the record straight on his position: 'O People of the Scripture, do not exaggerate in your religion nor say anything about God except the truth. The Messiah, Jesus son of Mary, was only a messenger of God, and his word which he conveyed to Mary, and a spirit from him. So believe in God and his messengers, and do not say "Three". Cease! It will be better for you. God is only one god. He is exalted far above having a son' (Q 4:171). However, the adoption of terms like 'word' and 'spirit', so frequently used in Christian dogma, could hardly resolve the issue, and discussion continues. Similarly the complexity of the statements about the death of Jesus (Q 3:55; 4:157–9) has opened the way to a variety of opinions in the commentary literature. The most widely held opinion is that the Qur'ān denies Jesus' death and that, therefore, he is alive and will return, undergoing death before being raised alive with the rest of creation on the day of judgement. Others hold that it is only the reality of the crucifixion that is denied, leaving open the possibility that Jesus died another kind of death, perhaps natural. Others still would interpret the verses in Q 4 as denying neither Jesus' death itself nor the reality of the crucifixion. They see there only an assertion that, even though Jesus died, the end result was that the Jews did not succeed in doing away with him, since God raised him up.[16] Though they boasted of having done so 'it was only made to seem so to them' (Q 4:157).

According to Q 5:116 Jesus will be asked on the day of judgement whether he encouraged people to worship himself and his mother as deities. He will deny it, adding, 'I told them only what you commanded me: "Worship God, my lord and your lord." Whether you punish them or pardon them, they are after all your servants, you are the mighty, the judicious (*al-ḥakīm*)' (Q 5:117–18).

GOD GIVES LIFE, CAUSES DEATH AND RAISES UP

Two major strands of thought in the qur'ānic treatment of death and afterlife should be underlined. They correspond to two major audiences of the qur'ānic discourse: first the Arab polytheists and second the new believers. The early sūras are clearly addressed to those who do not believe in any existence beyond the grave. It is none other than time itself (*al-dahr*) – often seen by the pre-Islamic Arabs as a kind of blind fate – that is responsible for death. In its characteristic manner, the Qur'ān quotes its opponents: 'And they say: There is nothing but our life in the world; we die and we live, and nothing destroys us but time' (Q 45:24). The Qur'ān announces, however, that it is God rather than some impersonal agency that governs the world. God is repeatedly named as the one who gives life and brings death – *yuḥyī wa-yumīt* (e.g., Q 2:28). Even if the pre-Islamic Arabs were correct in thinking that one's days are numbered and one's death irrevocably determined, still it is God who determines the moment, literally 'the span of time that has already been nominated' (*ajal musammā*, e.g., Q 6:2). The word *ajal* carries the sense of being a postponement, a putting off until later of something inevitable and perhaps also deserved. God is forbearing and patient, refusing to bring death sooner than its moment, even if the person has done wrong. The idea is not only personal; each nation also has its determined time (e.g., Q 7:34; 10:49; 23:43).

This determined moment is not, however, the end of all life. Death is seen as a step before resurrection to a new life: 'And he it is who gave you life, then he will cause you to die, and then will give you life (again). Humanity is indeed ungrateful' (Q 22:66). The Qur'ān repeatedly reminds the sceptic that God is able to bring life from apparent death, so it is not difficult for God to raise the dead to life: 'And God it is who sends the winds and they raise a cloud; then we bring it to a dead land and with it we revive the earth after its death. Such is the resurrection' (*al-nushūr*, Q 35:9).

GOD IS THE MOST JUST OF JUDGES

The announcement of the resurrection from the dead is both good news and bad – in traditional Islamic terms a promise (*waʿd*) and a threat (*waʿīd*) – for this is resurrection to judgement, to reward or punishment, to the gardens of paradise or the fires of hell. This was a central theme in the early preaching of the Prophet and the basis of his ethical appeal to those who had no fear of an eschatological punishment (see, for example, Q 6:30–2). Earthly creation is seen as a testing ground for humanity: 'God made the heavens and the earth in truth, so that each soul could be rewarded for what it earned' (Q 45:22). 'And he it is who created the heavens and the earth in six days – and his throne was upon the water – that he might test you, as to which of you is best in conduct' (Q 11:7).

The resurrection to judgement will take place at 'the hour' or on a particular day (*yawm al-dīn*, 'the day of judgement'; *yawm al-faṣl*, 'the day of harvest, separation, or sorting out'; *yawm muḥīṭ*, 'an all-encompassing day') known only to God (Q 33:63). The Qur'ān is replete with cataclysmic details of the end of the world – trumpet blasts, the splitting of the heavens (e.g., Q 55:37) and the rolling up of the heavens like a scroll (Q 21:104); the rolling up of the sun; an enormous earthquake. An extended example is Q 81:1–14. No one, we are assured repeatedly, will escape death, and so it is understood that at a certain point everything will perish – except the face of God (Q 28:88; 55:26–7). Then all will be brought to life once more and gathered for judgement before the throne of God. It is important to note that the Qur'ān teaches a belief not in immortality but rather in resurrection. Nothing is eternal but God. Life is God's gift, not an inherent attribute of the soul or spirit.

The experience of judgement and the reckoning (*ḥisāb*) will be terrifying even for those who are to be rewarded (e.g., Q 21:103; 37:20). Each will be presented with the record of his or her deeds – in the right hand for those to be saved, in the left for those to be damned (see, for example, Q 69:19–37). The text also speaks (Q 101:6) of the scales that will weigh with minute precision the deeds of those being judged. Being damned to hell is a kind of living death from which there is no escape: 'He who will be flung to the great fire, wherein he will neither die nor live' (Q 87:12–13; see also Q 14:17).

The Qur'ān stresses the justice of God's judging and the individual's responsibility for his or her deeds. Some verses seem to exclude the possibility of intercession, and substitution is not admitted (Q 39:41; 9:74; 2:48). Other verses, however, have been interpreted to mean that Muḥammad and the angels will be permitted to intercede and that their intercession will be effective, at least in the case of those who have not fallen into polytheism. Although without an unequivocal basis in the Qur'ān, this has become an important belief for the Muslim community, and numerous traditions (*aḥādīth*) speak of it.

GOD IS MERCIFUL

In the final analysis, the Qur'ān is concerned to assert God's tendency to forgive rather than to condemn. More than five hundred times it characterises God as forgiving (*ghafūr*, ninety-one occurrences, e.g., Q 2:173; also *ghāfir*, Q 40:3; *ghaffār*, Q 20:82; and *ʿafuww*, Q 4:43), often turning back (*tawwāb*, Q 49:12) towards sinners, generous (*karīm*, Q 27:40), kind (*ra'ūf*, Q 2:143) and loving (*wadūd*, Q 11:90). Virtually every sūra begins by naming God 'the merciful, the compassionate' (*al-raḥmān al-raḥīm*). God even claims to have prescribed mercy as a duty for himself (Q 6:12, 54). Moreover, this mercy is not incompatible with the power and command of God – it is the magnanimous, unconstrained mercy of the absolute sovereign.

An important aspect of God's mercy is the sending of prophets with revelation. Both the scriptures and the messengers are referred to as a mercy (e.g., Q 31:2–3; 44:2–6) since they provide God's warning against evil and God's guidance towards the promised reward. The reward of paradise is described in concrete detail, especially in the chapters normally dated to the earliest period: regal splendour (Q 83:24), costly robes, perfumes and jewellery. The texts lay emphasis on visions of elaborate banquets (e.g., Q 52:22–4), where the elect will rejoice in the company of their parents, their wives and children who were faithful (Q 13:23; 36:56, 40:8; cf. 43:70). They will praise their lord (Q 35:34), leaning towards each other in love, conversing in joy and recalling the past (e.g., Q 15:47; 52:25, etc.). 'Pure consorts' are promised (Q 2:25; 3:15; 4:57) and a happy life, without hurt or weariness, neither sorrow, fear nor shame, where every desire is fulfilled (Q 16:31, 39).

'[The pious] will there enjoy what they desire and we will grant still more (*mazīd*)' (Q 50:35). This 'more', like the 'addition' (*ziyāda*) of Q 10:26, is usually associated with the 'approval' (*riḍwān*) from God foretold to the elect in Q 3:15. 'To believers, God has promised gardens beneath which rivers flow, where they will rest immortal. He has promised them goodly dwellings in the gardens of Eden. [But] the approval of God is greater. That will be the great victory' (Q 9:72). The fruits of it will be nearness to God. God will bring the elect near to his throne (passim), and 'on that day some faces will shine, looking towards their lord' (Q 75:22–3). The theologians argued at length as to whether the vision of God (*ru'yat Allāh*) in paradise would be sight or insight.

The other major element in the Qur'ān's discussion of death is the question of warfare 'in the way of God'. The text witnesses to considerable resistance on the part of the new believers to the idea of risking their lives in the warfare that became a regular part of the life of the young community after its emigration to Medina. 'Have you not seen those to whom it was said, "Withhold your hands, establish worship and pay the poor due." When fighting was prescribed [lit. 'written'] for them, a party of them fear mankind as much as they fear God or even more, and they say, "Our lord, why have you prescribed fighting for us? If only you would give us a little more time"' (Q 4:77). The believers are told not to consider those who have died 'in the way of God' as being dead. They are alive with God (Q 2:154; 3:169). They should not be like the unbelievers of old who said of those killed in war, 'If they had been here with us they would not have died or been killed' (Q 3:156). Since it is God who gives life and brings death at a determined moment that cannot be escaped, it makes no difference whether those men answered the call to war or not; if their time had come, they would have died even at home in bed.

Taken all together, the major preoccupation of the qur'ānic teaching is to underline the sovereignty of God over life and death – as a theological affirmation, as a spur to moral seriousness and as an encouragement to risk all for the cause of God.

GOD IS GUIDE

The general moral and spiritual guidance offered in the earlier parts of the Qur'ān become ever more specific and detailed in the later period, reflecting a developing relationship between the Prophet and his hearers. In this period obedience to God and to messenger become closely identified – fifty-seven times the Medinan sūras speak of obedience and disobedience, assistance and opposition to 'God and his messenger'. This repeated identification then becomes the basis in the tradition for the authority of the prophetic word and example – the *sunna* – alongside the Qur'ān, to complete it and to give its definitive interpretation. The longest sūras all contain legislative material, covering marriage and family law (especially in Q 4), inheritance (e.g., Q 4:176), food (e.g., Q 5:1–5) and drink (e.g., Q 5:90–1), worship and purity (e.g., Q 2:140–4, 187), the conduct of warfare (e.g., Q 2:190–4), stipulated punishments (*ḥudūd*) for unlawful intercourse (Q 24:2), unsubstantiated accusation of such (Q 24:4), drinking alcohol (Q 5:90–1), theft (Q 5:38) and brigandage (Q 5:33–4).

The regulation of the community's affairs is sometimes surprisingly concrete and detailed, and no small part of this is concerned with women – particularly the wives of the Prophet, for whom very specific restrictions and privileges are established. Several parts of qur'ānic teaching use both the masculine and feminine forms of participles in addressing the believers (e.g., Q 33:35 where there are ten such pairings), underlining the equality of men and women before God. Mary (Ar. Maryam), the virgin mother of Jesus, is cited by God as an example to all believers because of her chastity, faith and obedience (Q 66:11–12). Along with Moses' mother and Abraham's wife Sara, she receives revelation or inspiration from God, though the consensus of the tradition is that they are not prophets. Muḥammad's wives are singled out in the qur'ānic legislation as 'mothers of the believers' and thus the restrictions placed on them in clothing and seclusion (cf. Q 33:32–3, 53) become generalised in the Muslim tradition to all women.

Much of the Qur'ān's legal material is not univocal, and so the tradition has had to try and discern the development in order to understand God's final word on the subject. In the case of wine (*khamr*) the progression from praise of it (Q 16:67), through reservations about it (Q 2:219; 4:43), to outright condemnation (Q 5:90–1) seems clear enough. With the somewhat tangled explanations of inheritance obligations and shares (Q 2:180; 4:11–12, 33, 176) more elaborate analysis was required.

These rules could be seen as an essential part of the process of defining the identity of the community that has accepted to be guided by God and the messenger. Thus the legislative material is interspersed with verses contending against other groups of believers, pagans and hypocrites. Sūrat al-Māʾida ('The Table', Q 5), for example, brings together a large number of commands and prohibitions in a context marked by contention with the Jews and Christians. Each of the three groups has been given its own law (Q 5:48), and the new community must judge by what has specifically been given to it.

'UNTIL RELIGION IS ALL FOR GOD'

The Qurʾān evinces little doubt about the outcome of the conflicts it observes and in which it takes part. God is 'the one, the vanquisher' and will brook no opposition. Once it has established itself, the community of believers is commanded to struggle 'in the way of God'. Though the command to fight is clear and repeated, so too are the exceptions to be made and the conditions to be observed in that fighting: 'fight those who fight you, but do not begin the hostilities' (Q 2:190); 'if they desist, then God is forgiving, merciful' (Q 2:192); 'if they are inclined to making peace, then you too should lean that way' (Q 8:61). Struggle (*jihād*) or fighting (*qitāl*) in the way of God is not intended merely for defence against persecution (Q 22:39). It means putting one's life and livelihood at the service of that divine sovereignty which is the Qurʾān's constant theme, to ensure that it is everywhere recognised.

Notes

1. W. C. Smith, 'The true meaning of scripture: An empirical historian's nonreductionist interpretation of the Qurʾān', *International Journal of Middle East Studies* 11 (1980), 504.
2. Even though the word *raḥmān* comes to function almost like an adjective, unlike many of the other adjectives and participles that become divine names it is never used of anyone but God.
3. See also Q 2:22, 29, 164; 10:67; 16:5–8, 10–18, 80–1; 17:12; 20:54–5; 22:65; 23:17–22; 67:15; 78:6–13; 79:32–3.
4. Q 2:30–9; 7:11–25; 15:28–43; 17:61–5; 18:50; 20:116–23; 38:71–85.
5. The word applied to God in all but six of its 140 occurrences, often paired with another adjective in a rhyming verse ending characteristic of the Qurʾān.

6. See A. K. Reinhart, *Before revelation: The boundaries of Muslim moral thought* (Albany: SUNY Press, 1995), ch. 6; also his 'Ethics and the Qur'ān', in J. D. McAuliffe (ed.), *Encyclopaedia of the Qur'ān,* 5 vols. (Leiden: Brill, 2001–6), vol. II, pp. 57–8; J. I. Smith, 'Faith', in McAuliffe (ed.), *Encyclopaedia of the Qur'ān,* vol. II, pp. 164–5.
7. Some of the more important passages of this kind are Q 2:164; 3:190–1; 6:95–9; 10:5–7; 13:2–4; 16:10–16, 78–81; 23:21–2; 26:7–8; 27:86, 93; 29:44; 30:20–8, 46; 32:27; 34:9; 36:33–47; 39:21; 41:37, 39, 53; 42:29–34; 45:1–6, 12–13; 50:6–11; 51:20.
8. On this subject see G. R. Hawting, *The idea of idolatry and the emergence of Islam: From polemic to history* (New York: Cambridge University Press, 1999) and his 'Idolatry and idolaters', in McAuliffe (ed.), *Encyclopaedia of the Qur'ān,* vol. II, pp. 475–80.
9. The longest listings of prophets are in Q 21:48–91 and Q 6:83–7.
10. Q 2:41, 89, 91, 97, 101; 3:3, 81; 4:47; 5:48; 6:92; 10:37; 12:111; 35:31; 46:12, 30.
11. Q 7:85–93; 11:84–95; 26:176–91.
12. Q 7:65–72; 11:50–60; 26:123–40; 46:21.
13. Q 7:73–9; 11:61–8; 26:141–59; 27:45–53.
14. For a synthetic presentation of the material, see R. Firestone, 'Abraham', in McAuliffe (ed.), *Encyclopaedia of the Qur'ān,* vol. I, pp. 5–11.
15. Q 2:135; 3:67, 95; 6:79, 161; 16:120, 123; cf. 4:125.
16. For discussions of this complex issue, see K. Cragg, *Jesus and the Muslim* (London: George Allen & Unwin, 1985) and N. Robinson, *Christ in Islam and Christianity* (Albany: SUNY Press, 1991), or his shorter treatment, 'Jesus', in McAuliffe (ed.), *Encyclopaedia of the Qur'ān,* vol. III, pp. 7–21.

Further reading

Izutsu, T., *Ethico-religious concepts in the Qur'ān,* Montreal: McGill-Queen's University Press, 2002 (1966[1]).

God and man in the Koran: Semantics of the koranic Weltanschauung, Tokyo: Keio Institute of Cultural and Linguistic Studies, 1964.

McAuliffe, J. D. (ed.), *Encyclopaedia of the Qur'ān,* 5 vols., Leiden: Brill, 2001–6.

Mir, M., *A dictionary of qur'ānic terms and concepts,* New York: Garland Pub., 1987.

Rahman, F., *Major themes of the Qur'ān,* second ed., Minneapolis: Bibliotheca Islamica, 1989.

Stowasser, B. F., *Women in the Qur'an, traditions and interpretation,* New York: Oxford University Press, 1994.

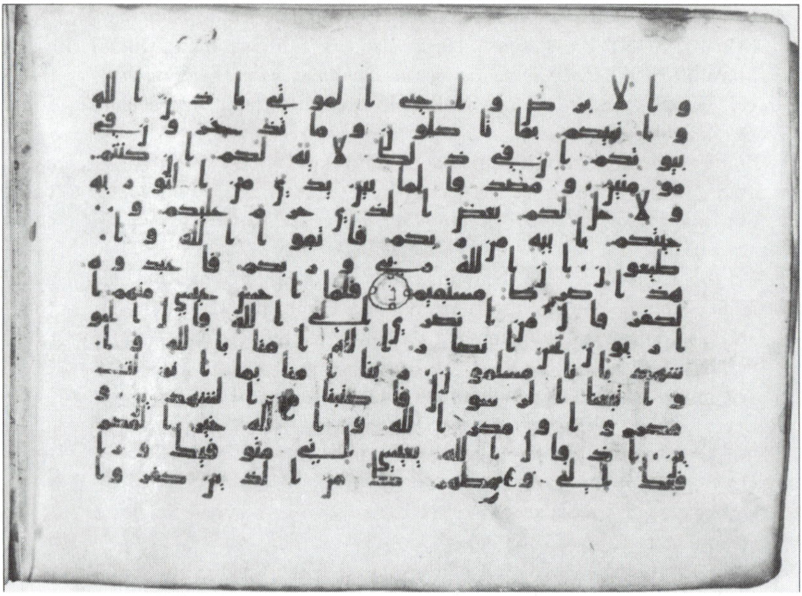

Fig. 5 Folio from an eighth-century *ḥijāzī* Qur'ān manuscript, depicting Q 3:49–55. Like the inscriptions on the Dome of the Rock, this early manuscript demonstrates a scribal method of distinguishing between the Arabic letters *fā'* and *qāf* by placing a dash above the former, and below the latter (Cod. Mixt. 917, fol. 27v). Courtesy of the Österreichische Nationalbibliothek, Vienna

5 Structural, linguistic and literary features

ANGELIKA NEUWIRTH

THE CODEX OF THE RECEIVED TEXT (*MUṢḤAF*)

The qur'ānic text transmitted to us betrays a peculiar composition, essentially different from that of the Hebrew Bible, which pursues salvation history through a roughly chronological sequence of events, and equally different from the Gospels that narrate the essential stages of the founding history of the Christian faith. The Qur'ān does not present a continuous narrative of the past, but in its early texts conjures the future, the imminent day of judgement, and later on enters into a debate with various interlocutors about the implementation of monotheist scripture in the present.

External subdivisions

In terms of form, the Qur'ān is not a sequentially coherent book, made up of sub-units that build on each other, but rather consists in a collection of 114 independent text units, sūras (*sūra*, pl. *suwar*) with no evident external link to each other. A sūra is marked by a heading giving its name, and by an introductory invocation, the so-called *basmala*: 'in the name of God, the compassionate and merciful' (*bi-smi llāhi l-raḥmāni l-raḥīm*). The term sūra is used in the Qur'ān, though originally referring to undetermined text units, smaller than the eventually fixed sūras. Whereas in some cases the names of the sūras are contested, several sūras being known under more than one name, the introductory formula – that is missing in only one sūra, Q 9 – goes back to the recitation practice of the Prophet's community itself. The sūras vary in length from two-sentence statements to lengthy polythematic communications. They are arranged in the qur'ānic corpus roughly according to their length: the longest sūras are placed first, the shorter ones following in a generally descending order. The vast majority of the sūras are neatly composed texts that may be understood to constitute a literary genre in themselves. Although a large number of sūras appear to have been expanded during the period of their oral transmission, even in their compounded version they appear to follow particular rules of composition. Only some of the long sūras appear to be haphazard compilations of isolated text passages, their shape due to the redaction process itself.

Sūras are composed of verses (*āya*, pl. *āyāt*), varying in size from one single word to an entire, complex pericope. The term *āya*, which corresponds to Syriac *āthā* and Hebrew *ōth*, meaning a 'visible sign of a transcendental reality', is first used in the Qur'ān to denote markings of divine omnipotence, such as are manifest in nature or in history. In the course of the Qur'ān's communication process, the concept came to designate a miraculous sign apt to prove the truth of the prophetic message, and could thus be eventually identified with a qur'ānic verse. The early short sūras are styled in a kind of rhymed prose, labelled *saj'*, known as the medium of the ancient Arabian soothsayers (*kahana*, sing. *kāhin*). *Saj'* is a particularly succinct rhythmic diction where single phrases are marked by prose-rhyme, *fāṣila*. This pattern of phonetic correspondence between the verse endings is not only looser than poetic rhyme (*qāfiya*) but also more flexible, thus allowing semantically related verses to be bracketed by a rhyme of their own and clearly distinct verse-groups to be marked off. The highly sophisticated phonetic structures produced by this style have been evaluated by Michael Sells.[1] Though the *saj'* style gave way at a later stage of qur'ānic development to a more smoothly flowing prose allowing for complex periods to form a single verse, closed by only a phonetically stereotypical rhyming syllable, the unit of the verse as the smallest compositional entity is an essential element of qur'ānic literary structure. It not only facilitates the act of memorising but constitutes the backbone of qur'ānic recitation (*tartīl, tajwīd*), the essential format of self-manifestation for the Muslim scripture. The numbering of qur'ānic verses is a modern phenomenon whereas other technical subdivisions, like the partitioning of the entire text into seven *manāzil* (sing. *manzila*, i.e., station), or into thirty *ajzā'* (sing. *juz'*, i.e., part) which, in turn, are subdivided into two *aḥzāb* (sing. *ḥizb*, part) – divisions governed by quantitative criteria without concern for the rhetorical and semantic disposition of the sūras – stem from the early post-redactional period and were introduced to facilitate memorising and reciting.

The compositional sequence of the qur'ānic sūras does not follow any logical, let alone theological, guideline and betrays both a conservative and a theologically disinterested attitude on the part of the redactors. It suggests that the redaction was carried out without extensive planning, perhaps in a hurry, at a stage of development prior to the emergence of the elaborate conceptions of prophetology that underlie the *sīra*, the biography of the Prophet that was fixed about a century and a half after his death. The fixation of the qur'ānic text must also have occurred before the great conquests, since a unification of various textual traditions dispersed over the ever-extending territories would have been difficult to implement. The traditional scenario of the ʿUthmānic redaction, the hypothesis that the texts of the Prophet's recitations were collected some twenty-five years after his death by the third caliph ʿUthmān to form the corpus we have before us, is thus not implausible, though impossible to prove positively.

Codification and its impact

The Arabic script used for the earliest codification only incompletely rendered the phonetic shape of the text. What was later to become a consonantal system combined with the obligatory notation of long vowels was, in the seventh century, yet an ambiguous representation of the phonetics of Arabic words. A number of consonants were rendered by a single homograph that only later was differentiated, through points placed above or below the letter form, into specific graphemes. Long vowels were not presented unambiguously and short ones were not yet marked by the strokes that later came into use. The earliest written codification of the qur'ānic texts could not, therefore, serve as more than a mnemonic-technical support for a continuing tradition of oral recitation. Despite the preliminary format of the first redaction, however, with the consonantal fixation of the text and with its arrangement as a sequence of sūras, a fixed text had been established.

At the same time, a decisive course had been set with regard to the literary character of the Qur'ān. The combined codification of loosely composed texts consisting of diverse, often conceptually isolated communications – characteristic of the Medinan 'long sūras' – together with the complex polythematic structures of the mnemonic and technically sophisticated short and middle-sized Meccan sūras, resulted in a very heterogeneous ensemble. This textual diversity certainly had a hermeneutical impact on the perception of the text. The individual texts became disconnected from their earlier communicational context during the period of the emergence of the community and this changed them from inter-depending prophetic communications into isolated sections of a book. Neatly composed sūras also lost much of their significance as literary texts once they were juxtaposed in the same codex with other units also labelled 'sūras', but whose constituent passages had not been formulated to create a coherent literary structure. The loosely composed sūras thus invalidated the structural claim conveyed by the neatly composed ones. The genre 'sūra' that had been established during the activity of the Prophet became blurred in the consciousness of the later community. It is not surprising then, that the sūra as a unit played only a minimal role in Muslim reading of the Qur'ān, and did not attract attention as a literary phenomenon in classical Muslim qur'ānic scholarship but had to be rediscovered in modern times.

THE PRE-CANONICAL QUR'ĀN

Controversial issues

The presentation of qur'ānic developments in this chapter presupposes the reliability of the basic data of traditional accounts about the emergence of the Qur'ān, assuming the transmitted qur'ānic text to be the genuine collection of the communications of the Prophet as pronounced during his activities at Mecca (about 610–22 CE), and again at Medina (1/622 until his death in 11/632). It is true that the earlier consensus of scholarly opinion on the origins of Islam has, since the publication of John Wansbrough's *Quranic studies*[2] and Patricia Crone and Michael Cook's *Hagarism*,[3] been shattered, and that various attempts at a new reconstruction of those origins have been put forward. As a whole, however, the theories of the so-called sceptic or revisionist scholars who, arguing historically, make a radical break with the transmitted picture of Islamic origins, shifting them in both time and place from the seventh to the eighth or ninth century and from the Arabian peninsula to the Fertile Crescent, have by now been discarded, though many of their critical observations remain challenging and still call for investigation. New findings of qur'ānic text fragments, moreover, can be adduced to affirm rather than call into question the traditional picture of the Qur'ān as an early fixed text composed of the sūras we have. Nor have scholars trying to deconstruct that image through linguistic arguments succeeded in seriously discrediting the genuineness of the Qur'ān as we know it. These include the work of Christoph Luxenberg,[4] who views the Qur'ān as an originally Syriac–Arabic melange later adapted to the rules of classical Arabic, and Günter Lüling,[5] who reads the Qur'ān as a collection of hymns composed in a Christian Arabic dialect and later revised to fit the grammatical rules newly established in the eighth and ninth centuries. Whereas Lüling's reference to the earlier hypothesis by Karl Vollers,[6] who had identified the original language of the Qur'ān as broadly dialectal, points to a yet unresolved problem, Luxenberg's assumption of a Syriac–Arabic linguistic melange as the original language of the Qur'ān lacks a methodologically sound basis. The alternative visions about the genesis of the Qur'ān presented by Wansbrough, Crone and Cook, Lüling and Luxenberg are not only mutually exclusive, but rely on textual observations that are too selective to be compatible with the comprehensive qur'ānic textual evidence that can be drawn only from a systematically microstructural reading.

Orality, scripturality

In spite of the etymology of its earliest self-designation as *qur'ān*, which is a loanword from Syriac *qeryānā*, meaning a lectionary, recital or pericope to be recited in liturgical services, far too often the Qur'ān is implicitly treated as a written literary work, imagined to have been authored by Muḥammad. This approach is apparent in frequent criticisms that blame the text for not fulfilling particular literary standards. Since the quest for an '*Ur*-text' has long been prevalent in historical-critical studies, qur'ānic speech has usually been investigated according to the criteria of written compositions unrelated to oral performance. This view has met with criticism in more recent scholarship, which has demanded that the quest for original meaning be replaced by a consideration of the Qur'ān's socio-cultural context as a necessary prelude to its interpretation. Some scholars have criticised the neglect of the ritual-recitational dimensions of the Qur'ān, others have stressed 'the abiding and intrinsic orality of the Qur'ān as a scriptural book of revelation and authority'.[7] Oral composition such as has been claimed for ancient Arabic poetry by Michael Zwettler and James Monroe on the basis of the thesis presented by Milman Parry[8] and followed by Albert Bates Lord,[9] although not immediately applicable to the case of the Qur'ān, still needs debate. According to Parry and Lord, 'oral poetry' is characterised by being composed (and recomposed) during performance, a procedure which is supported by a thesaurus of formulaic phrases. Though such a performance practice may apply to many early sūras, it can hardly be assumed for the bulk of the qur'ānic corpus. Some early sūras that were already composed without written assistance attest to an origin in nocturnal vigils, rather than in public performances. Later sūras, comprised of multipartite verses with little poetic shaping and thus devoid of effective mnemonic technical devices, strongly suggest an almost immediate fixation in writing, or may even have been written compositions to begin with.

To investigate the full scope of this development one has, however, to go beyond the mere technical aspects. It is true that the distinction between two decisive periods for the genesis of the Qur'ān – a purely oral phase, where the message refers to itself as '*qur'ān*' and a later phase where '*kitāb*' becomes the term of reference for new texts whose length and structure presuppose the use of writing as a mnemonic-technical device – has been accepted in historical-critical scholarship on the Qur'ān. Yet, this double modality of the qur'ānic text has not been explored for the implications that it poses to notions about the development of the Qur'ān as moving from oral recitals to the manifest status of a holy scripture, a development that has to be viewed as a process of gradual canonisation. One has to keep in mind, however, that the qur'ānic terms '*qur'ān*' and '*kitāb*' denote very different concepts. The first points to a communal event that is in progress and that involves a number of *dramatis personae* – a speaker reciting a message received from an 'absent' commissioner that he is charged to communicate to a plurality of listeners. It thus stresses a horizontal human interaction. This dynamic, thanks to the striking phenomenon of qur'ānic self-referentiality, is mirrored clearly in the early sūras themselves, which have preserved lively scenarios of the reception of the qur'ānic revelation.[10]

The second concept focuses on the hierarchical quality of a transcendent message presupposing a vertical relationship between a divine 'author' and his 'readers'. Thus, as Nicolai Sinai phrased it, whereas *al-kitāb* designates a heavenly medium of storage, *qur'ān* points to an earthly medium of display.[11] A distinctive relation between the divine and the prophetic speaker is, in the early phase, not yet elaborated. It is only with the '*kitāb*-phase' that it becomes a distinct sender–receiver relation. In itself, the notion of a *kitāb* clearly implies a strong claim to canonicity. Indeed, it was realised as such by the early community who first understood *kitāb* to be a transcendent scripture that both was manifested in the texts held sacred by the adherents of the older religions (who used to 'read' these in their services) and was being communicated to them in subsequent messages. These messages took the form of narrative pericopes conveying biblical stories and occupying the centre of the more complex liturgical recitals communicated by the Prophet as '*qur'ān*'. During the Meccan periods, therefore, *kitāb* was not yet identified with the qur'ānic message as a whole but only with the qur'ānic narratives familiar from biblical and apocryphical lore. The community only later conceived *kitāb* to cover their own growing corpus of divine communications, although during the lifetime of the Prophet they obviously did not expect a written corpus of these revelations to materialise. What was *qur'ān*, recital, in the beginning developed into *kitāb*, a virtual scripture, in the end, both concepts eventually merging. In turn, the qur'ānic *kitāb* preserves much of its *qur'ān*-ness, since throughout the process of revelation the anticipated presence of listeners is sustained. Among these listeners, the believers, i.e., the community, even step into the text, not only as protagonists in new scenarios of salvation history but also as conscious voices in an ongoing debate. Thus the entirely vertical relationship between the sender and the recipients, which prevails with the absence of the Prophet and the closure of the corpus, is not really pertinent to the preceding, pre-redactional stages.

To reclaim the pre-redactional Qur'ān, it is essential to understand that the Qur'ān is not meant to be a book to study but a text to recite. Kristina Nelson, who researched the recitation of the Qur'ān, has stressed that the transmission of the Qur'ān and its social existence are essentially oral. 'Qur'ānic rhythm and assonance alone confirm that it is meant to be heard ... The significance of the revelation is carried as much by the sound as by its semantic information.'[12] This observation has important implications. If the Qur'ān was meant to be recited, its actualisation as oral performance should be evident in the composition of the text itself. Where can we trace the intrinsic orality of the Qur'ān?

As was mentioned above, the early – and densely structured – parts of the Qur'ān reflect an ancient Arabic linguistic pattern, termed *saj'*, a prose style marked by very short and concise sentences with frequently changing patterns of particularly clear-cut, often expressive rhymes. In the later sūras once this style has given way to a more loosely structured prose, with verses often exceeding one complete sentence, the rhyme end takes the form of a simple *–ūn-* or *–īn-* pattern. In most cases this is achieved through a morpheme denoting masculine plural. One wonders how this rather mechanically achieved and inconspicuous ending could suffice to fulfil the listeners' anticipation of an end marker for the long verse. Upon closer investigation, however, it is apparent that the rhyme as such is no longer charged with this function, but there is now another device to mark the end. An entire, syntactically stereotypical, rhymed phrase concludes the verse. It is tempting to call this a cadenza in analogy to the final part of speech units in Gregorian chant which, through their particular sound pattern, arouse the expectation of an ending. In the Qur'ān what is repeated is not only the identical musical sound, but a linguistic pattern as well – a widely stereotypical phrasing. The musical sound pattern enhances the message encoded in the qur'ānic cadenza-phrase that, in turn, may introduce a meta-discourse. Many cadenza-phrases are semantically distinguished from their context and add a moral comment to it, such as 'verily, you were sinning' (*innaki kunti min al-khāṭi'īn*, Q 12:29). They thus transcend the main – narrative or argumentative – flow of the sūra, introducing a spiritual dimension, i.e., divine approval or disapproval. They may also refer to one of God's attributes, like 'God is powerful over everything' (*wa-kāna llāhu 'alā kulli shay'in qadīrā*, Q 33:27), which in the later stages of qur'ānic development have become parameters of ideal human behaviour. These meta-narrative insertions into the narrative or argumentative fabric would, in a written text meant for silent reading, appear rather disruptive, delaying the information process. They add essentially, however, to the impact of the oral recitation. The Qur'ān thus consciously styles itself as a text evolving on different, yet closely intertwined levels of discourse and mediation. Although it is true that not all multipartite verses bear such formulaic endings, cadenzas may be considered characteristic of the later Meccan and all the Medinan qur'ānic texts. The resounding cadenza, thus, replaces the earlier expressive rhyme pattern, marking a new and irreversible development in the emergence of the text and of the new faith.

THE ELEMENTS AT STAKE IN THE STRUCTURING OF THE SŪRA

Eschatological prophecies

The Qur'ān has developed diverse motifs and structures not known from earlier Arabic literature.[13] Among the most prominent are eschatological prophecies in early Meccan sūras, where they most frequently occur in the beginning. They are often introduced by oath clusters conjuring apocalyptic scenarios (e.g., Q 100:1–5). Contrary to biblical oath formulas, these do not function as invocations of a supra-natural authority external to the text. As Nicolai Sinai has stressed, the claim to validity of 'the early sūras . . . is not anchored in something beyond the text. One might speak of a poetic, rather than a theological truth-claim' of the early texts.[14] The sūras may equally be introduced by clusters of *idhā* ('when . . .')-phrases (Q 81:1–13), predicting the apocalyptic events of the last day. Both types of clusters create a pronouncedly rhythmical beginning to the sūra. In some cases the *idhā*-phrases are not confined to natural and cosmic phenomena but depict the preparations for the final judgement, such as the blowing of the trumpet, the positioning of the throne, the opening of the account books, etc. They are followed by a 'then . . .'-phrase, focusing on the behaviour of people in the apocalyptic setting and their separation into the groups of the blessed and the condemned. The ensuing descriptions of the hereafter are strictly divided into two contrasting parts. Introduced by phrases like *fa-ammā/. . . wa-amma* ('as to those who . . . they will', Q 101:6–9) or *wujūhun . . . wujūhun* ('faces will that day look . . . and other faces will look', Q 80:38–42), they juxtapose the situation of the believers in the garden of paradise with that of the disbelievers or evildoers suffering in the tribulations of the fire of hell. It is noteworthy that both depictions are particularly rich in imagery and together form a double image, consisting of either an equal number of verses, or of two verse-groups displaying a proportional relation to each other. As such, they remind us of the juxtaposed pictorial representations of both forms of the hereafter depicted in Christian iconography, thus suggesting the designation of 'diptycha'. Not infrequently, diptycha comprise recollections of the representative behaviours of the inmates of the two abodes during their worldly life, serving to justify their eschatological fate. These flashbacks are sometimes interspersed with direct speech; some of them merge into a catalogue of virtues to be emulated or vices to be avoided.

Signs

Signs implied in nature

Several descriptions of the 'biosphere', of copious vegetation, fauna, an agreeable habitat for humans, the natural resources at their disposal and the like, are incorporated into paraenetic appeals to recognise divine providence and accept divine omnipotence, since all these benefits are signs (*āyāt*) bearing a coded message. Properly understood they will evoke gratitude and submission to the divine will. The perception of nature, which in pre-Islamic poetry appears as alien and threatening, and as challenging the poet's heroic defiance of its hardships, has, by middle Meccan times, transmuted into the image of a meaningfully organised habitat ensuring human welfare and arousing an awareness of belonging. Although extensive *āyāt* passages reminiscent of the appraisals of divine creation to be found in the Psalms do not occur before the middle Meccan times, they are previewed by earlier enumerations of divine munificence, such as in Q 76:6–16 and others. In comparison to ancient Arabic poetry, *āyāt* passages clearly express an essential change in attitude towards nature and they soon become qur'ānic stock inventory, cf. Q 15:16–25 and 25:45–50. Although signs do occur in polemical contexts like Q 21:30–3, hymnal *āyāt* predominate.

Closely related to the hymnal *āyāt* is the hymn as such. Verses praising God's benevolence, omnipotence and his deeds in history occur predominantly in introductory sections like Q 87:1–5. They are also found distributed within the sūras like the early Q 53:43–9, and the later Q 32:4–9. Loosely related to the hymn in a structural sense, but serving a different purpose – namely to present a moral example for the community – is the catalogue of virtues which already appears in early sūras and is frequent in later texts (Q 23:57–61); its counterpart is the catalogue of vices which can be traced through the entire corpus (Q 68:8–16).

Signs implied in history: retribution legends

Short narratives – the invasion of Mecca (Q 105), the Thamūd myth (Q 91:11–15), the story of Pharaoh and Moses (Q 79:15–26) – or ensembles of narratives like that in Q 51 including Abraham and Lot, Moses and Pharaoh, the ʿĀd, the Thamūd, Noah, or evocations of stories (Q 52, 53, 69) occur from the earliest sūras onward. The latter sometimes form lists (Q 89). Longer narratives are introduced by the formula known from *āyāt* in nature, 'have you not seen' (*a-lam tara* . . .), later 'and when . . .' (*wa-idh* (*faʿala*) . . .), i.e., they are assumed to be known to the listeners. It is noteworthy that the longer narratives from early Meccan texts onward are split into equal halves, thus producing proportionate structures (Q 79:15–26; 51:24–37; 68:17–33). Narratives develop into retribution legends or punishment stories, serving to prove that divine justice is at work in history, the unjustly harassed being rewarded with salvation, the transgressors and the unbelievers punished by annihilation. At the same time, legends that are located in the Arabian peninsula may be read as reinterpretations of ancient Arabian poetic representations of deserted space. Sites no longer lie in ruins due to preordained natural processes, but because God is maintaining an equitable balance between human actions and human welfare. Deserted sites thus acquire a meaning, they are carrying a divine message. From Q15 onward, retribution legends no longer focus predominantly on ancient Arabian lore but increasingly include biblical narratives.

A related genre in terms of function, which also serves paraenetic purposes, is the parable, *mathal*, like that about the owners of the blighted garden (Q 68:17–33), the good and corrupt trees (Q 14:24–27), or the unbelieving town (Q 36:13–32). Parables are, however, less frequent than myths and historical narratives.

Narratives of salvation history

In contrast to the meticulous shaping of personages and the sophisticated coding and de-decoding of their motives, which characterise biblical narrative, qurʾānic narrating pursues complex 'para-narrative' aims. Narratives, at least insofar as they are developed and recall plots already known from biblical literature, are presented as excerpts or messages from the 'book' which, in turn, is clearly understood to be a corpus of literature apart from the rest of the known stories currently available through oral tradition. The dignity of these '*kitāb*-generated' narratives certainly has a strong bearing on the style of the stories presented as *kitāb* readings, not only forcing on them a distinct linguistic code to distinguish them from profane narrative, but also imbuing these narratives with the new message of imminent eschatological catastrophe, a message which brings the narrative close to an exhortative appeal or, later, a sermon.

It is exactly these discursive elements, so marginal in biblical narrative, that figure centrally in the qur'ānic narrative: the explicit presentation of the moral or theological implications for the community – often coded in the cadenza-phrases – that can be deduced from the narrated facts or speeches.

The Qur'ān is often accused of lacking a chronological framework for the events of pre-qur'ānic history that it narrates and the narration is frequently criticised as excessively repetitive. While this may hold true for the earliest discourse of the Qur'ān, the situation changes substantially when a new paradigm is adopted, switching the focus from the deserted sites of the real homeland to the realm of the messengers to the People of the Book, whose discourse as intermediaries between God and humankind is much more sophisticated.

Although initially embedded in narrative catalogues that include extra-biblical tradition, stories about major biblical figures like Moses and several patriarchs known from Genesis gradually gain a function of their own. They become the stock inventory of the central section of longer Meccan sūras and only rarely appear in other positions. Sūras from the second Meccan period onward often form a composite that mirrors the enactment of a monotheistic liturgical service where the central position is occupied by the reading of scriptural texts. They are embedded in a more extensive recital, whose initiatory and concluding section may contain liturgical material but also less universal elements such as debates about ephemeral issues facing the community. The ceremonial function of the biblically inspired narrative as a festive presentation of the book is underlined by introductory formulas. At a later stage, when the particular form of revelation communicated to the Muslim community is regarded as a virtual scripture of its own, i.e., when community matters are acknowledged as part of salvation history, whole sūras figure as manifestations of *al-kitāb*.

The phenomenon of recurring narratives, retold in slightly variant fashion, has often been dismissed as mere repetitions, i.e., as a deficiency. They deserve, however, to be studied as testimonies of the consecutive stages of the emergence of a community and thus reflective of the process of canonisation. They point to a successively changing narrative pact, to the continuing education of listeners and the development of a moral consensus that is reflected in the texts. In later Meccan and Medinan sūras, when a large number of narratives are assumed to be well known to the listeners, the position acquired by salvation history narratives is occupied by mere evocations and debates about them.

Debates

It has been argued that debate is one of the essential elements of the Qur'ān.[15] This is certainly true for the sūras from the middle Meccan period onward. In early Meccan texts, polemical utterances are more often than not directed against listeners who do not comply with the behavioural norms of the cult. These listeners are reprimanded by the speaker who is explicitly addressing them (Q 53:59ff.). Sometimes curses are uttered, against absent persons (Q 111:1ff.), or against humankind in general (Q 80:17). In other cases menacing words are directed at the ungrateful or pretentious (Q 114:1) and these may merge into a catalogue of vices (Q 107:2–7). Whereas in most of the early cases the adversaries are not granted an opportunity to reply, later sūras present the voices of both sides. Lengthy polemics are addressed to the unbelievers, sometimes in the presence of the accused, more often in their absence. During the middle and later Meccan periods, however, when the community had to struggle against a stubborn opposition, they needed to be trained in dispute. Meccan sūras often begin and end with polemical debates, treating diverse points of dissent. In some cases, the absent adversaries are verbally quoted, while in other cases the simulation of a debate is presented, instructing the addressee and his listeners to react to a given statement by their adversaries with a particular response: 'when they say . . ., respond . . .' (*wa-yaqūlūna . . . fa-qul*, Q 10:20). These instances, classified by Welch as 'say-passages', are to be regarded as virtual debates performed in the absence of one party to the encounter. In other cases, there are *qul*-verses that do not refer to a debate, but serve to introduce prayers or religious mottos. Often polemics respond to the unbelievers' rejection of the Qur'ān, again figuring at the beginning or the end, or in the conclusions to main parts of sūras.

Like polemics, apologetic sections frequently appear as framing parts of a sūra. From early Meccan texts onward they ordinarily serve to affirm the rank of the Qur'ān as a divine revelation, usually constituting the nucleus of concluding sections (Q 74:54–5). In later sūras these concluding affirmations of the revelation tend to merge into exhortations of the Prophet (Q 11:109–23). It is noteworthy that affirmations of the revelation finally become a standard *incipit* of sūras (Q 12:1–3), again often merging into exhortations.

In some cases, sūras are framed by two affirmations of revelation (Q 41:1–5, 41–54). In later developments, such introductory affirmations are reduced to mere evocations of the book. By far the majority of these sūras start with a pathos-arousing evocation of the book, often introduced by a chiffre, i.e., a combination of letters from the Arabic alphabet devoid of semantic meaning – an underscoring of divine authorship that is still missing in the early sūras. This *incipit* seems to hint at a newly achieved cultic function for the recited text, one which is no longer understood as the direct and immediate communication of a divine message to the community, but as a recital from a sacred scripture that is assumed to be pre-existing and reproduced only through recitation.

Additional elements: Regulations and reports about contemporary events

The form and structure of Medinan sūras have not yet been studied thoroughly. Summary analyses are presented by Theodore Nöldeke and Neal Robinson. Matthias Zahniser has discussed single sūras. A systematic investigation of their building blocks is still lacking. It may, however, be stated that, with a few exceptions, all the Meccan elements are met again in Medinan sūras, although the eschatological sections and the *āyāt* are no longer expressed at length, but rather are summarily evoked. This should not be taken as a decisive shift in theological interest. While new topics which occupy the focus of the community's attention do emerge, the earlier topics remain present, enshrined in the partial corpus of the early sūras that have been committed to memory by the believers and that serve as the textual basis for the emerging ritual prayers.

Although occasional regulations – mostly about cultic matters – do occur in Meccan sūras, more elaborate regulation concerning not only cultic but also communal affairs figure in the Medinan context. Their binding force is sometimes underlined by a reference to the transcendent source, e.g., 'it is prescribed for you' (*kutiba ʿalaykum*, Q 2:183–7). Medinan regulations do not display any structured composition nor do they form part of neatly composed units. They suggest, rather, later insertions into loosely connected contexts.

A new element that appears in Medinan sūras is what tradition has understood to be allusions to contemporary events experienced or enacted by the community, such as the Battle of Badr (Q 3:123), Uḥud (Q 3:155–74), the expulsion of the Banū Naḍīr (Q 59:2–5), the siege of Khaybar (Q 48:15), the expedition to Tabūk (Q 9:29–35) or the farewell sermon of the Prophet (Q 5:1–3). It is noteworthy that these reports do not display an obvious literary shaping. Nor do they betray any particular pathos. It does not come as a surprise, then, that unlike the situation in Judaism and Christianity, where the individual elements of biblical history have been fused to form a mythical drama of salvation, no such great narrative has arisen from the

Qur'ān itself. A metahistorical blueprint of the genesis of Islam was constructed only later, through the biographical construction of the Prophet (*sīra*).

THE SŪRA AS A GENRE

Types of early Meccan sūras

The spectrum of different themes, and their combinations, is very broad in early Meccan times. Sūra types range from single-part pieces – pure lampoon, *hijā'* (Q 111), pure exhortations through the Prophet (Q 94), pure eschatological discourse (Q 95, 100, 101) – to bipartite ones – oath cluster (Q 92:1–13) and eschatological section (Q 92:14–21) – to the later standardised tripartite sūra: exhortation (Q 74:1–10), polemics (Q 74:11–48) and affirmation of the Qur'ān (Q 74:49–56). Characteristic of this group as a whole is their striking self-referentiality. The sūras reflect a scenario situated locally in a Meccan public place, most probably close to the Ka'ba, as can be gathered from their decidedly articulate references to sacred space and human behaviour therein, as well as to sacred time. The rites at the Ka'ba seem to be the *Sitz im Leben* of many early sūras, the Ka'ba serving not only as the locale for the performance of their recitation, but its rites also marking particular times of the day respected by the community as ritually significant. Since these sūras were memorised without any written support, their distinct proportions were effective as mnemonic-technical devices.

Types of later Meccan sūras

Things change substantially in later Meccan times. We may localise the disjunction with Q 15, where, for the first time, an allusion is made to the existence of a particular form of liturgical service in which scripture functions as the cardinal section. In these sūras, references to the Meccan sanctuary (*ḥaram*) as the central warrant for the social coherence of the community have been replaced by new symbols. Instead of introductory allusions to liturgical times and sacred space, we encounter an evocation of the book, be it clad in an oath (Q 36:2; 37:3; 38:1; 43:2; 44:2; 50:1) or in a deictic affirmation of its presence (Q 2:2; 10:1; 12:1; 13:1, etc.).

Moreover, the message assumes a new scope and spatial extension. Later Meccan sūras have broadened the horizon for the listeners, who are led away from their local surroundings to a distant landscape, the holy land, familiar as the scenery where the history of the community's spiritual forebears had taken place. The introduction of the Jerusalem prayer orientation (*qibla*), alluded to in Q 17:1, is an unequivocal attestation of this change. In view of the increasing interest in the biblical heritage, it comes as no surprise that the bulk of the middle and late Meccan sūras seem to mirror a monotheistic service, starting with an initial dialogical section (apologetic, polemic, paraenetic) and closing with a related section, most frequently an affirmation of the revelation. These framing sections have been compared to the Christian Orthodox *ecteniae*, i.e., initial and concluding *responsoria* recited by the priest or deacon with the community. The centre of the monotheistic service and, similarly, of the fully developed sūra of the middle and late Meccan period is occupied by a biblical reminiscence – in the case of the liturgical service, a scripture reading (*lectio*), in the case of the sūra, a narrative focusing on biblical protagonists. Ritual coherence has thus given way to scriptural coherence, the more complex later sūras referring to scripture both by their transmission of scriptural texts and by their being dependent on the mnemonic technicalities of writing for their conservation. Already in later Meccan sūras, however, the distinct tripartite composition often becomes blurred, with narratives gradually being replaced by discursive sections. Many compositions also display secondary expansions – a phenomenon that still needs further investigation. Yet, for the bulk of the middle and late Meccan sūras, the claim to a tripartite composition can be sustained.

Types of Medinan sūras

In Medina, however, sūras have not only given up their tripartite scheme but also display much less sophistication in the patterns of their composition. One type may be summarily termed the 'rhetorical' sūra or sermon (Q 22, 24, 33, 47, 48, 49, 57, until 66); they consist of an address to the community whose members are called upon directly by formulas such as 'O people' (*yā ayyuhā l-nāsu*, Q 22:1). In these sūras, which in some cases (Q 59, 61, 62, 64) are stereotypically introduced by initial hymnal formulas strongly reminiscent of the biblical Psalms, the Prophet (*al-nabī*) appears no longer as a mere transmitter of the message but as personally addressed by God: 'O Prophet' (*yā ayyuhā l-nabiyyu*, Q 33:28), or as an agent acting in combination with the divine persona: 'God and his messenger' (*Allāhu wa-rasūluhu*, Q 33:22). Unlike these intended monolithic addresses, the bulk of the Medinan sūras are the most complex. Most of the so-called 'long sūras' (Q 2–5, 8, 9) cease to be neatly structured compositions but appear to be the result of a process of collection that we cannot yet reconstruct. As pointed out earlier, a systematic study of these sūras is still an urgent desideratum in the field.

Notes

1. M. Sells, 'Sound, spirit and gender in Surat al-Qadr', *Journal of the American Oriental Society* 11 (1991), 239–59.
2. J. Wansbrough, *Quranic studies: Sources and methods of scriptural interpretation* (Oxford: Oxford University Press, 1977).
3. M. Cook and P. Crone, *Hagarism: The making of the Islamic world* (Cambridge: Cambridge University Press, 1977).
4. Ch. Luxenberg, *Die syro-aramäische Lesart des Koran: Ein Beitrag zur Entschlüsselung der Koransprache* (Berlin: Das Arabische Buch, 2000).
5. G. Lüling, *Über den Ur-Qur'ān: Ansätze zur Rekonstruktion vorislamischer christlicher Strophenlieder im Qur'ān* (Erlängen: H. Lüling, 1974).
6. K. Vollers, *Volkssprache und Schriftsprache im alten Arabien* (Strassburg: K. J. Trübner, 1906).
7. Cf. W. Graham, *Beyond the written word: Oral aspects of scripture in the history of religion* (Cambridge/New York: Cambridge University Press, 1989).
8. M. Parry, *Studies in the epic technique of oral verse-making* (n.p., 1930–2).
9. A. Lord, *The singer of tales* (Cambridge, MA: Harvard University Press, 1960).
10. These have been collected by the author in 'Vom Rezitationstext über die Liturgie zum Kanon: Zur Entstehung und Wiederaufloesung der Surenkomposition im Verlauf der Entwicklung eines islamischen Kultus', in S. Wild (ed.), *The Qur'ān as text* (Leiden: Brill, 1996), pp. 69–105.
11. N. Sinai, 'From qur'ān to kitāb', forthcoming in M. Marx, A. Neuwirth and N. Sinai (eds.), *The Qur'ān in context: Historical and literary investigations into the cultural milieu of the Qur'ān* (Beirut).
12. K. Nelson, *The art of reciting the Qur'an* (Austin: University of Texas Press, 1985; repr. Cairo/New York: American University in Cairo Press, 2001), p. xiv.
13. These have been analysed by A. Neuwirth in *Studien zur Komposition der mekkanischen Suren* (Berlin: W. de Gruyter, 1981).
14. Sinai, 'From qur'ān'.
15. See J. D. McAuliffe, '"Debate with them in the better way": The construction of a qur'ānic commonplace', in A. Neuwirth, B. Embalo, S. Guenther and M. Jarrar (eds.), *Myths, historical archetypes and symbolic figures in Arabic literature: Towards a new hermeneutic approach* (Beirut: Orient-Institut der Deutschen Morgenländischen Gesellschaft, 1999), pp. 163–88. See also R. Gwynne, *Logic, rhetoric and legal reasoning in the Qur'ān* (London: Routledge, 2004).

Further reading

Cook, M. and P. Crone, *Hagarism: The making of the Islamic world*, Cambridge: Cambridge University Press, 1977.

Graham, W., *Beyond the written word: Oral aspects of scripture in the history of religion*, Cambridge/New York: Cambridge University Press, 1989.

Gwynne, R., *Logic, rhetoric and legal reasoning in the Qur'ān*, London: Routledge, 2004.

Horovitz, J., *Koranische Untersuchungen*, Berlin/Leipzig: W. de Gruyter and Co., 1926.

Lüling, G., *Über den Ur-Qur'ān: Ansätze zur Rekonstruktion vorislamischer christlicher Strophenlieder im Qur'ān*, Erlängen: H. Lüling, 1974.

Luxenberg, Ch., *Die syro-aramäische Lesart des Koran: Ein Beitrag zur Entschlüsselung der Koransprache*, Berlin: Das Arabische Buch, 2000.

McAuliffe, J. D., '"Debate with them in the better way": The construction of a qur'ānic commonplace', in A. Neuwirth, B. Embalo, S. Guenther and M. Jarrar (eds.), *Myths, historical archetypes and symbolic figures in Arabic literature: Towards a new hermeneutic approach*, Beirut: Orient-Institut der Deutschen Morgenländischen Gesellschaft, 1999, pp. 163–88.

Nelson, K., *The art of reciting the Qur'an*, Austin: University of Texas Press, 1985; repr. Cairo/New York: American University in Cairo Press, 2001.

Neuwirth, A., 'Myths and legends in the Qur'ān', in J. D. McAuliffe (ed.), *Encyclopaedia of the Qur'ān*, 5 vols., Leiden: Brill, 2000–6, vol. III, pp. 477–97.

'Qur'an and history – a disputed relationship', *Journal of Qur'anic Studies* 5 (2003), 1–18.

Studien zur Komposition der mekkanischen Suren, Berlin: W. de Gruyter, 1981.

'Vom Rezitationstext über die Liturgie zum Kanon: Zur Entstehung und Wiederauflösung der Surenkomposition im Verlauf der Entwicklung eines islamischen Kultus', in S. Wild (ed.), *The Qur'ān as text*, Leiden: Brill, 1996, pp. 69–105.

Nöldeke, Th., *Geschichte des Qorāns*, rev. ed. by F. Schwally, G. Bergsträsser and O. Pretzl, 3 vols., Leipzig: T. Weicher, 1909–38.

Robinson, N., *Discovering the Qur'an: A contemporary approach to a veiled text*, London: SCM Press, 1996.

Sells, M., 'Sound, spirit and gender in Surat al-Qadr', *Journal of the American Oriental Society* 11 (1991), 239–59.

Sinai, N., 'From qur'ān to kitāb', forthcoming in M. Marx, A. Neuwirth and N. Sinai (eds.), *The Qur'ān in context: Historical and literary investigations into the cultural milieu of the Qur'ān*, Beirut (forthcoming).

Vollers, K., *Volkssprache und Schriftsprache im alten Arabien*, Strassburg: K. J. Trübner, 1906.

Wansbrough, J., *Quranic studies: Sources and methods of scriptural interpretation*, Oxford: Oxford University Press, 1977.

Zahniser, A. H. M., 'The word of God and the apostleship of 'Īsā: A narrative analysis of Āl 'Imrān (3) 33–62', *Journal of Semitic Studies* 37 (1991), 77–112.

Fig. 6 Folio from a ninth-century Kūfic Qur'ān on dyed blue parchment (the so-called 'Blue Qur'ān'). Depicted here is Q 2:120–4 (Khalili Collection, KFQ 53, 1a). Courtesy of the Nasser D. Khalili Collection of Islamic Art, London

6 Recitation and aesthetic reception

WILLIAM A. GRAHAM AND NAVID KERMANI

For Muslims, the Qur'ān is not only a much-recited sacred text; it is '*the* reciting' (*al-qur'ān*). Specifically, it is God's 'reciting', his verbatim speech, his eternal, uncreated word. As such, it has been the medium *par excellence* of divine–human encounter for Muslims of all times, places and persuasions. It mediates the presence of God, just as it does his will and blessing. The revelations to Muḥammad were from the outset intended to be rehearsed and recited – first by the Prophet who received them, then by his followers. They were given as an audible text, not as 'a writing on parchment' (Q 6:7). The Qur'ān has always been primarily recited, oral scripture and secondarily inscribed, written scripture, and thus its spiritual and aesthetic reception as the most beautiful of all texts has been linked with its orality. Tradition ascribes to the Prophet the dictum: 'You can return to God nothing better than that which came from him, namely the recitation (*al-Qur'ān*).' Accordingly, every generation of Muslims has scrupulously memorised, recited and transmitted the Qur'ān as scripture, psalter, prayerbook and liturgical text all in one.[1] How Qur'ān recitation has been cultivated and used and what its corresponding aesthetic impact on and among Muslims has been are the central themes of what follows.

PART ONE: RECITATION OF THE QUR'ĀN

Recitation as a formal discipline

The intrinsically oral/aural character of the Qur'ān is evident in its own use of a verbal-noun form, *qur'ān*, 'reciting, recitation, lection' (from the verb *qara'a*, 'to read aloud, recite') to refer to itself as God's culminating revelation.[2] The term used for qur'ānic recitation generally is *qirā'a*, which, like *qur'ān*, is a verbal noun of *qara'a*.[3] It is used to refer to (1) the reciting aloud of the Qur'ān (and hence to the art or science of doing this), and also to (2) a particular 'reading' of any qur'ānic word or phrase, i.e., a 'variant' reading of any element of the text. This is the sense in which its plural, *qirā'āt*, is used, to refer collectively to all the variant 'readings' of the Qur'ān. *Qirā'a* can also be used by extension for (3) a single 'reading' of the entire qur'ānic text according to one of the main traditions of oral transmission. All such traditions are traced to prominent reciters or 'schools' of recitation in the first two centuries AH (seventh and eighth centuries CE). Thus one can speak of the *qirā'a* of Ibn Kathīr, of 'Āṣim, or of 'the people of Kūfa'.[4]

The formal discipline of reciting/reading (*'ilm al-qirā'a*) encompasses both study of the variant readings (*qirā'āt*) of the written codex or *muṣḥaf* and also the methods and rules of oral recitation (cantillation), or *tajwīd* ('rendering excellent' the Qur'ān). *Tajwīd* in turn comprises various traditions of vocal rendering of the recited text. Often referred to as a joint discipline, the *'ilm al-qirā'āt wa-l-tajwīd* ('discipline of readings and recitation') represents the heart of the long Muslim tradition of study, preservation and oral presentation of the Qur'ān. It both relies upon and contributes to scriptural exegesis (*tafsīr*) and various other Islamic linguistic disciplines, from grammar (*naḥw*) and philology (*lugha*) to rhetoric (*balāgha*) and orthography (*rasm*). Like these other disciplines, recitative studies have an extensive literary tradition of scholastic complexity. Muslim piety relies on them as the guarantor of the rendering and preserving of God's word as it 'came down' orally to Muḥammad.[5]

The recitative traditions

The importance of the recited Qur'ān does not obviate the importance of the written Qur'ān, but it reminds us that the written text is always secondary – a support to the orally transmitted text, not a determinant of it. If the traditional account of the codification of the authoritative *muṣḥaf* under 'Uthmān (r. 23–35/644–56) be accepted, this would have occurred before an Arabic orthography was developed that enabled accurate reading of a text. Therefore, the written *muṣḥaf* could never have sufficed without an accompanying mnemonic recitative tradition. Hence it is not surprising that Islamic accounts report that when 'Uthmān sent copies of his new Qur'ān text to the cities of the young empire, he also sent knowledgeable reciters who could teach the text orally. Its defective orthography would have allowed for variant readings not only of vowels and inflectional endings, but even of many of the still unpointed consonants themselves. For these reasons, the Qur'ān had to be transmitted primarily as it had originally come: as a recited text. The consonantal text could serve as an aide-memoire but not a stand-alone document.[6] To read the bare, unpointed text, one had to know it already by heart, or very nearly so.

The enduring importance of the recitative traditions can be vividly seen in the way leading Muslim scholars prepared the now generally accepted 'standard' text of the Qur'ān, the 'Cairo' or Egyptian official version of 1342/1923–4.[7] In over a decade of collaboration on an authoritative printed edition of the Qur'ān, these scholars did not depend upon collation of the earliest Qur'ān manuscripts and fragments for the base text. Instead, they relied on their extensive knowledge of the most venerable traditions of variants (*qirā'āt*) and of the accompanying literature. Even the orthography of their edition was based not on manuscripts but on the traditions of the *ʿilm al-qirā'āt* ('science/discipline of readings'). Although this procedure went against many canons of Western text-critical scholarship, it yielded a text widely recognised, even in non-Muslim scholarship, as the most authoritative version available.[8]

Qirā'āt and *qirā'a*

The early Muslims apparently accepted from the outset that there could be various readings of the same divine text, whether because of dialectical differences among the transmission traditions or because even the Prophet was said to have recited the same passage differently at times. Even the ʿUthmānic reform was not able to eradicate the early qur'ānic texts or text traditions of various prophetic Companions that it had excluded from the 'official' version – most prominently the codex of the famous Companion Ibn Masʿūd, which long continued to be popular in Kūfa and among some Shīʿīs. How much more impossible must it have been that a single oral 'reading' of even the 'standard' written text could have won the day across the already vast Islamic empire. This was especially so because the defective script of the ʿUthmānic *muṣḥaf* allowed, as noted above, for considerable variety in recitation of particular words and phrases, even if none of these variations seriously altered the Qur'ān's content.

In the end, Muslims interpreted this variety of possible readings as a blessing, not a curse for the community, and all accepted readings were deemed to have come ultimately from Muḥammad himself.[9] The consensus eventually allowed for the 'preference' of a capable scholar-reader in choosing to recite the text according to one *qirā'a* from among the various ones generally recognised – such recognition eventually being based formally upon adherence to (1) linguistic correctness, (2) the accepted ʿUthmānic text and (3) a sound tradition of transmission from the earliest authorities.[10] Muslims based this acceptance of divergent oral readings on the enigmatic statement ascribed to Muḥammad, that 'the Qur'ān was sent down according to seven *aḥruf*' (lit.: 'letters'; usually taken as 'dialects' or 'modes').[11]

As the traditional accounts of the preparation of the ʿUthmānic codex have it, both recitation, *qirāʾa*, and the individual *qirāʾāt*, or variant readings, were important from early on because of the concern with accurate preservation of the revelations and exclusion of interpolated readings after Muḥammad's death. Although treatises are ascribed to experts on *qirāʾa* in the first two Islamic centuries, the crystallisation of *qirāʾa* as a more formal science probably occurred only in the third/ninth century.[12]

Whatever its origin, this process culminated in the efforts of Abū Bakr b. Mujāhid (d. 324/936) of Baghdād to systematise rules for proper recitation.[13] He is credited with winning recognition (albeit not without contestation[14]) for seven different 'traditions' (*riwāyāt*; pl. of *riwāya*) of 'readings' as valid modes of transmitting the Qur'ān. Later scholars added three, or even seven, further 'authentic' traditions. Accordingly, seven, ten or fourteen traditions of accepted 'readings' are cited in the Muslim literature, and even these have sub-traditions. Thus the variant *riwāyāt* that the expert must master are numerous, even though they represent relatively minor actual textual variations and do not threaten the general meaning of the sacred text.[15]

The art of *tajwīd*

Within the general science of recitation, the study of the *qirāʾāt* is, as indicated, inextricable from the science or art of *tajwīd*, the recitative cantillation of the Qur'ān.[16] For Muslims, *tajwīd* is the attempt to preserve the living word of God in the full beauty with which it was given to and transmitted by the Prophet. Chanting the Qur'ān is potentially an actualisation of the revelatory act itself, and thus how the Qur'ān is vocally rendered not only matters, but matters ultimately. It is no wonder, therefore, that among Muslims, Qur'ān cantillation has its own forms that set it forever apart from all other recitation and all musical forms.

The traditional authority for *tajwīd* (literally, 'making beautiful' the sacred text, and hence its artful cantillation) is from the Qur'ān itself, namely its exhortation (Q 73:4) to 'chant the recitation in measured, clear chant' (*wa-rattili l-qurʾāna tartīlan*).[17] Although the word *tartīl* refers traditionally to carefully enunciated, measured chanting, the verse is widely interpreted as referring more broadly to *tajwīd* as cantillation according to formal rules.

As the general art of recitation, *ʿilm al-tajwīd* encompasses many traditions and modes of recitation. The basic mode is the *murattal*, or measured, less melodic cantillation (sometimes called *tartīl*, as noted above; both words are from the Arabic root, *r-t-l*). As the style of reciting normally used in the ritual prayer (*ṣalāt*), personal devotion and education, it has been the primary form of reciting in general use.[18] At its most 'ornamented' (*mujawwad* – from *tajwīd*), recitation includes more melodically modulated and musically cadenced forms of cantillation that are closer to singing. Such forms are specifically referred to as 'recitation with melodies' (*qirā'a bi-l-alḥān*), and in some places, such as Cairo today, these are by far the most popular recitative modes. Sometimes, however, *tajwīd* is even used specifically for such melodically embellished recitative modes, in which vocal quality and musical ability figure more prominently than they do in the *murattal* form of chant.[19]

Within the range of recognised recitative styles, opinions differ as to what constitutes acceptable modes of chanting. Some feel that only the melodic *mujawwad* styles render the beauty of the sacred text; others think these slide dangerously close to secular music and hence prefer the less embellished *murattal* form. None would deny, however, that all forms of qur'ānic chanting involve attributes beyond the fundamentals of *tartīl* or *murattal* chanting: accurate memorisation, knowledgeable technique, careful comprehension and sensitive interpretation of the whole text. Qur'ān recitation is finally a devotional, spiritual act before it is a technical, artistic performance.[20]

The chanting of the Qur'ān is viewed as a vocal form *sui generis*: its modes and possibilities come from the divine text itself, not from its reciters. In more musical forms of *tajwīd* the beauty of a good voice is joined ideally with technical accuracy to produce melodically sophisticated cantillation. Nevertheless, as we shall see in Part Two of this chapter, below, Muslim tradition refuses to describe any Qur'ān recitation as 'music' or as analogous to secular singing. Rather, the Qur'ān is 'inimitable' *(mu'jiz)*, and this miraculous quality inheres not simply in its literal written wording, but also its vocal rendering. By observable criteria and established tradition, it is in its oral recitation that the Qur'ān is most clearly experienced as divine. The ontological distinction between qur'ānic recitation and all other recitation reflects the strong Muslim sense of the holiness of this text of texts.

The recitative sciences in Muslim piety and practice

From the foregoing, we can see that, alongside exegesis *(tafsīr)*, knowledge of both *tajwīd* and the *qirā'āt* has sustained the Qur'ān as living scripture. To understand the Qur'ān's place in Muslim societies, we must attend both to these traditional disciplines and to the living tradition of Qur'ān recitation as it is found in contemporary centres such as Cairo. The work of Muslim textual scholars has never been isolated in the academy in the way modern biblical studies sometimes have been in the West. The study of *qirā'āt* and *tajwīd* finds practical application in the Islamic public domain through the popular oral recitation that has been a hallmark of Islamic culture wherever it has spread. This public recitation, whether in devotional or artistic performance (and the two are never easily separated), is in turn only the most formal part of the larger, functional role of the recited Qur'ān in Muslim life more generally.

An anonymous Muslim devotional pamphlet describes the Muslims as having their sacred texts 'in their hearts while others read them from sacred volumes'.[21] The formal disciplines of readings and cantillation could not have been sustained as vibrantly as they have been over the centuries had not Qur'ān memorisation (*ḥifẓ*) and recitation (*qirā'a* or *tilāwa*) always been central to the daily and seasonal round of life in Islamic societies. Here we can touch only briefly upon the place of memorisation and recitation in Muslim life, but any discussion of the recited Qur'ān would be sorely deficient without treating its active oral/aural presence among Muslims of diverse times, places and stations.

Recitation in worship (*ṣalāt*)

The Qur'ān is the one essential of Muslim ritual and devotional life. Unlike Jewish or Christian scriptures, the Qur'ān must be memorised and recited in the original to fulfil even the minimum requirements of worship. No *ṣalāt* is valid without recitation of at least the Fātiḥa, or 'Opening' (Q 1), and it is expected that one or more shorter sūras or verses will also be recited.[22] The functional distinction for purposes of valid worship between the Qur'ān and all other religious texts, even the ḥadīth, is striking. And unlike the Hindu Vedas, the qur'ānic text belongs to all the faithful, whatever their social status or education, even those who know no Arabic. The theological doctrine of 'inimitability' (*i'jāz*; see Part Two of this chapter, below) notwithstanding, it is the practical, ritual function of the Arabic Qur'ān as recited word in worship that distinguishes it from all other texts: recitation of the Qur'ān is what one student of Muslim piety has called 'the very heart of the prayer-rite'.[23] It is also quite common to precede or to follow the *ṣalāt* ritual proper with substantial recitation from the Qur'ān,[24] just as most Muslim celebrations and commemorations (e.g., funerals) involve recitation of shorter or longer qur'ānic passages.[25] Qur'ān recitation in general is a preferred form of religious devotion at any time – in many ways an extension of the *ṣalāt* into the other parts of the day for its practitioners.

The sacrality of recitation

As already noted, the acceptance of the Qur'ān as God's word in the form of 'an Arabic recitation' (*qur'ānan ʿarabiyyan*)[26] has deterred Muslims from translating it from the original Arabic. Conversely, it has spurred even Muslims who know no Arabic to memorise shorter or longer passages as they are able, not only for *ṣalāt*, but also to internalise the very speech of God. A nineteenth-century French traveller reports that an elderly Malay Muslim teacher, who could not read Arabic, said that he recited the Arabic Qur'ān for his Malay pupils because: 'the sons of the Prophet ought to have this word in their memory so that they can repeat it often. These words are endowed with a special virtue . . . In translating we might alter the meaning, and that would be a sacrilege.'[27] Here the inherent sacrality of the original Arabic sounds – and their meaning as well, even if that meaning is not understood literally, word-for-word – is eloquently affirmed. The sense of the holiness, or *baraka* ('blessing'), of the sounded holy text seems to penetrate into every corner of the Islamic world. In most Muslim contexts, the sounded strains of God's word are held to be powerful – especially so when sounded with full voice – and are therefore widely disseminated, in local mosques and by radio, television and tape or disk players daily and, still more prominently, on special occasions. To dismiss the quotidian ubiquity of the Qur'ān as superstition, merely 'background noise', or only a taken-for-granted habit, is to miss the perceived power and genuine spiritual function of such recitation quite apart from the understanding of every word of the Arabic text.

In education

Qur'ān recitation is the backbone of Muslim education. There is an enduring Muslim conviction that Muslims need to be able, as early as possible, to recite from the Qur'ān in its original form.[28] Memorising the Qur'ān has always been basic to child-rearing in Muslim societies, and there are few sounds more constant, from Morocco to Indonesia, than the singsong chant of children as they recite sacred scripture in the neighbourhood Qur'ān school (*kuttāb* or *maktab*). Centuries ago, Ibn Khaldūn (d. 784/1382) remarked that 'teaching the Qur'ān to children is one of the signs of [the] religion (*shaʿāʾir al-dīn*) that Muslims profess and practise in all their cities'.[29] Even though many children do not stay in school the five or more years needed to memorise the whole Qur'ān or to become literate in Arabic,[30] learning at least some part of the divine word by heart is the single most common early experience shared by most Muslims.[31]

More significantly, the universality of some kind of childhood 'rote' learning of the Qur'ān – principally by boys, but also girls – has provided a common Islamic cultural heritage as well as religious training. Familiarity with the qur'ānic text and its values, as well as appreciation for its melodic recitation, have been not only signs of Muslim faith, but shared threads of 'islamisation' in the diverse fabric of Islamic societies, across barriers of language, colour and custom, as well as time and place. 'The Muslim does not put a child in a Qur'ān school simply to teach him, but rather also to form him according to the immutable tradition that was that of his own parents and that of theirs.'[32] In other words, this schooling is 'a mechanism of total formation' of the person.[33] In Islamic societies, 'a firm discipline in the course of learning the Quran is culturally regarded as an integral part of socialisation . . . the discipline of Quranic memorisation is an integral part of learning to be human and Muslim.'[34]

Memorisation and recitation of the Qur'ān have traditionally been matters of great pride and status in Muslim communities. One of the most cherished honorifics a Muslim can earn is that of *ḥāfiẓ* (fem. *ḥāfiẓa*), 'one who preserves, has by heart' (the entire scripture). Sometimes the *ḥāfiẓ* is even addressed as *shaykh*, 'master'. Traditionally, such mastery of the Qur'ān has been a prerequisite for becoming a scholar (*ʿālim*; pl. *ʿulamā'*) in any of the religious sciences (it is obviously required for serious study of *tajwīd*). Of those children who stay long enough in school, some manage this by age ten or twelve, a few earlier. Even many who never control the entire text can quote and recite substantially from it, if they have studied in the *kuttāb* and beyond. It is not unusual for a 'layperson' in a secular profession and without advanced religious education to be a *ḥāfiẓ/ḥāfiẓa*.[35]

At higher levels of education, the writing and speech of scholarship is traditionally based in large degree on the vocabulary, phraseology and diction of the Arabic scripture. One need not have extensive contact with an *ʿālim* to note how echoes of the memorised, recited Qur'ān cadence the scholar's thinking, writing and speaking. The *ʿālim* has to be able to quote and recite the Qur'ān at will even to begin to hold his own among colleagues. Muslim scholarship reflects the acceptance of the Prophet's adage that 'knowledge shall not perish so long as the Qur'ān is recited'.[36]

In communal life

Qur'ān recitation occupies a public place in Muslim societies and forms a significant part of the auditory 'background' of everyday life. Its virtual omnipresence has intensified in recent decades through radio, television and other electronic media. The oral world of traditionalists in particular is still saturated with the sound of the Qur'ān – in worship, conversation and devotional practice. They have taken to heart the ḥadīth that says, 'the most excellent form of devotion (*ʿibāda*) among my people is reciting the Qur'ān'.[37]

In that most communal of all Muslim religious observances, the Ramaḍān fast, the nights are filled with public Qur'ān recitation. Muslim interpretation has traditionally found in Q 97 a reference to the night in which the Qur'ān was first revealed: 'Truly, we sent it down on the Night of Power (*laylat al-qadr*) . . .' (Q 97:1). Traditions identify this night as one of the odd-numbered nights (most often the 27th) of the last third of Ramaḍān, which is consequently deemed especially auspicious for recitation. The recitation of one of the Qur'ān's thirty 'parts' on each night of Ramaḍān is also widely practised.[38] However handled, the recitation of the divine word is the most salient public activity of this special month, and Muslims have delighted in finding different ways of making a complete recitation, or *khatma*, of the Qur'ān during Ramaḍān.[39]

Another popular form of public *tilāwa* is the group chanting of both formal *dhikr* sessions of Ṣūfī brotherhoods and popular *dhikr* sessions at particular mosques, especially tomb-mosques. *Dhikr*, the 'remembrance' of God in litanies of devotion, involves the chanting of formulas and texts either drawn from the Qur'ān or steeped in its language.[40] A contrast to such group chanting is found in the *maqra'*, or 'recitation session', wherein the Qur'ān is recited by individual practitioners of *tajwīd*. Cairo is especially well known for its varied forms of this kind of event, many of which are associated with particular mosques and take place regularly. One of the most prestigious occurs weekly at the Imām Shāfiʿī tomb-mosque, but there are many smaller, local-mosque or private sessions as well.[41] Still another kind of *maqra'* is the *nadwa*, or 'gathering', a listening session held often in private homes and attended by cognoscenti of the recitative art.[42] In a *nadwa* the musical aspects of recitation often receive special attention, although it is never easy to distinguish the aesthetic from the religious in Qur'ān reciting, as we shall see in Part Two of this chapter, below. The few studies available point up the degree to which recitation is at once art form, popular entertainment and performing contest, as well as pious observance.

In private life

The active role among Muslims of the recited Qur'ān is still more pervasive than the preceding conveys. From birth to death, virtually every action a Muslim makes, let alone every solemn event in his or her life, is potentially an occasion for qur'ānic recitation, whether of entire passages or simply discrete phrases that have passed into everyday usage. Most frequent is the simple *basmala*, 'In the name of God, the merciful, the compassionate', which precedes countless daily acts such as drinking or eating, just as it precedes all but one sūra of the Qur'ān. Alternatively, it may be the ubiquitous *mā shā' llāh* ('whatever God wills!') of Q 18:39 and *al-ḥamdu lillāh* ('praise be to God!') of Q 1:2, which punctuate Muslim speech even among non-Arabic speakers, as do qur'ānic expressions invoking God's mercy (*raḥma*) or forgiveness (*istighfār*). Also frequently heard is the affirmation of God's omnipotence in Q 2:156, 'Truly we are God's and unto him we return.'[43]

The best example of longer qur'ānic texts recited in daily life is surely the Fātiḥa, Q 1, which every Muslim knows by heart and which is recited not only in *ṣalāt* but on virtually every formal occasion, be it the signing of a wedding contract, closing of an agreement or prayer at a tomb.[44] There is also the powerful Q 112, Sūrat al-Ikhlāṣ ('Unity' or 'Purity'), which enters into most *ṣalāt* performances and countless litanies of praise; or the final two sūras, Q 113 and 114 (*al-muʿawwidhatān*), which 'deliver from evil' and hence serve as talismanic recitations; or the prayer for forgiveness in the final verses of Q 2, 'The Cow' (Sūrat al-Baqara), known as 'the seals of the Baqara' and often recited before going to sleep; or the powerful strains of Q 36, Sūrat Yā Sīn, recited at burials, on the approach of death and on the 'Night of Quittance' (*laylat al-barāʾa*, a kind of Muslim All Souls' Night).[45] These are but a few of many possible examples, as anyone is aware who knows how popular the 'Throne Verse' (Q 2:255) and Sūrat al-Nūr ('Light', Q 24) are.

What al-Ghazālī said of the Qur'ān still holds today: 'Much repetition cannot make it seem old and worn to those who recite it.'[46] The powerful presence of the rhythmic cadence of qur'ānic recitation is everywhere evident in traditional and much of modern Muslim society: 'the book lives on among its people, stuff of their daily lives, taking for them the place of a sacrament. For them these are not mere letters or mere words. They are the twigs of the burning bush, aflame with God.'[47]

PART TWO: AESTHETIC RECEPTION OF THE QUR'ĀN

The Qur'ān on its own aesthetic reception

The first suggestions about the Qur'ān's aesthetic reception occur in the text itself, e.g., in Q 39:23: 'God has sent down the most beautiful word (*aḥsan al-ḥadīth)*; a scripture consistent in its repetition, at which the skins of those who fear their lord crawl (*taqshaʿirru*); but then their skins and their hearts are softened for the remembrance of God.' It is worth taking a closer look at the last three lines, especially the verb *taqsha'irru*, 'crawl' (of skin), 'become raw'. Here the effect claimed for qur'ānic recitation is specified as giving the hearer goosebumps (literally what *taqsha'irru julūd* denotes)[48] – before it softens or calms body and soul, thereby preparing him to remember God. This expresses clearly the idea that religious perception of the Qur'ān is the aesthetic experience of a discourse described as the most beautiful (*aḥsan al-ḥadīth*) and communicated in a flesh-tingling auditory experience. Yet this text declares that the final aim of this act of communication is not mere satisfaction, or the 'disinterested pleasure' (*interesselose Wohlgefallen*) that Kant mentions in his treatment of aesthetics, but a cathartic process that prepares one 'for remembering God' (*ilā dhikri llāhi*).

It can be inferred from the Qur'ān that, during the first years of his calling, the Prophet regularly went to the Ka'ba to recite the revelations.[49] Around him gathered the (initially few) believers, who would prostrate themselves or cry during the recitation, as well as a growing number of spectators (often including Muḥammad's adversaries).[50] While his opponents from the outset scorned the new harbinger of salvation, they seem to have reacted to his growing audience with increasing insecurity and hostility. They could not accept his claim to be endowed with divine authority, so they tried to discredit him as a common soothsayer, magician, madman and, specifically, poet, as the Qur'ān itself clearly shows.[51]

Although in later sūras the response to the accusation that Muḥammad is a poet is rather stereotypical, the amount of detail, especially in early passages, indicates that this allegation must have been seen as a real threat. Had there been nothing in his performance to evoke this comparison, his opponents would have sought other ways of undermining his claim to prophethood. They could have accused him of being a liar, a thief or a charlatan, 'but they said: . . . he just composes poetry, he is a poet' (Q 21:5).[52] Up to this point, the description given by the later records concurs with the scenario of Muḥammad's recitations as presented in the Qur'ān.[53]

The Qur'ān's aesthetic reception in Islamic literature

Going beyond the information in the Qur'ān, one can see how this scenario was embellished in collective memory and how the story of the Qur'ān's reception – only hinted at in the text itself – was perceived as the story of the impact of an aesthetic miracle. In the Muslim community's cultural memory,[54] the attraction that the Qur'ān exerts, and which is confirmed in the text itself in several phrases, was poetically interpreted and described with loving attention to every detail and facet. Extra-qur'ānic sources place a much higher emphasis than the text itself on the fact that the revelation was not just convincing in its content but to a high degree in its aesthetics. In the course of the first several centuries after the emigration from Mecca to Medina (*hijra*), a history was constructed in which the Qur'ān's stylistic form was a fundamental element of the salvation history (*Heilsgeschichte*) and its metaphysical quality perceived as a historical fact. The relevant sources for this construction were the biographies and ḥadīth works, treatises and commentaries on the Qur'ān and Muḥammad's miraculous character, as well as books on prophethood (*nubuwwa*). In subsequent eras, much of the writings on Muḥammad and his life – be they composed in a devotional vein or written with a more scientific intent – have only supported the earlier texts. All offer examples of the overwhelming effects of reciting the Qur'ān.

With time, the significance of the Qur'ān's aesthetic impact was increasingly emphasised. Modern authors such as Muḥammad Abū Zahra (d. 1974), Ṣādiq al-Rāfiʿī (d. 1937), (the early) Sayyid Quṭb (d. 1966), Rashīd Riḍā (d. 1935) or Maḥmūd Rāmiyār have regarded the literary supremacy of the text as at least as crucial as the actions and speeches of Muḥammad for the triumphant advance of Islam – an emphasis not found in the Qur'ān, nor even in the early tradition. Although the Qur'ān hints at its own aesthetic reception, it still leaves the role of its literary quality in Muḥammad's mission unexplored. In the books on the Prophet's biography (*sīra*), the attraction supposedly emanating from qur'ānic recitation is explained in greater detail. But the subtext of the Meccan-period reports is that the Prophet met mostly with rejection, the best-known consequence of which was the *hijra*. Except for a few followers – mostly from the lower strata of society (*qalīlan min al-mustaḍʿafīn*), Meccans refused to acknowledge Muḥammad's message.[55] During this phase, the irresistibility of the recited Qur'ān described above was the exception rather than the norm.

In retrospect, however, this changed: the miraculous power of the qur'ānic recitation came to the fore. In later days, the Arab-Muslim community found in its own sources the record of the aesthetic power of the Qur'ān, and in the course of its reception history this power became increasingly important for its self-understanding – examples are not only to be found through comparison of qur'ānic passages and later commentaries and biographical classifications. In the course of time, extra-qur'ānic traditions about individual instances of recitation that confirm the irresistibility of the Qur'ān were increasingly embellished.

The aesthetic power of the Qur'ān in Muslim salvation history

Two premises are fundamental for the early history of the Qur'ān's reception as preserved in the cultural memory of the Muslim community: first, the notion that the pre-Islamic Arabs formed a cultural community distinguished essentially by its cultivation of language and poetry, and, second, the tremendous and irresistible fascination said to be elicited among hearers by recitation of the Qur'ān. These two premises underlie all reports about individual instances of reception and together yield particular topoi that recur in these reports: the opponents who publicly denounce the Prophet, yet secretly yearn to listen to the Qur'ān; the villains who cannot defend themselves against the power emanating from the Qur'ān other than by attacking anyone who recites it; the poets who cannot succeed in meeting the qur'ānic challenge with poetry of equal literary perfection and secretly hang around the Kaʿba when the Prophet recites the Qur'ān; and the Prophet's supporters who outdo each other in their love for Qur'ān recitation. In addition, there are anecdotes about the artistry of individual reciters and, of course, the Prophet, who is credited with the most beautiful of all voices yet who never misses an opportunity to listen to a skilful recitation. There are also testimonies to the curiosity that brings people from all over the Arabian peninsula and even from distant lands to Mecca or Medina to listen to the Qur'ān; and, simultaneously, the frantic attempts of the Quraysh to discourage locals and foreigners alike from doing just that.

Another central topos of the early history of reception is the consternation caused by the language of the Qur'ān because it does not correspond to any known genre of metrical language, yet is extraordinarily, if inexplicably, attractive. Early Muslim sources mention repeatedly that the people of Mecca consulted poets and other literary masters for advice on how technically to categorise Muḥammad's recitations. These 'experts' most often replied – both astonished and fascinated – that the Qur'ān was neither poetry nor rhyming prose, thus establishing the boundaries for evaluating the Qur'ān as literature. The famous poet Walīd b. al-Mughīra remarked, 'I know many *qaṣīdas* and *rajaz* verses, and am even familiar with the poems of the jinn. But, by God, his recitation is like none of them.'[56] He echoes here a common point of view among Muḥammad's contemporaries as remembered by later generations. Yet while sources consistently insist that poets and orators were aware of the stylistic difference of the Qur'ān from the poetry and oratory with which they were familiar, they concede that simple people found it hard to distinguish clearly between poetry and revelation. Tradition tells how the poet and Companion ʿAbdallāh b. Rawāḥa was surprised and challenged by his wife as he was leaving a concubine's chambers.

She had long harboured the suspicion that he was having a clandestine affair, and knowing that ʿAbdallāh had sworn never to recite the Qurʾān unless he was ritually pure (which he would not have been after an act of adultery), she asks him to recite from the Qurʾān. The poet immediately recited three verses of a poem that sounded so much like the Qurʾān that his wife exonerated him, 'thinking it was a *qurʾān*' (*ḥasibat hādhā qurʾānan*).[57]

Perhaps the most striking motif related to the aesthetic reception of the Qurʾān in early Islamic history is that of spontaneous conversion upon hearing the recitation: one or more unbelievers who are hostile to the Prophet, or do not know him, hear the Qurʾān being recited and instantly become Muslims, citing the beauty of the verses. The peculiarity of such tales of conversion – always uniformly structured and frequently found in later centuries in Islam as well[58] – becomes especially clear when one looks for similar reports in other religions. For example, while there are instances of conversions to Christianity resulting from an aesthetic response to its scripture, reports about this do not represent a significant part of the corpus of Christians' testimonies about the spread of their faith; they do not form a topos of salvation literature. This is not to imply that religious practice in Christianity, or other traditions, could be imagined without the aesthetic fascination of particular spaces, rituals, texts, sounds, songs, pictures, or even colours, acts, fragrances and gestures;[59] or that Protestantism could have spread so tremendously fast in German-language areas without the literary power of Martin Luther's translation of the Bible. Yet in the perception that Christian and especially Protestant communities have of their own past, the aesthetic of scripture plays a subordinate role, however relevant it may be for religious practice.

The theory of the Qurʾān's inimitability (*iʿjāz*)

In Muslim self-conceptions, the aesthetic fascination elicited by the Qurʾān recurs as a basic constituent of faith. It is this theological reflection and understanding about the importance of the aesthetic dimension of scripture that is characteristic of Muslim faith, rather than the experience of beauty itself that occurs in the reception of the sacred text (something, as noted above, that can be found in other traditions). Only in Islam did the rationalisation of this aesthetic experience culminate in a distinct theological doctrine of scriptural poetics, the notion of *iʿjāz*, or inimitability, based on the superiority and unique, *sui generis* power of the qurʾānic discourse.[60] For a Christian, the reasoning behind *iʿjāz* is peculiar: I hear in the Qurʾān the word of God because its language is too perfect to have been composed by a human being. While one can find similar ideas about the perfection of scriptural word in the veneration in Buddhist tradition of sutras, most vividly the Lotus Sutra, as sublime expressions of the Buddha-word (*buddhavacana*), or in the concept in Brahmanic tradition of Veda as the eternal sound (*śabda*) of truth, such notions are still quite differently developed doctrines from that of *iʿjāz* and have little of the latter's aesthetic emphasis.

Functionally, the *iʿjāz* concept serves as an aesthetic proof of God. In Western civilisation, virtually no equivalent exists in the religious sphere. The nearest we get is perhaps our subjective response to certain works of, say, Bach or Mozart, to which audiences often refer as 'divine' in their beauty. Muḥammad is known not to have healed the sick nor to have walked on water; his single miraculous 'proof' of his status as a prophet was the Qur'ān itself. An oft-cited ḥadīth says: 'There is no prophet but signs were given to him so that people would believe in him. I have been given nothing but the words that God has revealed to me, and I hope to have the greatest following on the day of resurrection.'[61] Al-Bāqillānī (d. 403/1013), author of the classical formulation of *iʿjāz*, wrote that every prophet is granted a specific miracle as his individual sign, since 'a prophet's mission is not authentic without his giving some evidence and legitimising himself through a sign. He does not distinguish himself from a liar by his features, nor by what he himself says, nor by anything else but by the proof (*burhān*) which has appeared for him so that through it he can prove the validity of his mission.'[62]

It is only because people are incapable of imitating a prophet's signs that they recognise his divine calling. In this general prophetology, the fact that Muḥammad's adversaries were incapable of producing speeches of a comparable literary quality is taken to be Muḥammad's miracle of 'accreditation' – quite in accordance with the Hebrew Bible's line of reasoning. To cite al-Bāqillānī again: 'When the native speakers of this language saw that all of them were incapable of challenging, finding fault with, or imitating the Qur'ān, they found themselves in the same situation as those who had seen the white hand or the staff changing into a snake, which revealed their lies.'[63]

Had Muḥammad's adversaries been able to meet the challenge (*taḥaddī*) as mentioned in the qur'ānic text,[64] al-Bāqillānī argues, their triumph would have been secure. They would have been spared all that followed – the quarrels and wars, migration and captivity, the total loss of power, esteem and wealth. For had they really been able to surpass the Qur'ān stylistically, Muḥammad's claims would have been invalidated. But even though they tried as hard as they could; even though they lacked neither time nor ambition; even though they were masters of eloquence – they remained silent and silent they remain unto this day.[65] That the adversaries remain silent until today is taken to be the proof of the Qur'ān's literary composition being a miracle transcending human capabilities and invalidating each and every attempt at denigrating or belittling it. Indeed, the precise meaning of *iʿjāz* is not 'inimitability', but 'invalidation' or 'prevention' of any attempt at a challenge. Part of the line of reasoning that establishes the Qur'ān as a miracle is that the Arabs accepted the Qur'ān as a divine creation because of its (Arabic) stylistic perfection; it had to be the Arabs who acknowledged this literary miracle, for they were the most poetically and linguistically sophisticated of peoples, the people who above all treasured and mastered the art of eloquence, and who could be convinced only by a literary miracle.

The connection between the Arabs' literary mastery and the idea of qur'ānic *iʿjāz* was first formulated by al-Jāḥiẓ (d. 255/868–9), well before al-Bāqillānī, and it is his formulation that appears whenever Muslim scholars are concerned with dogmatic arguments. This formulation runs as follows: God gave to each prophet the gift most highly valued by his people. Moses was legitimised as prophet by turning a staff into a snake, thereby surpassing the magic practised at the Pharaoh's court in Egypt where magic was held in high esteem. Jesus' miracle was raising people from the dead at a time when healing was highly valued. And Muḥammad was prophet to a people who valued their poets most of all; thus his miracle had to be a literary one.[66]

The Qur'ān and literature

In order to prove that such a book could in no way have come from a human author, ever since the early ninth century Muslim scholars have made tremendous efforts to explore the Qur'ān's formal perfection in every conceivable detail. In fact, Arab literary studies as such owe their very existence to the Qur'ān. If the miracle of Islam is the language of revelation, then the language of the Qur'ān has to be analysed in literary terms and, to prove its superiority, be compared to other texts, above all poetry. The initial thrust was apologetic, but literary interest soon departed from the theological context. From the tenth and twelfth centuries onward, great works on Arabic poetics were produced, anticipating many of the findings of modern linguistics and literary studies. Arabic rhetoricians discussed the Qur'ān and poetry together, refusing to play one off against the other – an interweaving of theology and literary studies hardly conceivable in today's Arabic-speaking world, in terms of both academic precision and theological legitimacy. A brilliant exponent of this kind of scholarship can be found in the Iranian ʿAbd al-Qāhir al-Jurjānī (d. 471/1078), who consistently focused on the specific merits of the poetical language as such – be it in the Qur'ān or in poetry. His book, *Dalā'il fī i'jāz al-Qur'ān* ('Evidence of the Qur'ān's miraculous character'), is not only remarkable for the striking precision and attention to detail which characterises his analysis of particular stylistic phrases; Jurjānī was the first to outline a poetic theory both comprehensive and systematic that is based on *naẓm* (order, system) and on several basic insights in the field of textual linguistics. In his poetic theory, he emphatically rejects the old dualism of form and content, arriving at an almost structuralist theory of language and poetry, the quality of the methodology of which has rarely been reached again in Arab literary studies.[67]

The Qur'ān has enriched Arabic poetry more than any other Arabic literary genre. Apart from frequent references to qur'ānic verses or images throughout Arabic or Persian literature, the Qur'ān liberated Arabic poetry from the narrow framework of existing genres and inspired new approaches to language, imagery and the use of motifs. Conventional standards, and the theoretical analysis of language and literature, can both be traced to the hermeneutics of the Qur'ān.[68] Just as theologians referred to poetry to analyse the language of the Qur'ān, the reverse also happened – and does still. One example of poets and literary scholars using the Qur'ān to analyse poetry was the movement of so-called 'modernists' (*muḥdathūn*) in Arabic poetry, who dominated literary debates in the eighth and ninth centuries. The imagery of the Qur'ān and its stylistic departures from the strict formal rules of poetry inspired 'modernists' such as Ibn al-Mu'tazz to introduce new rhetorical devices and to replace traditional norms. In the modernists' purely literary-aesthetic discussion of poetry, the Qur'ān was the obvious key point of reference because of its poetic quality.[69] Even in our times, a poet like Adonis, one of the leading and most controversial figures of contemporary Arabic literature, analyses the Qur'ān as the source of modernity in Arabic poetry. In his theoretical work, Adonis discusses and praises the language of the Qur'ān in detail, its provocative literary and aesthetic power, and its breaking with traditional norms.[70]

Qur'ān recitation and music

Nowhere is the aesthetic dimension of the reception of the Qur'ān more clearly seen than in the difficulties that Muslims have had with the musical aspect of Qur'ān recitation and its powerful effectiveness. While Muslims are usually careful not to call qur'ānic recitation music (*ghīnā*), nor to refer to the reciter (*muqri,' qāri'*) as singer (*mughannī*), in order to avoid any identification of the holy text with songs created by human beings, a strong melodic element is not only tolerated by theologians for reasons of popular appeal, but is even a prerequisite of the ideal recitation as conceptually determined in countless writings on *tajwīd* and *ādāb al-tilāwa*. Logically enough, the musical quality of recitation is one of the determining criteria of those institutions that train, test and distinguish reciters. Likewise, reciters and their audience make use of a terminology that is, in great part, synonymous with that used for music. An anecdote told by Ibn ʿAbd Rabbih from early Islamic times illustrates that the relation of qurʾānic recitation and music has always been ambivalent: a man is arrested because he is supposed to have been found singing loudly in a mosque, thereby breaking the rules of proper conduct. Fortuitously, a noble of Quraysh praying in the mosque rushes to his aid and explains to the police that the accused was only reciting the Qurʾān. The misunderstanding thus resolved, the detainee is released. Once outside again, the noble tells the miscreant: 'Had you not sung so well, I would not have protected you.'[71]

This ambivalence makes itself felt on the side of the recipients as well. To outside observers, their behaviour often appears to be that of participants at a musical function, however much that may run contrary to the theological guidelines for proper reciting. As noted above, in a country like Egypt, qurʾānic recitation by a well-known singer is more than just a religious matter. It ranks among the society's important artistic events and is frequented by Christians and Muslims, secular intellectuals and ordinary believers. The best reciters participate in live-broadcast international competitions and are revered throughout the country. Audience response to recitations hardly differs at times from that of audiences for music: shouts, clapping and signs of pleasure abound at concerts; star status is attributed to some reciters by their fans as well as in yellow press and musical magazines; spectacular appearances and important releases parallel those of pop artists; and the regular *nadwa*s (see above) bring aficionados together to listen to live recitations and recordings of the Qurʾān and to discuss their respective musical merits. In all these one finds numerous examples of the Qurʾān being received in a way that is outside a clearly religious domain, one that in many ways can only be called aesthetic or artistic.[72] The polemics against *qirāʾa bi-l-alḥān* (see above) show that already at the caliphs' courts the Qurʾān was performed as mere chamber music, even accompanied by dancing.[73] Typical is the indignation of Ibn al-Jawzī (d. 597/1200) about those who 'recite the Qurʾān with melodies and thereby exceed common norms, as they have made out of it a singing (*ghināʾ*)'.[74]

Even if scholarly tradition has not wanted to identify Qurʾān recitation with musical performance, the aesthetic power of the melodically recited scripture has been, so far as we can judge, an undeniable fact of Muslim piety and practice from the earliest days of Islam to the present moment. The recited Qur'ān is and has ever been the epitome of aesthetic as well as spiritual perfection for the faithful.

Notes

1. See the comments of S. D. Goitein, *Studies in Islamic history and institutions* (Leiden: Brill, 1966), p. 364.
2. Concerning the early meaning and derivation of *qur'ān*, see W. Graham, 'The earliest meaning of "Qur'ān"', *Die Welt des Islams* n.s. 23/24 (1984), 364.
3. The other general term often used in Arabic for recitation of the Qur'ān is *tilāwa*. While both *qirā'a* and *tilāwa* can sometimes be interchangeable, the former is the term used for the technical discipline of recitation and in phrases referring to a particular recitative style (e.g., *'ilm al-qirā'a* and *qirā'a bi-l-alḥān*, for both of which see below), while *tilāwa* is, as K. Nelson notes, 'always general' (*The art of reciting the Qur'ān* (Austin, TX: University of Texas Press, 1985), p. 73; for examples, see pp. 72–7). Cf. L. al-Fārūqī, 'Tartīl al-Qur'ān al-karīm', in K. Ahmad and Z. I. Ansari (eds.), *Islamic perspectives: Studies in honour of Mawlānā Sayyid Abul A'lā Mawdūdī* (Leicester: Islamic Foundation, 1979), pp. 106–7.
4. R. Paret, 'Ḳirā'a', in *Encyclopaedia of Islam*, new ed., 11 vols. (Leiden: Brill, 1979–2002), vol. V, pp. 127–9; R. Blachère, *Introduction au Coran* (Paris: G. P. Maisonneuve, 1947), p. 103; Th. Nöldeke et al., *Geschichte des Qorāns*, second rev. ed., 3 vols. (Leipzig: T. Weicher, 1909–38), vol. III, pp. 160–90. On particular 'readings' of individuals, see G. Bergsträsser, 'Die Koranlesung des Hasan von Basra', *Islamica* 2 (1926), 11–57; E. Beck, 'Die b. Mas'ūdvarianten bei al-Farrā'', *Orientalia* 25 (1956), 353–83; 28 (1959), 186–205, 230–56.
5. On the science of *qirā'a* generally, with primary emphasis on the *qirā'āt*, see Nöldeke, *Geschichte*, vol. III; Blachère, *Introduction*, pp. 103–35, 199–210; O. Pretzl, 'Die Wissenschaft der Koranlesung . . .', *Islamica* 6 (1933–4), 1–47; I. Goldziher, *Die Richtungen der islamischen Koranauslegung*, repr. ed. (Leiden: Brill, 1952, 1920[1]), pp. 1–54; F. M. Denny, 'Exegesis and recitation', in F. E. Reynolds and T. M. Ludwig (eds.), *Transitions and transformations in the history of religions* (Leiden: Brill, 1980), esp. pp. 109ff. Further literature may be found in Paret, 'Ḳirā'a', p. 128a. The traditional Muslim source is Shams al-Dīn Abū l-Khayr Muḥammad b. Muḥammad b. al-Jazarī, *al-Nashr fī l-qirā'āt al-'ashr*, ed. 'A. M. al-Dabbā' (Cairo: Maṭba'at Muṣṭafā Muḥammad, n.d.). See also L. al-Sa'īd, *The recited Koran*, trans. and ed. B. Weiss et al. (Princeton: Darwin Press, 1975), pp. 15–60.
6. Al-Sa'īd, *Recited Koran*, pp. 19–50. This is not to deny that the early specialists in Qur'ān recitation used the orthography of the 'Uthmānic text in devising or defending variant readings: see, e.g., the comments of G. Bergsträsser on the Qur'ān readings of al-Ḥasan al-Baṣrī ('Koranlesung des Hasan', 54).
7. There is some lack of clarity as to whether the Cairo edition was first published in 1337, 1342, 1343 or 1344 (i.e., between 1919 and 1926 CE); 1342/1923–4 seems the most accepted date for the first public printing. See W. Graham, *Beyond the written word: Oral aspects of scripture in the history of religion*, (Cambridge: Cambridge University Press, 1987), p. 211 n. 2.

8. When the edition appeared, a major European Qur'ān scholar declared that Western textual scholarship could not have produced a more exact or critically scrupulous edition than had these leading exponents of the highly oral and highly mnemonic *'ilm al-qirā'āt*; see G. Bergsträsser, 'Koranlesung in Kairo', *Der Islam* 20 (1932), 10–12. On the 'official Qur'ān', see the entire discussion in Bergsträsser, 'Koranlesung in Kairo', 1–13. Cf. also O. Pretzl's similar comments in Nöldeke, *Geschichte*, vol. III, pp. 273–4.
9. Bergsträsser, 'Koranlesung des Hasan', 53–5; cf. 25.
10. Ibn al-Jazarī, *al-Nashr*, vol. I, p. 9. Cf. Nöldeke, *Geschichte*, vol. III, pp. 118–29; A. Jeffery, *The Qur'ān as scripture* (New York: R. F. Moore Co., 1952), p. 98; Nelson, *Art of reciting*, pp. 2–3.
11. Abū 'Abdallāh Muḥammad b. Ismā'īl al-Bukhārī, *al-Jāmi' al-ṣaḥīḥ*, ed. H. al-Nawāwī, 9 vols. (Cairo: Muṣṭafā al-Bāb al-Ḥalabī wa-Awlāduhu, 1378/1958?), 44.4, 59.6, 66.5, 88.9, 97.53. For other occurrences of this tradition in the classical ḥadīth collections, see A. J. Wensinck et al., *Concordance et indices de la tradition musulmane*, 4 vols. (Leiden: Brill, 1988), vol. I, p. 448b. Cf. Ibn al-Jazarī, *al-Nashr*, vol. I, pp. 19–22; Goldziher, *Richtungen*, pp. 3ff., 36ff.; Nöldeke, *Geschichte*, vol. I, pp. 48–52; Nelson, *Art of reciting*, app. B, pp. 199–201.
12. F. Sezgin, *Geschichte des arabischen Schrifttums*, 9 vols. (Leiden: Brill, 1967–84), vol. I, pp. 4–13; Paret, 'Ḳirā'a', pp. 127b–128a; Pretzl, 'Wissenschaft der Koranlesung', 4ff.
13. Sezgin, *Geschichte*, vol. I, p. 14; Blachère, *Introduction*, pp. 127–9.
14. Such as the trial and flogging of Ibn Shanabūdh (d. 328/939) which forced him to recant his Qur'ān readings, or the public hearing on the readings of Ibn Miqsam (d. 354/965) and his subsequent disavowal of these. See Ibn al-Jazarī, *Ghāyat al-nihāya fī ṭabaqāt al-qurrā'*, ed. G. Bergsträsser and O. Pretzl, 3 vols. in 2 (Cairo: Maktabat al-Khānjī, 1932–5), vol. II, pp. 52–6, 123–5; Nöldeke, *Geschichte*, vol. III, pp. 12, 122–3; R. Paret, 'Ibn Shanabūdh', in *Encyclopaedia of Islam*, new ed., vol. III, pp. 935–6.
15. On the 'seven', 'ten' and 'fourteen' *qirā'āt*, see Abū 'Amr 'Uthmān al-Dānī, *al-Taysīr fī l-qirā'āt al-sab'*, ed. O. Pretzl (Leipzig/Istanbul: Maṭba'at al-Dawlat, 1930), pp. 4–16; Blachère, *Introduction*, pp. 116–32; Nöldeke, *Geschichte*, vol. III, pp. 186–9; al-Sa'īd, *Recited Koran*, pp. 53–6, 127–30. On actual variations on particular passages, see esp. Goldziher, *Richtungen*, pp. 4–32; A. Jeffery (ed.), *Materials for the history of the text of the Qur'ān* (Leiden: Brill, 1937); al-Dānī, *Taysīr*; Bergsträsser, 'Koranlesung des Hasan'. On other variant readings, see Abū 'Abdallāh al-Ḥusayn b. Aḥmad b. Khalawayh, *Mukhtaṣar fī shawādhdh al-Qur'ān min Kitāb al-Badī'*, ed. G. Bergsträsser (Leipzig/Cairo: Deutsche morgenländische Gesellschaft, im Kommission bei F. A. Brockhaus, 1934); E. Beck, 'Der 'uṯmānische Kodex in der Koranlesung des zweiten Jahrhunderts', *Orientalia* 14 (1945), 355–73. Further literature in Paret, 'Ḳirā'a'.
16. See Nelson, *Art of reciting*, ch. 2; F. M. Denny, 'The adab of Qur'ān recitation', in A. H. Johns (ed.), *International Congress for the Study of the Qur'ān* (Canberra: Australian National University, 1980; second ed. 1981); Cf. Bergsträsser, 'Koranlesung in Kairo', 110–34 (including section by K. Huber, 113–33).
17. Cf. Q 25:32. *Tartīl* is hard to translate adequately here; it intensifies the verb *rattala*, of which it is the verbal noun (*masdar*) used as a cognate accusative.

On the sense of *tartīl* as measured or slow, distinctly uttered chant, see E. W. Lane, *An Arabic–English lexicon* (London/Edinburgh: Williams and Norgate, 1863–93), p. 1,028; Nelson, *Art of reciting*, pp. 83–7; al-Fārūqī, 'Tartīl al-Qur'ān', esp. pp. 106–7; M. Ben Cheneb, 'Tadjwīd', in *Encyclopaedia of Islam*, new ed., vol. IV, p. 601.

18. Cf. Nelson, *Art of reciting*, pp. 86–7.
19. For a detailed discussion of *murattal* and *mujawwad* styles, see ibid., pp. 101–35. Cf. also pp. 14–18, 83–100. Note that the terminology – not only with respect to *tajwīd* but also *tartīl* – can vary in meaning from context to context. Cf. also H. H. Touma, 'Die Koranrezitation', *Baessler-Archiv* 48 (n.s. 23) (1975), 87–8; M. Talbi, 'La qirā'a bi-l-alḥān', *Arabica* 5 (1958), 183–90. For a good practical grasp of the common distinction between *tartīl* (i.e., *murattal* recitation) as the accurate and measured, but less musically modulated and embellished recitation, and *tajwīd* (i.e., *mujawwad* recitation) as artistically embellished, highly euphonic cantillation, see Denny's description of two different recitation sessions in modern Cairo ('Adab', pp. 149–58). Denny's exclusive use of the terms *tartīl* and *tajwīd* in this article is somewhat at odds with K. Nelson's description of the usage in the same environment; his article equates *tartīl* with *murattal* and *tajwīd* with *mujawwad*, as is often done.
20. Nelson, *Art of reciting*, esp. ch. 4, pp. 52–100; cf. pp. 184–7. As a whole, Nelson's fine study shows how a variety of skills and disciplines, as well as more intangible qualities of mind and feeling, are involved, both in theory and practice, in *tajwīd* (see esp. chs. 2–5, 7).
21. Cited and translated without page reference from *Munājāt Sayyidinā Mūsā* (Damascus/Cairo, n.d.) by C. Padwick, *Muslim devotions* (London: SPCK, 1961), p. 114.
22. Bukhārī, *Ṣaḥīḥ*, 10.94; Muslim b. al-Ḥajjāj, *al-Ṣaḥīḥ*, ed. 'Abd al-Bāqī, 5 vols. (Cairo: Dār Iḥyā 'al-Turāth al-'Arabī, 1374–5/1975–6), bk. 6, nos. 254–6; Abū 'Īsā Muḥammad b. 'Īsā al-Tirmidhī, *al-Jāmi' al-Ṣaḥīḥ (K. al-Sunan)*, ed. 'Abd al-Bāqī, 5 vols. (Cairo: Muṣṭafā al-Bāb al-Ḥalabī wa-Awlāduhu, 1356–95/1937–75), vol. II, p. 69; 'Abdallāh al-Dārimī, *al-Sunan*, ed. M. Dahmān, 2 vols. (Cairo (?): Dār Iḥyā 'al-Sunna al-Nabawiyya, n.d.), vol. II, p. 36. Cf. Abū Ḥāmid Muḥammad b. Muḥammad al-Ṭūsī al-Ghazālī, *Iḥyā' 'ulūm al-dīn*, 5 vols. (Beirut: Dār al-Ma'rifat lil-Ṭabā'at wa-l-Nashr, n.d.), vol. I, p. 4.
23. Padwick, *Muslim devotions*, p. 108. Cf. al-Ghazālī on *qirā'a* in *ṣalāt* (*Iḥyā'*, vol. I, p. 4).
24. Cf. al-Ghazālī, *Iḥyā'*, vol. I, p. 4.
25. For specific examples of traditional funeral recitation practices, see the description of Moroccan usage at the end of the nineteenth century by B. Meakin, *The Moors* (London: Swan Sonnenschein & Co., 1902), pp. 377–86, and that of funerary practices in nineteenth-century Cairo by E. W. Lane, *An account of the manners and customs of the modern Egyptians* (London: C. Knight and Co., 1836; repr. ed. New York: Dover Publications, 1973), pp. 511–28.
26. Q 12:2; 20:113; 39:28; 41:3; 42:7; 43:3.
27. M. Yvan, *Voyages et récits*, 2 vols. (Brussels: Meline, Cans et Cie., 1853–5), vol. II, p. 76. Thanks to William Roff (pers. commun., 14 July 1980) for calling attention to this passage from an English translation unavailable to the present authors.

28. On traditional Muslim education, see I. Goldziher, 'Education (Muslim)', in J. Hastings (ed.), *Encyclopaedia of religion and ethics*, 13 vols. (Edinburgh: T. & T. Clark, 1908–26), vol. V, pp. 198–207, as well as the works cited hereafter. Cf. also, on Moroccan education: E. M. Bellaire, 'L'enseignement indigène au Maroc', *Revue du monde musulman* 15 (1911), 422–52; on late-nineteenth-century education in Morocco, see Meakin, *The Moors*, pp. 325ff.; and the brief general survey of B. Dodge, *Muslim education in medieval times* (Washington: Middle East Institute, 1962).
29. ʿAbd al-Raḥmān b. Khaldūn, *Al-Muqaddimah*, ed. M. Quatremère, 3 vols. (Paris: Benjamin Duprat, 1858), vol. III, p. 260. On memorisation and recitation in Islamic education, see also D. F. Eickelman, 'The art of memory', *Comparative Studies in Society and History* 20 (1978), 485–516, and his *Knowledge and power in Morocco* (Princeton: Princeton University Press, 1985), pp. 57–71. On teaching the Qur'ān in traditional elementary schools, see L. Brunot, 'Maktab', in *Encyclopaedia of Islam*, new ed., vol. III, pp. 178a–179a; J. Sharīf, *Islam in India, or the 'Qanūn-i-Islam'*, trans. G. Herklots, rev. W. Crooke (London: Oxford University Press, 1921; repr. ed. New Delhi: Oriental Books Reprint Corp., 1972, 1832[1]), pp. 51–2; L. Sanneh, *The Jakhanke* (London: International African Institute, 1979), pp. 154–71 and 'The Islamic education of an African child', in G. N. Brown and M. Heskett (eds.), *Conflict and harmony in education in tropical Africa* (London: Allen and Unwin, 1975), pp. 168–86.
30. Cf. D. A. Wagner and A. Lotfi, 'Traditional Islamic education in Morocco', *Comparative Education Review* 24 (1980), 241–2; also, their 'Learning to read by "rote"', *International Journal of the Sociology of Language* 42 (1983), 112–15; Eickelman, 'Art of memory', 492–3.
31. One of the best-known descriptions of this experience is that by the great Egyptian educational reformer Ṭāhā Ḥusayn (1889–1973), *al-Ayyām* I (1926–7) (Cairo: Dār al-Maʿārif, 1962), pp. 28–72 (=Eng. trans. E. H. Paxton, *An Egyptian childhood* (London: G. Routledge, 1932; repr. ed. London: Heinemann, 1981), pp. 13–33).
32. Cited from Haut Comité Méditerranéen et de l'Afrique du Nord, *l'Islam dans les colonies françaises*, p. 32, by R. Santerre, *Pédagogie musulmane d'Afrique noire* (Montreal: Presses de l'Université de Montréal, 1973), p. 13.
33. Santerre, *Pédagogie*, p. 145 ('un méchanisme de formation totale'). See also pp. 13–17, 111–14, 122ff., 145–50. Cf. Santerre's comment (Santerre, *Pédagogie*, p. 123): 'L'enfant jadis était confié au mallum [the Qur'ān teacher] pour être initié non seulement au Coran, mais aussi à l'ensemble de la vie sociale. Le maître devait se charger de le socialiser et d'en faire un homme.'
34. Eickelman, *Knowledge and power*, pp. 62–3.
35. F. Denny, 'Types of Qur'ān recitation sessions in contemporary Cairo' (unpublished paper) includes interesting examples from Cairo.
36. Dārimī, *al-Sunan*, sect. 18, ḥadīth 8 of the introduction (*muqaddima*).
37. Cited by al-Ghazālī, *Iḥyā'*, vol. I, p. 8. This tradition is also found in the ḥadīth (see, e.g., Wensinck, *Concordance*, vol. I, p. 275b).
38. Or on each night of any month: Cf. al-Ghazālī, *Iḥyā'*, vol. I, p. 8. The thirtieths (*ajzā'*, pl. of *juz'*) are not the only divisions of the Qur'ān for recitative purposes: see the entire section in al-Ghazālī's *Iḥyā'*(vol. I, p. 8) on recitative divisions of

the text. Cf. E. Sell, *The faith of Islam*, third rev. ed. (Madras: SPCK Depôt, 1907, 1880[1]), app. A.

39. The term *khatma* (lit. 'sealing') is used to designate the conclusion of the recitation of the entire qur'ānic text from beginning to end. *Khatma*s are often performed over the whole month, the last ten days or during the single 'Night of Power'. Cf. Sharīf, *Islam in India*, pp. 206–8. For another testimony (from west Africa) to the importance of Ramaḍān recitation, especially on *laylat al-qadr*, see Santerre, *Pédagogie*, p. 108.
40. L. Gardet, 'Dhikr', in *Encyclopaedia of Islam*, new ed., vol. II, pp. 223–7; T. P. Hughes, *A dictionary of Islam*, rev. repr. ed. (Lahore: Premier Book House, n.d., 1885[1]), s.v. 'Zikr'; K. Nakamura, *Ghazali on prayer* (Tokyo: University of Tokyo, Institute of Oriental Culture, 1973), pp. 10–18 (further literature, p. 11 n. 4).
41. Denny, 'Adab', and esp. 'Types of Qur'ān recitation sessions'; Nelson, *Art of reciting*, esp. pp. 157–73.
42. Nelson, *Art of reciting*, pp. 167ff.
43. On widely used qur'ānic expressions, see J. Jomier, 'La place du Coran dans la vie quotidienne en Egypte', *Institute des belles lettres arabes* (Tunis) 58 (1952), 131–65. Cf. M. Piamenta, *Islam in everyday Arabic speech* (Leiden: Brill, 1979), pp. 10, 73, 75, 86, and passim (see also the index, pp. 263–4, s.v. 'Qur'ān'); Padwick, *Muslim devotions*, pp. 108ff.
44. C. Snouck Hurgronje, *Mekka in the latter part of the 19th century*, Eng. trans. J. Monahan (Leiden: Brill, 1931, 1889[1]), p. 29; Hughes, *Dictionary*, pp. 45–6; R. Paret, 'Fātiḥah', in *Encyclopaedia of Islam*, new ed., vol. II, p. 841; Jomier, 'Place du Coran', 141, 149; Piamenta, *Islam in everyday speech*, p. 87.
45. See Jomier, 'Place du Coran', esp. 148–65, and B. A. Donaldson, 'The Koran as magic', for diverse examples of the popular use of particular sūras and verses. See also Padwick, *Muslim devotions*, pp. 109–20, esp. pp. 117ff., and Piamenta, *Islam in everyday speech*, p. 114, on Yā Sīn. On the *laylat al-barā'a*, the 15th of the month of Sha'bān, see Piamenta, *Islam in everyday speech*, pp. 117–18; Hughes, *Dictionary*, p. 570 (s.v. 'Shab-i-barāt'); Mrs Meer Hasan Ali, *Observations on the Mussulmauns of India*, 2 vols. (London: Parbury, Allen and Co., 1832), pp. 300–3; Sharīf, *Islam in India*, pp. 203–4; Snouck Hurgronje, *Mekka*, p. 61.
46. al-Ghazālī, *Iḥyā'*, vol. I, p. 8.
47. Padwick, *Muslim devotions*, p. 119.
48. See Fakhr al-Dīn al-Rāzī, *al-Tafsīr al-kabīr*, 30 vols. (Tehran: Dār al-Kutub, n.d.), ad Q 39:23.
49. Q 11:16; 34:43; 37:36; 38:6; 74:24.
50. Q 5:83; 32:15; 17:107–9; cf. 84:21.
51. E.g., Q 11:7ff.; 34:43; 37:36; 38:4; 74:24.
52. Cf. M. Zwettler, 'A mantic manifesto', in J. Kugel (ed.), *Poetry and prophecy* (Ithaca, NY: Cornell University Press, 1991), pp. 75–120; A. Neuwirth, 'Der historische Muhammad im Spiegel des Koran – Prophetentypus zwischen Seher und Dichter?', in W. Zwickel (ed.), *Biblische Welten: Festschrift für Martin Metzger* (Freiburg, Switzerland: Universitätsverlag, 1993), pp. 83–108.
53. A detailed analysis of this scenario may be found in A. Neuwirth, 'Vom Rezitationstext über die Liturgie zum Kanon: Zu Entstehung und Wiederauflösung

der Surenkomposition im Verlauf der Entwicklung eines islamischen Kultus', in S. Wild (ed.), *The Qur'ān as text* (Leiden: Brill, 1996), pp. 69–105.
54. For methodological background to this concept, cf. J. Assmann's work, *Das kulturelle Gedächtnis: Schrift, Erinnerung und politische Identität in frühun Hochkulturen* (Munich: C. H. Beck, 1992).
55. See 'Abd al-Malik b. Hishām, *al-Sīra al-nabawiyya,* 2 vols., ed. M. Saqqā, I. al-Abyārī and 'A. Shalabī (Cairo: Muṣṭafā al-Bābī al-Ḥalabī, 1355/1937), vol. I, p. 422 (trans. A. Guillaume, *The life of Muhammad* (London: Oxford University Press, 1955), p. 194); N. Kermani, 'The aesthetic reception of the Qur'ān as reflected in early Muslim history', in I. J. Boullata (ed.), *Literary structures of religious meaning in the Qur'ān* (Richmond, Surrey: Curzon, 2000), pp. 255–76.
56. 'Imād al-Dīn Ismā'īl b. 'Umar b. Kathīr, *al-Sīra al-nabawiyya,* ed. M. 'Abd al-Waḥīd, 4 vols. (Beirut: n.p., 1407/1987), vol. I, p. 499.
57. Muḥammad b. al-Mukarram b. Manẓūr, *Lisān al-'arab,* 15 vols. (Beirut: Dār Ṣādir, 1375/1956), vol. VII, p. 183.
58. The most famous of the later adherents who supposedly converted to Islam because of the linguistic quality of the Qur'ān is probably 'Alī b. Rabbān al-Ṭabarī, who writes about the conversion in his *Kitāb al-Dīn wa-l-dawla = The book of religion and empire,* ed. and trans. A. Mingana (Manchester: Manchester University Press, 1923), pp. 44ff.
59. See H. Wenzel, *Hören und Sehen, Schrift und Bild: Kultur und Gedächtnis im Mittelalter* (Munich: C. H. Beck, 1995); J. Mukarovsky, *Kapitel aus der Ästhetik,* fourth ed. (Frankfurt: Suhrkamp, 1982), pp. 27ff.
60. On the doctrine of *i'jāz,* see T. Andrae, *Die Person Muhammeds in Lehre und Glaube seiner Gemeinde* (Stockholm: Norstedt, 1918), pp. 92–123; A. Aleem, 'I'jazu 'l-Quran', *Islamic Culture* 7 (1933), 64–82, 215–33; G. E. von Grunebaum, 'I'djāz', in *Encyclopaedia of Islam,* new ed., vol. III, pp. 1,018–20 and his 'Der Begriff der Unnachahmlichkeit des Korans in seiner Entstehung und Fortbildung', *Archiv für Begriffsgeschichte* 13 (1969), 58–72; A. Neuwirth, 'Das islamische Dogma der "Unnachahmlichkeit des Korans" in literaturwissenschaftlicher Sicht', *Der Islam* 60 (1983), 166–83; I. J. Boullata, 'The rhetorical interpretation of the Qur'ān: *I'jāz* and related topics', in A. Rippin (ed.), *Approaches to the history of the interpretation of the Qur'ān* (Oxford: Clarendon Press, 1988), pp. 139–57; M. Larkin, 'The inimitability of the Qur'ān: Two perspectives', *Religion and Literature* 20 (1988), 31–47; N. Kermani, *Gott ist schön* (Munich: C. H. Beck, 1999), pp. 233–314.
61. Bukhārī, *Ṣaḥīḥ,* 97.1 (no. 7274).
62. Abū Bakr al-Bāqillānī, *I'jāz al-Qur'ān* (Beirut: 'Ālam al-Kutub, 1988), p. 230.
63. Ibid.
64. Initially, the passages that are most often used as documentary evidence for the Qur'ān's *i'jāz* (the so-called *taḥaddī* verses, in which God 'challenges' the infidels to present a sūra that would equal the verses in the Qur'ān) did not refer to the stylistic perfection of the qur'ānic language, but only later were understood as an aesthetic challenge. Cf. M. Radscheit, *Die koranische Herausforderung: Die Taḥaddī-Verse im Rahmen der Polemikpassagen des Korans* (Berlin: Klaus Schwarz, 1996).

65. Radscheit, *Die koranische Herausforderung*, pp. 35ff. The line of argument here presented may already be found in the works of earlier authors, the earliest of them probably ʿAmr b. Baḥr al-Jāḥiẓ: see *Hujjaj al-nubuwwa*, in *Rasāʾil al-Jāḥiẓ*, 4 vols., ed. ʿA. S. M. Hārūn (Cairo: n.p., 1399/1979), vol. III, pp. 273ff., and the quotes in Jalāl al-Dīn al-Suyūṭī, *al-Itqān fī ʿulūm al-Qurʾān*, third ed., ed. A. S. ʿAlī, 2 vols. (Cairo: al-Ḥalabī, 1370/1951), vol. II, pp. 117ff.
66. See al-Jāḥiẓ, *Hujjaj al-nubuwwa*, pp. 278ff.
67. On al-Jurjānī, see K. Abu Deeb, *Al-Jurjānī's theory of poetic imagery* (Warminster: Aris and Phillips, 1979); Kermani, *Gott ist schön*, pp. 253–314.
68. Cf. M. Zaghlūl Sallām, *Athar al-Qurʾān fī taṭawwur al-naqd al-ʿarabī ilā ākhir al-qarn al-rābiʿ al-hijrī*, second ed. (Cairo: Dār al-Maʿārif, 1961); W. Heinrichs, 'Literary theory: The problem of its efficiency', in G. von Grunebaum (ed.), *Arabic poetry: Theory and development* (Wiesbaden: Harrassowitz, 1973), pp. 28ff.; G. von Grunebaum, *Kritik und Dichtkunst: Studien zur arabischen Literaturgeschichte* (Wiesbaden: Harrassowitz, 1955), pp. 87ff.
69. Abū l-ʿAbbās ʿAbdallāh b. Muʿtazz, *Kitāb al-Badīʿ*, ed. I. Kratschkovsky (London: Luzac, 1935); I. Kratschkovsky, 'Die arabische Poetik im IX. Jahrhundert', *Le monde oriental* 23 (1929), 23–39; J. C. Bürgel, 'Die beste Dichtung ist die lügenreichste', *Oriens* 23/24 (1970–1), 7–102.
70. Adūnīs (Adonis), *al-Shiʿriyya al-ʿarabiyya* (Beirut: Dār al-Ādāb, 1985), pp. 50ff.
71. Quoting from A. Shiloah, 'L'Islam et la musique', in J. Porte (ed.), *Encyclopédie des musiques sacrées*, 4 vols. (Paris: Editions Labergerie, 1968–70), vol. I, p. 418.
72. Cf. Bergsträsser, 'Koranlesung in Kairo'; Touma, 'Die Koranrezitation'; see also Nelson, *Art of reciting*; L. al-Saʿīd, *al-Taghannī bi-l-Qurʾān* (Cairo: al-Hay ʾa al-ʿĀmma lil-Taʾlīf wa-l-Nashr, 1390/1970); A. Kellermann, 'Koranlesung im Maghreb' (Ph.D. diss., Freie Universität Berlin, 1996).
73. Talbi, 'La qirāʾa bi-l-alḥān'.
74. Abū l-Faraj ʿAbd al-Raḥmān b. ʿAlī b. al-Jawzī, *Kitāb al-Quṣṣāṣ wa-l-mudhakkirīn*, ed. M. L. Swartz (Beirut: Dar el-Machreq, 1391/1971), p. 118.

Further reading

Assmann, J., *Das kulturelle Gedächtnis: Schrift, Erinnerung und politische Identität in frühun Hochkulturen*, Munich: C. H. Beck, 1992.

al-Bāqillānī, Abū Bakr, *Iʿjāz al-Qurʾān*, Beirut: ʿĀlam al-Kutub, 1988.

Bergsträsser, G., 'Koranlesung in Kairo' (with a contribution by K. Huber), *Der Islam* 20 (1932), 1–42; 21 (1933), 110–40.

Boullata, I. J., 'The rhetorical interpretation of the Qurʾān: Iʿjāz and related topics', in A. Rippin (ed.), *Approaches to the history of the interpretation of the Qurʾān*, Oxford: Clarendon Press, 1988, pp. 139–57.

Denny, F. M., 'The adab of Qurʾān recitation', in A. H. Johns (ed.), *International Congress for the Study of the Qurʾān*, Ser. 1, Canberra: Australian National University, 1980, second ed. 1981.

'Qurʾān recitation: A tradition of oral performance and transmission', *Oral Transmission* 4 (1989), 5–26.

'Qurʾān recitation training in Indonesia: A survey of contexts and handbooks', in A. Rippin (ed.), *Approaches to the history of the interpretation of the Qurʾān*, Oxford: Clarendon Press, 1988, pp. 288–306.

Eickelman, D. F., 'The art of memory', *Comparative Studies in Society and History* 20 (1978), 485–516.

al-Fārūqī, L., 'Tartīl al-Qur'ān al-karīm', in K. Ahmad and Z. I. Ansari (eds.), *Islamic perspectives: Studies in honour of Mawlānā Sayyid Abul A'lā Mawdūdī*, Leicester: Islamic Foundation, 1979, pp. 106–7.

Gade, A. M., *Perfection makes practice: Learning, emotion and the recited Qur'ān in Indonesia*, Honolulu: University of Hawai'i Press, 2004.

Goldziher, I., *Die Richtungen der islamischen Koranauslegung*, repr. ed., Leiden: Brill, 1952, 1920[1].

Graham, W., *Beyond the written word: Oral aspects of scripture in the history of religion*, Cambridge: Cambridge University Press, 1987.

Grotzfeld, H., 'Der Begriff der Unnachahmlichkeit des Korans in seiner Entstehung und Fortbildung', *Archiv für Begriffsgeschichte* 13 (1969), 58–72.

Heinrichs, W., 'Literary theory: The problem of its efficiency', in G. von Grunebaum (ed.), *Arabic poetry: Theory and development*, Wiesbaden: Harrassowitz, 1973, pp. 28–69.

Ibn al-Jazarī, Shams al-Dīn Abū l-Khayr Muḥammad b. Muḥammad, *Ghāyat al-nihāya fī ṭabaqāt al-qurrā'*, ed. G. Bergsträsser and O. Pretzl, 3 vols. in 2, Cairo: Maktabat al-Khānjī, 1932–5.

al-Nashr fī l-qirā'āt al-'ashr, ed. *'A. M. al-Dabbā,'* Cairo: Maṭba'at Muṣṭafā Muḥammad, n.d.

Jomier, J., 'La place du Coran dans la vie quotidienne en Egypte', *Institute des belles lettres arabes* (Tunis) 58 (1952), 131–65.

Juynboll, G. H. A., 'The position of Qur'ān recitation in early Islam', *Journal of Semitic Studies* 19 (1974), 240–51.

Kellermann, A., 'Koranlesung im Maghreb', Ph.D. diss., Freie Universität Berlin, 1996, Microform.

Kermani, N., *Gott ist schön: Das ästhetische Erleben des Koran*, Munich: C. H. Beck, 1999.

Mulder, D., 'The ritual recitation of the Quran', *Nederlands Theologisch Tijschrift* 37 (1983), 247–52.

Nelson, K., *The art of reciting the Qur'ān*, Austin, TX: University of Texas Press, 1985.

Neuwirth, A., 'Das islamische Dogma der "Unnachahmlichkeit des Korans" in literaturwissenschaftlicher Sicht', *Der Islam* 60 (1983), 166–83.

'Vom Rezitationstext über die Liturgie zum Kanon: Zu Entstehung und Wiederauflösung der Surenkomposition im Verlauf der Entwicklung eines islamischen Kultus', in S. Wild (ed.), *The Qur'ān as text*, Leiden: Brill, 1996, pp. 69–105.

Padwick, C., *Muslim devotions*, London: SPCK, 1961.

Piamenta, M., *Islam in everyday Arabic speech*, Leiden: Brill, 1979.

Radscheit, M., *Die koranische Herausforderung: Die Taḥaddī-Verse im Rahmen der Polemikpassagen des Korans*, Berlin: Klaus Schwarz, 1996.

Rasmussen, A., 'The Qur'ān in Indonesian daily life: The public project of musical oratory', *Ethnomusicology* 45 (2001), 30–57.

al-Sa'īd, L., *al-Jam' al-ṣawtī l-awwal lil-Qur'ān al-karīm aw al-muṣḥaf al-murattal*, Cairo: Dār al-Kātib al-'Arabī, 1967; Eng. trans. B. Weiss, M. A. Rauf and M. Berger, *The recited Koran*, Princeton: Darwin Press, 1975.

al-Taghannī bi-l-Qur'ān, Cairo: al-Hay'a al-ʿĀmma lil-Ta'līf wa-l-Nashr, 1390/1970; Eng. trans. *The recited Koran*, trans. and ed. B. Weiss et al., Princeton: Darwin Press, 1975.
Santerre, R., *Pédagogie musulmane d'Afrique noire*, Montreal: Presses de l'Université de Montréal, 1973.
Shiloah, A., 'L'Islam et la musique', in J. Porte (ed.), *Encyclopédie des musiques sacrées*, 4 vols., Paris: Editions Labergerie, 1968–70, vol. I, p. 418.
Talbi, M., 'La qirā'a bi-l-alḥān', *Arabica* 5 (1958), 183–90.
Touma, H. H., 'Die Koranrezitation: Eine Form der religiösen Musik der Araber', *Baessler-Archiv* 23 (1975), 87–120.
Zwettler, M., 'A mantic manifesto', in J. Kugel (ed.), *Poetry and prophecy*, Ithaca, NY: Cornell University Press, 1991, pp. 75–120.

Part III

Transmission and dissemination

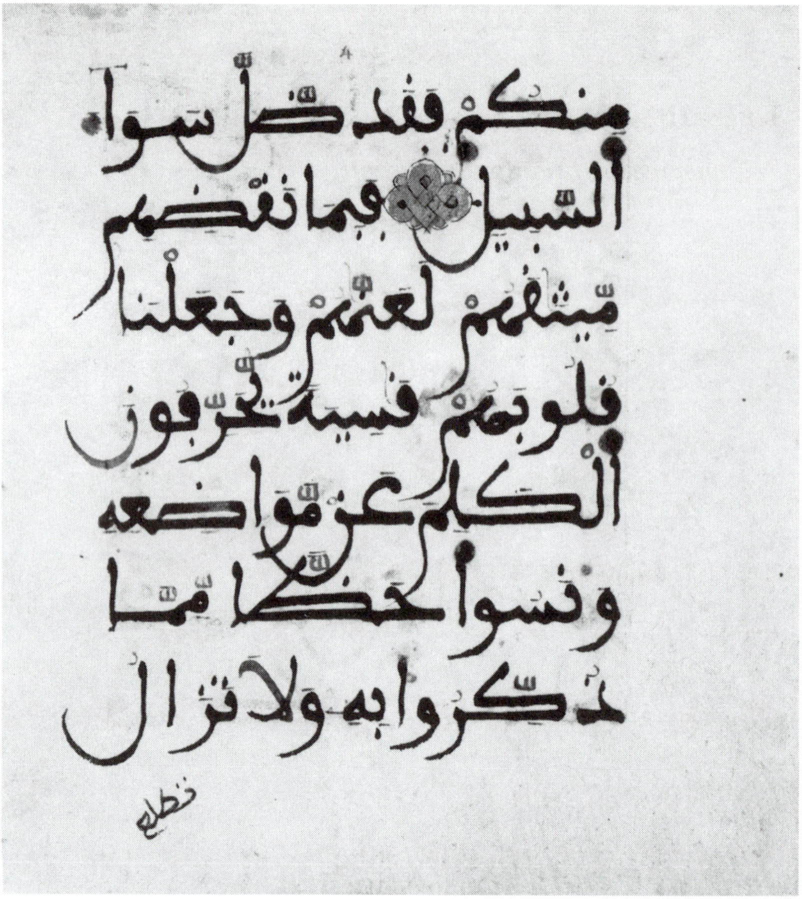
منكم فقد ضل سوا
السبيل فبما نقضهم
ميثقهم لعنهم وجعلنا
قلوبهم قسية يحرفون
الكلم عن مواضعه
ونسوا حظا مما
ذكروا به ولا تزال

Fig. 7 Detached folio from a thirteenth-century north African Qur'ān, containing a portion of Q 5:12–13 (F1929.69b). Courtesy of the Freer Gallery of Art and the Arthur M. Sackler Gallery, Washington, DC

7 From palm leaves to the Internet

FRED LEEMHUIS

From its beginnings the Qur'ān was first and foremost an oral text. When the prophet Muḥammad received a revelation, he spoke or recited the revealed text. It is not clear how long these original, spoken units of revelation were, or whether their length was variant or invariant. The relation between these spoken units and qur'ānic sūras is also unknown. According to the Islamic tradition, however, the revelation of the different sūras followed a chronology of roughly shorter to longer. The earlier ones were rather short and they tended to become longer as Muḥammad's mission and prophetic preaching continued.

CODIFICATION AND RECITATION

In addition to being memorised and transmitted orally, these revealed texts were written down during the life of Muḥammad, a process that probably began at an early stage. At least, that is what reports about the collection of the Qur'ān after the Prophet's death relate. The commission under Zayd b. Thābit (d. 32/652–3), which provided the edition of the qur'ānic text that subsequently became known as the ʿUthmānic codex, based its work on oral material, and on all kinds of written material, such as texts on scraps of wood, palm leaves, bark and bones. Zayd himself is said to have been ordered by Muḥammad to record verses of the Qur'ān on the shoulder blade of a camel immediately after a revelation. An older Companion of Muḥammad, ʿAbdallāh b. Masʿūd, is reported to have said that he had already written down seventy sūras from the mouth of the Prophet when Zayd was still playing with other little boys.

Although the reports about the collection of the Qur'ān are conflicting, it appears that soon after the death of Muḥammad one or more *muṣḥaf*s or codices of the Qur'ān existed. These were manuscript books of which the individual leaves were collected between two boards. Although some old manuscript scrolls of the Qur'ān – originally from the Umayyad mosque of Damascus but now housed in Istanbul[1] – are known, it is chiefly in the conventional book form that the written text of the Qur'ān was recorded and propagated. Only in modern times has the written text of the Qur'ān become available in new formats like the CD-ROM and various online versions.

From the beginning of its codification, the oral tradition about how the Qur'ān was to be recited played an important part. This may have been for theological reasons, but also for compelling practical reasons. The old Arabic script did not notate vowels and it distinguished only eighteen different characters, whereas the full alphabet has twenty-eight consonants. It should be borne in mind that this limitation applies to all the early graphic representations of the text of the Qur'ān, the ʿUthmānic redaction, as well as alternative redactions, like Ibn Masʿūd's. In general, this would not have been a serious problem as long as a written text was used as a kind of aide-memoire to reproduce the contents of a text, be it a message or a poem. In the case of the Qur'ān, however, this became a problem, because its text was not only meant to be read for its contents, its meaning, but also to be accurately reproduced in liturgical recitation. That mandate was complicated by the fact that there was not only one common form of Arabic in which the Qur'ān could be read and recited. Although precise knowledge of the elevated style of Arabic in the early period of Islam is unclear, it is certain that there were different accents and pronunciations. A case in point is the word for a written copy of the Qur'ān. The pronunciations *muṣḥaf, miṣḥaf* and *maṣḥaf* are all recorded.

Exactly what the earliest copies of the Qur'ān looked like is hard to say, because there is no agreement among specialist scholars about the dating of early Qur'ān manuscripts. A fairly large number of early manuscript fragments, many of them quite extensive, are known. There have been many attempts to date these, mainly on the basis of palaeographical evidence or with respect to the development of their decoration. Thus a few qur'ānic manuscripts have been attributed by some specialists to the seventh century, but as yet no extant manuscript has been unequivocally dated to a period before the ninth century on the basis of firm external evidence. Such external evidence would provide a powerful argument in the controversy that exists in Western scholarship about when the codification of the Qur'ān took place, whether this was at the beginning of Islamic history, as postulated by the traditional view, or about two centuries later, according to John Wansbrough's hypothesis.

EARLY QUR'ĀN MANUSCRIPTS

The past decades have witnessed ever-increasing work on the earliest manuscripts of the Qur'ān and there is an emerging consensus on a rough, relative chronology of these first qur'ānic manuscripts. The significant quantity of early qur'ānic fragments that were discovered in 1973 in a cache of manuscripts under the roof of the Great Mosque of Ṣanʿāʾ in Yemen has certainly furthered the art-historical analysis. An important feature, the transitions between sūras, is regarded as perhaps a more convincing marker of their antiquity than palaeographic arguments. These transitions evolved from rather simple markings of sūra endings to ever more elaborate and colourful headings, which included the names of the sūras and other data such as the number of verses. Also different types of codices could be distinguished, with their own peculiarities of script, sūra headings, verse markings, etc. Of two such groups that were identified by Estelle Whelan, it appears that a rather large, vertical format without features such as sūra titles, liturgical and verse-group markings, can be associated with the earlier strata of qur'ānic manuscripts.[2]

The style or styles of the script used for these early manuscripts seems to have been or to have become more or less specific for manuscripts of the Qur'ān and appears to be different both from the more cursive styles that are known from early papyri and from the lapidary ones that were used in most inscriptions incised in stone. In this early qur'ānic style of writing additional signs were introduced to distinguish characters that were used for more than one consonant. Little dashes or dots were added above or under the letters to identify them. The system that is found in the early qur'ānic manuscripts is basically the same as the one still in use, except for the treatment of the two letters *fā'* and *qāf*, which have the same initial and medial form. For some time three methods existed: (1) one dash above for the *fā'* and two for the *qāf*; (2) one dash underneath for the *fā'* and one above for the *qāf*; and (3) one dash above for the *fā'* and one underneath for the *qāf*. The first method has become the standard for eastern styles of Arabic and for its printed forms. The second became the norm in the Arab west and can still be found in lithographed editions of the Qur'ān in use in the Maghrib.

The third method did not survive and probably was followed for only a short time, possibly in the Ḥijāz and Yemen. It is, however, significant because it was also used in the inscriptions in the Dome of the Rock in Jerusalem. The mosaic inscriptions in the Dome of the Rock, which consist mainly of qur'ānic quotations, quite clearly imitate a style of writing that is very close to the style we know from early qur'ānic manuscripts. Where *fā'* and *qāf* are punctuated, they have their dashes exactly according to this third method. This external evidence leads to the conclusion that early Qur'ān manuscripts with the same method of punctuation date roughly from the same short period, i.e., from around 692 CE when the Dome of the Rock was built.

To date, I am aware of only four manuscripts in which this method is adopted. They are preserved in Istanbul (Saray, Medina 1a[3]), Ṣanʿā' (Dār al-Makhṭūṭāt, Inv. No. 01–29.2[4]), St Petersburg (Inv. No. E-20[5]) and Vienna (Fig. 5; Cod. Mixt. 917[6]). Two of these manuscripts are fairly long; of the Viennese codex 104 leaves are extant, and of the St Petersburg one, 81 leaves. As all early qur'ānic manuscripts appear to do, these two manuscripts also represent the ʿUthmānic redaction. This suggests that the ʿUthmānic redaction already enjoyed a degree of acceptance at that early period. The redaction of Ibn Masʿūd, which had probably been a rival of the ʿUthmānic redaction only in Iraq, disappeared after Ibn Mujāhid's proposal at the beginning of the fourth/tenth century that only seven ways of reciting the Qur'ān were to be accepted. As far as is known, no manuscript containing Ibn Masʿūd's redaction has been preserved, although there are some early manuscripts – for example, some among those discovered in the Great Mosque of Ṣanʿā' – that partially agree with the different order of the sūras that Ibn Masʿūd's codex is reputed to have had.[7]

In addition to signs that distinguish letters used for more than one consonant, vowel signs were also introduced. Initially, coloured dots were employed to indicate *a*, *i* and *u*, respectively, by putting the dot above, under or after the consonant with which they were to be pronounced. It is not clear whether the introduction of these vowel signs happened at about the same time as the distinction of consonants. There are manuscripts without vowel signs, but with consonant punctuation, but the opposite is also true. Interestingly, in quite a few early manuscripts different possible readings are indicated by dots of different colour. Most of these alternative readings appear to conform to readings that were later acknowledged as readings fit for recitation, but readings which later became known as *shadhdh*, 'solitary, isolated', i.e., not validated by a sufficient number of authoritative transmission chains, also appear.[8] Besides vowel signs, *ālif*s were added, usually in red, to make up for a consonantal skeleton that did not denote a long *a* as well as signs to indicate the pronunciation of a glottal stop where the Meccan pronunciation would not have had one, but where they were required according to a more normative pronunciation of Arabic.

READING TRADITIONS

In the beginning of the tenth century, readings which were based on the ʿUthmānic redaction finally eclipsed the alternative redaction of Ibn Masʿūd. This was largely due to the activities of Ibn Mujāhid (244–324/859–936) whose view on the admissibility of variant readings was enforced by the ʿAbbāsid authorities. An opponent of Ibn Mujāhid, Ibn Shanabūdh, who in public worship had confidently recited readings of Ibn Masʿūd and other early reciters that were not in accordance with the ʿUthmānic redaction, was brought to trial and punished with flogging, whereupon he recanted his defence of the non-ʿUthmānic readings. From then on the codified text in the form of the ʿUthmānic redaction was *de facto* the primary text and the only one admissible for reciting the Qurʾān. In other words, the written text of the Qurʾān became more than an aide-memoire for its recitation; it became the official score for the performance of its recitation. This did not mean that only one way of reciting the Qurʾān was accepted. Ibn Mujāhid approved of seven systems of reciting the Qurʾān that were based on the ʿUthmānic text. These seven systems of reading were allowed in recitation because Ibn Mujāhid considered them authoritatively transmitted and broadly authenticated. At the same time, he took care to identify these seven reading systems with the transmitted readings of famous readers who had lived in the second Islamic century and who were associated with the places that had received the first five copies of the ʿUthmānic codex: from Medina, Nāfiʿ b. ʿAbd al-Raḥmān (d. 169/785); from Mecca, ʿAbdallāh b. Kathīr (d. 120/738); from Kūfa, ʿĀṣim b. Abī l-Najūd (d. 127/745), Ḥamza b. Ḥabīb al-Zayyāt (d. 156/773) and ʿAlī b. Ḥamza al-Kisāʾī (d. 189/805); from Baṣra, Abū ʿAmr b. al-ʿAlāʾ (d. 154/770); and from Damascus, ʿAbdallāh b. ʿĀmir (d. 118/736).

In the course of time, three additional systems of reading also became widely accepted because they too were considered to satisfy Ibn Mujāhid's criteria. Less widely accepted, but still enjoying some authority are another four systems, each of which, however, could be viewed as a subset of one of the other ten. These systems of reciting the Qurʾān became known as the 'readings of the seven', of the 'three after the seven' and the 'four after the ten'. The knowledge of the other ways of reading the Qurʾān did not disappear. They were not allowed in recitation of the Qurʾān, but they survived in specialists' works, especially when these readings had a bearing on the meaning of the text of the Qur'ān. Ibn Mujāhid himself is reported to have composed a large work about these so-called *shadhdh*-readings, but it has not survived.

After Ibn Mujāhid's intervention, a copy of the Qur'ān would normally render one of the accepted readings. Increasingly, copies of the Qur'ān were produced with complete punctuation and full vocalisation. Additional signs were created to record the chosen reading as precisely as possible and to prescribe how it should be recited. Besides vowel signs, a whole range of signs was developed to indicate doubling of consonants, nasal pronunciation of case endings, prolonged pronunciation of vowels and where it was permissible to pause in reciting, where it was not and where it was obligatory. The development of signs to indicate peculiarities of the recitation actually continues today. For example, a recent edition of the Qur'ān published in Syria indicates vowels subject to prolongation by printing the letters in different colours. Other specifics of Qur'ān reciting, such as words where the vowel *a* should be pronounced more like an *e*, were not, however, indicated by signs. Although copies of the Qur'ān increasingly acquired the characteristics of a full musical score, the oral tradition remained important for teaching the finer points of recitation.

Not much can be said with certainty about the actual utilisation of the different readings and whether most of them had anything more than theoretical significance. At first, most readings appear to have been favoured by the regions where they originated, and more is known about some regions than others. In north-west Africa, Ḥamza's reading was supplanted by Nāfiʿ's which was also the favoured reading in Muslim Spain. Nowadays, the most widespread reading in west and north Africa, except Egypt, is Warsh's transmission of Nāfiʿ. In Libya and in parts of Tunisia and Algeria, Qālūn's transmission of Nāfiʿ also has some following. In Egypt the reading of Nāfiʿ according to Warsh's transmission was equally well spread until about the sixteenth century, but also the reading of Abū ʿAmr was not unknown. For example, the famous Qur'ān commentary *al-Jalālayn* by Jalāl al-Dīn al-Maḥallī (d. 864/1459) and Jalāl al-Dīn al-Suyūṭī (d. 911/1505) follows this reading. The reading of Abū ʿAmr is said to have been dominant in the Ḥijāz, Syria and Yemen from the eleventh century when it superseded Ibn ʿĀmir's until it, in turn, was superseded by Ḥafṣ on the authority of ʿĀṣim. Yet Ibn ʿĀmir's reading is still reported to be followed in some parts of Yemen. Nowadays one of the Abū ʿAmr readings appears to be used in parts of west Africa, Sudan, Somalia and Haḍramawt. Specific data are not really known, however, because almost no research has been done to establish the distribution in time and space of the different readings that can be found in the enormous mass of historical Qur'ān manuscripts of a known origin.

A preliminary investigation of a group of manuscript fragments found in the ruins of Ḍawrān Anis suggests that the historical situation was not so clear that sweeping statements about readings favoured by certain regions can be sustained. This little town about 60 kilometres south of Ṣan'ā' was destroyed in the earthquake of 1983 and the manuscripts were found in the ruined mosque.[9] The manuscripts all appear to be late, probably from later than the sixteenth century. Among them, three have the reading of Nāfi', one Ḥamza's, one 'Āṣim's and one is perhaps a mixture of two readings.[10]

Some not yet published leaves of a Qur'ān manuscript that were found during emergency excavations in the little town of al-Qaṣr in the Dakhla oasis in the western desert of Egypt show an interesting, and apparently eclectic, reading. In a number of cases, this manuscript – which generally follows Abū 'Amr – adopts a Meccan[11] reading for the pronunciation of the *hamza* or glottal stop. This manuscript was probably in use before or during the nineteenth century.

The great unifying change came in the sixteenth century with the hegemony of the Ottoman empire which had adopted the transmission of Ḥafṣ from 'Āṣim's reading. In the course of time this reading became the most widespread and has remained so. Only at the fringes of the Ottoman empire or beyond it, as in north-west Africa, have other readings remained in use.

THE QUR'ĀN IN EVERYDAY LIFE

Printing

For a long time after printing had become the normal form of book production in Europe, the Islamic world continued to produce handwritten copies of books. Printing in Arabic had begun in Europe at the beginning of the sixteenth century and the first Qur'ān was printed in Venice in 1537 CE, but apparently this was not a great success. In 1694 Abraham Hinckelmann in Hamburg published a complete edition of the Qur'ān in Arabic. Later, Russian editions appeared and in 1834 the first edition of Gustav Flügel's Qur'ān was published, a text used by Western scholars until well into the twentieth century.

In the Islamic world religious motives played their part in the initial aversion to printing, but social motives were probably at least as important. The industrial production of books by manual copying continued to employ a large number of people. In the late fifteenth century the Ottoman sultan forbade Muslims to print texts in Arabic. This prohibition lasted until 1726 when an official press was established. The printing of Qur'āns in the Ottoman empire, however, began only in the second half of the nineteenth century both in Egypt and Istanbul. At about the same time Qur'āns were also printed in India. Some of the early Muslim printings of the Qur'ān were done with movable type, but most were lithographed. Often they were accompanied by the commentary of al-Bayḍāwī (d. prob. 716/1316–17) or that known as *al-Jalālayn*. The advantage of these lithographed editions was not only that they had the look and feel of manuscripts, but also that all the special recitational signs that had been developed could be included. Apart from the fact that the Flügel Qur'ān did not reproduce the readings dominant in the Ottoman empire, for Muslims its major deficit was the lack of the special signs that had been developed for the Qur'ān text, such as those for nasalisation and pauses.

The Egyptian-government edition of the Qur'ān, which was typeset in Cairo and printed in Gizeh in 1923 and which followed the dominant Ottoman reading of Ḥafṣ' transmission of ʿĀṣim, greatly advanced the spread of this reading, even after the fall of the empire. This text, which was typeset from a movable typeface for which a number of special signs were developed, adhered to both the written and the oral tradition and could rightly be acclaimed as a scholarly achievement, a fact that was acknowledged by some of the leading non-Muslim, European Qur'ān scholars, such as Gothelf Bergsträsser.[12] Until the present day, this text has been reprinted and copied numerous times in the whole Islamic world and nearly everywhere it has more or less eclipsed other readings. The only exception is north-west Africa, where the Nāfiʿ reading, available in printed form according to both of its transmissions, has been embedded strongly enough to resist being supplanted.

Sound media

Today, of course, the oral tradition is surviving in a totally different way, because it can be captured on a sound-recording medium. This started in the 1920s with recordings of Qur'ān recitation on gramophone records. The first complete recording of the Qur'ān in the *murattal*, or formal, recitation style according to both the Ḥafṣ transmission of ʿĀṣim and the Warsh transmission of Nāfiʿ was executed in the 1960s by the Egyptian *shaykh* of Qur'ān readers Maḥmūd Khalīl al-Ḥuṣarī (d. 1980). Since then, numerous recitations of the Qur'ān have become available, especially on audiocassettes and compact discs. By far the majority of these recordings follow the reading of the Ḥafṣ transmission of ʿĀṣim, but recitations according to the readings of both transmissions of Nāfiʿ and of both transmissions of Abū ʿAmr also exist. In addition to their transmission on general radio and television stations, Qurʾān recitations are also broadcast on special radio stations, like the Egyptian *Idhāʿat al-Qurʾān al-karīm*, which started in 1964. And now there is, of course, the Internet which offers an enormous number of sites dealing with things Islamic and qurʾānic.[13] Many sites offer a searchable text of the Qurʾān, various translations, recitations in different styles (and from a growing number of reciters) and even courses on how to recite.[14] This contemporary development is reviving the diversity of what is essentially an oral tradition.

Epigraphy

Apart from its manifestation as a recited text, the Qurʾān in its written form figured largely in Muslim society from a very early time and it still does. Many copies of the holy text were produced in a remarkable variety of formats. Paper and parchment were used in this production but other materials as well. Passages from the Qurʾān of varying lengths were also written or inscribed on a variety of media. The Dome of the Rock in Jerusalem is probably the earliest example of a religious building with extensive quotations from the Qurʾān and, interestingly, it clearly shows that the inscription is the monumental imitation of an early qurʾānic script. As such, it set an example for many Islamic buildings and monuments. Somewhat later, between 87/706 and 91/710, the Mosque of the Prophet in Medina was reconstructed and provided with a long qurʾānic inscription, possibly containing the whole text of the Qurʾān.[15] In the history of Islam all kinds of buildings, religious or otherwise, have been adorned with qurʾānic quotations, usually in a script that derives from a book script, be it the angular Kūfic or the cursive styles like *naskhī* or *thuluth*.

Amulets and talismanic uses

The text of the Qurʾān was also considered to have potent magical qualities. Especially the two last sūras, known as *al-muʿawwidhatān*, 'the two sūras of taking refuge', have, since the time of the Prophet, been used as incantations and protective formulas to avert evil influences or bad luck. Although they may be pronounced aloud in appropriate situations, like other formulas they were (and still are) ordinarily written on pieces of paper to be worn as amulets. Such amulets could even take the form of complete garments, e.g., for warriors to wear below their armour for superior protection. A special characteristic of this use of written text from the Qur'ān is that these apotropaic texts are often written with unconnected letters.

TRANSLATIONS OF THE QUR'ĀN

The Qur'ān is an Arabic text and from a very early period the question was asked: How should the Qur'ān, God's revelation in Arabic to the 'seal of the prophets', be made known to those who did not understand it? In the early days of Islam some Arab Muslims held the opinion that this most recent version of God's revelation was addressed only to them, the Arabs. They did not mean that non-Arabs need not take notice of God's message. Rather, these groups were to observe the uncorrupted version of the revelations that had been directed to them. Of course, this view was based on the Qur'ān itself, on passages like Q 14:4: 'We have sent no messenger save with the tongue of his people, that he might make all clear to them.' Q 5:44–8, as part of one of the last sūras to be revealed, appeared to suggest the same; it could be taken to mean that Jews and Christians had to adhere to the uncorrupted Torah and Gospel, respectively.

If they just did that, they could, according to some early authorities, even be called Muslims. This view is expressed in two traditions which go back to Mujāhid (d. 104/722) and which are mentioned in al-Ṭabarī's (d. 310/923) commentary on Q 5:66, where the Qur'ān says about the People of the Book: 'Among them there are people who are moderate, but many of them are of evil conduct.'[16] In interpreting the expression 'people who are moderate' these two traditions state: 'these are the Muslims of the People of the Book'. One of the two traditions defines them as those who say that Jesus is God's servant and his spirit and who do not claim that he is God or the son of God.

Nevertheless, the idea that the message of God that was given to Muḥammad was intended for the whole of humankind became generally accepted. Many qur'ānic passages were considered to have a universal scope, especially passages like Q 7:158: 'Say [O Muḥammad]: "O humankind, I am the messenger of God to you all"' and Q 14:52: 'This is a message to be delivered to humankind.'

Even at the beginning of the fifth/eleventh century, however, this kind of exegesis was not entirely self-evident as is demonstrated by its discussion in the important theological compendium of the great Muʿtazilī thinker ʿAbd al-Jabbār al-Hamadhānī (d. 415/1025). He felt it necessary to remonstrate against the view that if Muḥammad had been sent to all humanity, he should have addressed them all in their own languages.[17]

Qur'ān translations within the Islamic world

The question, however, remained. How should non-Arabs become acquainted with the message of the Qur'ān? There are two reasons why a wholly satisfactory solution was not found. In the first place, the doctrine of the inimitability of the Qur'ān was, from an early period, coupled with a belief in the singular qualities of Arabic. The Qur'ān was thought to demonstrate and employ all the superior peculiarities of the Arabic language and thus it could not be rendered into another language, as the Gospel had been rendered from Syriac into Ethiopic and Latin, and as the Torah and the Psalms had been rendered into Arabic. An accurate rendering was thought to be impossible because it was believed that non-Arabic languages did not have at their disposal such extensive possibilities for the use of figurative language.[18]

In the second place, the Arabic word for 'translation' (*tarjama*) apparently meant a literal translation. If one were able to make a literal translation of the Qur'ān, a translation that manifested all the subtleties of the original Arabic text, then the miracle of the Qur'ān would be equalled. This was impossible because the Qur'ān declares, for instance in Q 17:88: 'Say: "If humans and jinn banded together to produce the like of this Qur'ān, they would never produce its like, even though they backed one another."' It could not be done and thus it should not be done.

Of course, practical solutions were found and over the centuries many translations of the Qur'ān have been made by both Muslims and non-Muslims. If a translation could be considered a kind of commentary, 'an exegesis' in another language that was not meant to replicate the original text, but was only to aid understanding, then it was permitted.

The whole discussion about the admissibility of translating the Qur'ān flared up again in the second decade of the twentieth century, because the Turkish leader Atatürk wanted to nationalise Islam in Turkey. Nationalisation in this respect meant 'turcification': the text of the ritual prayer, the *ṣalāt*, had to be pronounced in Turkish and translations of the Qur'ān in Turkish were to replace the original text. The challenge was taken up mainly by Egyptian Muslim leaders and old arguments were dug up and repeated but with different emphases. The classical position was asserted by Muḥammad al-Zurqānī (d. 1122/1710). In the 1943 edition of his handbook for students at al-Azhar, a long section is devoted to the problem.[19] He concluded that a translation of the Qur'ān in the sense of a rendering of all its meanings and intentions is impossible and should not be attempted. In his view it does not matter whether it claims to be a literal or an explanatory translation. A translator may not aspire to produce the equivalent of the Qur'ān in another language, but only the equivalent of a *tafsīr* of the Qur'ān in another language. As such it is not a translation of the Qur'ān, but a translation of a *tafsīr* of the Qur'ān and that is acceptable because it is not meant to be a substitution for the original text.

Al-Zurqānī was reacting to the more inflexible view taken by Muḥammad Rashīd Riḍā (d. 1935) in the *Tafsīr al-Manār.* In connection with Q 7:158 Rashīd Riḍā had stated that the language of Islam should be Arabic and that, accordingly, the Turkish government must decide that the Qur'ān is untranslatable. The message of Islam could and might be rendered in another language for missionary purposes, but at the same time, Arabic should be compulsory in all schools of the Muslims in order to reinstate the unity of Islam. For Muḥammad Rashīd Riḍā, translation meant only a literal translation, which he considered always to be wrong because it was impossible and thus forbidden. He did not consider a 'translation pertaining to meaning' (*tarjama maʿnawī*) to be forbidden.

In the end, the view of authoritative scholars like Muḥammad Muṣṭafā al-Marāghī (d. 1945) and Maḥmūd Shaltūt (d. 1963), both of whom had been *shaykh al-Azhar,* won the day. They considered it unrealistic to expect that the vast majority of Muslims had to learn Arabic in order to understand the Qur'ān and thus acknowledged the appropriateness of translations of the Qur'ān. Although a translation of the Qur'ān is not the Qur'ān and cannot be the Qur'ān, this did not mean, as Maḥmūd Shaltūt stated, 'that the translation of the Qur'ān, in the sense of an enunciation into a language other than Arabic of its meanings and of the morals and guidance that it contains, should be forbidden. On the contrary, it could, in our view, perhaps even be a necessary means to spread the dogmas, the morals and the precepts that it contains.'[20]

The present view of mainstream Islam appears to be in agreement with these principles. At most, we find that in non-Arabic Muslim countries there is a tendency to be somewhat less strict about the rule that the Arabic text should be printed alongside the translation. There seems to be no disagreement, however, about the rule that a translation can never be a source of legislation. Finally, only the Ḥanafīs allow the text of the Fātiḥa, the first sūra of the Qur'ān, to be recited in a language other than Arabic.

Non-Muslim translations of the Qur'ān

If Muslim translators have been concerned about rendering the message of the Qur'ān for those who do not master Arabic, the concern of non-Muslim translators of the Qur'ān has been different. The first Latin translation was commissioned by Peter the Venerable in the twelfth century and a number of early west European translations seem to be derived from it. They all appear to serve the purpose of facilitating its refutation. Later on, and especially after the publication of the Dutch scholar Adrian Reland's famous book, *De Religione Mohammedica,* in 1705, other motives came into play. From that time on, according to the German scholar Rudi Paret who published his own translation of the Qur'ān in 1962, serious European scholars aimed at 'tracing back the individual qur'ānic utterances of Muḥammad to specific historical situations and from these to understand them in their entire liveliness and actuality'.[21] In this vein most European Arabists have studied and translated the Qur'ān in order to reconstruct the genesis and development of the religious concepts of what Paret called 'the astonishing and, at the same time, the respect- and awe-commanding phenomenon of a religious genius'.[22] It is from that perspective that the translations of scholars like Bell, Blachère, Kramers and Paret should be viewed.

Scholars in the European philological tradition generally set great store by the philological insights of the Muslim commentaries, but attached much less value to later dogmatic developments. Thus, many of these translations fail to convey what, in the minds and hearts of Muslims, the Qur'ān means as holy scripture. It is nevertheless interesting that in the later European Arabist tradition someone like the great August Fischer felt bound to remark in 1937 that it had been wrong not to take the 'indigenous Qur'ān commentaries' sufficiently into account. He believed that European scholarship could not dispense with them, notwithstanding their shortcomings. Even more interesting is his view that 'one will never be able to understand the Qur'ān in all its details with certainty',[23] a view that could have come from the mouth of al-Zurqānī, even if the reasons why this should be so were certainly not the same for both.

Notes

1. S. Ory, 'Un nouveau type de muṣḥaf: Les Corans en rouleaux conservés à Istanbul', *Revue des études islamiques* 33 (1965), 87–149.
2. E. Whelan, 'Writing the word of God: Some early Qur'ān manuscripts and their milieux', *Ars Orientalis* 20 (1990), 113–47.
3. Photograph in G. Bergsträsser and O. Pretzl, *Die Geschichte des Korantexts* (vol. III of Th. Nöldeke, *Geschichte des Qorāns,* new ed., Leipzig: T. Weicher, 1938), fig. 10 (plate VIII).

4. Ṣanʿāʾ, Dār al-Makhṭūṭāt. Photograph and description on p. 105 in H.-C. Graf von Bothmer, 'Vroege Qurʾānmanuscripten, aangetroffen in de Grote Moskee van Sanaʾa, Jemen', in M. B. Piotrovski and John Vrieze (eds.), *Aardse schoonheid, hemelse kunst: Kunst van de islam* (Amsterdam: V + K Publishing, 1999).
5. St Petersburg branch of the Institute of Oriental Studies. Photograph and description on pp. 120–1 in J. A. Petrosjan et al. (eds.), *Von Bagdad bis Isfahan: Buchmalerei und Schriftkunst des Vorderen Orients (8.–18. Jh) aus dem Institut für Orientalistik, St Petersburg* (Lugano: ARCH Foundation, 1995).
6. Austrian National Library in Vienna. Photograph on table 1a and description on p. 76 in T. al-Samman and O. Mazal, *Die arabische Welt und Europa: Ausstellung der Handschriften- und Inkunabelsammlung der Österreichischen Nationalbibliothek* (Graz: Akademische Druck- und Verlagsanstalt, 1988).
7. G.-R. Puin, 'Observations on early Qurʾān manuscripts in Ṣanʿāʾ', in S. Wild (ed.), *The Qurʾān as text* (Leiden: Brill, 1996), pp. 110–11.
8. Y. Dutton, 'Red dots, green dots, yellow dots & blue: Some reflections on the vocalisation of early qurʾānic manuscripts', *Journal of Qurʾānic Studies* 1 (1999), 115–40; 2 (2000), 1–24.
9. J. J. Witkam, 'Qurʾān fragments from Ḍawrān (Yemen)', *Manuscripts of the Middle East* 4 (1989), 155–74.
10. The photographs published by Witkam ('Qurʾān fragments') show enough to determine the following six fragments: no. 1, the transmission of Ḥafṣ from ʿĀṣim; no. 7, Qālūn from Nāfiʿ; no. 16, Ḥamza; no. 22, Qālūn from Nāfiʿ; no. 31, Nāfiʿ or Abū Jaʿfar, one of the 'three after the seven'; and no. 32, Qālūn from Nāfiʿ except for one place where the reading of the other six is followed.
11. Ibn Kathīr of the 'seven' and Ibn Muḥayṣin of the 'four after the ten'.
12. See his 'Plan eines Apparatus Criticus zum Qurʾān', repr. in R. Paret (ed.), *Der Koran* (Darmstadt: Wissenschaftliche Buchgesellschaft, 1975), pp. 389–97.
13. On 5 June 2005 'Koran' gave 6,440,000 Google hits, 'Quran' 3,890,000, 'Qur'an' 1,400,000, and 'Qur'ân' 864,000. At the same time 'Bible' scored 34,800,000 hits.
14. It is not feasible to give a balanced opinion about the usefulness of all Internet sites that deal with the text or translations of the Qurʾān. Nevertheless, the sites mentioned in the bibliography appear to offer material of a good quality and/or useful links. The caveat expressed by A. Rippin in 'The study of tafsīr in the 21st century: E-texts and their scholarly use', *MELA Notes* 69–70, on http://www.lib.umich.edu/area/Near.East/MELANotes6970/tafsir.html about e-texts of qurʾānic commentaries (sing. *tafsīr*), at least in a number of cases holds true for e-texts of the Qurʾān as well.
15. See E. Whelan, 'Forgotten witness: Evidence for the early codification of the Qurʾān', *Journal of the American Oriental Society* 118 (1998), 1–14.
16. Cf. J. D. McAuliffe, *Qurʾānic Christians: An analysis of classical and modern exegesis* (Cambridge: Cambridge University Press, 1991), ch. 6.
17. ʿAbd al-Jabbār al-Hamadhānī, *al-Mughnī fī abwāb al-tawḥīd wa-l-ʿadl*, 14 vols. in 16 (Cairo: Wizārat al-Thaqāfa wa-l-Irshād al-Qawmī, al-Idāra al-ʿĀmma lil-Thaqāfa, 1960), vol. XVI (*Iʿjāz al-Qurʾān*), pp. 424–33.

18. Abū Muḥammad ʿAbdallāh b. Muslim al-Dīnawarī b. Qutayba, *Taʾwīl mushkil al-Qurʾān*, ed. S. A. Ṣaqr (Beirut: Dār al-Kutub al-ʿIlmiyya, 1981^3), p. 21.
19. Muḥammad ʿAbd al-ʿAẓīm al-Zurqānī, *Manāhil al-ʿirfān fī ʿulūm al-Qurʾān*, 2 vols. (Cairo: Dār Iḥyāʾ al-Kutub al-ʿArabiyya, n.d.), vol. II, pp. 107–73.
20. M. Shaltūt, *al-Islām: ʿAqīda wa-sharīʿa* (Cairo: Dār al-Qalam, 1990^{16}), p. 473.
21. R. Paret, 'Besprechung von: Arthur J. Arberry, *The Koran interpreted* (London 1955)', in Paret (ed.), *Der Koran*, p. 29.
22. Ibid.
23. A. Fischer, 'Der Wert der vorhandenen Koran-übersetzungen und Sure 111', in Paret (ed.), *Der Koran*, pp. 8–9.

Further reading

ʿAbd al-Jabbār al-Hamadhānī, *al-Mughnī fī abwāb al-tawḥīd wa-l-ʿadl*, 14 vols. in 16, Cairo: Wizārat al-Thaqāfa wa-l-Irshād al-Qawmī, al-Idāra al-ʿĀmma lil-Thaqāfa, 1960 (vol. XVI, *Iʿjāz al-Qurʾān*).

Abou Sheishaa, M., *The translation of the Qurʾān: A selective bibliography*, on http://www.quran.org.uk/ieb_quran_bibliography.html.

Bergsträsser, G., 'Plan eines Apparatus criticus zum Koran', repr. in R. Paret (ed.), *Der Koran*, Darmstadt: Wissenschaftliche Buchgesellschaft, 1975, pp. 389–97.

Bergsträsser, G. and O. Pretzl, *Die Geschichte des Korantexts*, new ed., Leipzig: T. Weicher, 1938 (vol. III of Th. Nöldeke, *Geschichte des Qorāns*, new ed., 3 vols. in 2, Leipzig: T. Weicher, 1938).

von Bothmer, H.-C. Graf, 'Vroege Qurʾānmanuscripten, aangetroffen in de Grote Moskee van Sanaʾa, Jemen', in M. B. Piotrovski and John Vrieze (eds.), *Aardse schoonheid, hemelse kunst: Kunst van de islam*, Amsterdam: V + K Publishing, 1999, pp. 98–105.

Dutton, Y., 'Red dots, green dots, yellow dots & blue: Some reflections on the vocalisation of early qurʾanic manuscripts', *Journal of Qurʾānic Studies* 1 (1999), 115–40; 2 (2000), 1–24.

Fischer, A., 'Der Wert der vorhandenen Koran-übersetzungen und Sure 111', in R. Paret (ed.), *Der Koran*, Darmstadt: Wissenschaftliche Buchgesellschaft, 1975, pp. 3–10.

Ibn Qutayba, Abū Muḥammad ʿAbdallāh b. Muslim al-Dīnawarī, *Taʾwīl mushkil al-Qurʾān*, ed. S. A. Ṣaqr, Beirut: Dār al-Kutub al-ʿIlmiyya, 1981^3, p. 21.

İhsanoğlu, E. (ed.), *World bibliography of translations of the holy Qurʾān in manuscript form*, Istanbul: Research Centre for Islamic History, Art and Culture, 2000.

World bibliography of translations of the meanings of the holy Qurʾān: Printed translations, 1515–1980, Istanbul: Research Centre for Islamic History, Art and Culture, 1986.

Kriss, R. and H. Kriss-Heinrich, *Volksglaube im Bereich des Islam.* II. *Amulette, Zauberformeln und Beschwörungen*, Wiesbaden: O. Harrassowitz, 1962.

Leemhuis, F., 'Codices of the Qurʾān', in J. D. McAuliffe (ed.), *Encyclopaedia of the Qurʾān*, 5 vols., Leiden: Brill, 2001–6, vol. I, pp. 347–51.

'Readings of the Qurʾān', in J. D. McAuliffe (ed.), *Encyclopaedia of the Qurʾān*, 5 vols., Leiden: Brill, 2001–6, vol. IV, pp. 353–63.

McAuliffe, J. D., *Qur'ānic Christians: An analysis of classical and modern exegesis*, Cambridge: Cambridge University Press, 1991.

Neuwirth, A., 'Koran: Textgeschichte', in H. Gätje (ed.), *Grundriss der arabischen Philologie. II. Literaturwissenschaft*, Wiesbaden: Reichert, 1987, pp. 106–13.

Ory, S., 'Un nouveau type de muṣḥaf: Les Corans en rouleaux conservés à Istanbul', *Revue des études islamiques* 33 (1965), 87–149.

Paret, R., 'Besprechung von: Arthur J. Arberry, *The Koran interpreted* (London 1955)', in R. Paret (ed.), *Der Koran*, Darmstadt: Wissenschaftliche Buchgesellschaft, 1975, pp. 27–30.

Pearson, J. D., 'Al-Ḳur'ān. 9. Translation of the Ḳur'ān', in *Encyclopaedia of Islam*, new ed., 11 vols., Leiden: Brill, 1979–2002, vol. V, pp. 429–32.

Petrosjan, J. A. et al. (eds.), *Von Bagdad bis Isfahan: Buchmalerei und Schriftkunst des Vorderen Orients (8.-18. Jh) aus dem Institut für Orientalistik, St Petersburg*, Lugano: ARCH Foundation (Art Restoration for Cultural Heritage), 1995.

Puin, G.-R., 'Observations on early Qur'an manuscripts in Ṣan'ā'', in S. Wild (ed.), *The Qur'ān as text*, Leiden: Brill, 1996, pp. 107–11.

Rippin, A., 'The study of tafsīr in the 21st century: E-texts and their scholarly use', *MELA Notes* 69–70, on http://www.lib.umich.edu/area/Near.East/MELANotes6970/tafsir.html.

al-Samman, T. and O. Mazal, *Die arabische Welt und Europa: Ausstellung der Handschriften- und Inkunabelsammlung der Österreichischen Nationalbibliothek*, Graz: Akademische Druck- und Verlagsanstalt, 1988.

Shaltūt, M., *al-Islām: 'Aqīda wa-sharī'a*, Cairo: Dār al-Qalam, 1990^{16}.

Smitshuijzen AbiFares, H., *Arabic typography: A comprehensive sourcebook*, London: Saqi, 2001.

Welch, A. T., 'Al-Ḳur'ān: History of the Ḳur'ān after 632', in *Encyclopaedia of Islam*, new ed., 11 vols., Leiden: Brill, 1979–2002, vol. V, pp. 404–9.

Whelan, E., 'Forgotten witness: Evidence for the early codification of the Qur'ān', *Journal of the American Oriental Society* 118 (1998), 1–14.

'Writing the word of God: Some early Qur'ān manuscripts and their milieux', *Ars Orientalis* 20 (1990), 113–47.

Witkam, J. J., 'Qur'ān fragments from Ḍawrān (Yemen)', *Manuscripts of the Middle East* 4 (1989), 155–74.

al-Zurqānī, Muḥammad 'Abd al-'Aẓīm, *Manāhil al-'irfān fī 'ulūm al-Qur'ān*, 2 vols., Cairo: Dār Iḥyā' al-Kutub al-'Arabiyya, n.d.

Internet sites about qur'ānic matters

www.islamic-awareness.org/Quran/

www.islamicfinder.org/quran/quran.php?lang=englishetext.virginia.edu/Qur'an.html.

www.islamicity.com/mosque/quran/

www.kitabullah.com/

www.quran.org

www.quran.org.uk

www.sacred-texts.com/isl/htq/
www.salamiran.org/Religion/Quran/
www.solidine.com/kb/turkey/Qur'an_quran.htm
www.thesaudi.net/quran/
www.yildun.com/quran.html.

Fig. 8 Section from a fourteenth-century (Mamlūk) Egyptian Qur'ān scroll containing the end of Q 12:64. The border contains repetitions of Q 112 (Sūrat al-Ikhlāṣ) (CBL Is. 1625, detail). Courtesy of the Trustees of the Chester Beatty Library, Dublin

8 Inscriptions in art and architecture

SHEILA BLAIR AND JONATHAN BLOOM

Qur'ānic inscriptions are ubiquitous, found on buildings and objects produced in many media throughout the Islamic lands from the earliest times to the present. The first example of Islamic architecture, the Dome of the Rock built by the Umayyad caliph 'Abd al-Malik (r. 65–86/685–705) in Jerusalem in 72/692, is decorated with a long band of qur'ānic verses. So are many recent buildings, such as the mosque built in 1983 at the King Khaled International Airport north of Riyadh. These qur'ānic inscriptions are, quite naturally, used more frequently in religious settings, especially mosques and their furnishings. But they were not exclusive to such sites, and buildings like the Alhambra Palace in Granada also bear qur'ānic inscriptions deemed suitable for a ceremonial setting. Nevertheless, qur'ānic inscriptions were not commonly found in utilitarian contexts, where the mundane function of the object might compromise the sanctity of the text. Despite their ubiquity, the study of qur'ānic inscriptions is a relatively new field, and this chapter begins with a survey of the subject and its history before turning to the question of how and why patrons and artisans selected specific qur'ānic texts and adapted their form to decorate these myriad objects.

THE STUDY OF QUR'ĀNIC INSCRIPTION

The study of qur'ānic inscriptions began in earnest only in the past half century, as the first scholars who studied Arabic epigraphy at the beginning of the century concentrated on historical inscriptions containing names and dates. This was only natural as many of these scholars were historians who used inscribed objects to verify or flesh out information from written chronicles. Medieval chroniclers themselves did not usually mention qur'ānic inscriptions or give the reasons for selecting a particular text. The few exceptional cases stand out for their rarity, as with the Nilometer (*miqyās*) in Cairo. According to Ibn Khallikān's (d. 681/1282) thirteenth-century biographical dictionary, its engineer is said to have selected appropriate qur'ānic passages to decorate it, and that statement is confirmed by the marble plaques inside the building that are inscribed with numerous qur'ānic verses about God's gift of water and the fecundity it brings (e.g., Q 14:37; 32:27; 16:10–11; 22:63; 25:50; 42:28; 22:5; 50:9), though they are carved in relief and not inset in the marble and tinted with lapis lazuli as described in the text.[1] This medieval description, like the building itself, is singular, and Ibn Khallikān may have felt compelled to explain its uniqueness. Virtually no other such examples are known, perhaps because medieval chroniclers deemed the reasons behind the choices of specific qur'ānic text obvious. Hence, some early scholars even went so far as to dismiss qur'ānic inscriptions as banal or irrelevant, and their study, like the study of expressions of good wishes or supererogatory prayers (*du'a*) commonly inscribed on objects, was typically relegated to the back burner.

Examining the objects themselves, however, shows the importance of qur'ānic inscriptions. They are very common, used more frequently than historical inscriptions. The list compiled by Erica Dodd and Shereen Khairallah in 1981 contains some 4,000 examples culled from architecture, and those mainly from buildings in the central Islamic lands up to Ottoman times.[2] Size, placement and technique also point to the importance of qur'ānic inscriptions. They are often large, sometimes occupying almost the entire surface to be inscribed. They are also placed in the most prominent positions. On architecture, for example, they encircle buildings, surmount entrances, ring the bases of domes and frame *miḥrāb*s. Bands with qur'ānic inscriptions are the exclusive decoration on the *kiswa*, the cloth draping the Ka'ba in Mecca, the holiest spot in Islam. Qur'ānic inscriptions are also executed in more costly techniques. Stone and brick examples are typically sculpted in relief, a more time-consuming (and hence expensive) technique than the incising typically used for less important texts like artisans' signatures. On the *kiswa*, they are embroidered in gold thread. Furthermore, qur'ānic inscriptions are sometimes set off by a different script. In later times, whereas most historical texts were typically written in the round script known as *thuluth*, qur'ānic inscriptions were often written in the angular script commonly called Kūfic. They are sometimes enhanced by different colours or shapes as well.

Several examples prove the rule. The lower shaft of the extraordinary 60-metre minaret of Jām, erected at the end of the sixth/twelfth century in a remote valley in Afghanistan by the Ghūrid ruler Muḥammad b. Sām, is encrusted with the entire Q 19 (Sūrat Maryam, 'Mary'), all 976 words inscribed in relief in interlacing bands of Kūfic script. The wooden frieze with qur'ānic text that runs around the ceiling of the mosque of Ibn Ṭūlūn in

Cairo measures almost 2 kilometres long, a wealth of timber in a forest-less land. The qur'ānic band with the opening verses of Q 57 (Sūrat al-Ḥadīd, 'Iron') around the base of the geodesic dome in the mosque at the King Khaled Airport covers an area of 240 square metres (2,600 sq. ft), with letters measuring over 4 metres (nearly 15 ft) high. It is said to be the largest of its kind ever produced, outdoing the already large inscriptions that had been used in medieval buildings such as the *madrasa* and tomb complex for Sulṭān Ḥasan in Cairo (757–64/1356–62), which has the Light Verse (Q 24:35) inscribed below the *muqarnas* dome over the entrance, Q 48:1–6, the opening verses of Sūrat al-Fatḥ ('Victory') ringing the *qibla īwān*, and the 'Throne Verse' (Q 2:255) encircling the domed tomb. These qur'ānic inscriptions on architecture are so large and prominent that Erica Dodd coined the term 'the image of the word'.[3]

Similar cases can be made for the inscriptions on objects. To take but one example: the large and splendid *minbar* ordered on the 1st of Muḥarram 532/19 September 1137 in Córdoba for the Kutubiyya mosque in Marrakesh. The edge of the stepped frame is inscribed with Q 7:54–61, written in Kūfic script in black wood letters outlined in bone and set against a marquetry ground of tiny wooden tiles. Material and colour heighten legibility. So does the positioning, for when the inscribed panels were attached to the frame, they were tilted slightly forward to better display the broad lower surface on which the letters lie. This qur'ānic inscription is the masterpiece of Almoravid (al-Murābiṭūn) epigraphy and one of the finest from all the western Islamic lands.[4]

Coins also show the importance of qur'ānic inscriptions and the significance of choosing particular ones.[5] The first silver and gold coins issued by Muslims were imitations of those minted earlier in the region, notably the silver dirhams depicting the Sasanian emperor and the Zoroastrian fire altar, and the gold solidi depicting Christ, the cross and the Byzantine emperor. At first Muslims adapted these prototypes, replacing the Pahlavi or Greek inscriptions with Arabic and switching the images to show the current caliph. These experiments in figural iconography were short-lived, and after a brief period of experimentation in the 70s/690s, the Umayyad caliph ʿAbd al-Malik had the various adaptive types replaced by a startlingly new type of purely epigraphic coin. These were decorated mainly with qur'ānic texts that were intended to convey the essence of the community's faith in the same way that images had for earlier rulers. The text on the obverse or front bears a statement about God's uniqueness, stating that there is no god but God alone, without associate, and is surrounded by a marginal inscription with the prophetic mission (Q 9:33) saying that Muḥammad is the messenger of God who sent him with guidance and the religion of truth that he might make it supreme over all other religions, even though polytheists might object. The field on the reverse is inscribed with Q 112 (Sūrat al-Ikhlāṣ, 'Unity': 'Say, "He is God. One, God, the everlasting refuge, who has not begotten and has not been begotten, and no one is equal to him'"), a direct rejection of the Christian Trinity. These epigraphic coins, with their polemical qur'ānic messages, were so successful that this type of coin was issued until the end of the dynasty in 132/750, and the obverse remained standard throughout the ʿAbbāsid period.

In the past half century scholars have begun to recognise the importance of qur'ānic inscriptions in elucidating the meaning and function of objects and buildings. This new interest in the subject can be marked by the 1959 publication of Oleg Grabar's landmark study on the Dome of the Rock, in which he used the 240-metre inscription band on the interior, whose text is drawn heavily from the Qur'ān, as evidence that the building was originally meant to be a symbol of the new faith directed not only to Muslims but also to Jews and especially Christians.[6] He was led to study the inscriptions because other contemporary evidence about the building was lacking: few chronicles survive from the Umayyad period, and those written in ʿAbbāsid times by the Umayyads' successors and rivals presented conflicting evidence that is tainted by an anti-Umayyad bias. His study was significant in showing that qur'ānic texts, previously dismissed as unimportant, might help in placing an object or building – in this case, one of the holiest in Islam – in context.

Grabar's 1959 study was soon followed by others, most of them concentrating on a single important landmark, such as the Dome of the Rock, the Nilometer, the hospital of Nūr al-Dīn in Damascus and the tomb complex of Sulṭān Ḥasan in Cairo.[7] These studies of individual monuments face the problem of generalising from the particular and of isolating the specific from the general (or the forest from the trees). The difficulties inherent in such a methodology are exemplified by Wayne Begley's 1979 study of the Taj Mahal, in which he used the qur'ānic inscriptions as part of his argument to reinterpret the building, traditionally understood as the tomb built by Shāh Jahān for his wife, as a symbolic replica of the heavenly throne of God set above the gardens of paradise.[8] His argument is vitiated by the fact that the qur'ānic inscriptions found on the building, including sūras 36, 48, 67 and 76, are some of the most common in qur'ānic epigraphy. They add little to his speculative and somewhat dogmatic (and to some Muslims even blasphemous) argument, which also overlooks one of the most important features of qur'ānic inscriptions: their multivalent meanings and the different ways that they could be interpreted by different audiences.

To confront this very problem – the relative frequency of any particular qur'ānic text on architecture – Dodd and Khairallah compiled their index of qur'ānic inscriptions on buildings.[9] Volume I contains essays on various buildings. Volume II contains the documentation which includes three lists of qur'ānic inscriptions: a numerical index arranged by number of sūra and verse; a geographical index arranged by country; and a typological index arranged by location within a particular building type (*madrasa*, mausoleum, mosque, etc.). This important work is the first source to consult for anyone studying qur'ānic inscriptions on architecture.[10]

Unfortunately, Dodd and Khairallah's corpus is not without its problems. Its scope is necessarily limited to inscriptions published before that date, mainly those in the *Matériaux pour un Corpus Inscriptionum Arabicarum*, founded by Max van Berchem at the end of the nineteenth century, and the *Répertoire chronologique d'épigraphie arabe*, published since 1931.[11] Dodd and Khairallah's corpus concentrates, therefore, on inscriptions from Egypt and Syria, with few inscriptions from the outlying lands (a mere eight buildings from Afghanistan, three from Morocco). Furthermore, it does not include citations from any works published in Arabic, Persian or Turkish. It is an ambitious beginning, but we still await a more comprehensive treatment of qur'ānic inscriptions on buildings, let alone on any other media, including coins. The need for such studies, and the interest in them, is clear from the recent colloquium, *Word of God, art of man: The Qur'ān and its creative expressions*, held at the Ismaili Centre in London in October 2003, which included a handful of papers that dealt with individual media in a very limited time or place (early Islamic or Fāṭimid numismatics, woodwork from Malaysia and Kaʿba covers from the Ottoman period).[12]

PRINCIPLES OF SELECTION

Even without such hard data as well as comprehensive studies drawn from material found across the Islamic lands over the centuries, it is possible to assess the material at hand to suggest principles that patrons and designers might have used in selecting the many qur'ānic inscriptions found on works of Islamic art and architecture, illustrating each with a few representative examples. It is important to remember that these principles are not exclusive but overlapping, and that just as architects who design a building today are subject to many constraints – including space, money, client and clientele – so too patrons and designers may have had multiple motives in selecting the qur'ānic verses they used.

Space

A first group of considerations is practical, for the text selected had necessarily to fit the surface available. Short sūras that could be written out in their entirety were popular, especially the Fātiḥa (Q 1), which is often considered a prayer, and the poetic ones from the end of the text, notably Q 97, which describes the mystical Night of Power when the revelation descended, and Q 112, the pre-eminent statement of God's oneness.

Longer texts were often shortened. Thus, all thirty-one verses of Q 76 (Sūrat al-Insān, 'Humankind'), describing the two classes of good and evil men, or all twenty-nine verses of Q 48 (Sūrat al-Fatḥ, 'Victory'), describing victory through courage, devotion, faith and patience, are sometimes inscribed on buildings like the Taj Mahal. Similarly, all ninety-eight verses of Q 19 (Sūrat Maryam, 'Mary') encircle the minaret of Jām, but these buildings are exceptional. Far more frequently only the opening verses were used, presumably to stand in synecdoche for the whole. Such shortening is clear from lustre tiles, which were produced in great quantities at Kāshān in central Iran in the thirteenth and early fourteenth centuries.[13] Painted over the glaze with a central design surrounded by an inscribed border, these star- and cross-shaped tiles were fitted together to make dados that, like wallpaper, revetted the interiors of important buildings. Tiles with figural scenes typically are inscribed with Persian poetry; those with floral or animal scenes typically have qur'ānic verses and were used in shrines, mosques, tombs and other religious settings. The 70-centimetre-long band around the rim of these tiles provides space for only a handful of verses, and an analysis of the some 300 star tiles found *in situ* in the mosque at Quhrūd included twenty-seven examples with Q 48:1–3, twenty-four examples with Q 76:1–3 and eleven examples with Q 36:1–6.[14]

Lustre tiles also suggest that bracketing was another method that could be used to contain long qur'ānic texts in short spaces. By using the first and last sūras, one might be said to have written the entire text of the Qur'ān, and these chapters were among the most commonly found at Quhrūd (twenty-four and six examples, respectively). Selective sampling was another way to condense longer texts. The wooden frieze around the mosque of Ibn Ṭūlūn is often said to have included the entire text of the Qur'ān, but this is unlikely and the carvers must have used selected verses to stand for the whole, though it remains to be documented exactly which of the more than 6,200 verses they chose.

Yet another method of fitting qur'ānic texts to available space was conflation, a technique that seems to have been more common in early Islamic times. The first Islamic coins issued from 77/697 bear a conflated statement about God's uniqueness, combining part of Q 37:35 with a phrase from Q 2:163. The long inscription around the Dome of the Rock not only repeats the same conflated statement five times, but also contains other passages using similar techniques such as juxtaposition of disparate passages, shift of person and the occasional addition or omission of brief phrases. Graffiti scratched on the rocks in the Ḥijāz often show similar manipulations of the qur'ānic text.[15] Such variations attest to the oral tradition of using qur'ānic and other familiar texts in persuasive messages and speeches. With the increasing regularisation of the qur'ānic text in the form of canonical readings and, in the twentieth century, standardised and printed editions, such variations have disappeared from the epigraphic record.

The qur'ānic text could also serve as the inspiration for inscriptions which were not strictly qur'ānic but whose texts were drawn from qur'ānic vocabulary or invoked qur'ānic imagery. The ninety-nine beautiful names of God, for example, are not found in a single specific place in the Qur'ān, but lists of them were often compiled and inscribed in tiny script on amulets, particularly those made in later times of semi-precious stones like carnelian or nephrite.[16] Texts on tombstones often invoke the paradisiacal garden (*janna*) or its gate (*mudkhal*), terms that run through the Qur'ān. They represent the deceased as desiring to be reunited with the Prophet (*alḥiqhu bi-nabiyyihi*), a phrase recalling Q 26:83 (*alḥiqnī bi-l-ṣāliḥīn*; 'unite me with the righteous'), or to be instructed in God's proof, a reference to such verses as Q 6:83 ('This is our proof which we bestowed on Abraham') and Q 6:149 ('To God belongs the conclusive proof').

Glorification of the faith

A second principle that underscores the choice of many qur'ānic inscriptions is the general glorification of Islam. This was most easily obtained by citing familiar verses, such that the recognition of a single word might clue the viewer or reader synecdochically to the whole. Such an approach was practical not only with the well-known short sūras at the beginning and end of the text (notably Q 1, 97 and 112), but also with verses so well known that they have acquired their own names. These include the Throne Verse (Q 2:255), probably the most eloquent evocation of God's majesty, inscribed in mosaic on the Umayyad mosque of Damascus, in stucco around the entrance courtyard or Cuarto Dorado at the Alhambra, and in stone over Bāb Zuwayla, the southern gate to the Fāṭimid city of Cairo; the prophetic mission (Q 9:33), found already on the first Islamic coins and common on tombstones erected in Egypt in the ninth century; and the Light Verse (Q 24:35), in which God is extolled as the light of the heavens and the earth, often found on minarets and mosque lamps. Another common verse is Q 3:18, saying that God, his angels and the knowing attest (*shahida*) to his uniqueness, a paraphrase of the *shahāda* (profession of faith), already used on the Dome of the Rock.

Function

Particular verses could also be chosen to suit the specific function of the object on which they were inscribed. The best example is Q 9:18, a declaration that the person to maintain God's mosques is he who believes in God, prays and gives alms, found some four times as frequently as any other qur'ānic inscription on buildings. The reason is clear. It is one of three qur'ānic verses that refer specifically to God's mosques (*masājid Allāh*). Furthermore, it is the only one that refers to the duties of Muslims in them. The other two verses about God's mosques are patently unsuitable: Q 2:114 mentions the unjust forbidding worship in mosques; Q 9:17 refers to polytheists. Hence Q 9:18 became the favourite text to decorate congregational mosques, ranging from the Umayyad Mosque of the Prophet in Medina to the seventeenth-century Ḥīra Masjid in India. But this verse was never limited to mosques alone. It was also common in multi-part complexes, such as the tomb complex for the Mamlūk emirs Sālār and Sanjar in Cairo (703/1303), or spaces that might be considered mosques, such as the Temple Mount (Ḥaram) in Jerusalem.

Parts of buildings were also distinguished by particular texts. Doors might be inscribed with Q 17:80, which asks God to lead with a just ingoing and a just outgoing. This text is found, for example, at the entrance to the stairway in the north minaret added to the mosque of al-Ḥākim in Cairo in 393/1002–3 and over the doorway to the courtyard of a *madrasa* constructed in the same city by the emir Ūzbak al-Yūsufī in 900/1495.

Many *miḥrāb*s are adorned with a verse that includes the word for ritual prayer (*al-ṣalāt*), not surprisingly because the term occurs sixty-seven times in the qur'ānic text. The text most commonly used is Q 17:78, in which the believer is enjoined to perform prayer (*al-ṣalāt*) from the setting of the sun to the darkness of the night as well as the dawn recitation of the Qur'ān, for that action is particularly attested. This verse is found in many far-ranging places, such as the Kisimkazi Mosque (500/1106) in Zanzibar, but it was particularly popular in Iran. It was used not only on plaster *miḥrāb*s installed *in situ*, as at the mosque of Zawāra (561/1156) and the mosque of Warāmīn/Varamin (722/1322), but also on lustre-tile *miḥrāb*s, such as the large and magnificent one made for the Maydān Mosque at Kāshān in 623/1226 and now in the Berlin Museum. Again the choice is not surprising. Q 17:78 is one of only two indisputable instances in the Qur'ān – the other, Q 75:16–18, is not suitable to inscribe on a *miḥrāb* as it refers to moving the tongue – in which the word *qur'ān* functions as a true verbal noun denoting an activity, not an object.[17] This particular verse was chosen because it conveys the verbal force of qur'ānic recitation. The choice of verse, in this case then, highlights not the architecture, but the believer's action that will take place in it.

Objects, particularly those used in a sacred context, could be similarly inscribed with qur'ānic inscriptions related to their function. For example, the *ḥizām* (literally, belt) or inscribed band on the *kiswa* contains Q 3:95–7, a text referring to Abraham's construction of the first house at Mecca. Keys to the Kaʿba are often inscribed with Q 3:96–7, referring to God's house.[18] The text around the rim of the gigantic cauldron for drinking water (*siqāya*) that the warlord Tīmūr donated to the shrine of Aḥmad Yasawī on 20 Shawwāl 801/25 June 1399 opens with Q 9:19 about giving water (*siqāya*) to pilgrims. Seals and amulets were often inscribed with prophylactic verses, including the four that contain the word *shifā'* (healing or cure): Q 10:57, which promises a healing for the diseases in your hearts; Q 16:69, which mentions a drink that is a healing for people; and Q 17:82 and 41:44, which describe the Qur'ān as a mercy and a guide to those who believe. Talismanic shirts worn in battle were frequently inscribed with verses about victory, not only the sūra of victory (Q 48) but also Q 61:13, a verse that promises help from God and a forthcoming victory (*fatḥun qarībun*). Endowment texts often contain Q 2:181 (*fa-man baddalahu baʿda mā samiʿahu fa-innamā ithmuhu ʿalā lladhīna yubaddilūnahu*: 'Whoever alters [a will] after hearing it shall be accountable for his crime'), a warning about the inviolability of *waqf*. Decrees might include similar warnings to potential violators, such as Q 26:227 ('Wrong-doers will come to know by what a great reverse they will be overturned') or the last phrase from Q 3:173 ('God is sufficient for us and most excellent as a protector').

These qur'ānic inscriptions could also be integrated into the architecture in a way that enhanced their content. The throne room at the Alhambra Palace, known as the Salón de Comares or Hall of the Ambassadors, is inscribed with Q 67, a well-known sūra that opens with a description of God's power over all things, including life and death, and his creation of the seven heavens. The magnificent ceiling above is composed of many thousands of individual wooden elements painstakingly fitted together into a pyramidal vault with six tiers of stars around a central small cupola. It is surely a physical realisation of the verses inscribed below.[19] Architectural form thus underscores content.

So too the material, colour and script of qur'ānic inscriptions on objects could be manipulated to enhance the message. Glass mosque lamps provide a good example. The typical lamp has a wide and flaring neck above a bulbous body. A small glass container for water and oil with a floating wick was inserted inside the lamp, which was suspended by chains from the ceiling. The lamps are typically inscribed with the Light Verse (Q 24:35), which literally says that 'God is the light of the heavens and the earth, the likeness of his light is as a wick-holder wherein is a light, the light in a glass, the glass as it were a glittering star.' The verse thus literally describes God's light through the metaphor of the wick floating in a dish of oil inside of a glass mosque lamp. This inscription is painted around the neck in thick blue letters. Encircling the body is a second inscription, with the patron's name and titles painted in reserve against a blue ground. When the lamp was lit, the patron's name and titles would glow with divine light, a stunning visual realisation of the qur'ānic metaphor inscribed above.

Grave markers, including tombstones and cenotaphs, comprise another type of object typically inscribed with qur'ānic verses.[20] These markers served a dual purpose – to record the name of the deceased and to bear witness to his faith – and hence they were typically inscribed with the deceased's name and genealogy and some sort of qur'ānic text. Sometimes the qur'ānic verses were general evocations of the faith, such as Q 112, the Throne Verse (Q 2:255) and especially Q 3:18, whose reference to testifying was particularly appropriate when the verb used to introduce the name of the deceased was 'testified' (*shahida*). Other verses on grave markers went in and out of popularity. Q 22:7, saying that the hour is undoubtedly coming and that God will raise those who are in their graves, was popular in the eighth and ninth centuries, reflecting the nascent Muslim community's preoccupation with eschatological questions.[21] Q 55:26–7, saying that all is perishable except God's face in majesty and magnificence (*kullu man ʿalayhā fānin wa-yabqā wajhu rabbika dhū l-jalāli wa-l-ikrāmi*), becomes increasingly popular across the Islamic lands from the mid-ninth century not only for the gravestones erected in cemeteries but also on tombs themselves. The same holds for the phrase saying that 'every soul shall taste of death', found identically in Q 3:185, 21:35 and 29:57. Q 35:5, describing the vanity of earthly life, however, is found regularly on tombstones from Andalusia.

Sectarian

Qur'ānic verses were often chosen to highlight particular theological perspectives. Shīʿīs, for example, often had their objects and buildings inscribed with verses referring to the Prophet's family. Q 42:23, which asks for no recompense other than love of kin (*al-mawaddata fī l-qurbā*), was a slogan common to all advocates of rule by the Prophet's family and is found already on coins issued in the mid-eighth century by the Ṭalibid rebel ʿAbdallāh b. Muʿāwiya and Abū Muslim, the leader of the ʿAbbāsid revolution. Q 33:33, which commands obedience to 'God and his messenger' and states specifically that 'God wishes only to remove abomination from you, members of the family (*ahl al-bayt*), and to make you pure and spotless,' became a Shīʿī battle cry, especially for the Fāṭimid rulers of north Africa and Egypt. The text is inscribed in beautiful floriated Kūfic in the roundel over the main doorway of the Aqmar Mosque, built by the Fāṭimid vizier on the main street of medieval Cairo in 519/1125, and also on numerous tombs and mausolea.[22] The Fāṭimids were experts in selecting verses that supported their theological position. Another popular qur'ānic text on Fāṭimid mausolea is Q 7:54, which mentions God's creation of the world in six days. The Fāṭimids also exploited qur'ānic vocabulary. Shīʿīs extend the *taṣliyya*, the statement of blessings on the Prophet, to include his family. The Fāṭimids added the adjectives *al-ṭayyibīn* (good) and *al-ṭāhirīn* (pure), adjectives drawn from qur'ānic phrases like Q 33:33, to their tombstones and textiles.[23] Such phrases were then used by others like the Almohads (al-Muwaḥḥidūn), Berber reformers who ruled north Africa and Spain in the late twelfth and thirteenth centuries. Their coins were typically inscribed with the extended form of the *taṣliyya*, whose phraseology and distinct design of a square in a circle emphasised their dissident beliefs as repudiators of the ʿAbbāsid caliphate. The Almohads' zeal as reformers and their use of polemic inscriptions on coins was nothing new to the region. Their predecessors, the Almoravids (al-Murābiṭūn), had Q 3:85 ('Whoever desires a religion other than Islam, it will not be accepted from him and he will be lost at the end') added around the margin on the obverse of dinars struck in the eleventh and twelfth centuries to reflect their fervour for holy war. This message was directed at non-Muslims, for these gold coins circulated extensively among Spanish Christians who called them 'maravedis' and issued their own imitations of them.

Political and current events

Politics and current events could also enter into the choice of specific qur'ānic inscriptions, especially on coins, congregational mosques and other major monuments. Q 30:4–5 ('Command, past and future belongs to God, and on that day believers shall rejoice in the victory granted by God') was added to the margin on coins issued after the ʿAbbāsid al-Maʾmūn defeated his brother al-Amīn, and henceforth became standard on ʿAbbāsid coins. The first coins issued by the Ilkhānid sultan Abū Saʿīd (r. 716–36/1316–35), a twelve-year-old who came to the throne after four months of intrigue and squabbling following the unexpected death of his father, were inscribed with Q 57:1–2 ('Blessed is he in whose hands is the kingdom; he has power over all things'), surely intended as a warning to rival claimants to the throne.[24] The inscription around the doorway added on the north-east side of the congregational or Friday mosque at Iṣfahān in central Iran opens with Q 2:114, a warning that whoever destroys mosques will suffer grave punishment. This text must have been chosen because, as the end of the inscription states, the mosque had to be reconstructed after a fire in 515/1121–2, an event that Ibn al-Athīr (d. 630/1233) attributed to the Ismāʿīlīs, foes of the ruling Saljūqs.[25]

Puns and slogans

Patrons or designers might also select a particular verse as a play on words. Such punning was popular in Arabic because of its linguistic structure in which any root conveys a semantic concept that is transformed into regular grammatical forms. The Muẓaffarid prince Quṭb al-Dīn Maḥmūd might have chuckled to see the phrase at the end of Q 17:79, which asks God to raise one to a praiseworthy station (*maqāman maḥmūdan*), tucked into the *īwān* of the *madrasa* that he had built in Iṣfahān in 725/1325. The Fāṭimids were masters of such plays on words. Q 9:18, found frequently in Fāṭimid times and already appropriate because of its reference to God's mosques, also includes the word *al-muhtadīn* (the guided) and was therefore doubly suitable for the Fāṭimids, descendants of the *mahdī* (the right guide).

Some qurʾānic words or phrases were also adopted as slogans. The ʿAbbāsids, for example, took one of the longest words in the Qurʾān – *fasayakfīkahum* ('[God] will suffice you against them') from Q 2:137 – as their motto.[26] According to the court chronicler Hilāl al-Ṣābiʾ(d. 448/1056), it was inscribed on the standard that supported their famous black banner, and other objects inscribed with their motto have survived. Some are textiles, such as an official textile, or *ṭirāz*, dedicated to Hārūn al-Rashīd (r. 786–809) and painted *ikat* cottons made in Yemen from the late ninth to the late tenth century. Others are ceramics: fragments of tin-glazed earthenware bowls with this motto have been excavated at the ʿAbbāsids' ninth-century capital at Sāmarrāʾ on the Tigris River. On these ceramics the potter painted the word in cobalt blue to form three sides of a rectangle, so that the design of the text was as distinctive as its content. This is a rare instance of a qur'ānic text used on objects of daily use, and the regnal associations of the word seem to have outweighed any fears of defiling the sacred text by putting it in a mundane context.

The word *fasayakfikahum* acquired talismanic significance, and artisans in the thirteenth and fourteenth centuries elaborated its shape on objects. A more complicated design with the connectors between letters twisted so that the word forms a *miḥrāb*-shaped arch was reproduced in several media, ranging from stone tombstones found in a cemetery in Iṣfahān to lustre tiles and even coins minted for the Ilkhānid ruler Abū Saʿīd from 722/1322–3 to 727/1326–7. The word here cannot have regnal connotations, for objects like tombstones and lustre tiles were not made for use at court, so the choice of text can best be explained as a general evocation of faith in God. Such examples illustrate the varying significance of verses in differing contexts and the generalisation and routinisation of meaning that occurs with repeated use.

A final example

Such varied and changing meanings demonstrate how difficult it can be to figure out why a particular set of verses was chosen, and one final example – Q 62:1–7 inscribed at the congregational mosque erected at Warāmīn/Varamin (near Tehran) in 726/1326 – shows how multiple suggestions can be put forward.[27] The text opens with four verses glorifying God who sent a messenger with signs to instruct humankind and confer benefits upon them as part of his bounty, which he bestows on whomever he wills. This straightforward statement of God's power is followed by a more unusual text that compares Jews loaded with the Torah to an ass (*himār*) carrying books and states that God does not guide evildoers. Placement (around the top of the domed sanctuary in front of the *miḥrāb*), size (it measures nearly a metre high) and technique (relief carving) all suggest that the text was significant, and several explanations for its selection are possible. The opening verses about God's power are common, occurring even in a contemporary building in the same town, and the text may simply have been repeated in the nearby congregational mosque, with the extra verses about Jews added to fill the space. This explanation seems insufficient, however, as Ilkhānid stucco carvers were skilled at spacing inscriptions. The inscription on the portal to the chamber contains the last three verses of the sūra (Q 62:9–11), with an altogether appropriate text about Friday prayer, and so the two texts might be read in synecdoche as containing the entire chapter.

This explanation is similarly insufficient, for it suggests that the carver did not plan accordingly and had to omit verse 8 inadvertently. It has also been suggested that the reference to Jews was connected with an incident in which several local Jewish doctors had converted to Islam in Ramaḍān 705/March–April 1306. This suggestion too seems unlikely because of the two-decade gap between the events and the mosque's construction. Another possibility is that the text was chosen because it contained a pun on the word ass, for Quhad, the patron's home town, was sometimes called Quhad of the Asses (Quhad-i Kharān), either to distinguish it from a nearby Quhad of the Water (Quhad-i Māʾī) or because of the many Ḥanafīs there. This explanation, too, is difficult to accept, as it depends on punning in two languages. Finally, the text may have been chosen to please a Shīʿī audience, for verse 6 contains the phrase 'friends to God' (*awliyāʾ lillāh*), a term Shīʿīs interpreted to designate their special relationship through ʿAlī, who was God's friend (*walī Allāh*), and this was the very time that veneration of the Prophet's family was growing in Iran. Whichever explanation is correct – and it may well be true that several overlapping layers of meaning were intended – the qurʾānic text is a ringing statement of God's power that illustrates the glory and multivalent meanings of qurʾānic inscriptions on Islamic art and architecture.

Notes

1. This example was first cited in G. Wiet, *Matériaux pour un Corpus inscriptionum arabicarum I: Egypte 2* (Cairo: Imprimerie de l'Institut français d'archéologie orientale, 1929–30), pp. 19–21 and is often repeated, as in E. Dodd and S. Khairallah, *The image of the word: A study of qurʾānic verses in Islamic architecture*, 2 vols. (Beirut: American University of Beirut, 1981), vol. I, pp. 2–33; S. Blair, *Islamic inscriptions* (Edinburgh: Edinburgh University Press, 1998), p. 211; and R. Hoyland, 'Epigraphy', in J. D. McAuliffe (ed.), *Encyclopaedia of the Qurʾān*, 5 vols. (Leiden: Brill, 2001–6), vol. II, p. 27. These last three references form the basic material for studying qurʾānic inscriptions and contain full references to the many buildings and objects mentioned here.
2. Dodd and Khairallah, *The image of the word.*
3. E. Dodd, 'The image of the word: Notes on the religious iconography of Islam', *Berytus* 18 (1969), 35–62.
4. J. Bloom et al., *The minbar from the Kutubiyya mosque* (New York: Metropolitan Museum of Art, 1998).
5. The clearest introduction to Islamic coinage is M. L. Bates' handbook, *Islamic coins* (New York: American Numismatic Society, 1982); all of the examples cited in this essay are discussed and illustrated there. See also his article 'Numismatics', in McAuliffe (ed.), *Encyclopaedia of the Qurʾān*, vol. III, pp. 555–60.
6. O. Grabar, 'The Umayyad Dome of the Rock in Jerusalem', *Ars Orientalis* 3 (1959), 33–62.
7. All treated in Dodd and Khairallah, *The image of the word.*

8. W. Begley, 'The myth of the Taj Mahal and a new theory of its symbolic meaning', *Art Bulletin* 61 (March 1979), 7–37.
9. Dodd and Khairallah, *The image of the word*; see also the review by S. Blair in *Arabica* 31 (November 1984), 337–42. Their volume was compiled by 1974 but turmoil in Lebanon prevented its publication for nearly a decade.
10. It was the source exploited, for example, for R. Hillenbrand's article, 'Qur'ānic epigraphy in medieval Islamic architecture', *Revue des études islamiques* 54 (1986), 171–87.
11. For instructions on how to find and use these multi-volume works, often abbreviated *MCIA* and *RCEA*, see Blair, *Islamic inscriptions*, pp. 207–10.
12. The papers are to be published in the forthcoming volume, F. Suleman (ed.), *Word of God – art of man: The Qur'ān and its creative expressions: Selected proceedings from the International Colloquium held in London, 18–21 October 2003* (Oxford: Oxford University Press in association with The Institute of Ismaili Studies, forthcoming).
13. The basic study of Kāshān lustreware is O. Watson, *Persian lustre ware* (London: Faber and Faber, 1985).
14. See especially the article by O. Watson, 'The Masjid-i ʿAlī, Quhrūd: An architectural and epigraphic survey', *Iran* 13 (1975), 59–74.
15. See the many examples given in Hoyland, 'Epigraphy'.
16. For the use of qur'ānic inscriptions on seals and amulets, see the section by Venetia Porter in ibid., pp. 35–9 and her forthcoming *Catalogue of Arabic and Persian seals and amulets in the British Museum* (London: British Museum Press).
17. On the meaning of this verse, see W. A. Graham, *Beyond the written word: Oral aspects of scripture in the history of religion* (New York: Cambridge University Press, 1993), p. 82.
18. The basic study is J. Sourdel-Thomine, 'Clefs et serrures de la Kaʿba', *Revue des études islamiques* 39 (1971), 29–86.
19. For an interpretation of the iconography of the qur'ānic inscriptions at the Alhambra Palace, see O. Grabar, *The Alhambra* (Cambridge, MA: Harvard University Press, 1978).
20. There is as yet no comprehensive study of the qur'ānic verses on tombstones. Meanwhile, see the summaries in Blair, *Islamic inscriptions*, pp. 196–9, Hoyland, 'Epigraphy', pp. 32–3. The largest body of material from early times, the corpus of tombstones from Egypt, was published in ten volumes by H. el-Hawary and G. Wiet, *Les stèles funéraires* (Cairo: Imprimerie de l'Institut français, 1932–42).
21. R. Hoyland, 'The content and context of early Arabic inscriptions', *Jerusalem Studies in Arabic and Islam* 21 (1997), 77–102.
22. C. Williams, 'The cult of ʿAlid saints in the Fatimid monuments of Cairo', *Muqarnas* 1 (1983), 37–52 and 3 (1985), 39–60.
23. For tombstones, see G. Wiet, 'Stèles coufiques d'Egypte et du Soudan', *Journal asiatique* 240 (1952), 273–97, and J. Bloom, 'The mosque of the Qarafa in Cairo', *Muqarnas* 4 (1987), 7–20; for textiles, see, among others, the so-called Veil of St Anne of Apt, whose inscription is *Répertoire chronologique d'épigraphie arabe*, 2882.
24. S. Blair, 'The coins of the later Ilkhanids: A typological analysis', *Journal of the Economic and Social History of the Orient* 26 (1983), 295–317.

25. *Répertoire chronologique d'épigraphie arabe*, 2991.
26. S. Blair, 'Written, spoken, envisioned: The many facets of the Qur'ān in art', forthcoming in Suleman (ed.), *Word of God*. Cf. Q 15:22 with *fa'sqaynākumūhu*, which is identified by Badr al-Dīn al-Zarkashī (d. 794/1392) as the longest word: *al-Burhān fī 'ulūm al-Qur'ān*, ed. M. A. al-Faḍl Ibrāhīm, 4 vols. (Cairo: Maktabat Dār al-Turāth, 1959), vol. I, p. 252.
27. S. Blair, 'The religious art of the Ilkhanids', in L. Komaroff and S. Carboni (eds.), *The legacy of Genghis Khan: Courtly art and culture in western Asia, 1256–1353* (New York: Metropolitan Museum of Art, 2003), pp. 105–33.

Further reading

Blair, S., *Islamic inscriptions*, Edinburgh: Edinburgh University Press, 1998.

Combe, E., J. Sauvaget and G. Wiet, *Répertoire chronologique d'épigraphie arabe*, Cairo: Impr. de l'Institut français d'archéologie orientale, 1931.

Dodd, E. and S. Khairallah, *The image of the word: A study of qur'ānic verses in Islamic architecture*, 2 vols., Beirut: American University of Beirut, 1981.

Hillenbrand, R., 'Qur'anic epigraphy in medieval Islamic architecture', *Revue des études islamiques* 54 (1986), 171–87.

Hoyland, R., 'The content and context of early Arabic inscriptions', *Jerusalem Studies in Arabic and Islam* 21 (1997), 77–102, esp. 86–9.

'Epigraphy', in J. D. McAuliffe (ed.), *Encyclopaedia of the Qur'ān*, 5 vols., Leiden: Brill, 2001–6, vol. II, pp. 25–43.

Imbert, F., 'Le Coran dans les graffiti des deux premiers siècles de l'hégire', *Arabica* 47 (2000), 381–90.

Suleman, F. (ed.), *Word of God – art of man: The Qur'ān and its creative expressions: Selected proceedings from the International Colloquium held in London, 18–21 October 2003*, Oxford: Oxford University Press in association with The Institute of Ismaili Studies (forthcoming).

Part IV

Interpretations and intellectual traditions

Fig. 9 Folio from a fourteenth-century Iraqi Qur'ān manuscript in *muḥaqqaq* script, depicting Q 5:24–5 (Khalili Collection, QUR 162). Courtesy of the Nasser D. Khalili Collection, London

9 The tasks and traditions of interpretation

JANE DAMMEN McAULIFFE

Sometime towards the end of the sixth/twelfth century, a prominent preacher in Baghdād wrote the following:[1]

> *Say, 'O you unbelievers, (1) I do not worship what you worship (2) and you do not worship what I worship. (3) I am not a worshipper of what you worship (4) and you are not worshippers of what I worship. (5) Your religion is for you and mine is for me.'(6)*[2]

> There are two views about this verse: (1) Ibn Masʿūd, al-Ḥasan and the majority say that it is Meccan. (2) It was reported on the authority of Qatāda to be Medinan. There are three different opinions about the occasion of its revelation: (1) a group of Quraysh, including al-Walīd b. al-Mughīra, al-ʿĀṣ b. Wāʾil and al-Aswad b. ʿAbd Yaghūth met al-ʿAbbās b. ʿAbd al-Muṭṭalib and said, 'O Abū l-Faḍl, if your nephew had submitted himself to one of our gods then we would have believed in what he says and we would certainly have believed in his god.' So al-ʿAbbās came and told him [Muḥammad] this and at that this sūra was revealed. Abū Ṣāliḥ reported this on the authority of Ibn ʿAbbās. (2) ʿUtba b. Rabīʿa and Umayya b. Khalaf met God's messenger and said, 'O Muḥammad, we shall not leave you alone until you follow our religion and we follow yours. If ours is the right course, you will take your share of it. If yours is the right course, we will take our share of it.' At that this sūra was revealed. ʿUbayd b. ʿUmayr said so. (3) The Quraysh said to the Prophet, 'If it please you we will follow your religion for a year and you will return to our religion for a year.' At that this sūra was revealed. Wahb reported it. Muqātil reported others to have said: 'This sūra was revealed about Abū Jahl and about "the mockers". Of those about whom it was revealed, not one ever became a believer.'[3]

> God's [i.e., the Qur'ān's] saying '*what* I worship',[4] actually meaning '*whom* I worship', is set as counter to his saying '*what* you [plural] worship', which is idols.
>
> There are two views about the repetition of the statement: (1) to emphasise the matter and to put a stop to their ambitions. Al-Farrā' said this. We have already favoured the explanation of this in [our commentary on] Sūrat al-Raḥmān, 13. (2) That it means: *I do not worship what you worship* at the present time and *and you do not,* at the present time, *worship what I worship. And I will not worship what you worship* in the future and the same for *you.* God applied that negation to Muḥammad and to them [Quraysh] in the present and in the future.
>
> This [sūra] is about a group of their most eminent men, as we have mentioned on the authority of Muqātil: God informed Muḥammad that they would not become believers. So it is not, in this instance, a repetition. This is the view of Tha'lab and al-Zajjāj.
>
> God's saying *your religion is for you and mine is for me* is with short 'a' (*fatḥa*) on the 'y' (*yā'*) of *wa-liya.* Nāfi', Ḥafṣ and the 'two Abūs' [read this] on the authority of 'Āṣim. Ya'qūb read *yā'* as a long vowel in both cases. According to the commentators, this [verse] is abrogated by *āyat al-sayf.*

The above passage, for which I have provided a literal translation, is drawn from a famous Arabic commentary on the Qur'ān. It was written by Abū l-Faraj 'Abd al-Raḥmān b. 'Alī b. al-Jawzī who died in the first year of the thirteenth century (597/1200). Although this commentary was composed more than 800 years ago, it is still regularly reprinted. The edition that I have used runs to nine volumes and compared to other medieval and modern commentaries on the Qur'ān, it is neither among the largest nor the smallest. The author himself deserves a brief introduction.[5] Ibn al-Jawzī, as he is commonly called, was born in Baghdād in 1116. Although his father died when he was a very small child, his was a family of moderate wealth so he received a fine education in the 'religious sciences'. This means that by virtue of family connections, coupled with a clever and retentive mind, he was able to study with some of the leading scholars of his time in all of the expected subjects: Qur'ān, ḥadīth, jurisprudence (*fiqh*) and grammar. His intellectual lineage, and that of his family, was Ḥanbalī so he stands in a line of thinkers that would place Ibn 'Aqīl (d. 513/1119–20) and 'Abd al-Qādir al-Jīlānī (d. 561/1166) as predecessors and Ibn Taymiyya (d. 728/1328) and Ibn Kathīr (d. 774/1373) as successors.

In translating this passage from Ibn al-Jawzī's commentary on the Qur'ān, I have stayed very close to his original. If the result seems dense, elliptical and virtually incomprehensible to the contemporary reader, there are good reasons for that reaction.[6] Ibn al-Jawzī wrote his commentary for a particular audience. As he explains in its introduction, he had surveyed a large number of earlier qur'ānic commentaries and found them to be either too long or too short. Even 'those of average size', he notes, 'are of little benefit, being poorly arranged and sometimes neglecting the problematic while explaining the obvious'. His *Provisions for the journey in the science of exegesis* (*Zād al-masīr fī ʿilm al-tafsīr*) attempts to evade these deficiencies by charting a course of sufficient brevity that he could expect his readers to memorise the result: 'I have striven to keep it short, so try, to the extent of your God-given capacity, to memorise it.'[7] While memorising a work of this magnitude may seem a somewhat daunting task to the modern reader, it was not an uncommon achievement in the annals of medieval Islamic education. Concision, however, could not come at the cost of quality and Ibn al-Jawzī managed to pack a great deal of material into his relatively compressed production. A comparison of his commentary on Q 109 with those of some of his predecessors and successors proves how skilfully he contrived to balance size with substance.

WHAT COMMENTATORS DO

Commentaries on the Qur'ān, at least those that are full-scale, sequential commentaries, ordinarily conform to an expected structure. They are often very large works – upwards of twenty volumes would not be unusual – and they begin with the first sūra of the Qur'ān and go to the last. (The Arabic term used to describe such commentaries is *musalsal* or 'linked', meaning that each part connects with what follows.) Taking each sūra in turn, a commentator will usually move systematically from one verse to the next, although some commentaries gather a group of consecutive verses for consideration or offer prefatory and thematic remarks about sections of a sūra. At the level of the individual verse, however, the methods and procedures of commentators may vary considerably. Some, such as Ibn al-Jawzī, will treat a number of topics. Others will focus on a few. Both a commentator's predominant interest – for example, grammar, law, mystical reflection, theology – and the verse itself often guide the choice.

In the very few pages that Ibn al-Jawzī devoted to this sūra, he covered most of the major topics that had already surfaced over the centuries of its interpretation. For those who are not yet initiated into the technical vocabulary of the 'qur'ānic sciences', these subjects are best presented as a series of questions: Was this sūra revealed in Mecca or in Medina? What prompted its revelation? Can we explain the grammatical peculiarities in certain verses? Why is there repetition of words or phrases? Were there any variant readings for these verses, i.e., instances of different vocalisation? Does the passage continue to carry legal consequences or has it been abrogated? While a few additional topics occur in other commentaries, these are certainly the most prominent matters addressed in the exegetical tradition on this sūra.

Taking each of these in turn, I will expand a bit on Ibn al-Jawzī's terse treatment and bring some other commentarial voices into the conversation. The point of this exercise is to present a brief glimpse of the Muslim exegetical mind at work, to capture its principal activities and abiding concerns. By the end of this elaboration, the translated passage with which this chapter begins should be much easier to understand.

Was this sūra revealed in Mecca or Medina?

All 114 sūras of the Qur'ān have been classified by the Muslim exegetical tradition as either having been received by Muḥammad in Mecca, during the earlier years of his prophetic career and before his emigration (*hijra*) to Medina, or later during the period of the Medinan theocracy.[8] In contemporary copies of the Arabic text of the Qur'ān this chronological identification is often indicated next to the sūra title. Further refinements of this classification identify both Medinan interpolations in Meccan sūras (and vice versa) and allow the generation of a list of all the sūras of the Qur'ān according to the chronology of their revelation, rather than their present textual order. Consequently, Ibn al-Jawzī begins his commentary on Q 109 with both the majority and minority opinions about where it was revealed, Mecca and Medina, respectively. By contrast, some three quarters of a century later, the Andalusian commentator Abū ʿAbdallāh Muḥammad b. Aḥmad al-Qurṭubī (d. 671/1272) does not tip his hand to a majority opinion but rather names three early authorities who judge it to be a Meccan sūra (Ibn Masʿūd, al-Ḥasan and ʿIkrima) and an equal number who say that it is Medinan (Ibn ʿAbbās, Qatāda and al-Ḍaḥḥāk).[9]

What prompted its revelation?

This question opens a large field of exegetical inquiry, one that drew significant attention in the commentaries on this sūra. The technical term for this field, *asbāb al-nuzūl*, can be translated as the 'occasions' or 'circumstances' or 'reasons' for revelations. Succinctly put, it captures the historical and contextual investigations that various verses and sūras of the Qur'ān provoked. Ordinarily, these investigations point to particular experiences and episodes in the life of Muḥammad. According to the *asbāb al-nuzūl* literature,[10] a verse or sūra may have been revealed in response to a direct question put to the Prophet. Or a particular situation could have elicited a corresponding revelation. Even a cursory reading of the sacred text will indicate that not all verses fit this category. For many verses and sūras, there is no specific 'occasion'. On the other hand, for some verses the exegetical tradition has conveyed several contextual narrations. Such is the case with Q 109 and thus Ibn al-Jawzī has reproduced three of them. Each is a variation on a basic narrative: a group of Muḥammad's opponents in Mecca, the Quraysh, attempt to challenge or entice him into abandoning his belief in the oneness of God. Ibn al-Jawzī also adds an additional variant on the authority of Muqātil b. Sulaymān (d. 150/767), but without elaboration.

Muqātil himself, whose commentary is among the earliest available in a printed edition,[11] provides the elaboration. Identifying Abū Jahl and others as the Quraysh 'mockers' (*mustahzi'ūn*),[12] those who relentlessly confronted Muḥammad's preaching with aggressive derision, he presents the incident of the 'Satanic verses' as the precipitating cause of the wager.[13] Later commentaries fill in further details of Muḥammad's response to the Quraysh challenge. Aḥmad b. Muḥammad b. Ibrāhīm al-Tha'labī (d. 427/1035) notes that when Muḥammad stands in the mosque and recites this sūra to them as God's rejoinder to their challenge, they are roused to anger and attack the Prophet and his Companions.[14] The Shī'ī exegete Muḥammad b. al-Ḥasan al-Ṭūsī (d. 460/1067) – who dubs this wager a 'worship exchange' (*munāqala al-'ibāda*) – offers an account that also connects the revelation of Q 39:64 to these Quraysh 'mockers': an example of an 'occasion of revelation' (*sabab al-nuzūl*) that functions to explain two separate revelations.[15] Al-Qurṭubī cites Ibn 'Abbās as his authority for this communication: 'The Quraysh said [to Muḥammad], "We will give you enough money to make you the richest man in Mecca, we will wed you to whomever you wish, we will travel right after you, that is, we will walk right behind you, if you will stop cursing our gods."'[16]

Are there explanations for the grammatical peculiarities in these verses?

This topic can be rather complicated to convey in English but one issue that captured exegetical attention is the objective pronoun used in the third verse of Q 109, '*what* I worship'. Should not, the grammarians asked, the correct expression be 'You do not worship *whom* I worship?' After all, God is a 'who', not a 'what'. Al-Ṭūsī answers the question by explaining that '*what* I worship' stands as a counterpart to the earlier '*what* you worship', namely, idols, and is used so that the statements are comparable rather than incompatible.[17] Further, according to both al-Ṭūsī and al-Qurṭubī, these contrastive statements carry a verbal sense: 'You do not worship in the way that I do, which is by professing God's unicity (*tawḥīd*).'[18]

Why is there repetition in these verses?

The responses recorded by Ibn al-Jawzī reflect two of the principal answers provided by the exegetical tradition. The first of these simply notes that in Arabic – as in many other languages – repetition is a rhetorical device, a common way of emphasising a statement. Abū Jaʿfar Muḥammad b. Jarīr al-Ṭabarī (d. 310/923), for example, mentions this and supplies the additional qurʾānic instances of Q 94:5–6 and Q 102:6–7.[19] Al-Thaʿlabī adds to this other qurʾānic examples (Q 55; 77:15; 78:4–5 and 82:17), as well as illustrations from ḥadīth and poetry.[20]

Another pervasive explanation prefers to link the repetitions found in this sūra to past, present and future, i.e., to the persistence of unbelief. A common way of expressing this interpretation is paraphrase:

> Say, O Muḥammad, to those unbelievers who have asked you to worship their gods for a year on the condition that they would worship yours for a year: 'O you unbelievers, I do not worship the gods and idols you worship now and you do not worship what I worship now. I will not be a worshipper in the future of what you have worshipped in the past and you will never be worshippers in the future of what I worship now and in the future.'[21]

As Ibn al-Jawzī and others have remarked, there is a harsh severity and finality conveyed by this verbal reinforcement.

A third suggestion, but one to which Ibn al-Jawzī does not refer, connects the repetition to the dialogue with the Quraysh unbelievers that is implied in these passages. By this account, it is their repeated insistence upon the wager that prompts an equally insistent divine rejoinder.[22] Finally, the exegetical discussion of this issue also records voices, such as that of al-Ṭūsī, who deny that there is any repetition in this verse, at least as that rhetorical category is ordinarily understood. Rather, the temporal distinctions of present and future render such categorisation untenable.[23]

Are there any variant readings for these verses, i.e., instances of different vocalisation?

This short sūra also surfaced the very large and complex exegetical question of different qur'ānic 'readings'. As any traditional account of the early codification of the Qur'ān will explain,[24] the original, rudimentary orthography of initial manuscripts admitted of much more variation in consonant and vowel marking than the eventually ratified text. Occasionally, these variants were of semantic consequence but the vast majority, like those recorded for this sūra, were of recitational significance only. An example, and one which Ibn al-Jawzī records, is the pronunciation of the final word, *dīn,* and its appended pronominal adjective. Some authorities on the 'readings' of the Qur'ān pronounce this adjective as a long vowel, whether or not the recitation stops on this word or proceeds immediately to the next sūra.[25] Most authorities, however, shorten the vowel and that is the orthography of the standard, contemporary text of the Qur'ān.

Are there continuing legal consequences for these verses or have they been abrogated?

This is the final exegetical question that Ibn al-Jawzī tackles in his commentary on this sūra and his response is unequivocal: 'According to the commentators [i.e., his predecessors], this [i.e., the final verse of the sūra] is abrogated by *āyat al-sayf*.' An understanding of this terse statement requires some explanation of the concept of 'abrogation' as well as an identification of this 'verse of the sword' (*āyat al-sayf*). Put very simply, 'abrogation' refers to the exegetical conviction that some verses of the Qur'ān restrict, modify or even nullify other verses. The key texts upon which this principle has been built are Q 2:106 and 16:101 but the basic operational concept is the sequential nature of qur'ānic revelations.

The most oft-quoted example of 'abrogating' (*nāsikh*) and 'abrogated' (*mansūkh*) verses are those that convey the increasingly restrictive pronouncements on intoxicants.[26] While the classical discussions of abrogation became very complex and dealt extensively with forms of intra-qur'ānic abrogation as well as the connection between the Qur'ān and *sunna,* the historical trajectory of such scholarship has been to limit rather than to expand the number of verses designated as either 'abrogating' or 'abrogated'.[27] An interesting instance of such categorisation is the verse to which Ibn al-Jawzī refers, 'the verse of the sword'. This is the name given to Q 9:5, a verse that begins, 'And when the sacred months have passed, kill the idolators wherever you find them . . .' According to one of the standard treatises on this topic, Q 9:5 abrogates at least 124 other verses, the last of which is Q 109:6.[28]

There are a number of topics that Ibn al-Jawzī does not include in his exegesis of this sūra but that are found in the works of other commentators. A brief look at a few of these can round out this commentarial case study. For example, related to the notion of abrogation is that of how specifically, or generally, a verse must be read (*al-ʿamm wa-l-khaṣṣ*). The question that drives this area of exegesis is: does the verse apply to a single individual or a specific group of people or is its applicability far broader than that? Abū Bakr Aḥmad b. ʿAbdallāh al-Jaṣṣāṣ (d. 370/981) asks this question about those designated in Q 109:1 as 'unbelievers' (*kāfirūn*) and offers two options in response: (1) that it is of general application and means all unbelievers and (2) that it means only those who persist in their disbelief despite their recognition of the divine. He opts for this latter view on both rhetorical and historical grounds. Rhetorically, circumscription is achieved by use of the definite article (*al-*) in a vocative construction and historically it is verified by the existence of those former unbelievers who became Muslims.[29] Al-Jaṣṣāṣ also makes a different argument by insisting that all unbelievers, regardless of their various doctrinal or ritual affiliations (*madhāhibuhum*), constitute a single sect (*milla*) or religion (*dīn*) that stands contrary to the religion of Islam.[30]

Less directly exegetical, but interesting nevertheless, are reflections on this sūra which assess its spiritual value. In the five or six centuries following the codification of the Qur'ān, a rich body of literature developed which detailed the 'excellences' (*faḍā'il*) of the holy book. Much of this material takes the form of statements credited to the Prophet and his Companions that praise the efficacy of particular sūras and verses. Several such statements are associated with Q 109. The most common of these is the declaration that the recitation of this sūra is equivalent to the recitation of a quarter of the Qur'ān. Al-Thaʿlabī cites this on the authority of Malik b. Anas (d. 179/796) while al-Zamakhsharī (d. 538/1144) puts it in the mouth of Muḥammad.[31] Both al-Thaʿlabī and al-Qurṭubī reference Ibn ʿAbbās in professing that no sūra of the Qur'ān angers Satan (Iblīs) more than this one does.[32]

Finally, there is the extra-exegetical evidence of enumeration. A telling demonstration of the reverence with which the Qur'ān is endlessly examined may be found in the various forms of counting to which the exegetes set themselves. In his famous compendium of the 'qur'ānic sciences' Badr al-Dīn al-Zarkashī (d. 794/1392) devotes attention to numbering the sūras, verses, words and letters of the Qur'ān. To this he adds calculations for the longest sūra (Q 2, al-Baqara), the longest verse (Q 2:282 at 128 words), the shortest verse (either Q 89:1 or Q 93:1, each a verse of a single word) and even the longest word (*fa'sqaynākumūhu* in Q 15:22).[33] In this same spirit, al-Thaʿlabī (or his editor) has provided the statistics for this sūra: six verses, sixteen words and ninety-four letters.[34]

CHRONOLOGIES AND CATEGORIES

In this effort to expand upon Ibn al-Jawzī's terse explanation of Q 109 and to delineate the different exegetical tasks, I have mentioned the names of many other commentators. At this point it should be useful to shift from the micro level of textual analysis to the macro level of historical and thematic overview, to survey the subject of qur'ānic interpretation as a whole. Most contemporary efforts to provide a succinct introduction to commentaries on the Qur'ān begin, either explicitly or implicitly, with one of two basic works.[35] If you are an author writing for an Arabic-speaking audience, your primary source will likely be *al-Tafsīr wa-l-mufassirūn* ('Commentary and the commentators'), a work first published in 1961 by Muḥammad Ḥusayn al-Dhahabī, a professor of the qur'ānic sciences in the Faculty of Islamic Studies (Kulliyyat al-Sharīʿa) of the University of al-Azhar in Cairo.[36] (Or it will be one of the many short summaries and textbooks that have drawn upon this publication.) In his two-volume work, al-Dhahabī offers both a chronological and a thematic presentation of the history of qur'ānic commentary. After a prefatory section that deals with various terminological distinctions, he launches into what he calls the first stage of commentary on the Qur'ān, that which developed during the lifetime of the prophet Muḥammad and his closest Companions. Stage two is defined as the period of the successors to those Companions, while stage three, in al-Dhahabī's chronology, covers the many subsequent centuries of compilations and compendia. Here is where one finds a long list of famous figures whose names still feature prominently in any history of qur'ānic exegesis: al-Ṭabarī, al-Thaʿlabī, al-Zamakhsharī, Fakhr al-Dīn al-Rāzī, Ibn Kathīr.

In elaborating stage three of this chronology, al-Dhahabī adopts the standard distinction between *al-tafsīr bi-l-ma'thūr* and *al-tafsīr bi-l-ra'y*[37] and categorises his authors accordingly. In Muslim accounts of exegetical activity this is a fundamental distinction, at least at the level of classification. Briefly put, the first of these, *al-tafsīr bi-l-ma'thūr*, can be paraphrased as 'interpretation based upon transmitted sources' and refers to those commentaries that reproduce exegetical ḥadīth attributed to the Prophet, his Companions and other early authorities. The second, *al-tafsīr bi-l-ra'y*, or 'interpretation based on individual reasoning', carries both positive and pejorative connotations. To be acceptable, the process of reasoning must be well grounded in linguistic knowledge and the Islamic intellectual traditions. Unfounded or fanciful forms of exegetical speculation are severely condemned, as are sectarian forms of exegesis, such as that of the Muʿtazilīs. Al-Dhahabī devotes considerable coverage to Muʿtazilī commentary, to the negative judgements that have been rendered against it and to some of its more noted exponents, e.g., ʿAbd al-Jabbār (d. 415/1025) and al-Zamakhsharī.[38]

The second part of al-Dhahabī's survey divides itself into thematic subsections. These present major works and the principal emphases of the following forms of commentary: Shīʿī (Ithnā' ʿAshara, Ismāʿīlī, Bābī and Bahā'ī, Zaydī), Khārijī, Ṣūfī, philosophical (*tafsīr al-falāsifa*), legal, scientific (*al-tafsīr al-ʿilmī*). A final chapter on twentieth-century commentary and some of its major authors – Muḥammad ʿAbduh, Rashīd Riḍā and Muḥammad Muṣṭafā al-Marāghī – concludes the volume.

The only Western, non-Muslim work listed among the volumes in al-Dhahabī's bibliography is that of Ignaz Goldziher's *Die Richtungen der islamischen Koranauslegung*. This is the source from which most Euro-American summaries of the history of qur'ānic commentary start. Goldziher's work pre-dates that of al-Dhahabī by several decades and was initially conceived as a set of lectures. It was first published in 1920.[39] He, too, begins chronologically with a description of the earliest periods of exegetical development. The remaining chapters of Goldziher's book then set forth five 'directions' or orientations: traditional (based on exegetical ḥadīth), rationalist (particularly Muʿtazilī), mystical, sectarian (i.e., non-Sunnī) and modern. Each of these subdivisions allows Goldziher to present characteristic features of the 'orientation' as drawn from its most representative works.

INTRODUCING SOME COMMENTATORS

Following the models set by Goldziher and al-Dhahabī, recent summaries of the history of qur'ānic exegesis continue to combine chronological and thematic taxonomies. Four easily available encyclopaedia articles offer concise and comprehensive surveys of the principal commentators and commentaries so there is no need to replicate such efforts yet again.[40] For the purpose of this chapter it would be more useful to introduce significant figures from some of the major periods and genres of qur'ānic commentary and to indicate both their commonalities and their differences.

Even the briefest introduction to the chronology and classification of Muslim interpretation of the Qur'ān will mention **Abū Ja'far Muḥammad b. Jarīr al-Ṭabarī** (d. 310/923). Both his achievement and his methodology define a significant stage in the history of qur'ānic exegesis. Al-Ṭabarī died almost three centuries after the death of the prophet Muḥammad and those centuries witnessed the growth and consolidation of the major fields of Islamic intellectual endeavour: ḥadīth, jurisprudence (*fiqh*), grammar and lexicography.[41] He was born in what is now Iran but eventually settled in Baghdād. The journey that took him from his native city of Āmul to his eventual home at the centre of 'Abbāsid hegemony is replicated – with varying itineraries – countless times in the lives of medieval Muslim scholars.

The learned elite of that period, and those for centuries to follow, educated themselves by travelling from one city to another in search of the best teachers in specific areas of the religious sciences. It was a kind of student itinerancy through which an individual affiliated himself for a period of time with a leading teacher, listening to his lectures and dictations and participating in recitation sessions that assessed the student's ability to transmit accurately the information that he was hearing. Eventually, those students whose performance and mastery of the material were recognised as outstanding became, in turn, the scholars to whom the next generation of educational itinerants flocked. Biographical compendia that compiled information on thousands of medieval Muslim scholars record these intellectual lineages, listing the names of those with whom a particular scholar studied and those who later sought his tutelage.

While al-Ṭabarī's own education began close to home, subsequent stages took him to places like al-Rayy, Baṣra, Kūfa, Cairo and parts of Syria. Names of the scholars with whom he studied in these places are scattered throughout his works: Hannād b. al-Sarī (d. 243/857), Ḥumayd al-'Aqadī (d. 245/859–60), Muḥammad b. 'Abd al-A'lā al-Ṣan'ānī (d. 245/859), Abū Kurayb Muḥammad b. al-'Alā'(d. 247/861), Muḥammad b. Mūsā al-Ḥarashī (d. 248/862) and Muḥammad b. Bashshār (d. 252/866).[42] These represent but a fraction of al-Ṭabarī's teachers and informants but, if the biographical vignettes be true, they found him to be an exceptional student. One such account about his teacher in Kūfa, Abū Kurayb, captures some of the memorable aspects of these academic encounters.

Abū Kurayb was apparently a difficult person, but al-Ṭabarī managed to mollify him from the start of their acquaintance by the force of his extraordinary ability. When he came to his house together with other ḥadīth students clamouring for admission, he found the great scholar looking out of a window and asking for those who could recite from memory the traditions they had written down on his dictation. The assembled students looked at each other and then pointed to al-Ṭabarī as the one who would be able to do that. Abū Kurayb examined him and found him able to recite every tradition he was asked, with the exact day on which Abū Kurayb had taught it.[43]

After his extended and far-flung years of study, al-Ṭabarī settled in Baghdād and began a half century of teaching and writing. His students, who are duly listed in the biographical summaries about him, were many and his productivity as an author was apparently on a scale that can scarcely be believed. While boasts of prolificacy are not uncommon in the biographies of medieval Muslim scholars, those about al-Ṭabarī record astounding quantities of daily output. Chief among the products of this prodigious author are two multi-volume works that continue to exert scholarly influence even today. The first of these is his notional history of the world, *The history of messengers and kings* (*Ta'rīkh al-rusul wa-l-mulūk*), which begins with the divine act of creation and covers the long period of pre-Islamic prophets from Adam through Jesus until the time of Muḥammad.[44] Its real importance for contemporary historians, however, lies in the annalistic coverage of all the caliphates from the inception of this office until shortly before al-Ṭabarī's death. The second major work, and the one most relevant to this chapter, is al-Ṭabarī's lengthy commentary on the Qur'ān. Its title, *The comprehensive clarification of the interpretation of the verses of the Qur'ān* (*Jāmiʿ al-bayān ʿan ta'wīl āy al-Qur'ān*), signals its predominant quality – comprehensiveness. This work is ordinarily described as the summative repository of the first two and one half centuries of Muslim exegetical endeavour. Such characterisations are quickly qualified, however, with the observation that the author did much more than simply compile extant material.[45] His selection and ordering of his sources, as well as the judgements that he makes among differing interpretations, reveal both the extent of his exegetical expertise and his thorough understanding of the other major areas of Muslim intellectual endeavour.[46] In an illuminating article on the dynamics of classical Qur'ān commentary, Norman Calder has expressed this with particular felicity:

> The process of citing authorities and providing multiple readings is in part a declaration of loyalty: it defines the tradition within which one works. It is also a means to establish the individuality or the artistry of a given *mufassir*: the selection, presentation and organization of citations constitutes always a process that is unique to one writer. Finally, it is, of itself, one element in a theological message: the possibility of the community and the text to contain multiplicity while remaining one community and one text is thereby asserted.[47]

It would be difficult to overestimate the influence of al-Ṭabarī's *magnum opus*. Even the most modest Muslim bookstore will offer copies of current editions – these run to as many as thirty volumes – and frequent reprints are a standard feature of Islamic publishing. I still recall vividly an experience that highlights the ubiquity of this commentary. Walking into a supermarket in Amman, Jordan some years ago, I spotted a small book display at the side of the entrance and went over to take a look. Stashed in the middle of some piles of modern novels and contemporary textbooks was a complete edition of al-Ṭabarī's *Jāmiʿ al-bayān*. While selling books in supermarkets is not uncommon in North America, I have never run across a medieval biblical commentary in the midst of the mystery stories and paperback bestsellers.

An intriguing figure who died about a quarter century before al-Ṭabarī has captured a prominent place in the history of qur'ānic exegesis both because of his influence on the development of Ṣūfī thought and practice and because of the attention he has attracted in contemporary scholarship.[48] Like al-Ṭabarī, **Sahl al-Tustarī** (d. 283/896) spent his early years in a Persian-speaking area (Tustar, Khūzistān) but eventually settled and lived his remaining days in Baṣra, a town in the south of Iraq, about 450 kilometres south-east of Baghdād. Al-Tustarī's academic lineage includes Dhū l-Nūn al-Miṣrī (d. 246/861) as a predecessor, and ʿAbdallāh Muḥammad b. Aḥmad b. Sālim al-Baṣrī (d. 297/909) and al-Ḥallāj (d. 309/922) as disciples. Use of the word 'disciple' rather than 'student' points to al-Tustarī's status as a charismatic ascetic. Through the cultivation of spiritual disciplines such as fasting and prolonged prayer, he underwent some profound spiritual experiences that shaped his intellectual growth and development. Later sources recount the miraculous events in al-Tustarī's life, the wild and dangerous animals that visited him and the visions and raptures he experienced. Here is a representative report from one of the above-named disciples:

> Muḥammad b. Sālim said: 'Ecstasy (*wağd*) used to overpower Sahl b. ʿAbd Allāh, so that he remained for 24 or 25 days without eating food. And he used to perspire at the severe cold in winter while he was only clothed in a single shirt. When he was asked about anything pertaining to mystical knowledge (*ʿilm*), he would answer, 'do not question me, for in this mystical moment (*waqt*), you do not benefit from my utterance.'[49]

As the insights gained from such experiences matured within al-Tustarī, others were attracted to his mystical teaching as disciples and were willing to submit themselves to him for spiritual formation. These, in turn, shaped subsequent generations of al-Tustarī's followers who diverged into different groups, some remaining in Baṣra while others made Baghdād their home.

Unlike al-Ṭabarī, al-Tustarī was not primarily a scholar and an author. At least we have no extant works that can be reliably ascribed to him. What we have are works composed by his followers which collect and convey his sayings and his teachings. Among these is a commentary on the Qur'ān, or, more properly, a partial commentary.[50] Al-Tustarī's *tafsīr* treats about 1,000 qur'ānic verses or roughly one sixth of the total. For those verses selected, the kinds and forms of interpretation vary widely and include both literal and metaphorical elements: 'illustrations from the Prophet's normative and customary behaviour; examples from the legends of the prophets of old; traces of mystical views shared by earlier Ṣūfīs and anecdotes concerning their practical conduct; fragments of Tustarī's mystical themes, his religious thought, and ascetic practice; exhortations and guidelines for disciples and answers to their questions; and finally, episodes about Tustarī's life, glosses and explanatory insertions into the text'.[51]

Moving from the mystical to the legal, from east to west and from the ninth to the eleventh century brings us to the world of the Andalusian commentator and jurisprudent Abū Bakr Muḥammad b. ʿAbdallāh al-Maʿāfirī, known as **Ibn al-ʿArabī** (d. 543/1092).[52] The rich cultural heritage of Islamic Spain has long been a focus of historical, literary and art-historical scholarship. This is a world whose intellectual life would bear the influence of such towering figures as the chivalrous poet and Ẓāhirī theologian Ibn Ḥazm (d. 456/1064) and the Aristotelian philosopher Ibn Rushd (Averroes, d. 595/1198). Literary production in Muslim Spain began with works of Mālikī law and theology, an intellectual current imported to that area via Muslim settlements in north Africa. Ibn al-ʿArabī was formed and educated in that tradition, eventually serving as a judge (*qāḍī*) in his native Seville.[53] The years before this appointment, however, witnessed his own participation in the peripatetic educational pattern common to the medieval period. Quite expectedly, his journeys took him east, back to the long-standing centres of scholarship in Syria and Iraq. In Baghdād his teachers included the renowned theologian and philosopher Abū Ḥāmid al-Ghazālī (d. 505/1111). With his father, he travelled to Cairo and Alexandria and made the pilgrimage to Mecca but, after the death of his father in 493/1100, he returned to Spain. His years there were not without conflict and towards the end of his life he was imprisoned in north Africa, where he died.

Works in a number of different fields – law, ḥadīth, literature, grammar, history – are credited to Ibn al-ʿArabī, including an important and frequently cited commentary on the Qur'ān. Entitled *The legal rulings of the Qur'ān* (*Aḥkām al-Qur'ān*), it is commonly printed in a four-volume edition.[54] Like the commentary created from al-Tustarī's exegetical insights, this work of Ibn al-ʿArabī treats only selected verses, those which carry legal implications.[55] At the beginning of each sūra he notes the number of such verses in that particular sūra. For this subset of qur'ānic material, he then provides the standard exegetical elements, i.e., lexical identifications and glosses, occasions of revelation, judgements about abrogation, etc. Because of his Mālikī affiliation and orientation, the views of other Mālikī scholars are often brought forward in support of a particular interpretation. Some verses provide Ibn al-ʿArabī with an opportunity for extra-legal extrapolation. An example would be Q 7:180, famous for its mention of the 'beautiful names' of God: 'To God belong the most beautiful names, so use them to call upon him; but stay clear of those who bend his names to wrongful ends – they will be requited for what they do.'

Ibn al-ʿArabī signals the importance of this passage by mentioning others of his writings in which, he tells us, he has provided more elaboration than in his commentary.[56] He then launches into a seven-part analysis of the verse. These subsections treat topics such as terminology, the occasions of revelation and the question of categorisation, i.e., what are the divine designations that fall within the category of 'the beautiful names'? Ibn al-ʿArabī answers by first providing a sūra-by-sūra list of the divine names found in the Qur'ān. For example, he states that there are thirty to be found in the second sūra, seventeen in the sixth and three in the eighteenth. He then offers 146 names drawn from the Qur'ān and the *sunna* in a numbered list, with a brief explanatory gloss for some of them.

All of this digression on the 'beautiful names' could, however, equally well appear in a comprehensive commentary, such as that of al-Ṭabarī, or in a Ṣūfī one like that of al-Tustarī. What makes this verse a suitable entrant in a commentary devoted to the prescriptive statements in the Qur'ān are the two imperative statements – the two commands – that it contains, i.e., 'use them to call upon him' and 'stay clear of those', etc. Here Ibn al-ʿArabī takes pains to connect a particular divine name to what the worshipper seeks to secure in prayer, i.e., 'O Compassionate One, have mercy on me,' 'O Sustainer, give me sustenance.' The author of a contemporary monograph on Ibn al-ʿArabī and his commentary has added this about the commentator's treatment of Q 7:180: 'The most exalted name by which a person can pray is the name "Allāh", to which every other name returns and to whose interpretation every meaning is connected. When one prays to God by this name, he responds; when one asks of God by this name, he gives.'[57]

While legal commentaries and mystical commentaries constitute important subgenres of the library of qur'ānic exegesis, prime placement continues to be given to the comprehensive, ḥadīth-based commentaries that follow the model set by al-Ṭabarī. Every subsequent century saw the production of at least one such work but none has achieved more contemporary currency than that produced in the fourteenth century by **ʿImād al-Dīn Ismāʿīl b. Kathīr** (d. 774/1373). While four centuries separate al-Ṭabarī and Ibn Kathīr they share similarities of scholarly stature and productivity. The most famous works of each are a commentary on the Qur'ān and a world history. For Ibn Kathīr the respective titles are *The interpretation of the mighty Qur'ān* (*Tafsīr al-Qur'ān al-ʿaẓīm*) and *The beginning and the end* (*al-Bidāya wa-l-nihāya*), with his famous biography of the Prophet (*al-Sīra al-nabawiyya*) forming part of the latter.

The centre of Ibn Kathīr's scholarly life was not Baghdād – which had been sacked by the Mongols in 656/1258 – but Damascus. Although he was born in the Syrian citadel town of Boṣrā, he moved to Damascus as a young child and took full advantage of its thriving intellectual milieu. Certainly, his most famous teacher was the Ḥanbalī theologian and jurisconsult Taqī l-Dīn Aḥmad b. Taymiyya (d. 728/1328) and Ibn Kathīr studied with him during periods when Ibn Taymiyya was often under attack. This was a period of Mamlūk hegemony but also of Mongol invasions and Ibn Taymiyya's polemical preaching did not always fare well in this volatile mix. Several times he was imprisoned in the Damascus citadel and, towards the end of his life, the censorship of his work extended to the seizure of all his writing materials.

It is worth focusing for a moment on this controversial but critically important thinker because he figures so prominently in today's Muslim intellectual life. Ibn Taymiyya is perhaps most famous for his unrelenting attacks on all forms of religious 'innovation' (*bidʿa*). By 'innovation' he meant unwarranted accretions to the normative practice of the prophet Muḥammad and his closest Companions. A frequent target of his invective is what he deemed to be the excesses of Ṣūfī thought and devotion. Other examples would be such practices as saint veneration and tomb visitation, both of which were anathema to him. (Although, in an interesting twist of fate, after his death Ibn Taymiyya himself attracted the veneration of a saint and his tomb has been a locus of devotional visitation.) This same concern for continuity with the prophetic tradition marked Ibn Taymiyya's attitude towards the interpretation of the Qur'ān, an attitude that he transmitted to his student Ibn Kathīr. Although Ibn Taymiyya did not compose a comprehensive commentary, he did write about the hermeneutics or proper methodology of Qurʾān interpretation. His treatise on this topic, *An introductory essay on the principles of interpretation* (*Muqaddima fī uṣūl al-tafsīr*),[58] draws on a long tradition of exegetical reflection and has strongly influenced subsequent commentary work.

As elaborated in this treatise, Ibn Taymiyya sets forth a ranked sequence of exegetical steps which can be quickly summarised. (1) Start with intra-qurʾānic interpretation by looking for other verses that could clarify the one under consideration. As Ibn Taymiyya explains, 'what is summarily expressed in one place is expatiated upon in another. What is abridged in one place is elaborated upon in another.'[59] (2) Should that prove fruitless, then have recourse to the *sunna*, a practice that he justifies with assertions from both the Qurʾān and the ḥadīth. (3) If there is nothing of relevance in the Prophet's *sunna*, the next step is examining the statements of the Companions and (4) if that proves unsuccessful, then those of their Followers. Ibn Taymiyya includes in this methodological statement two cautionary remarks. One is about a genre of exegetical material known as *isrāʾīliyyāt* or 'tales of the Israelites' which, although it has been defined in various ways and often used in a pejorative sense, can best be understood as information or accounts attributed to Jewish and/or Christian sources.[60] Despite the widespread use of *isrāʾīliyyāt* in the many preceding centuries of Muslim commentary literature, a decided uneasiness about the advisability of reliance upon these 'external' sources began to emerge. Ibn Taymiyya's treatise captures this ambivalence as it cites a prophetic ḥadīth which authorises the practice while, at the same time, severely restricting its scope:

> Yet these Jewish and Christian accounts (*al-aḥādīth al-isrāʾīliyya*) should only be mentioned for purposes of attestation, not as a basis for belief. These accounts are essentially of three kinds. The first kind is what we know to be true because we already possess that which attests to its authenticity. That kind is sound. The second sort is that which we know to be untrue because of what we possess which contradicts it. The third type is that about which nothing can be said, being neither of the first kind nor the second. We should neither believe it nor declare it to be false. It is permissible to recount it, given what has just been said, but most of it provides no benefit in matters religious.[61]

The second issue to which Ibn Taymiyya addresses himself is the inadmissibility of speaking about the Qurʾān on the basis of personal opinion (*al-tafsīr bi-l-ra'y*), a category of exegetical activity which has been explained above. Rephrasing and expanding upon a famous ḥadīth, Ibn Taymiyya's rejection is unequivocal: 'Whoever does speak about the Qur'ān on the basis of his own personal opinion feigns a knowledge which he does not possess and acts contrary to the command he has been given. Even if, in actuality, he were to get the meaning right, he would still be erring, because he did not come at the matter in the proper way.'[62]

Ibn Taymiyya's hermeneutical principles and attendant cautions directly informed Ibn Kathīr's work as a commentator on the Qur'ān. In fact, Ibn Kathīr incorporates much of the section of Ibn Taymiyya's *Muqaddima* that discusses 'the best methods of interpretation' into the introduction to his own commentary and he does so verbatim.[63] Additionally, the hierarchy of exegetical valuation expressed in that hermeneutical manifesto deeply informs his work.[64] This is not to imply that he mechanically implements the suggested sequence with each successive verse. Rather he lets the primacy of *al-tafsīr bi-l-ma'thūr*, which these hermeneutical principles encapsulate, manifest itself in the overall orientation and achievement of his commentary.[65] Yet it is precisely the unassailable priority given to ḥadīth from the Prophet and those closely associated with him that separates Ibn Kathīr from many of his predecessors. Like his esteemed teacher, Ibn Kathīr advocates a radical return to the beginnings, one that implodes the present into the past and extrudes the exegetical accomplishments and accretions of the intervening centuries. He is particularly wary of those forms of interpretation which have been 'infected' by biblical narratives or other non-Muslim literary sources. The recognition and even celebration of exegetical diversity (*ikhtilāf*) wins no assent from him. In a trenchant comparison of Ibn Kathīr with such predecessors as al-Ṭabarī and al-Qurṭubī, the following judgement has been rendered:

> Ibn Kathīr's *Tafsīr* has many merits; but he has little respect for the intellectual tradition; he barely recognises its authority and is indifferent to the fact that the positions he takes up imply at least a disrespect for his predecessors. He does not generally like polyvalent readings, but argues vehemently for a single 'correct' reading. He is not even-handed in respect of the Islamic sciences, markedly preferring the dogmatic agenda over the narrative . . . It is difficult to avoid the conclusion that, in Ibn Kathīr's view, God has considerably less literary skill than the average human being, and very little imagination.[66]

Jumping almost six centuries to the world of contemporary qur'ānic exegesis presents us with both continuity and change. A twentieth-century Shīʿī commentator like **Muḥammad Ḥusayn Ṭabāṭabā'ī** (d. 1982) represents considerable continuity with the past. Born in Tabrīz, a city in north-western Iran, he studied and taught in the Shīʿī shrine cities of Najaf and Qumm, spending much of his life in the latter, still the intellectual centre of Iranian Shīʿism. His twenty-volume commentary, *The balance in the interpretation of the Qur'ān* (*al-Mīzān fī l-tafsīr al-Qur'ān*),[67] follows the standard model of commenting sequentially on the entire Qur'ān but, like some other commentators, both ancient and modern, he groups sections of consecutive verses for exposition and analysis. Ṭabāṭabā'ī deals with the standard topics, including lexicography, grammar and intra-qur'ānic connections and parallels, and also devotes attention to the relevant ḥadīth literature, particularly that transmitted on the authority of earlier Shīʿī commentators. Frequently cited are Muḥammad b. Masʿūd al- ʿAyyāshī (d. 320/932), ʿAlī b. Ibrāhīm b. Hāshim al-Qummī (d. 328/939) and Aḥmad b. ʿAlī l-Faḍl b. al-Ḥasan al-Ṭabarsī (d. 548/1153).[68] Ṭabāṭabā'ī is among the most noted Persian religious scholars of the past century. Several of his works, including an introduction to Shīʿī thought,[69] have been translated into English and a complete English translation of his *tafsīr* has been in progress for some time.

In the past few years the name of an activist Egyptian commentator who died in 1966, **Sayyid Quṭb**, has become well known to American and European audiences. A cover-page article in the *New York Times Magazine*, published in March 2003,[70] profiled Quṭb under the title 'The philosopher of Islamic terror' and his name has become closely identified in many minds with the form of Islamic thought that motivated the September 11 attacks. Quṭb, whose full name was Sayyid Quṭb Ibrāhīm Ḥusayn Shādhilī, was born in 1906 in Upper Egypt and educated in the village Qur'ān school.[71] Like many traditionally educated Muslim children, he is said to have memorised the complete Qur'ān before the age of ten. His subsequent studies took him to Cairo for secondary- and university-level work. Quṭb's early writings were literary efforts but increased attention to Egypt's social and political problems, as well as an opportunity for extended international travel, reoriented him both ideologically and professionally. He spent most of this travel period in the United States and studied at schools that eventually became the University of Northern Colorado and the University of the District of Columbia.[72] Disgusted by the racism and promiscuity that he saw in North America and Europe, Quṭb returned to Egypt with an even stronger sense of the need for radical social renewal. He joined the Muslim

Brothers and became its most prominent intellectual and writer. Shortly after Gamal Abdel Nasser's ascent to power in 1952, Quṭb was imprisoned and tortured. He spent much of his remaining years in prison and was executed by hanging in 1966.

Quṭb wrote his Qur'ān commentary, *In the shade of the Qur'ān* (*Fī ẓilāl al-Qur'ān*)[73] during his prison years. This work, along with his last book, *Milestones* (*Ma'ālim fī l-ṭarīq*), remain his most famous writings. The latter has often been described as the basic manifesto for contemporary Islamic fundamentalism. But it is his commentary on the Qur'ān that offers the richer and more nuanced version of Quṭb's religio-political reflection. At the core of this reflection is the line that Quṭb draws not between Muslims and non-Muslims but between those who can justifiably call themselves Muslims and those who have surrendered any right to this identification. This latter group constitute a new *jāhiliyya*, a new 'age of ignorance', not dissimilar to the ungodly and depraved society whom the prophet Muḥammad addressed as a 'warner'. This theme and its obverse, a call to Islamic reform and revitalisation, is sounded over and over again in Quṭb's commentary. There is no denying the near-apocalyptic urgency with which Quṭb repeats this summons.

In a manner reminiscent of Ibn Kathīr's – following Ibn Taymiyya – hermeneutics, Sayyid Quṭb spends little time reproducing the exegetical insights that accumulated during the centuries of medieval *tafsīr*. He puts far more emphasis on intra-qur'ānic interpretation and that which can be grounded in the statements of the Prophet and his closest Companions.[74] Like Ṭabāṭabā'ī, he divides the verses of many sūras into sections and these sections and their constituent parts then become the bases for extended excursus on themes that support Quṭb's social and political agenda. The use of a qur'ānic grid on which to plot this agenda gives the whole project a particular power. It allows Quṭb to consistently tie his critiques and his calls for reform to the most potent possible support, God's own word.

COMING BACK TO Q 109

With this introduction to qur'ānic commentators and to the questions that they pose to the text, Q 109 can now be re-read with greater understanding. I selected this sūra as a test case because its exegesis offers a succinct but multifaceted example of qur'ānic interpretation. But I also decided to focus on Q 109 because I have found that it is frequently misread, that it is often cited with a complete disregard of its exegetical tradition. An expanded, i.e., exegetically enhanced, presentation of the sūra provides a prelude to considering some instances of its misreading.

Taking account of the interpretative tradition on Q 109, it could be rendered in this way:

> During his years in Mecca (or, perhaps, Medina) a group of unbelievers tried to coax the Prophet into abandoning, either temporarily or permanently, his allegiance to the one God. Strongly rejecting such a suggestion, Muḥammad delivers a divinely inspired response and disassociates himself completely and absolutely from the idolatrous religion of his opponents: 'O you unbelievers, I do not worship what you worship and you do not worship the One whom I worship. Neither, in the future, will I worship what you worship nor will you worship the One whom I worship. Your false religion is for you and my true religion is for me.'

In the commentary tradition on this sūra there is no evidence of either equivocation or compromise. To use contemporary terminology, there is nothing that suggests an 'acceptance' of 'religious pluralism' or a desire to promote religious 'toleration'. Quite the contrary: the line between truth and falsehood, between what is from God and what is not from God, is clearly drawn.

Yet in current discussions of interreligious relations or in current efforts to support interreligious dialogue, Q 109 frequently figures as a textual support. Take, for example, the article by David Little, a prominent Christian ethicist, in which he seeks affirmation in the Qur'ān 'of religious tolerance and forbearance' and finds his first proof text in Q 109.[75] Or listen to Syed Barakat Ahmad as he argues that 'religious liberty is not an exclusively modern concept'. The initial qur'ānic argument to which he points is Q 109: 'The Sūrat al-Kāfirūn, revealed in the early period of the Prophet's ministry, is a most forthright statement of policy on the subject of freedom of conscience.'[76] Yet more recently, Salwa El-Awa cites Q 109:6 as evidence that the Qur'ān strongly discourages religious intolerance.[77] Increasingly, a connection is made between the sentiments of this sūra – as understood without recourse to the commentary tradition – and the articles pertinent to religious freedom in the Universal Declaration of Human Rights. Defining 'religious pluralism' as 'acknowledging the intrinsic redemptive value of competing religious traditions', Abdulaziz Sachedina points to Q 109 as countering the 'common attitude among the religious groups' that 'there is only one true religion and that competing traditions are false and valueless'.[78]

Rarely is an exegetically sensitive reading of Q 109 encountered in the contemporary discourse about pluralism, tolerance, human rights and religious freedom. One instance, however, is the work of Yohanan Friedmann. In his monograph on Islamic concepts of coercion and tolerance, Friedmann recognises that Q 109 'has sometimes been understood as reflecting an attitude of religious tolerance on the part of the Muslims' but rejects such understandings as textually and exegetically unwarranted.[79] Accepting Theodor Nöldeke's dating of this sūra to the first Meccan period,[80] Friedmann sees Q 109 as taking 'cognizance of the unbridgeable gap between Islam and the religion of the Meccans'.[81] He actually goes further than the commentators on this verse by insisting that the passage is 'best interpreted as a plea to the Meccans to refrain from practicing religious coercion against the Muslims of Mecca before the *hijra*'.[82]

But Friedmann is the exception to a general pattern of misreading this sūra in the name of religious diversity and toleration. By pointing to these misinterpretations, however, I do not mean to suggest that there are no qurʾānic or Islamic resources upon which a theology of religious and interreligious rights could be constructed.[83] Q 2:256 and its assertion 'there is no compulsion in religion' (*lā ikrāha fī l-dīn*) is the *locus classicus*, but there are others as well.[84] Yet for Q 109 the classical exegetical tradition is clear and attempts to deploy its verses to support contemporary principles of religious toleration contradict that tradition.

Of course, the extent to which that tradition should be respected and should remain an active factor in the contemporary conversation continues to be a compelling subject of debate and one that has captured the attention of many modern Muslim intellectuals. A 'back to the sources' sentiment that has become increasingly prominent over the past century or so seeks to collapse the distance between the contemporary context and the founding moment, disregarding the intellectual accomplishments of intervening centuries. Where medieval authorities are cited, the reference is limited to a handful of authors. It is easy to find al-Ghazālī quoted; rare to find reference to al-Fārābī (d. 339/950). Ibn Taymiyya's name appears everywhere, frequently bundled with other Ḥanbalīs like Ibn Qayyim al-Jawziyya (d. 751/1350), but al-Zamakhsharī is absent.

Nevertheless, the inherent dynamism of exegetical activity leaves it ever open-ended. Commentary begets commentary as each new generation of readers receives the text within its own frame of reference – and as that same community assimilates the multiple lines of interpretation that earlier readings have generated. But those lines of interpretation are not simply a series of parallel trajectories. There are instances of influence and points of confluence. There are also disjunctions or disruptions and even, as just mentioned, wholescale rejection of the accumulated consequences of centuries of exegetical activity. Yet the conversation continues, the tug of the text persists and the desire for intellectual engagement with the divine word remains irresistible.

Notes

1. Abū l-Faraj ʿAbd al-Raḥmān b. ʿAlī b. al-Jawzī, *Zād al-masīr fī ʿilm al-tafsīr,* 9 vols. (Beirut: al-Maktab al-Islāmī, 1984).
2. Q 109 (Sūrat al-Kāfirūn):1–6.
3. I have taken the alternate reading, *lam yuʾmin,* cited in the footnote from an Istanbul manuscript.
4. While the text reads *lā aʿbudu* here, a phrase from the second verse, the meaning requires *mā aʿbudu,* a phrase from the third verse.
5. For further details, see H. Laoust, 'Ibn al-Jawzī', in *Encyclopaedia of Islam,* new ed., 11 vols. (Leiden: Brill, 1979–2002), vol. III, pp. 751–2; J. D. McAuliffe, 'Ibn al-Jawzī's exegetical propaedutic: Introduction and translation', *Alif* 8 (Spring 1988), 101–14; and J. D. McAuliffe, *Qurʾānic Christians: An analysis of classical and modern exegesis* (Cambridge: Cambridge University Press, 1991), pp. 57–63.
6. A famous translator of the Qur'ān, the British scholar and convert Marmaduke Pickthall, spoke of a Qur'ān commentary as requiring 'another commentary of equal length to make its methods and mentality intelligible to English people who have never studied Quranic commentary'; 'Arabs and non-Arabs and the question of translating the Qur'an', *Islamic Culture* 5 (1931), 422.
7. McAuliffe, 'Exegetical propaedutic', 107.
8. Further to this see Badr al-Dīn Muḥammad b. ʿAbdallāh al-Zarkashī, *al-Burhān fī ʿulūm al-Qurʾān,* ed. M. A. Ibrāhīm, 4 vols. (Cairo: Dār al-Turāth, n.d.), ch. 9 and Jalāl al-Dīn ʿAbd al-Raḥmān al-Suyūṭī, *al-Itqān fī ʿulūm al-Qurʾān,* ed. M. A. Ibrāhīm, 4 vols. in 2 (Cairo: Dār al-Turāth, 1985), ch. 1. For a summary review of both Muslim and Western analyses of qur'ānic chronology, see G. Böwering, 'Chronology and the Qur'ān', in J. D. McAuliffe (ed.), *Encyclopaedia of the Qurʾān,* 5 vols. (Leiden: Brill, 2001–6), vol. I, pp. 316–35.
9. Abū ʿAbdallāh Muḥammad b. Aḥmad al-Anṣārī al-Qurṭubī, *al-Jāmiʿ li-aḥkām al-Qurʾān,* 20 vols. + 2 vol. index (Beirut: Dār al-Fikr, 1978), vol. XX, p. 224.
10. The most famous work in this genre is that of Abū l-Ḥasan ʿAlī b. Aḥmad al-Nīsābūrī al-Wāhidī (d. 468/1076): *Asbāb al-nuzūl* (Cairo: Mu'assassat al-Ḥalabī, 1968).
11. Muqātil b. Sulaymān, *al-Tafsīr,* ed. ʿAbdallāh Maḥmūd Shiḥāta, 5 vols. (Cairo: al-Hay'a al-Miṣriyya al-ʿĀmma lil-Kitāb, 1979–89).
12. For other instances of this term see Q 2:14; 15:95; cf. 4:140; 9:65; 11:8; 26:6; 36:30; 45:33.

13. Muqātil, *Tafsīr*, vol. IV, p. 887, which includes his citation of Q 53:19–20. Abū Jahl, who died in the Battle of Badr, was a noted enemy of the Prophet in Mecca and a figure against whom several qur'ānic revelations are credited.
14. Abū Isḥāq Aḥmad al-Thaʿlabī, *al-Kashf wa-l-bayān*, ed. A. M. b. ʿĀshūr and N. al-Sāʿidī, 10 vols. (Beirut: Dār Iḥyā' al-Turāth al-ʿArabī, 2002), vol. X, p. 315.
15. Abū Jaʿfar Muḥammad b. al-Ḥasan al-Ṭūsī, *al-Tibyān fī tafsīr al-Qur'ān*, 10 vols. (Beirut: Dār Iḥyā' al-Turāth al-ʿArabī, n.d.), vol. X, p. 420. Cf. Abū Jaʿfar Muḥammad b. Jarīr al-Ṭabarī, *Jāmiʿ al-bayān ʿan ta'wīl āy al-Qur'ān*, 15 vols. (Beirut: Dār al-Fikr, 1984), vol. XV, p. 331. Q 39:64 – 'Say [Muḥammad, to the unbelievers], "Do you command me to serve other than God? Oh, you fools!"'
16. al-Qurṭubī, *Jāmiʿ*, vol. XX, p. 227. Accounts of this and related scenarios can be found in the *sīra*, the biography of the Prophet. A. Guillaume (trans.), *The life of Muhammad: A translation of Sīrat Rasūl Allāh* (Oxford: Oxford University Press, 1955), p. 165 and pp. 132–5. See also the translated version of al-Ṭabarī's *Ta'rīkh* (full bibliographic information for the Arabic edition below, note 44): W. M. Watt and M. V. McDonald (trans.), *The history of al-Ṭabarī*, vol. VI, *Muḥammad at Mecca* (Albany: SUNY Press, 1988), p. 107.
17. al-Ṭūsī, *Tibyān*, vol. X, pp. 423–4.
18. al-Qurṭubī, *Jāmiʿ*, vol. XX, pp. 228–9.
19. al-Ṭabarī, *Tafsīr*, vol. XV, p. 332.
20. al-Thaʿlabī, *Tafsīr*, vol. X, pp. 316–17.
21. al-Ṭabarī, *Tafsīr*, vol. XV, pp. 330–1. Cf. Muqātil, *Tafsīr*, vol. IV, pp. 887–8; al-Qurṭubī, *Jāmiʿ*, vol. XX, p. 228.
22. al-Qurṭubī, *Jāmiʿ*, vol. XX, p. 228.
23. al-Ṭūsī, *Tibyān*, vol. X, pp. 420–1.
24. See Gilliot's contribution to the present volume, Chapter 2; cf. also G. Bergsträsser, 'Plan eines Apparatus criticus zum Koran', *Sitzungsberichte der Bayerischen Akademie der Wissenschaften, Philosophisch-historische Abteilung* 7 (1930); repr. in R. Paret (ed.), *Der Koran* (Darmstadt: Wissenschaftliche Buchgesellschaft, 1975), pp. 389–97; F. Déroche and S. Noja Noseda, *Sources de la transmission manuscrite du texte coranique*, vol. I, *Les manuscrits de style ḥiǧāzī*, 2 vols. (Lesa: Fondazione Ferni Noja Noseda, 1998–2001).
25. A. M. ʿUmar and ʿA. S. Mukkaram, *Muʿjam al-qirā'āt al-qur'āniyya*, 8 vols. (Iran: Uswah, 1991–7), vol. VIII, p. 257; ʿA. al-L. al-Khaṭīb, *Muʿjam al-qirā'āt*, 11 vols. (Damascus: Dār Saʿd al-Dīn, 2002), vol. X, pp. 617–19.
26. See K. M. Kueny, *The rhetoric of sobriety: Wine in early Islam* (Albany: SUNY Press, 2001); J. D. McAuliffe, 'The wines of earth and paradise: Qur'ānic proscriptions and promises', in R. M. Savory and D. A. Agius (eds.), *Logos islamikos: Studia islamica in honorem Georgii Michaelis Wickens* (Toronto: Pontifical Institute of Medieval Studies, 1984), pp. 159–74.
27. For a discussion of modern efforts to repudiate the doctrine of *naskh* see D. Brown, 'The triumph of scripturalism: The doctrine of naskh and its modern critics', in E. H. Waugh and F. M. Denny (eds.), *The shaping of an American Islamic discourse* (Atlanta, GA: Scholars Press, 1998), pp. 49–66.
28. Ibn Salāma, *al-Nāsikh wa-l-mansūkh* (Beirut: al-Maktab al-Islāmī, 1984), p. 184; D. Powers, 'The exegetical genre *nāsikh al-Qur'ān wa mansūkhuhu*', in A.

Rippin (ed.), *Approaches to the history of the interpretation of the Qur'ān* (Oxford: Clarendon Press, 1988), pp. 117–38; Muqātil, *Tafsīr*, vol. IV, p. 888.

29. Abū Bakr Aḥmad b. ʿAbdallāh al-Jaṣṣāṣ al-Rāzī, *Aḥkām al-Qur'ān*, 3 vols. (Cairo: Dār al-Fikr, n.d.), vol. III, p. 476. Cf. al-Ṭūsī, *Tibyān*, vol. X, p. 422; al-Qurṭubī cites al-Māwardī (d. 450/1058) in support of this position (*Jāmiʿ*, vol. XX, pp. 225–6).
30. al-Jaṣṣāṣ, *Aḥkām al-Qur'ān*, vol. III, p. 476.
31. al-Thaʿlabī, *Tafsīr*, vol. X, p. 314; Maḥmūd b. ʿUmar al-Zamakhsharī, *al-Kashshāf ʿan ḥaqā'iq ghawāmiḍ al-tanzīl wa-ʿuyūn al-aqāwīl fī wujūh al-ta'wīl*, ed. ʿĀ. A. ʿAbd al-Mawjūd and ʿA. M. Muʿawwaḍ, 6 vols. (Riyadh: Maktabat al-ʿUbaykān, 1998), vol. VI, p. 449.
32. al-Thaʿlabī, *Tafsīr*, vol. X, p. 315; al-Qurṭubī, *Jāmiʿ*, vol. XX, p. 225.
33. J. D. McAuliffe, 'Exegetical sciences', in A. Rippin (ed.), *Blackwell Companion to the Qur'an* (Oxford: Blackwell, 2006), pp. 403–19.
34. al-Thaʿlabī, *Tafsīr*, vol. X, p. 314.
35. J. D. McAuliffe, 'The genre boundaries of qur'ānic commentary', in J. D. McAuliffe, B. D. Walfish and J. W. Goering (eds.), *With reverence for the word: Medieval scriptural exegesis in Judaism, Christianity, and Islam* (Oxford: Oxford University Press, 2003), pp. 445–6.
36. al-Dhahabī, *al-Tafsīr wa-l-mufassirūn*, 2 vols. (Cairo: Dār al-Iḥyā' al-Turāth al-ʿArabī, 1976[3]).
37. In modern works on qur'ānic exegesis the pairing is usually given as *al-tafsīr bi-l-riwāya* and *al-tafsīr bi-l-dirāya*, respectively.
38. A. Lane, *A traditional Muʿtazilite Qur'ān commentary: The Kashshāf of Jār Allāh al-Zamakhsharī* (Leiden: Brill, 2006).
39. I. Goldziher, *Die Richtungen der islamischen Koranauslegung* (Leiden: Brill, 1920, repr. 1970).
40. A. Rippin, 'Tafsīr', in M. Eliade (ed.), *The encyclopedia of religion*, 16 vols. (New York: Macmillan Publishing Co., 1987), vol. XIV, pp. 236–44, and also his 'Tafsīr', in *Encyclopaedia of Islam*, new ed., vol. X, pp. 83–8, and Cl. Gilliot, 'Exegesis of the Qur'ān: Classical and medieval', in McAuliffe (ed.), *Encyclopaedia of the Qur'ān*, vol. II, pp. 99–124, and R. Wielandt, 'Exegesis of the Qur'ān: Early modern and contemporary', in McAuliffe (ed.), *Encyclopaedia of the Qur'ān*, vol. II, pp. 124–42.
41. The best, and most accessible, English-language biography of al-Ṭabarī may be found in the first volume of the translation of his world history. F. Rosenthal (trans. and annot.), *The history of al-Ṭabarī* (*Ta'rīkh al-rusul wa-l-mulūk*), vol. I, *General introduction and From the creation to the flood* (Albany: SUNY Press, 1989), pp. 5–80.
42. Ibid., pp. 20–1.
43. Ibid., p. 21, as cited from Yāqūt b. ʿAbdallāh al-Ḥamawī, *Irshād: al-arīb ilā maʿrifat al-adīb (Muʿjam al-udabā')*, ed. A. F. al-Rifāʿī (Cairo: Maṭbuʿāt Dār al-Māmūn, 1936–8).
44. Abū Jaʿfar Muḥammad b. Jarīr al-Ṭabarī, *Ta'rīkh al-rusul wa-l-mulūk*, ed. M. J. de Goeje et al., 15 vols. (Leiden: Brill, 1879–1901); ed. M. Abū l-Faḍl Ibrāhīm, 10 vols. (Cairo: Dār al-Maʿārif, 1960–9). For an approach to the *Ta'rīkh* that draws upon contemporary theories of linguistic and rhetorical construction, see

B. Shoshan, *Poetics of Islamic historiography: Deconstructing Ṭabarī's History* (Leiden: Brill, 2004).

45. The only major monograph on this commentary in Western languages is Cl. Gilliot's *Exégèse, langue, et théologie en Islam: L'exégèse coranique de Ṭabarī (m. 310/923)* (Paris: J. Vrin, 1990).
46. For more on al-Ṭabarī's exegetical methodology see J. D. McAuliffe, 'Quranic hermeneutics: The views of al-Ṭabarī and Ibn Kathīr', in A. Rippin (ed.), *Approaches to the history of the interpretation of the Qur'ān* (Oxford: Clarendon Press, 1988), pp. 46–62.
47. N. Calder, '*Tafsīr* from Ṭabarī to Ibn Kathīr: Problems in the description of a genre, illustrated with reference to the story of Abraham', in G. R. Hawting and A. A. Shareef (eds.), *Approaches to the Qur'ān* (London: Routledge, 1993), pp. 103–4.
48. G. Böwering, *The mystical vision of existence in classical Islam: The qur'ānic hermeneutics of the Sūfī Sahl at-Tustarī (d. 283/896)* (Berlin: de Gruyter, 1980).
49. Ibid., p. 73 as cited from Abū Naṣr ʿAbdallāh b. ʿAlī Sarrāj, *al-Luma' fī l-taṣawwuf*, ed. R. A. Nicholson (Leiden: Brill, 1914), p. 307.
50. Sahl al-Tustarī, *Tafsīr al-Qur'ān al-ʿaẓīm* (Cairo: Dār al-Kutub al-ʿArabiyya al-Kubrā, 1911).
51. Böwering, *Mystical*, p. 129.
52. Not to be confused with the later Andalusian, Muḥyī l-Dīn b. al-ʿArabī (d. 638/1240), an important Ṣūfī author.
53. Brief biographical information can be found in J. Robson, 'Ibn al-ʿArabī, Abū Bakr Muḥammad b. ʿAbd Allāh Maʿāfirī', in *Encyclopaedia of Islam*, new ed., vol. III, p. 707.
54. Abū Bakr Muḥammad b. ʿAbdallāh b. al-ʿArabī, *Aḥkām al-Qur'ān*, ed. M. ʿA. ʿAṭā, 4 vols. (Beirut: Dār al-Kutub al-ʿIlmiyya, 1988).
55. J. D. McAuliffe, 'Legal exegesis: Christians as a case study', in L. Ridgeon (ed.), *Islamic interpretations of Christianity* (Richmond, Surrey: Curzon, 2001), pp. 54–77.
56. The titles he gives are *Anwār al-fajr*, a work that is no longer extant but which is frequently mentioned in his *Aḥkām al-Qur'ān*, and *al-Amad al-aqṣā*, a commentary on the divine names and attributes, of which there are manuscripts in Rabat and Istanbul. See M. I. al-Mashnī, *Ibn al-ʿArabī al-Mālikī al-Ishbīlī wa-tafsīruhu* (Amman: Dār al-ʿAmmār, 1991), p. 32.
57. al-Mashnī, *Ibn al-ʿArabī*, p. 335.
58. Taqī l-Dīn Aḥmad b. ʿAbd al-Ḥalīm b. Taymiyya, *Muqaddima fī uṣūl al-tafsīr*, ed. A. Zarzūr (Beirut: Dār al-Qur'ān al-Karīm, 1971).
59. J. D. McAuliffe, 'Ibn Taymiya: Treatise on the principles of tafsir', in J. Renard (ed.), *Windows on the house of Islam: Muslim sources on spirituality and religious life* (Berkeley: University of California Press, 1998), p. 36.
60. J. D. McAuliffe, 'Assessing the Isrā'īliyyāt: An exegetical conundrum', in S. Leder (ed.), *Story-telling in the framework of non-fictional Arabic literature* (Wiesbaden: Harrassowitz, 1998), pp. 345–69.
61. McAuliffe, 'Ibn Taymiya', p. 38.
62. Ibid., p. 41.

63. Compare Ibn Taymiyya, *Muqaddima*, pp. 93–115 with Ibn Kathīr, *Tafsīr al-Qur'ān al-'aẓīm*, 4 vols. (Cairo: Maktaba Dār al-Turāth, 1980), vol. I, pp. 3–6. For a contemporary recap of Ibn Taymiyya's *Muqaddima* see A. Saeed, *Interpreting the Qur'ān: Towards a contemporary approach* (London: Routledge, 2006), pp. 42–9.
64. McAuliffe, 'Quranic hermeneutics', pp. 46–62.
65. Maḥmūd Shihāta, *Ta'rīkh al-Qur'ān wa-l-tafsīr* (Cairo: al-Hay'a al-Miṣriyya al-'Āmma lil-Kitāb, 1972), p. 176; al-Dhahabī, *al-Tafsīr wa-l-mufassirūn*, vol. I, p. 236.
66. Calder, '*Tafsīr* from Ṭabarī to Ibn Kathīr', p. 124.
67. Muḥammad Ḥusayn Ṭabāṭabā'ī, *al-Mīzān fī l-tafsīr al-Qur'ān*, 20 vols. (Beirut: Mu'assasat al-A'lāmī lil-Maṭbū'āt, 1974).
68. A significant concern in early Shī'ī exegesis was the textual integrity of the Qur'ān and the willingness, or not, to accept the canonical validity of the 'Uthmānic codex. Further to this, see J. Eliash, 'The Šī'ite Qur'ān: A reconsideration of Goldziher's interpretation', *Arabica* 16 (1969), 15–24; E. Kohlberg, 'Some notes on the Imāmite attitude to the Qur'ān', in S. M. Stern, A. Hourani and V. Brown (eds.), *Islamic philosophy and the classical tradition* (Columbia, SC: University of South Carolina Press, 1972), pp. 209–24; H. Modarressi, 'Early debates on the integrity of the Qur'ān', *Studia Islamica* 77 (1993), 5–39; M. M. Bar-Asher, *Scripture and exegesis in early Imāmī Shiism* (Leiden: Brill, 1999).
69. Muḥammad Ḥusayn Ṭabāṭabā'ī, *Shi'ite Islam*, trans. and ed. S. H. Nasr (Albany: SUNY Press, 1975).
70. http://www.nytimes.com/2003/03/23/magazine/23GURU.html. This article is drawn from the author's book-length study: Paul Berman, *Terror and liberalism* (New York: W. W. Norton and Co., 2003).
71. Two monographic studies are W. E. Shepard, *Sayyid Qutb and Islamic activism* (Leiden: Brill, 1996), with brief biographical information on pp. xi–xvii, and O. Carré, *Mystique et politique: Lecture révolutionnaire du Coran par Sayyid Quṭb, frère musulman radicale* (Paris: Editions du Cerf, 1984).
72. S. Akhavi, 'Quṭb, Sayyid', in J. Esposito (ed.), *The Oxford encyclopedia of the modern Islamic world*, 4 vols. (New York: Oxford University Press, 1995), vol. III, p. 401.
73. Sayyid Quṭb, *Fī ẓilāl al-Qur'ān*, 6 vols. (Cairo: Dār al-Shurūq, 1972). Much of this work has been translated into English and parts of it are still appearing. Sections of this translation are available online.
74. This approach has been characterised as 'the Islamist ideal of subordinating oneself to the divine word as immediately as the first Muslims had done'. See Wielandt, 'Early modern', p. 138.
75. D. Little, 'The development in the West of the right to freedom of religion and conscience: A basis for comparison with Islam: (1) The Western tradition', in D. Little, J. Kelsay and A. Sachedina (eds.), *Human rights and the conflict of cultures: Western and Islamic perspectives on religious liberty* (Columbia, SC: University of South Carolina Press, 1988), p. 28.
76. Syed Barakat Ahmad, 'Conversion from Islam', in C. E. Bosworth, C. Issawi, R. Savory and A. L. Udovitch (eds.), *The Islamic world: From classical to modern times* (Princeton: Darwin Press, 1989), p. 3.

77. S. El-Awa, 'Zealotry', in McAuliffe (ed.), *Encyclopaedia of the Qur'ān*, vol. V, pp. 572–4.
78. A. Sachedina, *The Islamic roots of democratic pluralism* (Oxford: Oxford University Press, 2001), p. 36.
79. Y. Friedmann, *Tolerance and coercion in Islam: Interfaith relations in the Muslim tradition* (Cambridge: Cambridge University Press, 2003), p. 88.
80. T. Nöldeke, *Geschichte des Qorans*, new ed. by F. Schwally, G. Bergsträsser and O. Pretzl, 3 vols. (Leipzig: T. Dieter, 1909–38), vol. I, p. 108.
81. Friedmann, *Tolerance and coercion*, p. 88.
82. Y. Friedmann, 'Tolerance and compulsion', in McAuliffe (ed.), *Encyclopaedia of the Qur'ān*, vol. V, pp. 290–4.
83. A concise, preliminary effort can be found in the article by R. Mottahedeh, 'Towards an Islamic theology of toleration', in T. Lindholm and K. Vogt (eds.), *Islamic law reform and human rights: Challenges and rejoinders* (Copenhagen et alia: Nordic Human Rights Publications, 1993), pp. 25–36.
84. See I. Goldziher, *Introduction to Islamic law and theology*, trans. A. and R. Hamori (Princeton: Princeton University Press, 1981), pp. 33–6; R. Paret, 'Sure 2, 256: *lā ikrāha fī d-dīni*: Toleranz oder Resignation?', in R. Paret (ed.), *Der Koran* (Darmstadt: Wissenschaftliche Buchgesellschaft, 1975), pp. 306–8 (repr. from *Der Islam* 45 (1969), 299–300); Friedmann, *Tolerance and coercion*, pp. 94–5 and 100–8. It must be noted that Q 2:256 has received quite restrictive readings and can also be found on the list of verses abrogated by Q 9:5.

Further reading

Bar-Asher, M. M., *Scripture and exegesis in early Imāmī Shiism*, Leiden: Brill, 1999.

Calder, N., '*Tafsīr* from Ṭabarī to Ibn Kathīr: Problems in the description of a genre, illustrated with reference to the story of Abraham', in G. R. Hawting and A. A. Shareef (eds.), *Approaches to the Qur'ān*, London: Routledge, 1993, pp. 101–40.

Gatje, H., *The Qur'ān and its exegesis: Selected texts with classical and modern Muslim interpretations*, A. T. Welch (trans.), London: Routledge & Kegan Paul, 1976.

Gilliot, Cl., 'Exegesis of the Qur'ān: Classical and medieval', in J. D. McAuliffe (ed.), *Encyclopaedia of the Qur'ān*, 5 vols., Leiden: Brill, 2001–6, vol. II, pp. 99–124.

Goldziher, I., *Die Richtungen der islamischen Koranauslegung*, Leiden: Brill, 1920, repr. 1970.

McAuliffe, J. D., 'The genre boundaries of qur'ānic commentary', in J. D. McAuliffe, B. D. Walfish and J. W. Goering (eds.), *With reverence for the word: Medieval scriptural exegesis in Judaism, Christianity, and Islam*, Oxford: Oxford University Press, 2003, pp. 445–62.

'Legal exegesis: Christians as a case study', in L. Ridgeon (ed.), *Islamic interpretations of Christianity*, Richmond, Surrey: Curzon, 2001, pp. 54–77.

Qur'ānic Christians: An analysis of classical and modern exegesis, Cambridge: Cambridge University Press, 1991.

'Quranic hermeneutics: The views of al-Ṭabarī and Ibn Kathīr', in A. Rippin (ed.), *Approaches to the history of the interpretation of the Qur'ān,* Oxford: Clarendon Press, 1988, pp. 46–62.

Rippin, A. (ed.), *Approaches to the history of the interpretation of the Qur'ān,* Oxford: Clarendon Press, 1988.

Wielandt, R., 'Exegesis of the Qur'ān: Early modern and contemporary', in J. D. McAuliffe (ed.), *Encyclopaedia of the Qur'ān,* 5 vols., Leiden: Brill, 2001–6, vol. II, pp. 124–42.

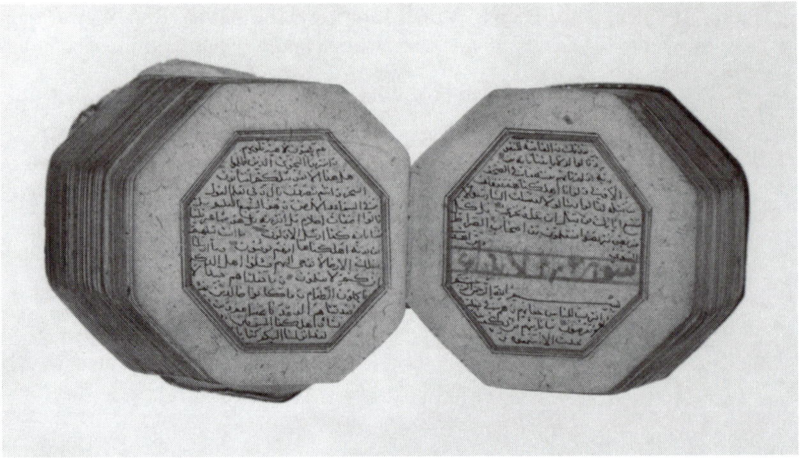

Fig. 10 A fifteenth-century miniature Iranian or Turkish Qur'ān in *naskhī* script. Shown here is the end of Q 20 (Sūrat Ṭā Hā) and the beginning of Q 21 (Sūrat al-Anbiyā', 'The Prophets') (Khalili Collection, QUR 371, fol. 235b–236a). Courtesy of the Nasser D. Khalili Collection of Islamic Art, London

10 Multiple areas of influence

ALEXANDER KNYSH

> So the book lives on among its people, stuff of their daily lives, taking for them the place of a sacrament. For to them, these are not mere letters or mere words. They are the twigs of the burning bush, aflame with God . . . 'It is recited by tongues, written in volumes, memorized in breasts.'[1]

'The overwhelmingly central role played by the Qur'ān in Muslim piety'[2] is an axiom that is recognised by both Muslims and outside observers. The book's profound and pervasive influence on all aspects of Islamic personal and communal life and its ubiquitous presence in Islamic sciences, arts, literatures, craftsmanship, devotional practices and everyday speech are richly attested. Less obvious and more difficult to gauge is its impact on the social, familial and political behaviour and on the spiritual and intellectual life of the average Muslim, although this, too, is easy to imagine. Whether the Qur'ān's significance for its followers is due to its irresistible attraction, inherent aesthetic appeal and persuasiveness, or to their 'Islamic' upbringing, schooling and socialisation, its overriding importance for the Muslim community is hardly in doubt. What follows is an attempt to examine the influence of the Qur'ān on such spheres of Arab/Islamic intellectual endeavour as philology, jurisprudence, theology/philosophy and literary production. Considerations of space will necessarily make this survey selective and incomplete.

PHILOLOGY

From the very outset, the fact that the Qur'ān – the literal and exact word of God – was, in its own words, revealed in 'clear Arabic', endowed this language with a sacred status in the eyes of Muslims. It was, according to the Islamic tradition, the language that God taught to Adam and of which the prophet Muḥammad was the most accomplished speaker. As such, it had to be protected from corruption and distortion, a danger that became a distinct possibility with the conversion to Islam of non-Arabic speakers.[3] Furthermore, the recitation of verses of the divine revelation was incumbent on every believer, so one had to have at least some knowledge of the Arabic language in order to utter them properly. The introduction in the middle of the first/seventh century of the canonical text of the Qur'ān – the first Arabic book – was but a partial solution to the problem, because the deficiencies of the Arabic script allowed for different readings of one and the same passage. The need to preserve this still mostly oral text and to standardise its recitation, which was so central to Muslim worship, prompted some concerned individuals – especially professional Qur'ān readers/reciters (*qurrā'*) supported by the Umayyad authorities – to undertake the first rudimentary analysis of its diction. It took four months for a committee of five leading Qur'ān experts and readers from Baṣra, who were appointed by the Iraqi governor al-Ḥajjāj (d. 95/714), to determine the number of words and letters in the caliph ʿUthmān's redaction of the qur'ānic text (77,439 and 323,015, respectively). (At about the same time, the Qur'ān was divided into thirty parts to facilitate its use in Muslim ritual practices, such as the recitation of one thirtieth on each day of the month.) The first attempt to introduce special coloured markings for the Arabic vowels and diacritical points for the consonants with a view to securing the correct recitation of the Qur'ān was undertaken in the second half of the second/seventh century. Such practices, however, acquired their final shape at the hands of the first Arab lexicographer al-Khalīl b. Aḥmad (d. 175/791). The importance of this innovation – which took place under the influence of Aramaic grammatical conventions[4] – is difficult to overestimate as it facilitated the establishment of Arabic as the official (and only) language of the state and its administration under the caliph ʿAbd al-Malik (r. 65–86/685–705). From that time on, it became the principal language of culture and communication in the rapidly growing Islamic empire.[5] Thus, one can argue that Arabic philology initially emerged as qur'ānic text linguistics *par excellence* and vice versa.

At the turn of the second/eighth century, the nascent Arabic philological science witnessed a gradual transition from a focus on orthography, which was necessitated by the immediate exigencies of qur'ānic recitation, to more abstract and sophisticated grammatical studies, which included discussions of 'difficult words' (*gharīb*), morphology and syntax (*iʿrāb*) and rhetorical features (*majāz*). Such studies were pursued by the growing circle of professional Qur'ān readers, who were based in the major religious and cultural centres of the Muslim world: Mecca, Damascus, Medina, Baṣra and Kūfa. Their activities prepared the foundation for the groundbreaking grammatical *summa* of Sībawayhi (d. around 180/796), who sought to highlight the 'correct diction and usage' of Arabic words by freely availing himself of extra-qur'ānic material, especially pre-Islamic poetry and the Bedouin language, whose 'pagan' status made it unacceptable to his more orthodox colleagues.[6] Sībawayhi's approach, nowhere explicitly stated, implied that the diction of some Bedouin tribes may occasionally be preferable to that of the Qur'ān and that it was thus equally valid as a source of linguistic material (pre-Islamic poetry being inferior to both). This idea was nothing short of revolutionary despite the fact that the great grammarian did not go so far as to replace a qur'ānic reading sanctioned by the readers' consensus with one that he considered to be more correct on purely linguistic grounds.[7] As grammatical theories grew more detached from the immediate exigencies of Qur'ān recitation and thus more abstract and sophisticated, a tension arose between the philologists' religious sentiments and their commitment to the philosophy of language at which they had arrived through a painstaking observation of linguistic phenomena. Overcome by remorse, some of them abandoned their 'ungodly' scholarly pursuits altogether, while others made it a habit to expiate their 'sins' by copying the text of the Qur'ān and donating it to the local community or by performing supererogatory acts of piety (e.g., Abū 'Amr b. al-'Alā', d. *c.* 154/770, Abū 'Amr al-Shaybānī, d. 213/828 and al-Zajjājī, d. *c.* 337/949, etc.).[8] Others (e.g., al-Aṣma'ī, d. 213/828) adopted an 'agnostic' position, arguing that they could explain the meaning of a certain word or phrase in common Arabic usage, but did not 'know what is meant by it in the Qur'ān and the Sunna'.[9] Still others were unapologetic. Thus, the renowned philologist Abū 'Ubayda (d. 209/824–5) argued that since God had spoken to the Arabs in their own language, it is only natural to interpret his revelation by means of their 'profane' diction and poetry. In line with this premise, he elucidated the grammatical and semantic intricacies of the Qur'ān by freely quoting linguistic evidence derived from pre-Islamic poetry.

Overall, however, the doctrinal constraints faced by the philologists were numerous and daunting, namely, the presence of foreign words in the Qur'ān, the tenet regarding the unsurpassed excellence of the Quraysh dialect in which, according to the tradition, the Qur'ān was revealed, and the conclusive character of the Arabic language as the repository of God's final revelation – a notion that precluded any possibility of its subsequent development. These challenges were, eventually, successfully met by Arab linguists and grammarians, who used all their ingenuity to bring their elegant philological constructions in line with religious dogma.[10] In the course of dealing with such dogmatic challenges the originally homogeneous class of Qur'ān experts split into the *qurrā'* proper, who viewed themselves as the custodians of the received linguistic lore relating to qur'ānic recitation and the dogmatic orthodoxies associated with it, and the 'grammarians' (*naḥwiyyūn*), who were anxious to assert their right to study the Qur'ān unencumbered by the dogmatic restraints imposed upon it by the 'readers'. This 'division of labour' within the early philological movement was accompanied by mutual recriminations. The readers/reciters accused the 'grammarians' of profaning the revelation by treating it as any man-made text and judging it with the criteria borrowed from the pre-Islamic ('pagan') poetic and oral corpus. The grammarians, for their part, ridiculed their opponents' 'poor understanding' of linguistic theory, while duly acknowledging their exemplary piety and unwavering loyalty to the primeval tradition of Qur'ān readings (*qirā'āt*), which were established on the basis of their compatibility with 'Uthmān's codex.[11] This acknowledgement, however, was not devoid of condescending overtones in that it implicitly denied the readers the authority to rule on the admissibility of linguistic usage outside and even inside the Qur'ān.[12] It should be pointed out that the grammarians were reluctant to recognise themselves as experts on language *par excellence*. Rather, they seem to have considered themselves as interpreters of the Qur'ān, who employed their sense of language and linguistic expertise to elucidate its underlying message, especially its legal implications, for their coreligionists.[13] In this regard, their philological elaborations constituted part and parcel of Muslim exegetical endeavour. Nevertheless, as time went on, qur'ānic philology evolved into a number of semi-independent disciplines such as phonology, morphology and syntax, lexicography, semantics, rhetoric, etc. While these disciplines were richly represented in the exegetical works of the third–fourth/ninth–tenth centuries, including al-Ṭabarī's (d. 310/923) monumental commentary *Jāmi' al-bayān*, they were no longer limited to the Qur'ān and their methods were equally applied to other linguistic phenomena, especially poetry. This non-qur'ānic application of philological science gave rise to literary criticism.

With time, systematic comparisons between the style of pre-Islamic poetry and Bedouin speech and that of the Qur'ān led to the emergence of Arabic rhetoric (*balāgha*) with its doctrine of the uniqueness and unmatchable eloquence of the scripture. It represents an elaborate synthesis of philology and theology aimed at asserting the absolute rhetorical and stylistic supremacy of the Qur'ān over any other text. On this view, the Qur'ān's unsurpassable excellence renders incapable (*i'jāz*) anyone who might dare to imitate it. According to a less popular opinion advanced by some Mu'tazilīs (e.g., al-Naẓẓām, d. 232/846, and al-Rummānī, d. 386/996), God miraculously prevented the Arabs from imitating his speech by depriving them of the requisite competence.[14] The conclusion, however, remains the same – the qur'ānic diction cannot be replicated by either spirits or human beings. Even its irregularities came to be seen as something miraculous and wonderful.[15] While the medieval linguists' overly rationalist and methodological approach to the qur'ānic text may have prevented them from 'exploring the imaginative richness and the boundless energy' of its metaphors,[16] they definitely succeeded in endowing it with an aura of sacredness and mystery. With al-Zamakhsharī (d. 538/1144), al-Bayḍāwī (d. prob. 716/1316–17) and Abū Ḥayyān al-Gharnāṭī (d. 745/1344), philological exegesis achieved unprecedented heights in both scope and detail. All later discussions of variant readings, grammar, syntax, rhetoric and 'unusual' words of the Qur'ān depend heavily on their works.[17] As for 'secular' Arabic philology, all of its branches are still deeply indebted to the terminology and methods developed by the early Muslim philologists in the course of their analysis of the revelation.

In sum, the study of the qur'ānic language, which was initially dictated by purely utilitarian considerations, engendered an impressive array of highly sophisticated philological disciplines and a philosophy of language whose creators still impress us with their 'remarkably modern approach' to their subject matter.[18] Thus, the sacred status of the Qur'ān encouraged the study and wide dissemination of the Arabic language among non-Arab Muslims. As a result, Arabic established itself as the language of scholarship, administration and culture throughout the Muslim world.[19]

JURISPRUDENCE AND ETHICS

The Qur'ān constitutes the first and foremost source of Islamic law (*al-sharīʿa*) which, unlike Western (Roman) secular law but like the Jewish *halakha,* contains not just precepts governing relationships among people (*muʿāmalāt*), but also religious duties and rules of worship (*ʿibādāt*). The Qur'ān itself did not sharply differentiate between law and ethics. As a book of moral and ethical guidance for individual Muslims and the Muslim community as a whole,[20] its legal subject matter, in the Western sense of the word, is relatively minor and does not exceed 500 verses. Therefore, from the very outset the Qur'ān's general legal principles had to be supplemented by the Prophet's more specific oral instructions as to what they meant and how they were to be applied to concrete cases. These instructions, known as the 'custom of the Prophet', or his *sunna,* became an indispensable part of legal theorising in the early Islamic community that culminated in the creation of a comprehensive system of law, the *sharīʿa*, around the end of the second/eighth century. Understandably, the notion of the Prophet as the divinely guided and infallible legislator was, in its turn, based on the carefully selected qurʾānic pronouncements to this effect (e.g., Q 4:13, 65, etc.).

It is often argued that the text of the Qurʾān reflects the gradual evolution of Muḥammad's self-perception from that of an admonisher who was sent to remind his pagan audience of the teachings of the earlier scriptures to that of a legislating prophet in his own right. This transition took place during the Medinan period of the Prophet's career, as evidenced by Q 5, which confirmed Muḥammad's status as the legislator for his community and marshalled an impressive array of legal commands concerning dietary prohibitions, hunting, theft, ritual ablutions and purity, retaliation for murder or injury, etc. Yet this same sūra expressed astonishment that the Jews should have recourse to Muḥammad,[21] 'seeing they have the Torah, wherein is God's judgement',[22] while also enjoining Christians to seek guidance and advice in their Gospels.[23] Thus, the status of the Qurʾān as the *Muslim* law was unequivocally articulated in its own text. Nevertheless, by any standard, the Qurʾān hardly provided the faithful with an unequivocal and comprehensive system of law, as its apparently contradictory statements about the status of alcoholic drinks (Q 16:67; 2:219; 4:43 and 5:90–1) and the punishment for adultery (Q 4:15–16 and 24:2) indicate. Even when a certain practice was roundly condemned, the Qurʾān stipulated no enforceable punishment. For instance, those who are accused of misappropriating the property of orphans are simply threatened with a painful torment in the hereafter,[24] and no concrete this-worldly sanction against them is stipulated. On the other hand, some issues, e.g., marriage and divorce, received a fairly detailed, if not always unequivocal, coverage.

Be this as it may, following the death of Muḥammad it fell to his Companions and their successors to fill gaps in qurʾānic legislation and to develop a clear and non-contradictory legal framework and penal code firmly rooted in the Qurʾān, yet flexible enough to respond to the new political and social realities as they arose. To this end, all relevant legal material had to be systematically arranged and analysed and on its basis human actions were to be classified as forbidden or permitted, disapproved or indifferent, commendable or obligatory. This analytical and classificatory endeavour required special expertise, or '[juridical] understanding' (*fiqh*). The individuals possessed of this expertise came to be known as *fuqahāʾ*. With time, the *fuqahāʾ*, who originally were private individuals versed in the Qurʾān and *sunna*, became professional legal experts, who strove to maintain independence vis-à-vis the imperial dynasties of the Umayyads and ʿAbbāsids.[25] They were largely responsible for generating 'an autonomous body of sacred law' in Islam[26] which, in theory, was supposed to govern all aspects of Muslim personal and communal life. On the practical level, the law developed by the *fuqahā'* on the basis of the Qur'ān was implemented by judges (*qāḍīs*), who were entrusted by the secular rulers with applying the will of God to concrete situations. Unlike the theoretically minded *fuqahā'*, who were less concerned with the law as it actually was than with law as it ought to be, in their adjudicatory activities the judges had to exercise constantly their personal discretion and understanding of the spirit of the divine legislation while simultaneously availing themselves of 'the norms of local custom'.[27] Since the judges were formally independent of those who studied and formulated the law, in addition to established custom they relied heavily on the legal precedents endorsed by the authoritative members of their juridical school, of which there were four in Sunnī Islam and one in Shīʿī. Periodically the *fuqahā'* made attempts to restrict the discretionary powers of the judges by inviting them to 'return' to the letter of the Qur'ān and *sunna*, but, for all intents and purposes, the latter remained the only interpreters of divine will to their communities. This situation changed with the advent of modernity and the introduction of European legal codes (criminal, commercial, etc.) which are still in force in the overwhelming majority of Muslim countries. As a result, Qur'ān-based jurisdiction, often substantially modified, is now almost everywhere restricted to the law of personal status and family.

Since qur'ānic prescriptions were often mutually contradictory, pioneers of Islamic jurisprudence had to exercise considerable ingenuity. Thus, they introduced the theory of abrogation (*naskh*), according to which earlier legal norms were superseded by later revelations, especially those that legal experts considered to be 'more in line with the prevailing customs'[28] of the day. The abrogation theory which, naturally, was justified by references to the Qur'ān (e.g., Q 2:106; 16:101 and 87:6–7), had ramifications beyond the strictly juridical field as it forced Muslim legal experts to establish the relative chronology of the 'abrogated' and the 'abrogating' verses. This required a thorough knowledge of the history of the first Muslim community in order to determine the time and circumstances (*asbāb al-nuzūl*) in which certain verses were revealed. Thus, the exigencies of legal exegesis gave impetus to the production and accumulation of historical knowledge, creating a fascinating symbiosis of legal, exegetical and historical expertise which is exemplified by the work of al-Ṭabarī (d. 310/923) – simultaneously a legal expert, an exegete and an historian. As mentioned earlier, exegesis, in turn, required of its practitioners a sure grasp of Arabic grammar, semantics and lexicology. Thus, one can say that all these sciences grew out of the Qur'ān, whereupon they acquired a semi-independent status and came to be applied to issues and phenomena not immediately germane to the scripture.

The abrogation theory achieved great sophistication at the hands of later legal scholars, who, for instance, argued that the famous 'Sword Verse' enjoining the believers to 'slay the idolaters wherever you find them' (Q 9:5) abrogated no fewer than 124 other verses commanding 'anything less than a total offensive against the non-believers'.[29] Subsequently, the abrogation theory was expanded to include 'replacing one legal ruling with another due to the termination of the effective period of the earlier ruling'.[30] Obviously, such an interpretation rendered Islamic legal theory much more flexible and accommodating, although some scholars had difficulty accepting the system of abrogation as worthy of God. Nor could they understand why God did not suppress the abrogated verses to avoid confusion among the faithful.[31]

When, at the early stage of legal theory building, a certain legal practice had to be implemented which had no explicit qur'ānic authorisation, one could 'remember' that it had originally been there but was somehow omitted at a later stage. This was the case with the notorious 'Stoning Verse' that was 'remembered' by the caliph 'Umar (d. 23/644) or the 'Suckling Verse' that was 'remembered' by 'Ā'isha (d. 58/678).[32] Instances such as these are an eloquent indication of the precedence of the Qur'ān over all other sources of juridical or moral authority.

Those qur'ānic conundrums that did not lend themselves to the abrogation theory were resolved by scholarly consensus which usually reflected the predominant ethos of the scholarly elite of the day. Thus in Q 4:3 Muslims are enjoined to take up to four wives, while verse 129 of the same sūra indicates that a man simply cannot treat several wives equally no matter how hard he tries. Historically these injunctions appear to have been revealed after the Battle of Uḥud in 4/625, during which many Muslims were killed, leaving their widows without sustenance. Hence the permission for the surviving Muslim men to take more than one wife, which may have been a temporary measure.[33] In the course of legal debates over the import of these verses this temporary injunction was taken out of its historical context and transposed on to all future situations. While for many centuries the permission of polygamy was not in question because it corresponded to the predominantly androcentric and patriarchal ethos of pre-modern Middle Eastern societies, with the military and political ascendancy of the West and its values in the nineteenth century some Muslim modernists offered a drastic reconsideration of this precept, arguing that Q 4:129 precludes a man from taking several wives due to his obvious inability to treat them equally.[34] The fact that in this and many other instances qur'ānic evidence has to be marshalled by modern Muslims to justify a certain practice or idea furnishes the most eloquent evidence of the Qur'ān's continual role – despite the intellectual and social upheavals brought about by modernity – as the ultimate source of authority and arbiter in matters pertaining to Muslim life. On the other hand, while pitched debates between Muslim conservatives and reformers that have raged over the past hundred years may appear to be about the correct understanding of the Qur'ān, 'in reality it is the extent to which parties approve of Western ideas that is [often] under discussion'.[35] This, of course, applies not just to questions of law, but also to those of theology, political legitimacy, 'just' government and social order, as will be demonstrated in the following section.

THEOLOGY AND PHILOSOPHY

As with legal theory, the Qur'ān did not provide its adherents with a systematic and unequivocal declaration of doctrine or with a fully formulated creed. It contained, however, numerous passages that could easily be construed as elements of one (e.g., Q 2:177 and 285; 4:136). Yet these passages were often inconsistent and, taken out of their original context, yielded themselves to a wide variety of different and occasionally diametrically opposed interpretations by Muslims who often knew the whole Qur'ān by heart and were anxious to appeal to its authority to justify their views or course of action. Practically every religious movement or school of thought that recognised the Qur'ān as the final divine communication with humankind could find in it statements that corroborated its religio-political convictions. Since such convictions were numerous and variegated, polemical and apologetic appeals to the Qur'ān became a standard feature of intra-Islamic theological debates, a feature that has not subsided down to the present day. Initially, these debates revolved around such issues as: (1) the essence of God and its relationship with his attributes; (2) human free will versus divine predestination; (3) faith and its prerequisites; (4) the createdness/uncreatedness of the Qur'ān; (5) the just and legitimate leadership of the Muslim community. Although the first four may strike modern-day Westerners as purely scholastic, with little relevance to the realities of everyday life, and the fifth as being mostly about politics, to the overwhelming majority of pre-modern Muslims they belonged to basically the same sphere and were fundamentally important.[36] In other words, the correct solution to each of them was essential for the all-important goal of personal or collective salvation in the hereafter. In any event, it is over these issues that the earliest theological and political factions in Islam locked horns. At first sight, it is sometimes difficult to determine what came first – the issue or the faction associated with it – and why exactly a given faction chose to advocate a certain doctrinal position. At issue, however, was invariably the 'correct' interpretation of God's will as expressed in his revealed book and how best to execute it. In the aftermath of the civil wars of the first decades of Islam, many Muslims were anxious to formulate their position vis-à-vis the authority of the Umayyads, who were viewed by many as illegitimate and unscrupulous usurpers. One solution was to accept Umayyad rule, no matter how imperfect, for the sake of the stability and unity of the Muslim state. On the theological level, this position was justified by reference to the inexorable and inscrutable workings of divine predestination, or 'compulsionism' (*al-jabr*). Its adherents supported their quiescent political stance by referring to the qur'ānic verses that imply God's absolute sovereignty over his creatures and the immutable nature of his foreordained decrees (e.g., Q 2:26–7; 7:30; 9:104; 14:4 and 27; 16:93; 17:13–14; 22:18, etc.).[37] Right next to these verses, however, we find others that assert exactly the opposite (e.g., Q 9:105–6; 14:30; 17:15, etc.), giving ammunition to those who advocated the doctrine of human free will (*al-qadariyya*), according to which God, being necessarily just, should grant his servants the freedom to do right or wrong, if they wished. Even one and the same passage may have been interpreted in either a predestinarian or an anti-predestinarian vein (e.g., 2:26–7; 9:105–6; 22:18) and thus used to justify diametrically opposed beliefs and courses of actions.

A radical interpretation of the Qur'ān was advanced by the Khārijīs – 'those who set out' (to right what is wrong) – who derived their name from Q 9:46–7. They refused to recognise any mundane authority, including ʿAlī and his Umayyad foes, and argued that allegiance was due not to any particular person or institution but only to the Qur'ān and *sunna*. In practice this meant 'setting out' in arms against any authority or religious faction and letting God determine the outcome on the battlefield. This militant stance comes to the fore in the Khārijī interpretation of the qur'ānic concept of faith: those who refused to embrace their radical religio-political programme, which in practice meant rebellion against any mundane authority, were declared grave sinners – a status that, in the eyes of some Khārijīs, mandated the miscreants' execution or enslavement. The Khārijī radicalism sprang, at least in part, from holding believers responsible for their actions and thus implicitly acknowledging their free will. Hence, an unjust ruler was seen by the Khārijī party as being deliberately in the state of grave sin and thus having forfeited his status as a believer. To such a one no allegiance was due; furthermore, he had to be deposed and his misguided followers eliminated. In the Khārijī interpretation of the Qur'ān the definition of faith was inextricably intertwined with the notion of just and legitimate leadership and both, in turn, intimately linked to the doctrine of divine predestination/human free will.

A similar activist position was maintained by some early Shīʿī groups, which, incidentally, also derive their name from the Qur'ān (Q 28:15 and 37:83). Their concept of legitimate leadership was quite different from that of the Khārijīs in that they considered direct male descendants of the Prophet to be the only eligible, legitimate and indispensable leaders (*imāms*) of all Muslims. Naturally, they found numerous allusions to the *imāms*' special role in the Qur'ān. Faced with the might of the Sunnī state, the majority of the Shīʿīs, who came to be known as 'Twelvers' after the number of *imāms* they gave allegiance to, abandoned the dream of attaining political sovereignty and embraced a sophisticated theology developed by their intellectual elite. It justified the Shīʿī belief in the special role of their *imāms* by presenting them as the only authentic interpreters of the qur'ānic message by virtue of a divinely inspired and infallible knowledge granted to them by God. In the absence of such a divinely guided interpreter the scripture remained 'silent' and was liable to misunderstanding and distortion, both of which were evident in the 'sinful' ways of the Sunnī state and its misguided supporters. Only those who had the divinely inspired and infallible interpreters – the so-called 'speaking Qur'ān' – in their midst knew exactly what God's will was and were thus destined to achieve salvation on judgement day.[38] The idea of salvation through the 'sacred' knowledge of the scripture by a divinely inspired *imām* also motivated the Ismāʿīlī community, whose leaders laid even more stress than the Twelver Shīʿīs on the 'interior' aspect (*bāṭin*) of the revelation, which they deemed accessible only to their divinely inspired *imāms* and their legatees through a process of esoteric interpretation. Whereas the 'exterior' (*ẓāhir*) revelation, which pertains to the apparent meaning of a given scripture and the obligations of its adepts, varies from prophet to prophet, 'the *bāṭin* remains unchanged and universally valid'. This is true of the Qur'ān, which contains both the 'external' message accessible to all and sundry and the 'secret' meaning accessible to the *imāms*, who impart it to their followers. Although some earlier Ismāʿīlī sects denied the *ẓāhir* any validity whatsoever, the majority of later Ismāʿīlīs eventually recognised the complementary character of *ẓāhir* and *bāṭin*, which they described as the 'body and soul' of the Qur'ān.[39]

Thus, for the Twelvers and the Ismāʿīlīs, the scripture – or rather its 'hidden', 'esoteric' meaning – is essential for self-definition. Both communities viewed those content with its literal – and thus one-sided and incorrect – interpretation as being beyond redemption. The Sunnī majority, on the other hand, were confident of the salvific role of the collective wisdom of its religious scholars which, in their view, guaranteed them the correct interpretation of the revelation and thus salvation in the hereafter. On the issue of God's predestination of events, the Shīʿī communities assumed a variety of different positions with preference usually given to the anti-predestinarian teaching as being more in line with their rejection of the Sunnī-dominated status quo.

Within the Sunnī community the anti-predestinarian interpretation of the Qur'ān did not necessarily entail armed rebellion against 'unjust' or 'illegitimate' authorities. Most scholars, however, reserved the right to criticise the powers that be for violating qur'ānic injunctions, while still remaining loyal subjects of the caliphal state as long as it declared its commitment to the implementation of the word of God – often quoted on its coins – and the teaching of his Prophet. A moderate stand on the issue of faith and the status of the grave sinner was maintained by the 'postponers' (*al-murji'a*), who argued that humans were in no position to judge the faith of their fellow-believers and thus such judgement should be 'deferred' to God. As with the Khārijīs, the denomination of this trend in early Islamic theology was derived from the Qur'ān (Q 9:106), which, as we have already determined, constituted the common frame of reference for all Muslim factions and schools of thought. Nevertheless, from this common source the Murji'a derived exactly the opposite conclusion to that of the Khārijīs: grave sinners do not forfeit their faith and remain within the community of faithful until God himself determines their fate in the hereafter. Finally, some scholars argued that the grave sinner occupied an intermediate position between faith and unbelief, thus being neither fully outside nor inside the community of faithful. This opinion became the hallmark of the school of theology known as Muʿtazilism which for several centuries successfully competed with its ideological rivals, the adherents of the Prophet's *sunna* (*ahl al-ḥadīth*) and the Ashʿarī theologians, with the latter eventually emerging as the winners. The Māturīdī theological school, which was active in the Ḥanafī-dominated lands of the eastern Muslim world, was but a variant of Ashʿarism.

The debates among these schools of theology over the issues just mentioned – combined with their self-imposed obligation to defend the Muslim faith against potential detractors – gave rise to Muslim speculative theology or *kalām*. It entered upon a period of rapid growth in the late second/eighth century and produced the several theological schools mentioned above by the end of the third/ninth century. While its practitioners, the *mutakallimūn*, probably borrowed some of their arguments and methods from their Christian (namely, Greek and Syriac) counterparts, their overriding commitment to the Qur'ān rendered their theological discussions recognisably and unmistakably Islamic.[40] Significantly, the very name of this discipline corresponds to a common designation of the Qur'ān as 'the speech of God' (*kalām Allāh*), although it is usually understood as 'discussion' (*kalām*) of various points of the Islamic creed. In any event, there is no reason to doubt that it developed first and foremost in response to the linguistic – as with exegesis and *fiqh*, its representatives were accomplished philologists who made extensive use of grammatical terminology in their deliberations – and doctrinal challenges of the qur'ānic text. No wonder that its major concepts, such as 'divine names and attributes' (*al-asmā'* (*al-ḥusnā*) *wa-l-ṣifāt*), 'acquisition [of divinely created actions by individual human beings]' (*kasb*), 'power [to act created by God in the human individual]' (*istiṭā'a*), 'the imposition of religious obligations' (*taklīf*), etc., derive their names from qur'ānic words (Q 7:180 and 17:110; 2:286 and 55:33; 5:112; 6:152; 7:42; 23:62, etc.). Whenever the *mutakallimūn* attempted to introduce terminology not explicitly mentioned in the Qur'ān, especially the Greek philosophical concepts such as 'essence', 'accidents', 'existence', 'non-existence', 'mode (of being)', etc., they were accused by conservative scholars of 'heretical innovation' or even outright 'unbelief'. Such accusations sprang from the belief that God can be described only by the names and epithets which are attributed to him in his revelation. The *mutakallimūn* accepted this belief and after analysing the panoply of attributes ascribed to God in the Qur'ān, concentrated on those of them which they considered to be essential to him, namely his being powerful, knowing, living, eternal, hearing, seeing and speaking. The last attribute was identified with the 'speech of God', i.e., the Qur'ān, giving rise to heated debates about whether the latter was created or uncreated. Such debates eventually led to the persecutions of advocates of both parties depending on whose side the ruler was. While, on the face of it, what was at stake was the possibility of co-existence of another eternal entity alongside God – an illogical absurdity to the Mu'tazilīs and a great mystery of God to the adherents of the Prophet's *sunna* – there were deeper reasons behind these momentous events (which unfolded in the first half of the third/ninth century), namely the caliph's control over the semi-independent and outspoken religious scholars and jockeying for power within the ruling elite. In any case, for those involved the recognition or denial of the created nature of the Qur'ān was not just an abstract theological principle, but also often a matter of life and death, not to mention career. Here the central position of the Qur'ān as the very essence of faith presents itself in all its magnitude.

Despite its growing sophistication and its reliance on 'alien' methods of argumentation, *kalām* remained a qur'ānic discipline *par excellence* in its commitment to the principle that 'there was nothing in the Qur'an that was repugnant to careful reasoning'.[41] Whether practised by the Muʿtazilīs or the Ashʿarīs, the aim of *kalām* was to establish an overall cosmology, which was both rational and free from the crude anthropomorphism of the adherents of the Prophet's *sunna,* while remaining in harmony with the Qur'ān.[42] The drive to bring the divine book in line with rational and logical criteria – for in the view of the *mutakallimūn* one cannot believe without good reason – compelled the majority of Muslim scholars to allow for a limited use of 'alien' methods of argumentation. Nevertheless, today as in the past, the scholars of *kalām* still give priority to the scripture over the most compelling and sophisticated human-made arguments. In any case, it goes without saying that their attempts to reconcile the illogical, poetic and often self-contradictory text of the revelation with Greek syllogistic reasoning has provided a major stimulus to the flourishing of intellectual and cultural life in Islam and, in the end, produced a powerful ideological foundation (and legitimation) of the religious, social, moral and political order associated with it. Whether these attempts have been successful and whether there can be a satisfactory solution, on rational grounds, to the issue of the qur'ānic God's omnipotence vis-à-vis the freedom of human beings to exercise their choice is a different matter.

Unlike *kalām,* which arose first and foremost in response to the necessity to defend the Muslim faith against its non-Muslim detractors and to make rational sense out of the revelation, Islamic philosophy (*falsafa*) derived its inspiration from the non-Islamic intellectual legacy of ancient Greece and its Hellenistic reworkings. This fact automatically made Muslim philosophers suspect in the eyes of mainstream theologians, including those who were ready to admit the Greek-inspired methods of *kalām* into their considerations. Yet, a few special cases apart, in a culture that rested on qur'ānic foundations, the majority of philosophically minded Muslim scholars remained loyal to their sacred book and worked hard to integrate it into their intellectual constructs. To justify their fascination with philosophical methods they invoked qur'ānic verses (e.g., Q 2:269; 3:48 and 81), in which, in their view, *falsafa* (referred to as 'wisdom') was mentioned alongside the Qur'ān itself.[43] Despite this fascination, some of them (e.g., Averroes (Ibn Rushd), d. 595/1198) recognised the sacred book as the most perfect way to guide the masses to happiness and salvation. Composed in a figurative and anthropomorphic language, it is easily accessible to all regardless of their intellectual capacities, whereas higher philosophical truths (understood as knowledge of human nature, syllogistic reasoning and universal laws that govern the universe) are confined to the elect few and should be concealed from the general public for fear of misunderstanding. It is this universalistic appeal of the qur'ānic message that makes it the greatest miracle of Islam, as is evident to every sensible person who cares to study it.[44] Nevertheless, lurking behind the philosopher's admiration for the Qur'ān is the belief that it is but an allegorical representation of philosophical truths by the prophet-populariser 'who translates his philosophical awareness of how people ought to live, what happiness really is, into a system of persuasive stories . . . and images of kings and prophets who existed in the past'.[45] The same task can be accomplished, at least in theory, by a philosophically trained legislator, who is in possession of both universal laws and the knowledge of human nature and can thus institute a virtuous and blissful society. Until such a society is instituted, the philosopher was morally bound to follow the popular religion of his community with its allegorical norms and values. Although the philosophers made every effort to accommodate their deliberations to the scriptural truths, the majority of Muslim scholars remained unconvinced, as demonstrated by the momentous critique of philosophy undertaken by al-Ghazālī (d. 505/1111). The only way for *falsafa* to survive was to be integrated with qur'ānic sciences such as *kalām* and exegesis. This integration was effected around the seventh/thirteenth century, giving rise to an elegant and seamless synthesis of qur'ānic sciences, Greek/Hellenistic logic and metaphysics and mystical thought which, some would argue, may have been too perfect for its own good in that it absolved its learned custodians from seeking creative solutions to new intellectual challenges as they arose.

LITERATURE AND RHETORIC

The influence of the Qur'ān upon 'profane' literature, no matter how profound, was incidental to its own purpose. In fact, imaginative literature, especially lyrical poetry, with its symbolic expressions of spiritual and aesthetic awareness was inevitably in competition with the qur'ānic demand for the believer's 'undivided attention to its single and total message'[46] and with its magnificent portrayal of the human condition and its moral and ethical implications. Hence the significance of an oft-quoted qur'ānic condemnation of (pagan) poets and poetry (Q 26:221–7), which may be interpreted as an expression of the monotheistic fear that the poets' art might distract the faithful from God rather than as a simple retort to the Prophet's detractors who had accused him of using his poetic skills to impose his will upon his followers (e.g., Q 21:5; 37:36–7, etc.).

In the light of the inherent tension between poetry and the Qur'ān it is all the more remarkable that the poetic art of pre-Islamic Arabia came to enjoy such high respect among Muslim philologists and exegetes who drew on it as a proof text and benchmark to explain obscure passages of the sacred text and to demonstrate the unsurpassed excellence of its language. As a result, paradoxically, the necessity to understand and elucidate the Qur'ān served as the major motivation to record and evaluate pre-Islamic poetry in written form, thereby facilitating the all-important 'switch from an oral to a written culture – from a culture of intuition and improvisation to one of study and contemplation'.[47] With time, Arabic-Islamic culture as a whole came to be dominated by the dual ideal of rhetorical and literary excellence that can be summarised as follows: 'The most beautiful form of human expression is pre-Islamic poetry, and in absolute form the most beautiful form of expression, human or divine, using the very language of this poetry, is the Qur'ān.'[48] In other words, the Qur'ān along with pre-Islamic poetry became the predominant force in shaping classical, post-classical and modern Arabic oral and literary culture and, with the spread of Islam to non-Arab cultural and linguistic areas, in the non-Arabic-speaking Muslim lands as well.

In poetry, the direct use of qur'ānic material was somewhat restricted by the exigencies of metre and rhyme as well as by the presence of the highly developed literary canon of pre-Islamic poetry, which, as mentioned, was elevated to the status of the unsurpassable model of poetic diction by the end of the second/eighth century. To comply with the formal requirements of this canon the poet had creatively to adjust his qur'ānic material by 'changing the vocalisation of the rhyme-word borrowed from the Qur'ān, or replacing it by another suitably rhyming word, a synonym or near-synonym, when necessary'.[49] On the thematic level, however, such restrictions did not apply, giving poets freedom to make use of qur'ānic topoi and reminiscences as they saw fit. The influence of qur'ānic themes, personages and imagery can be found in practically every genre of classical

Arabic poetry from the Umayyad and ʿAbbāsid periods. While some genres (e.g., the poems of ascetic self-reflection, which are 'but running commentaries on the Qur'an',[50] or mystical poetry) were more amenable to it than others, we find it in such unlikely places as odes in praise of a generous patron or wine poetry. In the latter, scandalously, wine may displace God as the object of veneration and the source of guidance, as in an elegantly blasphemous poem of Abū Nuwās (d. *c.* 198/813),[51] which features the poet's subtle (and risky) appropriation of qur'ānic motifs with a view to justifying his rakish lifestyle.[52] It is in the circles of ʿAbbāsid poets and literary critics that the Qur'ān received recognition not only for its sacred status, but also as a literary masterpiece in its own right. In his celebrated codification of figures of speech, the ill-fated caliph-poet Ibn al-Muʿtazz (d. 296/908) opens each category of poetic devices with samples of the 'excellences' of the qur'ānic style, thereby implicitly inviting his fellow-poets to imitate it – contrary to the doctrine of its inimitability which had taken shape about that time.

One can thus agree with the contemporary Arab poet Adonis that 'modernity in Arabic poetry . . . has its roots in the Qur'an' insofar as its study provided the critical impetus for the emergence of a new, bolder poetic idiom that was unrestricted by the rigid conventions of the pre-Islamic poetic canon.[53] Beginning with Amīn al-Rayḥānī (d. 1940) and ending with Nizār Qabbānī (d. 1998), the qur'ānic subtext has permeated modern Arabic poetry. It has been used for a wide variety of ends from advocating the Palestinian cause and bemoaning its fallen heroes (Maḥmūd Darwīsh and Muʿīn Basīsū) to critiquing social injustice (Amal Dunqul). Its uses may be irreverent or flippant (Qabbānī) and, occasionally, may feature a deliberate mockery of the qur'ānic diction (Ḥasan Ṭilib). If there is any common feature that is shared by all these poets it is probably their 'acceptance of the Koran as the fundamental text of Arabic culture and Arabo-Islamic religion'[54] and the recognition of its deep entrenchment in the Arab mentality and literary sensitivity.

In religious prose and rhetoric (e.g., sermons, invocations, incantations, exegesis, Ṣūfī manuals, epistles, testaments, etc.) qur'ānic influence is ubiquitous and easy to detect – here passages from the Qur'ān are quoted verbatim and Qur'ān-based formulas are cited at the opening and ending of a text or oration. The Qur'ān, quoted literally or by way of allusion, has determined the diction, style, images, symbols, word and sentence order of the whole of Arabic discourse. Such typical features of the qur'ānic style as parallelism (namely, the repetition of one meaning in two or more phrases), antithetical pairing, and rhymed prose with its musical cadence of sentences, figure prominently in Arabic prose from different periods, giving it an unmistakable qur'ānic flavour. One can thus argue that with the emergence of the Qur'ān '[Arabic] prose fell almost completely under its spell'.[55] Collections of qur'ānic verses to be used on various occasions were composed for the benefit of writers and speakers along with the advice as to where and when qur'ānic quotations were 'befitting', 'unbefitting, but permissible' and 'absolutely unbefitting' and thus forbidden.[56] Sermons of the Umayyad (e.g., al-Ḥasan al-Baṣrī, d. 110/728) and ʿAbbāsid epochs (e.g., Ibn Nubāta al-Khaṭīb, d. 374/984) abound in qur'ānic verses and themes, stressing fear of God and the necessity to observe his commands, the transience of earthly existence, the terrors of the judgement day, etc. Qur'ānic reminiscences and allusions also permeate the epistolary genre that was developed by secretaries employed by the caliph's chancellery, such as ʿAbd al-Ḥamīd b. Yaḥyā (d. 132/750) under the Umayyads and Abū Isḥāq al-Ṣābī (d. 384/994) under the ʿAbbāsids.

The earliest samples of Arabic prose, such as those by al-Jāḥiẓ (d. 255/868–9), also exhibit his deep indebtedness to the qur'ānic style and themes. On occasion, his use of qur'ānic material may appear irreverent, as in his 'Book of Misers' where the famous 'Light Verse' from the Qur'ān (Q 24:35) is quoted at the conclusion of the story of the miser who availed himself of his rhetorical skills in order to save oil in his lamp. Qur'ānic descriptions of the hereafter inspired another great Arab writer and poet, Abū'Alā' al-Maʿarrī (d. 449/1057), to compose an account of his imaginary visit to paradise and hell in order to interview its inhabitants, especially ancient poets, grammarians and linguists, about their experiences as well as various philological issues. Al-Maʿarrī's 'Book of Paragraphs and Endings' was composed as a deliberate imitation of qur'ānic verses, especially the so-called 'oracular' sūras of the early Meccan period.[57] In the celebrated 'sessions' (*maqāmāt*) of al-Hamadhānī (d. 398/1008) and al-Ḥarīrī (d. 516/1122), the Qur'ān's presence is conveyed both directly – through the use of rhymed prose which invokes 'the cadences of the sacred text' – and indirectly by means of Qur'ān-based homiletic orations of the picaresque characters, who used their mastery of religious rhetoric to cheat their gullible listeners of their money.[58] Even such a seemingly 'profane' narrative as the 'Thousand and one nights' has not eluded the influence of the Qur'ān, as the gloomy tale of the 'City of Brass' – a Qur'ān-inspired parable of the transience of earthly life – vividly testifies.[59]

The influence of the Qur'ān on modern Arabic literature (from the early twentieth century on) remains considerable. Qur'ānic allusions and themes are evident in the work of such Arab prose writers as Yūsuf al-Sibāʿī, ʿAbd al-Ḥamīd al-Jūda, Najīb Maḥfūẓ, Yūsuf Idrīs and Maḥmūd Diyāb. Their uses of the Qurʾān range from reverential (al-Sibāʿī, al-Jūda and Diyāb) to controversial (Maḥfūẓ in his *Children of our quarter* and *Children of Gebelawi*) to deliberately irreverent and subversive (Idrīs in his short stories 'The Greatest Sin', 'The House of Flesh' and 'The Egyptian Mona Lisa'[60] or Nawāl Saʿdāwī in her *Jannāt wa-Iblīs*[61]). Even francophone writers of the Maghrib with little or no knowledge of Arabic (e.g., Driss Chraïbi in his 'L'âne' and 'Muhammad') draw heavily on qurʾānic topoi albeit rendered into French – another testimony to the remarkable tenacity of the qurʾānic culture and idiom in the face of the seemingly irresistible forces of Westernisation and modernisation.

Needless to say, the impact of the Qurʾān was not limited to Arabic culture, but is richly attested in all major non-Arab literatures of the Muslim world from Persia/Iran to Malaysia.

Notes

1. C. Padwick, *Muslim devotions* (Oxford: Oneworld, 1996), p. 119.
2. M. G. S. Hodgson, *The venture of Islam*, 3 vols. (Chicago: University of Chicago Press, 1974), vol. I, p. 366.
3. K. Versteegh, *The Arabic language* (New York: Columbia University Press, 1997), pp. 50–1.
4. M. Carter, 'Les origines de la grammaire arabe', *Revue des études islamiques* 40 (1972), 93.
5. D. Frolov, 'K istorii slozheniia klassicheskoi arabskoi fililogii', *Vestnik Moskovskogo universiteta* 13/3 (1987), 60.
6. L. Kopf, 'Religious influences on medieval Arabic philology', *Studia Islamica* 5 (1956), 20–1.
7. A. Levin, 'Sībawayhi's attitude to the language of the Qurʾān', *Israel Oriental Studies* 19 (1999), 271.
8. Kopf, 'Religious influences', 20–1.
9. E. Almagor, 'The early meaning of *majāz* and the nature of Abū ʿUbayda's exegesis', in Y. Navon et al. (eds.), *Studia orientalia memoriae D. H. Baneth* (Jerusalem: Max Schloessinger Memorial Foundation, 1979), p. 325.
10. M. Shah, 'The philological endeavors of early Arabic linguists', *Journal of Qurʾanic Studies* 1 (1999), 27–46.
11. R. Baalbaki, 'The treatment of *qirāʾāt* by the second and third century grammarians', *Zeitschrift für arabische Linguistik* 15 (1985), 12.
12. Ibid., 28–9.
13. Carter, 'Les origines', 96–7.
14. I. Boullata, 'The rhetorical interpretation of the Qurʾān', in A. Rippin (ed.), *Approaches to the history of the interpretation of the Qurʾān* (Oxford: Clarendon Press, 1988), pp. 141–2.
15. Cl. Gilliot, *Exégèse, langue, et théologie en Islam: L'exégèse coranique de Ṭabarī (m. 311/923)* (Paris: J. Vrin, 1990), pp. 73–8.

16. K. Abu Deeb, 'Studies in the *majāz* and metaphorical language of the Qur'ān', in I. Boullata (ed.), *Literary structures of religious meaning in the Qur'ān* (Richmond: Curzon, 2000), p. 345.
17. J. J. Jansen, *The interpretation of the Koran in modern Egypt* (Leiden: Brill, 1974), p. 63.
18. S. Glaze, 'Abū Ḥayyān al-Gharnāṭī', in *Encyclopaedia of Islam*, new ed., 11 vols. (Leiden: Brill, 1979–2002), vol. I, p. 126.
19. A. Jones, 'The Qur'ān–II', in A. F. L. Beeston, T. M. Johnstone et al. (eds.), *Arabic literature to the end of the Umayyad period* (Cambridge: Cambridge University Press, 1983), p. 242.
20. N. Coulson, *A history of Islamic law*, repr. ed. (Edinburgh: Edinburgh University Press, 1997), p. 11.
21. W. Hallaq, *A history of Islamic legal theories* (Cambridge: Cambridge University Press, 1997), pp. 4–5.
22. Q 5:43.
23. Q 5:46.
24. Coulson, *A history*, p. 12.
25. B. Weiss, *The spirit of Islamic law* (Athens/London: University of Georgia Press, 1998), pp. 7–8 and 17.
26. Ibid., p. 3.
27. Ibid., p. 187.
28. Hallaq, *A history*, p. 9.
29. D. Powers, 'The exegetical genre *nāsikh al-Qur'ān wa mansūkhuhu*', in Rippin (ed.), *Approaches to the history of the interpretation of the Qur'ān*, p. 130.
30. Ibid., p. 122.
31. J. Burton, 'Abrogation', in J. D. McAuliffe (ed.), *Encyclopaedia of the Qur'ān*, 5 vols. (Leiden: Brill, 2001–6), vol. I, p. 17.
32. Ibid., pp. 17–18.
33. R. Paret, 'The Qur'ān–I', in Beeston, Johnstone et al. (eds.), *Arabic literature*, p. 224.
34. Jansen, *The interpretation*, pp. 91–3.
35. Ibid., p. 94.
36. P. Crone, *Medieval Islamic political thought* (Edinburgh: Edinburgh University Press, 2004), pp. 10–16.
37. For further examples see E. Beck, 'The dogmatic religious stance of the grammarian Yaḥyā b. Ziyād al-Farrā'', in A. Rippin (ed.), *The Qur'ān: Formative interpretation* (Aldershot: Ashgate, 1999), pp. 136–58.
38. M. Ayoub, 'The speaking Qur'ān and the silent Qur'ān', in Rippin (ed.), *Approaches to the history of the interpretation of the Qur'ān*, pp. 177–98.
39. I. Poonawala, 'Ismā'īlī *ta'wīl* of the Qur'ān', in Rippin (ed.), *Approaches to the history of the interpretation of the Qur'ān*, pp. 199–222.
40. R. Frank, *Beings and their attributes* (Albany: SUNY Press, 1978), p. 9.
41. Hodgson, *The venture*, vol. I, p. 437.
42. Ibid., p. 438.
43. S. H. Nasr, 'The Qur'ān and *ḥadīth* as source and inspiration of Islamic philosophy', in S. H. Nasr and O. Leaman (eds.), *History of Islamic philosophy*, 2 vols. (London/New York: Routledge, 1996), vol. I, p. 30.

44. O. Leaman, *An introduction to classical Islamic philosophy* (Cambridge: Cambridge University Press, 2002), pp. 101–2 and 186.
45. Ibid., p. 86.
46. Hodgson, *The venture*, vol. I, p. 368.
47. Adonis, *An introduction to Arab poetics* (London: Saqi, 1990), p. 37.
48. Ibid., p. 41.
49. W. al-Qāḍī, 'The limitations of qur'ānic usage in early Arabic poetry', in W. Heinrichs and G. Schöler (eds.), *Festschrift Ewald Wagner zum 65. Geburtstag*, 2 vols. (Beirut/Stuttgart: Franz Steiner, 1994), vol. II, p. 180.
50. Cl. Audebert, 'Emprunts faits au Coran par quelques poètes du iie/viiie siècle', *Arabica* 47 (2000), 461.
51. Ibid., passim.
52. Ph. Kennedy, *The wine song in classical Arabic poetry* (Oxford: Clarendon Press, 1997), pp. 17–18, 226–32 and passim.
53. Adonis, *An introduction*, p. 49.
54. S. Wild, 'The Koran as subtext in modern Arabic poetry', in G. Borg and E. de Moor (eds.), *Representations of the divine in Arabic poetry* (Amsterdam/Atlanta: Rodopi, 2001), p. 145.
55. W. Kadi (al-Qāḍī) and M. Mir, 'Literature and the Qur'ān', in McAuliffe (ed.), *Encyclopaedia of the Qur'ān*, vol. III, p. 219.
56. Cl. Gilliot, 'Un florilège coranique', *Arabica* 47 (2002), 488–500.
57. A. M. Zubaidi, 'The impact of the Qur'ān and *ḥadīth* on medieval Arabic literature', in Beeston et al. (eds.), *Arabic literature*, pp. 337–8.
58. R. Allen, *An introduction to Arabic literature* (Cambridge: Cambridge University Press, 2000), pp. 63–4; J. Bürgel, 'Language on trial, religion at stake?', in A. Neuwirth et al. (eds.), *Myths, historical archetypes and symbolic figures in Arabic literature* (Beirut/Stuttgart: Franz Steiner, 1999), pp. 200–2.
59. Allen, *An introduction*, p. 64.
60. R. Wise, 'Subverting holy scriptures', in J. Hawley (ed.), *The post-colonial crescent* (Berlin: Peter Lang, 1998), pp. 140–54.
61. W. Bodman, 'Stalking Iblīs: In search of an Islamic theodicy', in Neuwirth et al. (eds.), *Myths*, pp. 268–9.

Further reading

Abu Deeb, K., 'Studies in the *majāz* and metaphorical language of the Qur'ān', in I. Boullata (ed.), *Literary structures of religious meaning in the Qur'ān*, Richmond: Curzon, 2000, pp. 310–53.

Adonis, *An introduction to Arab poetics*, London: Saqi, 1990.

Allen, R., *An introduction to Arabic literature*, Cambridge: Cambridge University Press, 2000.

Almagor, E., 'The early meaning of *majāz* and the nature of Abū 'Ubayda's exegesis', in Y. Navon et al. (eds.), *Studia orientalia memoriae D. H. Baneth*, Jerusalem: Max Schloessinger Memorial Foundation, 1979, pp. 307–26.

Audebert, Cl., 'Emprunts faits au Coran par quelques poètes du iie/viiie siècle', *Arabica* 47 (2000), 457–72.

Ayoub, M., 'The speaking Qur'ān and the silent Qur'ān', in A. Rippin (ed.), *Approaches to the history of the interpretation of the Qur'ān*, Oxford: Clarendon Press, 1988, pp. 177–98.

Baalbaki, R., 'The treatment of *qirā'āt* by the second and third century grammarians', *Zeitschrift für arabische Linguistik* 15 (1985), 11–32.

Beck, E., 'The dogmatic religious stance of the grammarian Yaḥyā b. Ziyād al-Farrā'', in A. Rippin (ed.), *The Qur'ān: Formative interpretation*, Aldershot: Ashgate, 1999, pp. 136–58 (Eng. trans. of 'Die dogmatische religiöse Einstellung des Grammatikers Yaḥyā b. Ziyād al-Farrā'', *Le Muséon* 64 [1951], 187–202).

Bodman, W., 'Stalking Iblīs: In search of an Islamic theodicy', in A. Neuwirth et al. (eds.), *Myths, historical archetypes and symbolic figures in Arabic literature*, Beirut and Stuttgart: Franz Steiner, 1999, pp. 247–69.

Boullata, I., 'The rhetorical interpretation of the Qur'ān', in A. Rippin (ed.), *Approaches to the history of the interpretation of the Qur'ān*, Oxford: Clarendon Press, 1988, pp. 139–57.

Bürgel, J., 'Language on trial, religion at stake?', in A. Neuwirth et al. (eds.), *Myths, historical archetypes and symbolic figures in Arabic literature*, Beirut/Stuttgart: Franz Steiner, 1999, pp. 189–204.

Carter, M., 'Les origines de la grammaire arabe', *Revue des études islamiques* 40 (1972), 70–97.

Coulson, N., *A history of Islamic law*, repr. ed., Edinburgh: Edinburgh University Press, 1997.

Crone, P., *Medieval Islamic political thought*, Edinburgh: Edinburgh University Press, 2004.

Frank, R., *Beings and their attributes*, Albany: SUNY Press, 1978.

Frolov, D., 'K istorii slozheniia klassicheskoi arabskoi fililogii', *Vestnik Moskovskogo universiteta* 13/3 (1987), 59–70.

Gilliot, Cl., *Exégèse, langue, et théologie en Islam: L'exégèse coranique de Ṭabarī (m. 311/923)*, Paris: J. Vrin, 1990.

'Un florilège coranique', *Arabica* 47 (2002), 488–500.

Hallaq, W., *A history of Islamic legal theories*, Cambridge: Cambridge University Press, 1997.

Hodgson, M. G. S., *The venture of Islam*, 3 vols., Chicago: University of Chicago Press, 1974.

Jansen, J. J., *The interpretation of the Koran in modern Egypt*, Leiden: Brill, 1974.

Jones, A., 'The Qur'ān–II', in A. F. L. Beeston, T. M. Johnstone et al. (eds.), *Arabic literature to the end of the Umayyad period*, Cambridge: Cambridge University Press, 1983, pp. 228–45.

Kennedy, Ph., *The wine song in classical Arabic poetry*, Oxford: Clarendon Press, 1997.

Kopf, L., 'Religious influences on medieval Arabic philology', *Studia Islamica* 5 (1956), 19–45.

Leaman, O., *An introduction to classical Islamic philosophy*, Cambridge: Cambridge University Press, 2002.

Levin, A., 'Sībawayhi's attitude to the language of the Qur'ān', *Israel Oriental Studies* 19 (1999), 267–71.

Nasr, S. H., 'The Qur'ān and *ḥadīth* as source and inspiration of Islamic philosophy', in S. H. Nasr and O. Leaman (eds.), *History of Islamic philosophy*, 2 vols., London/New York: Routledge, 1996, vol. I, pp. 27–39.

Padwick, C., *Muslim devotions*, Oxford: Oneworld, 1996.

Paret, R., 'The Qur'ān–I', in A. F. L. Beeston, T. M. Johnstone et al. (eds.), *Arabic literature to the end of the Umayyad period*, Cambridge: Cambridge University Press, 1983, pp. 186–227.

Poonawala, I., 'Ismāʿīlī *ta'wīl* of the Qur'ān', in A. Rippin (ed.), *Approaches to the history of the interpretation of the Qur'ān*, Oxford: Clarendon Press, 1988, pp. 199–222.

Powers, D., 'The exegetical genre *nāsikh al-Qur'ān wa mansūkhuhu*', in A. Rippin (ed.), *Approaches to the history of the interpretation of the Qur'ān*, Oxford: Clarendon Press, 1988, pp. 117–38.

al-Qāḍī, W., 'The limitations of qur'ānic usage in early Arabic poetry', in W. Heinrichs and G. Schöler (eds.), *Festschrift Ewald Wagner zum 65. Geburtstag*, 2 vols., Beirut/Stuttgart: Franz Steiner, 1994, vol. II, pp. 161–81.

Shah, M., 'The philological endeavors of early Arabic linguists', *Journal of Qur'anic Studies* 1 (1999), 27–46.

Versteegh, K., *The Arabic language*, New York: Columbia University Press, 1997.

Weiss, B., *The spirit of Islamic law*, Athens/London: University of Georgia Press, 1998.

Wild, S., 'The Koran as subtext in modern Arabic poetry', in G. Borg and E. de Moor (eds.), *Representations of the divine in Arabic poetry*, Amsterdam/Atlanta: Rodopi, 2001, pp. 139–60.

Wise, R., 'Subverting holy scriptures', in J. Hawley (ed.), *The post-colonial crescent*, Berlin: Peter Lang, 1998, pp. 140–54.

Zubaidi, A. M., 'The impact of the Qur'ān and *ḥadīth* on medieval Arabic literature', in A. F. L. Beeston et al. (eds.), *Arabic literature to the end of the Umayyad period*, Cambridge: Cambridge University Press, 1983, pp. 332–43.

Fig. 11 Section from an eighteenth-century Indian Qur'ān manuscript. Depicted here are the opening verses of Sūrat Yā Sīn (Q 36:1–3, with the first word of verse 4) (CBL Is. 1563, fol. 1v). Courtesy of the Trustees of the Chester Beatty Library, Dublin

11 Western scholarship and the Qur'ān

ANDREW RIPPIN

Early in the twentieth century, the notion of what was meant by Western scholarship on the Qur'ān would not have created much discussion. It was quite obvious that the phrase referred to scholarly work on the Qur'ān undertaken by European academics who were not Muslims. Continuing with such an understanding in the twenty-first century is quite problematic, however, both for its suggestion that work by those who declare themselves to be Muslims cannot be included in such a category – this is evidently false as browsing the bookshelf of any scholar today will reveal – and for the vagaries of the term 'scholarly' when it is applied to an intellectual world that is increasingly diverse methodologically and culturally. How are we to distinguish in a meaningful way between the discipline of exegesis (*tafsīr*) as it might be exercised today by a Muslim living in Europe from that of an academic working in a North American university within the discipline of religious studies? The answer is not necessarily as apparent as both of those individuals may wish to assume.

One might argue that what is intended here by Western scholarship on the Qur'ān is simply that which adopts an approach that involves a non-confessional ('secular') attitude towards Islam. Such is the shorthand that would often be used in modern discussions. More elaborately, this might be described as 'the critical dispassionate (i.e., non-polemical) search for knowledge, unconstrained by ecclesiastical institutional priorities'.[1] Here too, the problem emerges of how then to distinguish such approaches from what might rightly be called secular polemic. Such a differentiation is increasingly crucial in modern academic circles in which polemic often masquerades as scholarship, especially on the Internet, but in traditional publishing activities as well. While it might be tempting to substitute a word such as 'disinterested' for 'non-confessional' in order to solve the problem, the issue of the motivation for undertaking studies on Islam in general has become far too political since the wake-up call sounded with the publication in 1978 of

Edward Said's *Orientalism* to allow for such easy resolution. The accusation is easily made that 'disinterested scholarship' is actually prompted by many conscious and subconscious political and social preconceptions and ideologies, many of which continue to reflect the ethos of the colonialist eras. Further, it may also be suggested that this is an issue that must be confronted in every study of religion. It is increasingly recognised within the discipline that the bare assertion that in the university we study religion from a secular viewpoint simply does not suffice: secularism, like religion, is a position with associated values for which the claim to universal truth is no more valid than it may be for religion itself.[2]

Some help in grappling with these problems may be found by putting aside the definitional issues and investigating some particular perspectives; it may thus be possible to enunciate some principles which will serve to define what is meant by Western scholarship on the Qur'ān without either a simple invoking of the insider–outsider dichotomy (and its presumption of a temporary epoché) or resorting to equally problematic conceptions that would define the notion of scholarly as 'secular' or 'academic' (while still recognising the pragmatic value of understanding a discipline as operating within a 'community of interpreters' with its own discourse[3]). A brief examination of approaches to the Qur'ān throughout history will display the emergence of a particular character in works that began to appear in the nineteenth century, a character that became identified as the 'scholarly' approach. This by no means judges what preceded that period to be of no value; rather, it suggests a shift in motivation and expression that matches the requirements of the modern ethos.

EVIDENCE FROM THE QUR'ĀN AND *SĪRA*

The Qur'ān itself recognises that people approach the text of scripture for different reasons but, as is undoubtedly appropriate to a text which is attempting to convey a message, it divides the world into those who respond to its message and those who do not. In doing so, it inherently recognises the interest that non-Muslims have in the scripture. The study and critique conducted by those who do not respond actively and positively to the religious claims of the text are presented as revolving around the concept of revelation and the various factors associated with that. From the perspective of the Qur'ān the issue is thus one of religious truth: those who challenge the Qur'ān are denying the truth of its religious message and, in some cases, even the existence of God. This is perhaps best summarised in the verses which are often referred to as the 'challenge' verses, those that imply an attack by non-believers on the truth claims of the Qurʾān: 'If you are in doubt concerning that which we have sent down on our servant, then produce a sūra like it and call on your witnesses other than God if you are truthful' (Q 2:23). In the exegesis of this verse, doubting the Qurʾān is usually understood to refer to its mode of production rather than its contents, but fundamentally the issue is one of the truth claims related to the divine. The Qurʾān pictures those who interact with the text as either accepting its divine status and its witness or not; the idea that one could simply be 'curious' about the book without responding to its truth claims does not seem to be entertained.

Likewise, within the life story of Muḥammad (*sīra*), non-Muslim groups play an important role in presenting a challenge to the Prophet and his credentials. The study of the Qurʾān in this context is once again portrayed as either an acceptance of its truths or as an antagonistic activity. For example, the Jews of Medina are pictured as challenging the meaning of the mysterious letters in the Qurʾān and using them to make numerical predictions.[4] In this episode, the truth of the text might seem to be accepted but the text is twisted so as to be used against Islam itself. Those who do not accept Islam on the basis of the clear evidence that the Qurʾān presents, it might be suggested, are portrayed as wanting to undermine Islam and the Qurʾān itself. Their approach to the text is destructive. This may well explain the emergence of a common sentiment, found expressed in early legal documents known as the 'Covenant of ʿUmar' which are treaties between Christians (usually) and their Muslim conquerors from the early centuries of Islam. In some versions of this document Christians are forbidden to teach their children the Qurʾān; the suspicion that teaching the Qurʾān to those who have not accepted Islam will prove destructive is at least one of the subtexts of such statements.

MEDIEVAL CHRISTIAN APOLOGETIC AND TRANSLATION

To some extent, these Muslim suspicions were certainly validated in the early centuries. Christians were quick to see the challenge that the new faith posed to the universal claims of their own faith. Early church leaders such as John of Damascus (fl. second/eighth century) seem to have spent a good deal of time studying the Qurʾān (either directly or indirectly through informants) in order to critique it. One of the best-known and more searing critiques is that found in a book known as *The apology of al-Kindī*, said to have been written in the year 215/830 as a defence of Christianity against Islam. Topics such as the materials and mode of collection of the Qur'ān and the contradictory passages found within the scripture are cited in order to disprove any sense of the divine source of the scripture.[5] The text demonstrates that the author has an intimate acquaintance with the text of the Qur'ān and much of the Islamic tradition about its history; that intimacy is used in an attempt to disprove the truth claims of the text.

Not all medieval work on the Qur'ān done by Christians, however, was superficial or conducted simply to attack Islam, especially as the centuries move into the European Middle Ages. Detailed studies of medieval translations of the Qur'ān reveal a much more complex picture. We begin to see a change in attitude, at least to the extent that suggests that understanding the Qur'ān is worthwhile, even if the end result may still lead to a denial of the truth of the message itself. For medieval writers, effective polemic was to be grounded in secure knowledge even if they conclude that the Qur'ān is a mixture of falsehood and truth and part of a conspiratorial plot against Christianity. At the same time, the Qur'ān was viewed by Christian writers as a source for enhancing the validity of Christian claims about Jesus and the Bible because of the testimony that the Qur'ān contains about Christian beliefs. It was, as has been pointed out, a 'simple, if seemingly self-contradictory, strategy'.[6] Underneath such attitudes were several very positive factors: an admiration for Arabo-Islamic learning and its transmission of the wisdom of the ancient Greeks, and a recognition of Arabic as a significant language. Greek, Hebrew and Arabic were all deemed essential for scholarly pursuits as early as the fourteenth century. On the basis of European works on the Qur'ān (especially translations) from the twelfth through the sixteenth centuries, evidence of what has been termed a 'philological reading' can be discerned.[7] A desire to understand the Qur'ān with all of its textual and linguistic difficulties led to investigations of the text that paralleled the intense study of the Bible taking place at the time, the latter often occurring in a Jewish context in order to come to a full appreciation of the Torah. Thus, medieval readers of the Qur'ān frequently had recourse to the Muslim exegetical tradition, for example, without any apparent polemical intent: their desire was to understand the text. '[P]olemical uses to which these translations were eventually to be put did not rule out an extensive and co-existent philological engagement with the text on the part of the translators themselves.'[8] Such writers certainly remained hostile towards Islam and the Qur'ān but investigative processes underlay their efforts.

THE EXPANSION OF EARLY MODERN SCHOLARSHIP

In the sixteenth century, Martin Luther argued that knowledge of the Qur'ān was essential, not so much to convert Muslims as to protect Christians from apostasy. That fear emerged within the context of significant anti-Trinitarian debates taking place within Christianity itself; if Christians were influenced by those debates within their own church, they might be tempted by the Islamic emphasis on the unity of God to abandon Christianity altogether. Such motivation was able to take advantage of the emergence of the printing press in this era, so that the first printed translation of the Qur'ān, commonly called the Bibliander edition, appeared in 1543.

In the seventeenth century, the printing of Qur'ān translations became widespread through the efforts of Ludovico Marracci (d. 1700). His work included a printed Arabic text but also interspersed refutations of qur'ānic claims with sections of translation and text. An edited version in 1721 by Christian Reineccius removed the extraneous parts of Marracci's work as well as the Arabic text, and it served as the basis for popular understanding of the Qur'ān in European circles for some time.

The rise in eighteenth-century Europe of historical-critical studies of the Bible had an effect on the study of all of the world's religions from that time on. The study of Islam did not immediately prosper in this context, perhaps because Islam's similarity to its biblical counterparts meant that earlier medieval attitudes to Islam which saw it as a secondary derivation lingered. The exception to this, and the most important element in the development of qur'ānic studies, would occur within the school of philological studies, especially as it developed in Germany. Three works are rightly regarded as fundamental in this respect.

NINETEENTH-CENTURY REORIENTATION

Abraham Geiger's book, known under its English title, *Judaism and Islam,* is a startling novelty within the history of qur'ānic studies because of its perspective and approach, although within the context of attitudes to religion developed within Reform Judaism the book fits very well. The University of Bonn in 1832 ran a contest for essays on Islam which called for 'an enquiry into those sources of the Qur'ān, that is, the Muhammadan law, which were derived from Judaism'.[9] Geiger's winning submission, written in Latin, was published in German in 1833 under the title *Was hat Mohammed aus dem Judenthume aufgenommen?* Geiger's goal was to trace the sources of the Qur'ān within Judaism especially, but also within Christianity. His was a historical approach that fitted with the perspective of *Wissenschaft des Judentums* and the founding principles of Reform Judaism: that religion in its various manifestations is a product of historical and social forces. In that context, Islam and the Qur'ān might be viewed as providing a 'test case' for Geiger's understanding of religion as the result of an initial religious revelation which is subject to human development. As such, a sympathetic approach to Islam was called for, one that did not raise the issue of its truth value, one that did not conceive of Muḥammad as an 'impostor' or false prophet, but rather one that saw the Prophet within the context of his time. Certainly, such a study is reductive in that notions of originality and creativity are put aside in the search for explanatory devices and this has been the tendency in the long line of works that followed Geiger's lead in this regard. The range of religious sources purported to have influenced the Qur'ān expanded over the following decades of research but the core concern remained the same.

The work of Gustav Weil, *Historisch-kritische Einleitung in den Koran*, first published in 1844, is another example of German scholarship of the period. Weil's intention was to place the Qur'ān in its historical context by refining the division of the sūras into Meccan and Medinan origins, already an inherent part of the Muslim tradition. Working from assumptions about the nature of the development of Muḥammad's life and the evolution of religion, Weil was able to correlate linguistic and semantic aspects of the qur'ānic text with three periods that fell within the Meccan segment of the Prophet's career.

Theodor Nöldeke's 1856 Latin dissertation and prize-winning essay, published in German in 1860 as *Geschichte des Qorāns* ('History of the Qur'ān'), is the work that set the tone, approach and agenda for most of the European and American scholarship that has been produced since. As the very title suggests, the book focused upon uncovering the historical processes behind the formation of the Qur'ān. A comparison of this work to that of al-Kindī in the third/ninth century displays the nineteenth-century sense of scholarship: the material and the topic are essentially the same but the end result is very different. For Nöldeke, the process of historical reconstruction is a rigorous one, based upon the weighing of the probability of accounts given in different sources. Historical judgements about the age of texts and the presence of obvious ideological biases, as well as notions of reasonable causality, allow an author such as Nöldeke to create an account with claims to be (close to) 'what really happened', as the famous phrase of nineteenth-century historiography has it. Questions of ultimate truth are displaced – some might say they are simply put to one side – by the quest to understand why and how events in human history unfolded as they did.

The work of both Weil and Nöldeke focused a good deal of attention on constructing the critical history of the text of the Qur'ān, a task that was already a topic of investigation as indicated by the publication in 1834 of the first scholarly edition of the Arabic text of the Qur'ān, edited (eclectically) by Gustav Flügel. Even more significantly, Flügel also published a concordance of the Qur'ān in 1842. The development of a tool such as this has an enormous impact on any scholarly community and the case for the Qur'ān was no different. The significance of such tools may be seen in the methodological presumptions that underlie their development and subsequent use. A concordance acts to define the corpus of a text as a subject of investigation in itself; the scholarly apparatus of the past tradition and its continuity of learning is thus displaced and a text-oriented study is substituted. The earlier approach of mixing text and tradition, as seen in polemic, is no longer deemed appropriate, and the canonical text itself, regardless of the way in which the community of believers may interact with its scripture, comes to the forefront. Such an attitude – a characteristic impetus of Protestant Christianity – is facilitated, institutionalised and recognised as scholarly through tools such as concordances.

These works, then, stand as major achievements in the philological study of the Qur'ān. They bring the critical tools of historical study to language and seek to understand thereby the development and the meaning of the text. Such a tendency has continued until today; most new introductions to the Qur'ān continue to be grounded in such an approach. The approach supports the particular interest that modern studies have shown in examining the sources of the Qur'ān, an investigation that has endured from medieval times, is continued in Geiger's work and has still not completely lost its polemical edges. In the absence of firm historical documentation, the exercise has been one of detecting parallels in a fairly random manner and trying to generalise beyond the point supported by specific instances. Thus, there are scholarly works that suggest Judaism as the core source. (Sometimes such works are tinged by a certain Christian anti-Judaism, while others embrace Jewish claims for the origin of all monotheism.) Other scholars have postulated Christianity in its various manifestations, or Qumran, or Zoroastrianism, or paganism as the major source. Such studies are grounded frequently in philology but also introduce elements of folklore.[10]

TWENTIETH-CENTURY CHALLENGES TO THE CONSENSUS

One of the more remarkable characteristics of this period of modern study of the Qur'ān is its incorporation of aspects of the Muslim perspective, sometimes subjecting these to a critique, but not moving outside the modernist framework. Richard Bell, for example, is famous for his attempt to understand the composition of the Qur'ān by means of dividing it up into little fragments. Bell's translation of the Qur'ān tries to reconstruct a document formed from scraps of parchment with writing on both sides and speculates about where scraps may have been misplaced and so forth.[11] Such an approach to the text has been sharply criticised – ridiculed even – for its destruction of the integrity of the Qur'ān and for its attitude towards the early Muslim community. Yet what strikes one in considering Bell's approach is the recognition that he is, in fact, merely taking one of the basic tenets of the Muslim tradition about the Qur'ān – that it was collected from text fragments 'on sheets, on palm-leaf stalks, on pumice stone, on baked clay, and on other items like that'[12] – and carrying it to its 'logical' extent. In that sense, Bell accepts the truth of the historical accounts of the emergence of the Qur'ān quite literally, at least once those basic stories have been collated into a single, historically coherent account. It might be said that Bell takes the tradition's own historical accounts more seriously than some adherents might wish them to be taken or than they even considered possible.

In a significant critique of the discipline of qur'ānic studies, Mohammed Arkoun[13] makes this same observation about the structure of the entire discipline and not simply the work of someone like Richard Bell. Arkoun notes that the topics discussed, the areas of concern and the fundamental assumptions of the scholarly discipline have not changed significantly from the outline of them provided by Jalāl al-Dīn al-Suyūṭī (d. 911/1505) in the fifteenth century, itself based on a long heritage of Muslim scholarship on the Qur'ān. When modern scholars approach the Qur'ān, the core assumptions of the Muslim tradition about the text are not challenged. Even certain methodological innovations which look at the Qur'ān in a broader perspective than the strictly philological, such as those connected to the semantic approach developed by Toshihiko Izutsu,[14] do not escape this basic orientation. They promulgate a view of the Qur'ān as a static, unchanging text, compiled in a clearly composed corpus that can be read against a background of Arabia in the seventh century. Despite the supposed 'secular' foundation of Western qur'ānic studies, even the process of revelation is discussed in terms consistent with those of the Muslim community, although recourse will virtually always be made to (the more rational and thus more suited to modern sensibilities) Muʿtazilī attitudes and conceptions of a 'created' Qur'ān. A basic affirmation of the 'religious' nature of Muḥammad's experiences, but one that ultimately remains a mystery to academic inquiry, links all scholarship that works within this presupposition and belies the easy assumption of a separation between insider–outsider perspectives and the like. The publication in 1980 of Fazlur Rahman's *Major themes of the Qur'ān* emphasises this point, for the book speaks from a Muslim perspective with the presuppositions of modern scholarship and is probably the most significant example of that tendency and one which has empowered many others to follow on in its path.

Some of the most successful and enduring of modern studies are those that bring a broad knowledge of religion in many cultures to particular questions about the Qur'ān. In doing so, the limits of traditional scholarship are overcome somewhat. Monographs by Geo Widengren on the notions related to Muḥammad as a prophet, his revelation and his book,[15] and, to a more limited extent in terms of study of the Qur'ān, the earlier work of A. J. Wensinck on images and symbols emerging from the natural world,[16] bring to the Islamic worldview the entire panoply of near and Middle Eastern religious mythology. This is not done in a reductive attempt to specify the roots of the Qur'ān and Islam, but rather in an effort to see both the variety and the parallels across cultures as human attempts to deal with the world in which we find ourselves, the human condition that we share and the images in which we portray ourselves to ourselves. In a work such as this, the Qur'ān gains its rightful place as an element in the study of world literature.

More recent times have produced significantly new initiatives. Starting in the latter part of the twentieth century, attempts were made to address questions not previously raised within the scholarly framework. Pivotal was the work of John Wansbrough, even though many of its results have been met with fierce resistance. Wansbrough's *Quranic studies: Sources and methods of scriptural interpretation* (1977) interrogates the grounding assumptions of scholarship on the Qur'ān, especially its unquestioned reliance on the dogmas of the Muslim tradition. Both in terms of the composition of the Qur'ān and the stabilisation of the text, Wansbrough proposed a historical development that extended far longer – both before and after the historical person of Muḥammad – than Muslim accounts of the life of the Prophet and the collection of the Qur'ān after his death had contemplated. Previous scholarship had subjected the Muslim accounts to critique, tried to resolve their internal contradictions and had produced a new unified vision of the historical process (on the basis of a reconstruction founded eclectically on the Muslim historical sources). Wansbrough argued that not only did the evidence that still exists suggest a different model, but later dogmatic assumptions underpinned the Muslim sources which were being used by scholars to re-establish the history of the earliest period. Wansbrough asked fundamental questions: does the structure of the text of the Qur'ān (in its form, literary features and linguistic aspects) really support the presumption of composition over a short period of time, as the Muslim accounts have it? Could those accounts be motivated by the desire to assert the integrity of the text, raising doubts about their historical value? Positive evidence, Wansbrough argued, was to be found in the exegetical tradition, the emergence of which testified to a gradual solidification of the Qur'ān over the period of several centuries.

What has lingered as the most profound impact of Wansbrough's work is the opening up of new modes of working with the Qur'ān that attempt to examine the text with a set of assumptions indebted to a broader range of religious and literary models. By far the most successful attempts are those being conducted by Angelika Neuwirth, whose work of looking at the literary structure of the Qur'ān started quite independently of Wansbrough. Neuwirth, however, has certainly recognised the impact of Wansbrough's work on new approaches in the discipline. As Neuwirth's work has evolved, stimulated quite explicitly by the issues that Wansbrough's work raises while rejecting his conclusions, she has suggested new models of understanding the text of the Qur'ān as liturgical units developed within the early community in the process of worship. Neuwirth's many contributions have focused on the literary processes that occur prior to the emergence of the qur'ānic text as a scripture. This she calls the pre-canonical phase of the Qur'ān and she argues that the text evolved and developed organically, sometimes through a process of inner exegesis, sometimes through liturgical iterations.[17]

A CONTEMPORARY CATHOLICISM

It may be that the discipline of qur'ānic studies today has matured to a stage where a certain catholicism prevails. The recent project of the *Encyclopaedia of the Qur'ān*[18] certainly illustrates the point that the insider–outsider divide has no relevance in scholarly assessment or, at least, that the approaches to be 'canonised' as constituting scholarly work can vary in the extent to which they will question basic Muslim assumptions about the Qur'ān. The common characteristic of all such work is that it takes its subject seriously and leaves its readers to draw their own conclusions as to whether (or to what extent) the Qur'ān is a work which will be life-motivating to the individual. That, of course, does reflect a modern attitude towards religion itself, and means that the study of the Qur'ān, as it is found in the academy today, is undoubtedly one fully imbued with the spirit of modernism that regards religion to be a personal matter for the individual. But that spirit of openness and seriousness is also what separates the work from contemporary polemic, where the underlying thrust is either the defence or the destruction of Islam, the tone is antagonistic, and respect for the position of one's 'opponent' is not valued. The volumes of collected articles by Ibn Warraq (pseud.)[19] represent the polemical face of scholarship, but also illustrate how fine the line remains between anti-religious polemic and the productions of the academic community. Ibn Warraq's republication of many classic articles of scholarship is contextualised as a challenge to the reader, forcing the question, 'What rational person could believe in a book such as the Qur'ān?' By juxtaposing Muslim dogma and modern scholarly investigation, the former is subject to ridicule as 'unscientific' and not worthy of belief. This is precisely the dilemma in which modern scholarship finds itself, with individual scholars claiming disinterestedness to excuse whatever conclusions the faithful may take from their studies.

As a consequence, critiques of contemporary qur'ānic studies come from many directions. Some object, from the perspective of Muslim orthodoxy, that a non-Muslim cannot and should not approach a text that means so much to so many people. To do so will surely misrepresent it and will be unacceptable to Muslims.[20] Others, such as Parvez Manzoor,[21] adopt the language of anti-Orientalism and see the destructive impact of such studies as resulting from a position grounded in an anti-religious and specifically anti-Islamic bias. Mohammed Arkoun has been perhaps the most insistent yet constructive voice within the boundaries of the discipline to call for developments in new directions. Writing in the *Encyclopaedia of the Qur'ān*, he sees a future that calls for 'a protocol of interpretation that is free from both the dogmatic orthodox framework and the procedural disciplines of modern scientism which is, it must be admitted, no less constraining'.[22] Seeking a deconstruction of all existing categories through which we approach the Qur'ān, Arkoun calls for a Nietzschean genealogy of values of the Qur'ān within the comparative context of religious societies which will be 'an interpretation that wanders', one in which each interpreter 'gives free rein to his or her own dynamic of associating ideas and representations, beginning from the freely chosen interpretation of a corpus of which the often imputed disorder, so often denounced, favours the freedom to wander'.[23]

As with most scholarly disciplines, the strength to withstand such critiques is enormous, given that the institutional contexts within which such academic activities take place have their own structures of logic and emotion. The resistance to the language of the post-modern critique exemplified by Arkoun is hardly unique to qur'ānic studies but certainly finds its place therein.[24] The much-debated divergence between the 'traditionalists' and 'revisionists'[25] (or the 'sanguine' versus the 'sceptic'[26]) epitomises the extent of intellectual disputation in the field, and even this disputation is conducted for the most part within the decorum and the standards expected for academic discourse (except when it transgresses by having attention thrust on it by the popular media) and rarely confronts the challenges of the serious critiques which are posed. Despite the pessimism implicit in this description of qur'ānic studies, the discipline does change substantially with each generation and there can be little doubt concerning the continued viability and increasing popularity of the field. The major dangers to the integrity and academic success of the discipline come from the more tangential pieces of work, especially when they attract public attention such as has been the case with the books of Christoph Luxenberg (pseud.),[27] Ibn Warraq[28] and Günter Lüling.[29] Luxenberg's work with its fanciful reconstructions of Syriac originals to the text of the Qur'ān captures a public sentiment that has been sensitised to embrace any claim that casts doubt on a religious orthodoxy that is characterised as 'old-fashioned' or 'fundamentalist'. Works such as Luxenberg's can be rehabilitated by incorporating some of their specifics within the tradition of scholarly discourse. For example, Neuwirth,[30] among others, has suggested that there is value in bringing issues to the fore that have been neglected in the flow of scholarly research. The tone of polemic, however, remains close to the surface of the works themselves and no amount of scholarly effort can ultimately take that away. Even the scholarly discussion of the issues raised in such works is perceived by some as raising questions of religious truth, thus evoking the spectre of the works of early medieval polemic.

One branch of qur'ānic studies that has attempted to circumvent some aspects of the problems raised here involves study of Muslim approaches to the text of scripture, especially as found in classical exegetical (*tafsīr*) literature. This kind of research, framed – usually implicitly – within a theoretical stance of 'reader response', views the Qur'ān not as a static text but as a dynamic entity constantly being (re-)formed by the community that interacts with it. Such a stance shows no likelihood of overcoming, in the near future, the fascination with the text of the Qur'ān itself as a scholarly object, although it certainly is a growing field of study.[31] Of course, this can only serve to remind us that medieval polemical writers were interested in the *tafsīr* tradition as well and that the marks of what we consider modern scholarly approaches to the Qur'ān remain ill-defined when difficult questions are asked of them. The modern study of *tafsīr* is not a simple answer to the dilemmas of the discipline, for each work that is written within the field, whether it aims to or not, adds to the collective human response to the text of the Qur'ān. What the study of *tafsīr* does show, however, is that humans, whether Muslim or not, interact with the text from the perspective of their own era, and that is just as true for modern scholars as it is for classical writers. Our era does not (or at least should not) allow us to confuse such conditioned interaction with notions of absolutes, whether they be deemed religious dogmas or scientific objectivity. It may well be only with the perspective of history that the true character of twenty-first-century Western scholarship on the Qur'ān can actually be appreciated.

Notes

1. A. Rippin, 'Introduction' to A. Rippin (ed.), *The Qur'ān: Style and content* (Aldershot: Ashgate Variorum, 2001), p. xi n. 2.
2. R. McCutcheon, *The discipline of religion: Structure, meaning, rhetoric* (London: Routledge, 2003).
3. S. Fish, *Is there a text in this class? The authority of interpretive communities* (Cambridge, MA: Harvard University Press, 1980).
4. A. Guillaume, *The life of Muhammad: A translation of Isḥāq's* [sic] Sīrat Rasūl Allāh (London: Oxford University Press, 1955), pp. 256–7.
5. W. Muir, *The Apology of al Kindy written at the court of al Mâmûn (AH 215; AD 830) in defence of Christianity against Islam* (London: Smith Elder, 1882), pp. 22–30, 41–6.
6. T. E. Burman, 'Polemic, philology, and ambivalence: Reading the Qur'ān in Latin Christendom', *Journal of Islamic Studies* 15 (2004), 182.
7. Ibid., 189.
8. Ibid., 195.
9. A. Geiger, *Judaism and Islam*, trans. F. M. Young, repr. with prolegomenon by M. Pearlman (New York: KTAV Publishing House, 1970, 1898[1]), p. xxix.
10. For a good overview of such studies, see T. Kronholm, 'Dependency and prophetic originality', *Orientalia Succana* 31–2 (1982–3), 47–70.
11. R. Bell, *The Qur'ān, translated, with a critical re-arrangement of the surahs* (Edinburgh: T. & T. Clark, 1937, 1939).
12. N. Calder, J. Mojaddedi and A. Rippin (eds.), *Classical Islam: A sourcebook of religious literature* (London: Routledge, 2003), p. 80 (from Ibn ʿAtiyya, d. 541/1147).
13. M. Arkoun, 'Introduction: Bilan et perspectives des études coraniques', in his *Lectures du Coran* (Paris: G. P. Maisonneuve et Larose, 1982), pp. v–xxxiii.

14. T. Izutsu, *God and man in the Koran: Semantics of the koranic Weltanschauung* (Tokyo: The Keio Institute of Cultural and Linguistic Studies, 1964), and his *Ethico-religious concepts in the Qur'ān* (Montreal: McGill University Press, 1966).
15. G. Widengren, *The ascension of the apostle and the heavenly book* (Uppsala: A. B. Lundequistska Bokhandeln, 1950); G. Widengren, *Muḥammad, the apostle of God, and his ascension* (Uppsala: A. B. Lundequistska Bokhandeln, 1955).
16. A. J. Wensinck, *Studies of A. J. Wensinck* (New York: Arno Press, 1978). This reprints articles from 1916, 1918 and 1921.
17. A. Neuwirth, 'Qur'ān, crisis and memory: The qur'ānic path towards canonization as reflected in the anthropogonic accounts', in A. Neuwirth and A. Pflitsch (eds.), *Crisis and memory in Islamic societies: Proceedings of the Third Summer Academy of the Working Group Modernity and Islam held at the Orient Institute of the German Oriental Society in Beirut* (Beirut/Würtburg: Ergon Verlag, 2001), pp. 113–52; and her 'Referentiality and textuality in *Sūrat al-Ḥijr*: Some observations on the qur'ānic "canonical process" and the emergence of a community', in I. J. Boullata (ed.), *Literary structures of religious meaning in the Qur'ān* (Richmond: Curzon Press, 2000), pp. 143–72.
18. J. D. McAuliffe (ed.), *Encyclopaedia of the Qur'ān*, 5 vols. (Leiden: Brill, 2001–6).
19. Ibn Warraq (pseud.) (ed.), *The origins of the Koran: Classic essays on Islam's holy book* (Amherst, NY: Prometheus Books, 1998), as well as his (ed.), *What the Koran really says: Language, text, and commentary* (Amherst, NY: Prometheus Books, 2002).
20. As an example, see M. Abdul-Rauf, 'Outsiders' interpretations of Islam: A Muslim's point of view', in R. C. Martin (ed.), *Approaches to Islam in religious studies* (Tucson: University of Arizona Press, 1985), pp. 179–88.
21. P. Manzoor, 'Method against truth: Orientalism and qur'ānic studies', *Muslim World Book Review* 7 (1987), 33–49.
22. M. Arkoun, 'Contemporary critical practices and the Qur'ān', in McAuliffe (ed.), *Encyclopaedia of the Qur'ān*, vol. I, p. 429.
23. Ibid. For an example of what this approach might look like in practice, see M. Fischer and M. Abedi, *Debating Muslims: Cultural dialogues in postmodernity and tradition* (Madison, WI: University of Wisconsin Press, 1990), ch. 2.
24. See D. Madigan, 'Reflections on some current directions in qur'ānic studies', *Muslim World* 85 (1995), 345–62.
25. Y. Nevo and J. Koren, *Crossroads to Islam: The origins of the Arab religion and the Arab state* (Amherst, NY: Prometheus Books, 2003).
26. H. Berg, 'Competing paradigms in Islamic origins: Qur'ān 15:89–91 and the value of *isnāds*', in H. Berg (ed.), *Method and theory in the study of Islamic origins* (Leiden: Brill, 2003), pp. 259–90.
27. Ch. Luxenberg (pseud.), *Die Syro-Aramäische Lesart des Koran: Ein Beitrag zur Entschlüsselung der Koransprache* (Berlin: Das Arabische Buch, 2000).
28. Ibn Warraq (pseud.), *The origins of the Koran* and his *What the Koran really says.*
29. G. Lüling, *A challenge to Islam for reformation: The rediscovery and reliable reconstruction of a comprehensive pre-Islamic Christian hymnal hidden in the Koran under earliest Islamic reinterpretations* (Delhi: Motilal Banarsidass, 2003). This work is based on earlier German versions.

30. A. Neuwirth, 'Qur'an and history – a disputed relationship: Some reflections on qur'anic history and history in the Qur'an', *Journal of Qur'anic Studies* 5 (2003), 1–18.
31. W. Saleh, *The formation of the classical* tafsīr *tradition: The Qur'ān commentary of al-Tha'labī (d. 427/1035)* (Leiden: Brill, 2004), provides a vivid example of what can be accomplished.

Further reading

Abdul-Rauf, M., 'Outsiders' interpretations of Islam: A Muslim's point of view', in R. C. Martin (ed.), *Approaches to Islam in religious studies*, Tucson: University of Arizona Press, 1985, pp. 179–88.

Arkoun, M., 'Contemporary critical practices and the Qur'ān', in J. D. McAuliffe (ed.), *Encyclopaedia of the Qur'ān*, 5 vols., Leiden: Brill, 2001–6, vol. I, pp. 412–31.

'Introduction: An assessment of and perspectives on the study of the Qur'ān', in A. Rippin (ed.), *The Qur'ān: Style and content*, Aldershot: Ashgate Variorum, 2001, ch. 18.

'Introduction: Bilan et perspectives des études coraniques', in M. Arkoun, *Lectures du Coran*, Paris: G. P. Maisonneuve et Larose, 1982, pp. v–xxxiii; Eng. trans.

Bell, R., *The Qur'ān, translated, with a critical re-arrangement of the surahs*, Edinburgh: T. & T. Clark, 1937, 1939.

Berg, H., 'Competing paradigms in Islamic origins: Qur'ān 15:89–91 and the value of *isnāds*', in H. Berg (ed.), *Method and theory in the study of Islamic origins*, Leiden: Brill, 2003, pp. 259–90.

Bobzin, H., 'Latin translations of the Koran: A short overview', *Der Islam* 70 (1993), 193–206.

'"A treasury of heresies": Christian polemics against the Koran', in S. Wild (ed.), *The Qur'ān as text*, Leiden: Brill, 1996, pp. 157–75.

Burman, T. E., 'Polemic, philology, and ambivalence: Reading the Qur'ān in Latin Christendom', *Journal of Islamic Studies* 15 (2004), 181–209.

'*Tafsīr* and translation: Traditional Arabic Qur'ān exegesis and the Latin Qur'āns of Robert of Ketton and Mark of Toledo', *Speculum* 73 (1998), 703–32.

Calder, N., J. Mojaddedi and A. Rippin (eds.), *Classical Islam: A sourcebook of religious literature*, London: Routledge, 2003.

Firestone, R., 'The Qur'ān and the Bible: Some modern studies of their relationship', in J. C. Reeves (ed.), *Bible and Qur'ān: Essays in scriptural intertextuality*, Atlanta: Society of Biblical Literature, 2003, pp. 1–22 (on the works of Geiger, Bell and Wansbrough).

Fischer, M. and M. Abedi, *Debating Muslims: Cultural dialogues in postmodernity and tradition*, Madison, WI: University of Wisconsin Press, 1990, ch. 2.

Fish, S., *Is there a text in this class? The authority of interpretive communities*, Cambridge, MA: Harvard University Press, 1980.

Flügel, G., *Concordantiae Corani arabicae*, Leipzig: Tauchnitz, 1842.

Corani textus arabicus, Leipzig: Tauchnitz, 1834.

Geiger, A., *Judaism and Islam*, trans. F. M. Young, repr. with prolegomenon by M. Pearlman, New York: KTAV Publishing House, 1970 (1898^1).

Guillaume, A., *The life of Muhammad: A translation of Isḥāq's* [sic] Sīrat Rasūl Allāh, London: Oxford University Press, 1955.

Ibn Warraq (pseud.) (ed.), *The origins of the Koran: Classic essays on Islam's holy book*, Amherst, NY: Prometheus Books, 1998.

(ed.), *What the Koran really says: Language, text, and commentary*, Amherst, NY: Prometheus Books, 2002.

Izutsu, T., *Ethico-religious concepts in the Qur'ān*, Montreal: McGill University Press, 1966.

God and man in the Koran: Semantics of the koranic Weltanschauung, Tokyo: The Keio Institute of Cultural and Linguistic Studies, 1964.

Kronholm, T., 'Dependency and prophetic originality', *Orientalia Succana* 31–2 (1982–3), 47–70.

Lüling, G., *A challenge to Islam for reformation: The rediscovery and reliable reconstruction of a comprehensive pre-Islamic Christian hymnal hidden in the Koran under earliest Islamic reinterpretations*, Delhi: Motilal Banarsidass, 2003 (based on German works written in 1974, 1993).

Luxenberg, Ch. (pseud.), *Die Syro-Aramäische Lesart des Koran: Ein Beitrag zur Entschlüsselung der Koransprache*, Berlin: Das Arabische Buch, 2000.

McCutcheon, R., *The discipline of religion: Structure, meaning, rhetoric*, London: Routledge, 2003.

Madigan, D., 'Reflections on some current directions in qur'ānic studies', *Muslim World* 85 (1995), 345–62.

Manzoor, P., 'Method against truth: Orientalism and qur'ānic studies', *Muslim World Book Review* 7 (1987), 33–49; repr. in A. Rippin (ed.), *The Qur'ān: Style and content*, Aldershot: Ashgate Variorum, 2001, ch. 21.

Muir, W., *The Apology of al Kindy written at the court of al Mâmûn (AH 215; AD 830) in defence of Christianity against Islam*, London: Smith Elder, 1882.

Neuwirth, A., 'Qur'an and history – a disputed relationship: Some reflections on qur'anic history and history in the Qur'an', *Journal of Qur'anic Studies* 5 (2003), 1–18.

'Qur'ān, crisis and memory: The qur'ānic path towards canonization as reflected in the anthropogonic accounts', in A. Neuwirth and A. Pflitsch (eds.), *Crisis and memory in Islamic societies: Proceedings of the Third Summer Academy of the Working Group Modernity and Islam held at the Orient Institute of the German Oriental Society in Beirut*, Beirut/Würtburg: Ergon Verlag, 2001, pp. 113–52.

'Referentiality and textuality in *Sūrat al-Ḥijr*: Some observations on the qur'ānic "canonical process" and the emergence of a community', in I. J. Boullata (ed.), *Literary structures of religious meaning in the Qur'ān*, Richmond: Curzon Press, 2000, pp. 143–72.

Nevo, Y. and J. Koren, *Crossroads to Islam: The origins of the Arab religion and the Arab state*, Amherst, NY: Prometheus Books, 2003.

Nöldeke, Th., *Geschichte des Qorāns*, Göttingen: Dieterichschen, 1860; second rev. ed. F. Schwally (ed., vols. I and II), G. Bergsträsser and O. Pretzl (eds., vol. III), Leipzig: Dieterichsche, 1909–38.

Rahman, F., *Major themes of the Qur'ān*, Minneapolis: Bibliotheca Islamica, 1980.

Rippin, A., 'Introduction', in A. Rippin (ed.), *The Qur'ān: Style and content*, Aldershot: Ashgate Variorum, 2001, pp. xi–xxvi.

'Literary analysis of Qur'ān, *tafsīr* and *sīra*: the methodologies of John Wansbrough', in R. C. Martin (ed.), *Approaches to Islam in religious studies*, Tucson: University of Arizona Press, 1985, pp. 151–63.

The Qur'ān and its interpretative tradition, Aldershot: Variorum, 2001 (includes reprints of Rippin, 'Literary analysis of Qur'ān, *tafsīr* and *sīra*' and 'Reading the Qur'ān with Richard Bell').

'Reading the Qur'ān with Richard Bell', *Journal of the American Oriental Society* 112 (1992), 639–47.

Said, E., *Orientalism*, New York: Pantheon Books, 1978.

Saleh, W., *The formation of the classical* tafsīr *tradition: The Qur'ān commentary of al-Tha'labī (d. 427/1035)*, Leiden: Brill, 2004.

Wansbrough, J., *Quranic studies: Sources and methods of scriptural interpretation*, Oxford: Oxford University Press, 1977; second ed. with foreword, annotations and glossary by A. Rippin, Amherst, NY: Prometheus Press, 2004.

Weil, G., *Historisch-kritische Einleitung in den Koran*, Bielefeld: Velhagen & Klasing, 1844.

Wensinck, A. J., *Studies of A. J. Wensinck*, New York: Arno Press, 1978.

Widengren, G., *The ascension of the apostle and the heavenly book*, Uppsala: A. B. Lundequistska Bokhandeln, 1950.

Muḥammad, the apostle of God, and his ascension, Uppsala: A. B. Lundequistska Bokhandeln, 1955.

Part V

Contemporary readings

Fig. 12 Section from an eighteenth-century Chinese Qur'ān manuscript. Depicted here is most of Q 5:83 (CBL Is. 1602 fols. 1v–2r). Courtesy of the Trustees of the Chester Beatty Library, Dublin

12 Women's readings of the Qur'ān

ASMA BARLAS

Some 1,400 years ago, when the Qur'ān was being revealed to the prophet Muḥammad, his wife Umm Salama reportedly asked him why it was not addressing women.[1] It seems she was not impressed by the fact that in the Arabic language, as in many others, the male gender is inclusive of the female and that in using it the Qur'ān was, in effect, addressing both. Of course if this had been an idle question on her part and nothing had come of it, the incident probably would not have found its way into Muslim tradition. Yet, not only does tradition record it, but many Muslims use it to explain the context in which the Qur'ān became the only scripture to speak directly to women.

WOMEN IN THE QUR'ĀN

Indeed, not only does the Qur'ān address women, but it frequently does so in a manner that should leave little room for doubt that it considers them equal to men. One example is Q 33:35: 'For Muslim men and women, for believing men and women, for devout men and women, for men and women who are patient and constant, for men and women who humble themselves, for men and women who give in charity, for men and women who fast (and deny themselves), for men and women who guard their chastity, and for men and women who engage much in God's praise; for them has God prepared forgiveness and great reward.' In spite of such verses, and the Qur'ān's counsel to read it for its best meanings, most Muslims continue to project sexual inequality, discrimination and even misogyny into it. Before considering why this is so, it seems appropriate to dwell for a bit on Umm Salama's question since it offers such compelling and potentially unending lessons for believers.

Most obviously, her question, and the responsiveness in divine discourse it seems to have evoked, shows that a spirit of critical inquiry may be essential for a meaningful encounter with God. That is, reason and faith may not necessarily be at odds with one another. In fact, the Qur'ān would have *all* Muslims cultivate a mode of critical engagement by using their own intellects and capacities to reason in order to decipher its verses or *āyāt*, literally, 'signs' of God.

Just as notably, Umm Salama's question establishes the value of a woman's critique to the community of believers since God answered her not only by making women the subjects of divine discourse but, as the Qur'ān makes clear, also by shaping its content in light of their concerns as they themselves expressed these concerns during the process of its revelation. Such receptiveness tells us that '*women too* are among those oppressed whom God comes to vindicate and liberate'.[2] Yet, later generations of Muslims would forget this lesson in their myopic belief that Islam privileges men and that women are morally and mentally defective and unfit to interpret religion, much less to pass judgement on the religious knowledge produced by men.

Umm Salama's question also reveals that long before the advent of modernity, feminism and disciplines based on studying 'the relationship between language and forms of human subjectivity, some pre-modern, illiterate, Muslim women were thinking critically about the role of language in shaping their sense of self'.[3] If that were not so, Umm Salama would probably not have asked her question, and if her question was not important, presumably God would not have heeded it. From the latter fact we can also infer that for divine discourse to speak to us, we must also continue asking questions of it.

WOMEN IN ISLAM

Regrettably, however, for most of their history Muslim women have not had much of an opportunity to ask the sort of question Umm Salama did. In fact, even as her intervention confirms the influence of some women (and among these one must include Khadīja and 'Ā'isha, the Prophet's first and last wives) on the formation of Islamic knowledge at the very inception of Muslim history, it also draws attention to the fact that there is little in the unfolding of that history, or in its recording, to suggest that their influence was anything but sporadic and short-lived. Even in the Prophet's own lifetime, some men sought to counteract the Qur'ān's provisions for women – such as those giving them the right to own property – by misinterpreting its verses.[4] By the second Islamic century (eighth century CE), male scholars, or *'ulamā'*, had managed to dilute 'the egalitarian impulse in various parts of tradition', and a hundred years later, even the egalitarianism that was once associated with the Qur'ān had lost its 'subversive connotation'.[5]

The growing social conservatism and political quietism of Muslims – reflected in a qur'ānic exegesis that became progressively more misogynistic over time – owed itself partly to the political aspirations and fortunes of successive dynasties. For instance, under ʿAbbāsid rule, the state itself became instrumental in suppressing certain interpretations of Islam in an effort to secure communal unity and thereby its own hegemony. Such measures impacted women disproportionately given that different readings of the same religious texts can yield 'fundamentally different Islams' for them.[6] The ʿAbbāsids also did irreparable harm to women by institutionalising female slavery and subordination to men through the practice of popularising limitless harems, the stuff of legends like the 'Arabian Nights'. As a result, over time, the 'tradition of historicizing women as active, full participants in the making of culture', came to be replaced by a 'memory in which women [had] no right to equality'.[7]

As individuals, certain women did continue to acquire learning and some gained renown either in their own right, as scholars, poets, Ṣūfīs and teachers (among his teachers, Ibn al-ʿArabī (d. 638/1240), for instance, counted a woman), or as politically powerful wives or concubines of this or that ruler. As a group, however, women were excluded from public life and from the processes of knowledge construction for the thousand or so years that the Muslim empire endured, in ever shifting and eventually attenuated forms.

Perhaps this is not very noteworthy given that all societies of that time were steeped in misogyny and traditional modes of patriarchy and there was no recognition of women's rights before the advent of women's and feminist movements in the twentieth century. Certainly, the European Middle Ages, with which the Muslim empire overlapped in its early phases, are not known for their emancipatory stance towards women. Yet, there is some irony in how women fared under Muslim rule given the rights the Qur'ān had extended to them and given too that, at its zenith, the Muslim empire was a dazzlingly rich mosaic of cultures, races and religions, as remarkable for its tolerant cosmopolitanism as for its inventiveness and openness to learning. And yet, in spite of this intellectual and cultural efflorescence, even exceptional women did not acquire the same stature as men in religious matters due to the nexus that developed between political and sexual power and between the growth of (all-male) interpretive communities and their control of religious knowledge.

This nexus survived the disintegration of Muslim power, with the collapse of the Ottoman empire after World War I, and even outlasted European colonialism that had enabled the Muslim collapse and followed on its heels. Yet, even though colonisation could not erode traditional structures of religious authority, and in some cases even strengthened them, it induced far-reaching changes that eventually led to self-critiques by Muslim intellectuals. In the ensuing debates, people also began to discuss women's rights and, for the first time, some women publicly joined in these debates.

RE-READING THE QUR'ĀN: SEXUAL EQUALITY?

While women's and feminist movements emerged decades ago in many Muslim countries and the numbers of scholars who work on gender and women's rights in Islam are legion (among the most famous being Leila Ahmed and Fatima Mernissi), it was only in the last quarter of the twentieth century that Muslim women took up the systematic study of the Qur'ān. Of course, several non-Muslim women have also analysed women-related themes in the Qur'ān and/or the ḥadīth literature (Yvonne Haddad, Jane Smith, Barbara Stowasser) and at least one is involved in theorising an Islamic feminism based on the Qur'ān's teachings (Margot Badran). Moreover, not just women, but also some Muslim men have offered re-readings of the Qur'ān (Farid Esack, Asghar Ali Engineer) or have done work that has paved the way for a modern qur'ānic hermeneutics (Fazlur Rahman). There are as yet, however, only a handful of Muslim women (notably, Azizah al-Hibri, Riffat Hassan, Amina Wadud and myself) who are involved in re-reading the Qur'ān, particularly its position on sexual equality, and this chapter focuses on their work.

Even though some women call themselves feminists and others do not,[8] their readings actually have a great deal in common. They all challenge the theme of male privilege that Muslims historically have read into the Qur'ān while also recuperating its teachings on sexual equality. They do this by offering a sustained critique of the theology and the interpretive methodology that have given rise to oppressive conceptions of God and patriarchal readings of divine speech, and by re-reading the so-called misogynistic verses relating to men's alleged superiority, 'wife-beating', polygyny, judicial evidence and veiling. In addition, women's scholarship reframes our understanding of the Qur'ān's position on sexual equality and patriarchy, thus opening up the liberatory possibilities of scripture.

Cumulatively, then, women's and feminist readings pose a challenge to dominant (and androcentric) modes of knowledge-construction and we can view them as comprising a single body of work. Within this shared framework, however, each theorist also has her own distinctive focus and critique, so it is important to note their differences as well. In what follows, I give some sense of both the collective and the individual aspects of their writings.

Theological critique

Hassan and al-Hibri were the first (in the early 1980s) to challenge patriarchal readings of the Qur'ān and to emphasise its stance on sexual equality. Hassan does this by critiquing the theological assumptions on the basis of which Muslims justify male superiority. As she points out, Muslims generally believe

> (1) that God's primary creation is man, not woman, since woman is believed to have been created from man's rib, hence is derivative and secondary ontologically; (2) that woman, not man, was the primary agent of what is generally referred to as 'Man's Fall' or man's expulsion from the Garden of Eden, hence 'all daughters of Eve' are to be regarded with hatred, suspicion, and contempt; and (3) that woman was created not only from man but also for man, which makes her existence merely instrumental and not fundamental. The three theological questions to which the above assumptions may appropriately be regarded as answers are (1) How was woman created? (2) Was woman responsible for the 'Fall' of man? and (3) Why was woman created?[9]

Each of these assumptions, argues Hassan, is false. To begin with, the Qur'ān locates the origins of both women and men in a single *nafs* (self). Moreover, the word 'Adam' as used in twenty-one out of twenty-five cases in the Qur'ān symbolises 'self-conscious humanity' and is 'a collective noun referring to "the human" rather than to a male person'. Further, there is no qur'ānic narrative about original sin or 'Eve's' culpability for the fall (as Smith and Haddad also argue).[10] Indeed, there is no concept of the fall in Islam. Rather, to Hassan, as to Muhammad Iqbal, on whose work she draws, the expulsion of the human pair from paradise marks the transition from consciousness to self-consciousness. Lastly, she contests the claim that women were created for men by pointing to the Qur'ān's teaching that humans were created 'for just ends' and 'in the best of moulds' and enjoined to 'live together in harmony and righteousness'.[11]

According to Hassan, it is the customary Muslim practice of interpreting the Qur'ān by way of the ḥadīth (pl. *aḥādīth*, narratives about the life, sayings and praxis of the Prophet), that leads to misogynistic interpretations. She believes the reason Muslim women as a whole have not contested such interpretations is that not only poor and illiterate women, but 'even privileged and educated Muslim women – like their counterparts in other major religious traditions – have been systematically denied the opportunity to acquire the critical tools whereby they can examine the roots of their tradition and discover how they became so disadvantaged'. As a result, they have been 'unable to refute the arguments that impose unjust laws and restrictions upon them in the name of Islam'.[12] For Hassan, a feminist theology alone can 'liberate not only Muslim women, but also Muslim men, from unjust social structures and systems of thought which make a peer relationship between men and women impossible'.[13] (She does not say, however, what she means by a feminist theology.)

The point of departure for al-Hibri's reading of the Qur'ān's position on sexual equality is different. To her, it is the principle of God's unity, or *tawḥīd*, that 'provides the basis for the fundamental metaphysical sameness of all humans as creatures of God'. As she too argues, this sameness is also a function of the fact that all human beings were created from the same *nafs*. Thus, while differences exist by divine will, as the Qur'ān teaches, the most honoured in God's sight is the most pious; as such, gender alone cannot render men superior to women.

In fact, al-Hibri derives the same moral from the story of Satan's fall from divine grace because of his refusal 'to bow to Adam in direct contravention of a divine order'. Satan's disobedience, she points out, stemmed from his belief that he was better than Adam 'because God created him from fire and Adam from clay'. She calls 'this mode of arrogant reasoning . . . "Satanic logic"' and maintains that it also underpins patriarchies. Early Muslim jurists, unaware of this logic, readily accepted 'the central thesis of patriarchy, namely, that males were superior to females'. She thus rejects patriarchal readings of Muslim law on the grounds that 'they are based on Satanic logic and conflict with *tawḥīd*'. Since such interpretive reasoning was a product of its own time, al-Hibri believes that it needs 'to be reexamined in light of the change in human consciousness'.[14]

Later works, by Wadud and myself, focus attention on this relationship between the content of knowledge and the methods by which and the contexts in which it is produced as a way to emphasise that what one understands the Qur'ān to be saying depends on who reads it, how and in what contexts. Since, historically, only men have read the Qur'ān, our understanding of it has been mediated by the 'male vision, perspective, desire, or needs', as Wadud argues. Women and their experiences have been either overlooked or excluded from the 'basic paradigms through which we examine and discuss the Qur'ān and qur'ānic interpretation'.[15] Since men's and women's experiences are, however, different, silencing the women not only keeps them, but also the men, from developing a 'holistic understanding of what it means to be Muslim'. More crucially, silencing the women violates the Qur'ān's designation of both men and women as God's vicegerents, or *khulafā'*, on earth, equally charged with moral responsibility. In light of this critique, Wadud self-consciously seeks to identify 'the significance of the female voice in the text and the female perspective on what it means to follow the guidance of the text'.[16] (She does not, however, define what she means by the female voice 'in' the text.)

While I agree with many aspects of Wadud's critique, I do not view the Qur'ān as a dual-gendered text (as having female and male voices). Rather, since God is beyond sex/gender, I believe that so is divine speech. While sex/gender does structure human experiences and understanding of the world, my own view is that women and men have a stake in reading texts differently, or in different readings of the same text. But I do not valorise women's voices as inherently liberatory (or men's as oppressive) given the Qur'ān's teaching that both women and men have been equally endowed with the capacity for moral choice and personality. I therefore focus more on the theology and interpretive strategies that generate patriarchal readings of scripture as well as on the fact that the Qur'ān 'happens against a long background of patriarchal precedent'[17] and has always been interpreted within patriarchies. (I define patriarchy as both a form of father-rule/husband-right and as a politics of sexual differentiation that privileges males.)

In this context, I make both a historical and a hermeneutic argument. The historical traces the gradual convergence of political power and religious authority that shaped how Muslims came to define religious epistemology and methodology and thus also how they came to read the Qur'ān as a patriarchal text. The hermeneutic proposes a method for reading the Qur'ān in contextually appropriate ways, as the text itself would have us do. Basically, I locate the hermeneutic keys for interpreting it in the nature of divine self-disclosure (how God describes God) since there is a relationship between God and God's speech. I also emphasise the need to begin with a sound theological conception of God that does not project a sexual identity or partisanship on to God. Indeed, I argue that qur'ānic epistemology is inherently antipatriarchal inasmuch as a qur'ānic worldview is based in an uncompromising rejection of the patriarchal imaginary of God the father, or prophets as fathers, or fathers/husbands as (divinely ordained) rulers. Instead, a qur'ānic perspective is based in the belief that God is beyond sex/gender and that divine justice lies in never doing any *ẓulm* to human beings (transgressing against their rights).[18]

Such a view of God has direct implications for relationships between women and men as well. At the very least, it undermines the legitimacy of patriarchy, given that patriarchies are based in valorisations of male authority and transgressing against women's rights. I thus argue that the Qur'ān cannot possibly endorse them, a claim that I also substantiate by examining the nature of divine ontology, the qur'ānic narratives of the prophets Abraham and Muḥammad, and its position on mothers and fathers, wives and husbands, sex and sexuality, and marriage and divorce.

Methodological critique

In addition to critiquing the theology that underpins anti-women readings of the Qur'ān, women's and feminist scholarship also takes issue with their methodology, in particular, with the interpretive practices of the exegetes of the classical period whose work has acquired a canonical status. These exegetes, it is argued, adopted a 'linear-atomistic' approach in which they studied 'one or a few verses . . . in isolation from the preceding and following verses'. As a result, they failed to recognise the Qur'ān's thematic and structural coherence.[19] To quote Wadud, they 'begin with the first verse of the first chapter and proceed to the second verse of the first chapter – one verse at a time – until the end of the Book. Little or no effort is made to recognise themes and to discuss the relationship of the Qur'ān to itself, thematically.' Even when they refer to the relationship of two verses (*āyāt*), they do not apply any hermeneutic principle to do so since a method 'for linking similar Qur'anic ideas, syntactical structures, principles, or themes together is almost nonexistent'.[20]

Also non-existent at that time was knowledge of linguistics and, as a result, much of the classical exegesis, or *tafsīr*, pays no attention to the 'language act, syntactical structures, and textual context' in which specific words are used in the Qur'ān, or to their larger textual development.[21] An inevitable, if ultimately unacceptable, result is a partial, piecemeal and decontextualised (mis)interpretation that not only fails to see hermeneutic connections between different themes in the Qur'ān, but which also projects patriarchal and misogynistic meanings into it.

Female subservience?

Thus, dominant readings of the Qur'ān rely, at best, on three or four words, or parts of a line in a verse, to establish the principle of male superiority and female inferiority and subservience to men. For instance, the claim that God has made men superior to women derives from Q 4:34: 'Men are "*qawwāmūn*" over women in matters where God gave some of them more than others, and in what they spend of their money.' Yet as al-Hibri argues, '"*qawwamun*" is a difficult word to translate. Some writers translate it as "protectors" and "maintainers". However, this is not quite accurate. The basic notion involved here is one of moral guidance and caring.' To maintain that men are superior to women in reason and strength, she argues, is both unwarranted and inconsistent with

> other Islamic teachings . . . To start with, nowhere in the passage is there a reference to the male's physical or intellectual superiority. Secondly, since men are *'qawwamun'* over women in matters where God gave *some* of the men more than *some* of the women, *and* in what the men spend of their money, then clearly men *as a class* are not *'qawwamun'* over women *as a class* . . . It is worth noting that the passage does not even assert that *some* men are inherently superior to *some* women. It only states that in certain matters some man may have more than some woman.[22]

Reading the theme of male superiority into this verse would also be inconsistent with the Qur'ān's other teachings, says al-Hibri, including Q 9:71 that says 'The believers, men and women, are "*awliyā'*" of one another.' She points out that *awliyā'* means '"protectors", "in charge", "guides". It is quite similar to "*qawwamun*"'. But how can 'women be "*awliyā'*" of men if men are superior to women . . . How could women be in charge of men who have absolute authority over their lives?'[23]

Female obedience?

Most Muslims also read Q 4:34 as mandating a wife's obedience (*qānitāt*) to her husband and giving him the right to beat (*ḍaraba*) a rebellious (*nushūz*) wife. Wadud, however, argues that *qānitāt* refers to an attitude of obedience to God on the part of all believers and not to a wife's obedience to her husband. As she says, the Qur'ān 'never orders a woman to obey her husband. It never states that obedience to their husbands is a characteristic of the "better women" (Q 66:5)' or makes it 'a prerequisite for women to enter the community of Islam'. Significantly, the Qur'ān did not force the Prophet's wives to obey him and neither did he. Nor did he deal with occasional marital discord (*nushūz*) by abusing them (in Wadud's reading *nushūz* refers to marital disorder and not specifically to a wife's rebellion). Similarly, *ḍaraba* can mean 'to strike', 'to set an example' and 'to separate' and is not the same as *ḍarraba* which means 'to strike repeatedly or intensely'. As such, Wadud reads the verse 'as prohibiting unchecked violence against females' and therefore as 'a severe restriction of existing practices'.[24]

Hassan, on the other hand, argues that the word '*ṣāliḥāt*, which is translated as "righteously obedient", is related to the word *ṣalāḥiya*, which means "capability" or "potentiality", and not obedience'. She reads this as a reference to women's child-bearing potential, also suggested by one of the meanings of *qānitāt*, which is a water container (a metaphor for the womb). In her view, then, the verse is referring to 'women's role as child-bearers' and only if *all* the women rebel against this role, can the community as a whole discipline them. But even this does not mean doing violence since, in a 'legal context' the word *ḍaraba* means 'holding in confinement'.[25] Even if one does not agree with her exegesis, the point is that projecting wife-beating into the Qur'ān is incongruent with the totality of its teachings, which emphasise love and mercy between spouses (Q 3:21; *mawaddatan wa-raḥmatan*), and enjoin restraint and liberality even when a husband suspects his wife of disloyalty or hates her and wants to divorce her.[26]

Male superiority?

Another verse that comes under scrutiny is Q 2:228 which Muslims customarily read as establishing men's ontological superiority, even if by a single degree (*daraja*), over women. As Wadud, however, argues, the subject of the verse is divorce and the 'degree' that men have refers specifically to the rights of a husband in a divorce and is not a universal statement about male ontology or biology, or even their rights in general.

Polygyny?

Women's and feminist readings have also focused on the verses relating to polygyny and evidence-giving. Although the right to take more than one wife is typically regarded as evidence of sexual inequality and male privilege, the Qur'ān's treatment of polygyny does not confirm such an assumption if we read the relevant verse in its entirety:

> Give the orphans their property, and do not exchange the corrupt for the good [i.e., your worthless things for their good ones]; and devour not their property with your property; surely that is a great crime. *If* you fear that you will not act justly towards the orphans, marry such women as seem good to you, two, three, four; but if you fear you will not be equitable, then only one, [*aw*][27] what your right hands own; so it is likelier you will *not be partial* (Q 4:2–3).[28]

As Wadud argues, polygyny in the Qur'ān is meant solely to secure justice for orphans and is not presented as a solution for men to have children or to satisfy their sexual desires.[29] Indeed, as I argue, the Qur'ān does not distinguish between male and female sexuality or needs and there is no contextual justification to assume that polygyny is meant to cater to male libidos, as most Muslims hold. Moreover, on my reading, polygyny is restricted to female orphans themselves and not to their mothers, as some commentators argue. Even if I am wrong, polygyny is permitted only

> in those cases where the guardian feels that (1) he may be unable to do full justice to his charge outside of marriage (the assumption being that marriage gives the husband a stake in the honest management of his wife's property), and, (2) if the marriage does not do injustice to the *wife*. If there is such a likelihood . . . then a man should marry only one wife. Indeed, the Qur'ān is clear that men in polygynous situations are never 'able to be equitable between your wives, be you ever so eager'.[30]

(It is also important to keep in mind that the Qur'ān's provisions put an end to the pre-Islamic practice of marrying an indefinite number of times.)

Female testimony?

As for evidence-giving, Muslims generally read Q 2:282 – that allows two women in place of one man to witness a financial transaction – as sanctioning a 'two-for-one formula', as Wadud puts it. If this, however, were the Qur'ān's intent then 'four female witnesses could replace two male witnesses. Yet, the Qur'an does not provide for this alternative.' Furthermore, she argues that the two-for-one formula draws on a simplified view of the Qur'ān's provisions about inheritance which Muslims read as giving a man twice the share of a woman in all circumstances. 'If there is one female child, her share is half the inheritance,' however, and the principle that a woman's share is half that of a man's 'is not the sole mode of property division, but *one* of several proportional arrangements possible'.[31]

Gendered language

In addition to contesting dominant readings of specific words or verses, some scholars have also analysed the role of language in creating gendered meanings, often in ways that undermine the Qur'ān's teachings. Thus Wadud points to the problems that result from using gendered language to speak about God. The fact that the Qur'ān refers to God as 'he' does not mean, she says, that we should interpret the language empirically and literally.[32]

Moreover, as I argue, while Muslim scholars and Ṣūfīs draw on the doctrines of divine transcendence and immanence (respectively) to emphasise God's masculine or feminine attributes, there is nothing in the ideas of transcendence and immanence or even in the attributes themselves that renders them intrinsically masculine or feminine. I also argue against engendering God (even if the Arabic word for God is gendered) since the Qur'ān tells us that God is unlike anything created and forbids using similitude to describe God.[33]

Significantly, as Wadud argues, the Qur'ān does not even define human beings in terms of feminine or masculine attributes. In other words, there is no '*concept* of woman' or of 'gendered man' in the Qur'ān. As such, whatever differences exist between them cannot indicate 'an inherent value' because, if they did, 'free will would be meaningless'.[34] On my reading, while the Qur'ān recognises sexual *differences,* it does not propagate a view of sexual *differentiation*; that is to say, the Qur'ān recognises sexual specificity but does not assign it any gender symbolism.[35] Inasmuch as the Qur'ān 'does not invest biological sex with content or meaning, being male or female does not in itself suggest what it means to be either'. And to the extent that one cannot theorise a determinate relationship between sex and gender based on the Qur'ān's teachings, one also cannot ascribe sex/gender hierarchies to the Qur'ān.[36] In light of this fact, we cannot simply assume that the Qur'ān's different treatment of women and men with respect to some issues means that it establishes them as being unequal. Not only does the Qur'ān not tie its different treatment of women and men to claims about biology or ontology, but difference in itself does not imply inequality.

Rethinking generalisations

Finally, some theorists criticise the pervasive tendency to generalise specific qur'ānic injunctions which, they argue, negatively impacts women. Wadud, in particular, focuses on this practice and it is one of her distinctive contributions to insist on the need for a 'hermeneutical model which derives basic ethical principles . . . by giving precedence to general statements rather than particulars'.[37] I ascribe the tendency to generalise the particular to the way that Muslims theorise the Qur'ān's universalism and to their understanding of sacred and secular time. Typically, Muslims defend the Qur'ān's universalism by '*de* historicising the Qur'ān itself, and/or by viewing its teachings ahistorically' because they believe that historicising its '*contexts* means also historicizing its *contents*, thereby undermining its sacred and universal character'.[38] Arguably, however, it is necessary to treat revelation as occurring within time because history, 'like Scripture, provides clear "signs" and lessons of God's sovereignty and . . . intervention in human development'.[39] This intervention not only shows that there is a connection between the contents and contexts of divine speech, but it also makes the speech *relevant*. Thus, it is 'precisely the location of the sacred within history that is critical to understanding its universal nature', which is why a 'historicizing understanding of revelation' need not undermine the doctrine of its universalism.[40]

Veiling

As an example of how Muslims collapse universal principles with specific teachings, Wadud takes the practice of 'veiling' (I put the word in quotes since the word 'veil' does not occur in the Qur'ān and while *ḥijāb* does, the Qur'ān does not use it to refer to women's dress.) She argues that what the Qur'ān means to universalise is the principle of sexual modesty, and not seventh-century Arab dress. Moreover, as I argue, there are two sets of verses dealing with the 'veil' and they embody two models, one particular and the other universal, of 'veiling'.

The first instructs the Prophet to tell his wives, daughters and believing women to cast 'their [*jalābīb*] over their persons (when abroad); that is most convenient, that they should be known [as free women, not slaves] and not molested [by the] hypocrites, . . . and those in whose hearts is a disease, and those who stir up sedition in the city [al-Madīna]'.[41]

The second reads: 'Say to the believing men that they should lower their gaze and guard their modesty: that will make for greater purity for them: . . . And say to the believing women that they should lower their gaze and guard their modesty; that they should not display their beauty and ornaments except what [must ordinarily] appear thereof; that they should draw their (*khumur*) over their bosoms and not display their beauty except to . . .'[42]

Even though 'the veil' has become so over-invested with meaning that it is difficult to talk about it without misrepresenting someone's position, it is clear from these verses that some forms of veiling and the ideology that justifies them, are innovations not sanctioned by the Qur'ān. The concept of 'veil' now comprises everything from a headscarf (*ḥijāb*) to a face-covering (*niqāb*) to a body-covering (*burquʿ*), and even gloves, and the dominant ideology behind these modes of veiling holds that women's bodies are pudendal hence corrupting for the male believer to view; he therefore needs to be protected from seeing them.

By contrast, the Qur'ān not only does not mandate covering the face, or even the head and hair in so many words, but it also does not suggest that the purpose of female sexual modesty is to protect men. Rather, in the first set of verses the function of the *jilbāb* was to make Muslim women *visible* to *non-Muslim* (*jāhilī*) men as being sexually unavailable because of the prevalent practice of molesting uncovered slaves in the public arena. That is, the Qur'ān explicitly links the *jilbāb* to a slave-owning *jāhilī* society, that no longer exists, not to the dangers posed to Muslim men by viewing an unveiled body. I thus read these verses as signalling a historically specific model of 'veiling'.

The second set of verses, on the other hand, refers to a general form of 'veiling' that extends to the gaze and applies to both men and women. The counsel to lower one's gaze makes sense only if men and women are indeed free to look upon one other in the public arena. And, yet, women are often forced to cover their faces or are confined to their homes in Muslim societies in the name of adhering to an Islamic ethic. Such practices, however, 'are both a cause and a consequence of redefining and universalizing the *jilbāb*'. In the Qur'ān, the injunction to don the *jilbāb* arose from a concern with *jāhilī* male corruption, but today many Muslims view it as proof of *female* immorality and inferiority. 'This perversion of the Qur'ān's teachings results also in ignoring the critical issue of what constitutes sexually appropriate behavior for *men*.'[43] One of the challenges for Muslims today, therefore, is to derive the general principles about which Wadud speaks rather than to universalise specific injunctions addressed to seventh-century Arabs.

CONCLUSION

In summary, women's and feminist scholarship on the Qur'ān is an attempt to read behind the text in order to make visible the historical contexts in which it was revealed and interpreted as a way of explaining its patriarchal exegesis. At the same time, women's and feminist scholarship on the Qur'ān is an attempt to read in front of the text in order to establish the continuing relevance of its teachings to the lives of believers today. In the process, these readings seek to rescue the Qur'ān from the sexism and misogyny that have marred our understanding of it for so many centuries on the grounds that God is above both sexual affinity (with men) and sexual hatred (for women).

Yet, for the most part, this liberatory endeavour remains confined to the margins of Muslim religious discourse because of the structure of religious authority in Muslim societies that allows only men, and only some men at that, to speak authoritatively in God's name. For this to change, there needs to be a far-reaching reform of Muslim societies and communal consciousness since one cannot read the Qur'ān for its best meanings in repressive and antidemocratic circumstances where one cannot ask some questions openly. In the very connectedness of hermeneutical and existential questions, then, Muslims have a reason to struggle against social and gender inequalities. The example of Umm Salama beckons to us from nearly a millennium and a half ago.

Notes

1. F. Mernissi, *The veil and the male elite* (New York: Addison-Wesley, 1991).
2. Rosemary Reuther quoted in G. O. West (ed.), *Biblical hermeneutics of liberation* (South Africa: Cluster Publications, 1995), p. 110; author's emphasis.
3. A. Barlas, *'Believing women' in Islam: Unreading patriarchal interpretations of the Qur'ān* (Austin, TX: University of Texas Press, 2002), p. 20.
4. Mernissi, *Veil.*
5. L. Marlow, *Hierarchy and egalitarianism in Islamic thought* (Cambridge: Cambridge University Press, 1977), pp. 93, 66.
6. L. Ahmed, *Women and gender in Islam* (New Haven, CT: Yale University Press, 1992).
7. F. Mernissi, *Women's rebellion and Islamic memory* (London: Zed, 1996), pp. 94, 79.
8. Since none of the women theorise feminism or womanism in their own work, I also do not attempt to give meaning to their understanding of these terms.
9. R. Hassan, 'Religious conservatism', on http://ncwdi.igc.org/html/Hassan.htm, 2.
10. J. Smith and Y. Haddad, 'Eve: Islamic image of woman', in A. al-Hibri (ed.), *Women and Islam* (Oxford: Pergamon Press, 1982), pp. 135–44.
11. Hassan, 'Religious conservatism', 5.
12. R. Hassan, 'Is family planning permitted by Islam?' in G. Webb (ed.), *Windows of faith: Muslim women scholar-activists in North America* (New York: Syracuse University Press, 2000), p. 235.
13. Hassan, 'Religious conservatism', 7.
14. A. al-Hibri, 'An introduction to Muslim women's rights', in Webb (ed.), *Windows*, pp. 52–4.
15. A. Wadud, *Qur'an and woman: Rereading the sacred text from a woman's perspective* (Oxford: Oxford University Press, 1999), p. 2.
16. A. Wadud, 'Alternative qur'anic interpretation and the status of Muslim women', in Webb (ed.), *Windows*, pp. 19, 16.
17. K. Cragg, *The event of the Quran* (Oxford: Oneworld, 1994), p. 14.
18. For this meaning of *ẓulm*, see T. Izutsu, *God and man in the Koran: Semantics of the koranic Weltanschauung* (Tokyo: Keio Institute of Cultural and Linguistic Studies, 1964).
19. M. Mir, *Coherence in the Quran* (Indianapolis: American Trust Publication, 1986), p. 24.
20. Wadud, *Qur'an and woman*, p. 2.
21. Ibid., p. xiii.

22. A. al-Hibri, 'A study of Islamic herstory', in al-Hibri, *Women and Islam*, pp. 217–18; the author's emphases.
23. Ibid., p. 218.
24. Wadud, *Qur'an and woman*, pp. 77, 76.
25. R. Hassan, 'An Islamic perspective', in K. Lebacqz (ed.), *Sexuality: A reader* (Cleveland: The Pilgrim Press, 1999), pp. 355–6.
26. See Barlas, *'Believing women'*, esp. ch. 6.
27. Women whom men's 'right hands own' are thought to be war captives, slaves and concubines, all part of seventh-century Arab social structure for whose equitable treatment the Qur'ān laid down guidelines. While commentators read the *āya* as permitting men to marry such women by translating *aw* as 'or', Muhammad Asad reads '*aw*' as 'that is'. In his view, the reference is to women whom men's right hands already possess, *that is*, their spouses; M. Asad, *The message of the Qur'ān* (Gibraltar: Dar al-Andalus, 1980), p. 519 n. 3.
28. Cf. trans. in A. J. Arberry, *The Koran interpreted* (New York: Allen and Unwin, 1955), p. 100; my emphases.
29. Wadud, *Qur'an and woman*, p. 83.
30. Barlas, *'Believing women'*, p. 191; Q 4:125.
31. Wadud, *Qur'an and woman*, pp. 86–7; her emphasis.
32. Barlas, *'Believing women'*, p. 11.
33. Q 16:74.
34. Wadud, *Qur'an and woman*, pp. xxi, 35; her emphasis.
35. I borrow this expression from E. Grosz, *Jacques Lacan: A feminist introduction* (New York: Routledge, 1990).
36. Barlas, *'Believing women'*, p. 165.
37. Wadud, *Qur'an and woman*, p. 30.
38. Barlas, *'Believing women'*, pp. 50–1.
39. B. Stowasser, *Women in the Quran, tradition and interpretation* (Oxford: Oxford University Press, 1994), p. 14.
40. Barlas, *'Believing women'*, p. 58.
41. Q 33:59–60.
42. Q 24:30–1. There follows a list of male relatives before whom women need not observe these restrictions.
43. Barlas, *'Believing women'*, p. 57.

Further reading

Ahmed, L., *Women and gender in Islam*, New Haven, CT: Yale University Press, 1992.

Barlas, A., *'Believing women' in Islam: Unreading patriarchal interpretations of the Qur'ān*, Austin, TX: University of Texas Press, 2002.

Esack, F., *The Qur'an: A short introduction*, Oxford: Oneworld, 2002.

Hassan, R., 'An Islamic perspective', in K. Lebacqz (ed.), *Sexuality: A reader*, Cleveland: The Pilgrim Press, 1999, pp. 355–6.

al-Hibri, A. (ed.), *Women and Islam*, Oxford: Pergamon Press, 1982.

Marlow, L., *Hierarchy and egalitarianism in Islamic thought*, Cambridge: Cambridge University Press, 1977.

Mernissi, F., *The veil and the male elite*, New York: Addison-Wesley, 1991.

Women's rebellion and Islamic memory, London: Zed, 1996.

Rahman, F., *Major themes of the Qur'ān*, Minneapolis, MN: Bibliotheca Islamica, 1980.

Smith, J. and Y. Haddad, *The Islamic understanding of death and resurrection*, Oxford: Oxford University Press, 2002.

Stowasser, B., *Women in the Qur'an, tradition and interpretation*, Oxford: Oxford University Press, 1994.

Wadud, A., *Qur'an and woman: Rereading the sacred text from a woman's perspective*, Oxford: Oxford University Press, 1999.

Webb, G. (ed.), *Windows of faith: Muslim women scholar-activists in North America*, New York: Syracuse University Press, 2000.

Fig. 13 Folio from an eighteenth- or nineteenth-century Indonesian Qur'ān in *naskhī* script, containing Q 1:1–2:3 (Khalili Collection, QUR 133). Courtesy of the Nasser D. Khalili Collection of Islamic Art, London

13 Political interpretation of the Qur'ān

STEFAN WILD

THE QUR'ĀN AS A POLITICAL FACTOR IN PRE-MODERN TIMES

After the 'emigration' (*hijra*) from Mecca to Yathrib (later Medina) in 622 CE, the Prophet became the acknowledged leader of a community. A fair number of Medinan passages in the Qur'ān are, therefore, of direct social and political relevance. Rules of conduct in relation to other religious groups, most notably Jews and Christians, laws of inheritance, marriage and divorce, but also financial and commercial regulations, rules of warfare and the distribution of booty, retaliation, the treatment of slaves, etc., became part of the holy text. Important basic divisions, social forces and regulations that operated in pre-Islamic society are reflected in the Qur'ān. Numerous customs of pre-Islamic times were absorbed, while others were modified or abrogated. Such customs and rulings constituted the social practices in a tribal, patriarchal and partly nomadic, partly agricultural society. They were designed to shape the life of the early Muslim community under the leadership of the prophet Muḥammad. The Qur'ān legitimised the Prophet as the absolute and divinely guided leader of the Muslim community. The frequent qur'ānic exhortation 'Obey God and his Prophet!' is the central political message to the community. When they were uttered and received as divine revelations, the Prophet's words and rulings were absolutely binding and were later collected in the Qur'ān. Even when the Prophet did not claim his words to be divinely inspired, his utterances were generally held to bind the community, but were regarded as belonging to a different and subordinate text-genre.

The Qur'ān in its present form is the outcome of a process of collection and redaction. This reshaping of verses, passages and sūras into the qur'ānic text as we know it had obvious political implications. The initial spread of variant forms of the qur'ānic text was perceived by the rulers as a direct political danger to the unity of the expanding Muslim community.

It was thus deemed indispensable that the emerging Muslim liturgy and the whole of revelation should be without major internal differences and contradictions. This aim was largely but never completely achieved.

In redacting the textual form of the Qur'ān, the Muslim community had to find a compromise between different local traditions of recitation and variant written texts. The earliest qur'ānic manuscripts were inscribed in archaic Arabic alphabets. These texts offered clusters of graphemes, which were not yet specified by the diacritic dots that distinguish certain consonants. Because of their polyvalence and the complete lack of vocalisation such rudimentary textual representations could not be much more than a mnemonic support for recitation. According to the most trusted Muslim sources, the third caliph ʿUthmān (d. 35/655) established one variant of these early collections as canonical. This version became known as the ʿUthmānic text and, according to the traditional reports, the caliph ordered all competing versions to be destroyed. Certain Western, mostly non-Muslim, scholars, however, date the final canonical form of the Qur'ān later, some only at the end of the second/eighth century. In any case, since the ʿUthmānic text suffered from the same polyvalence as its predecessors, local traditions of recitation re-emerged, which it seemed politically unwise to suppress. Scholarly tradition acknowledged these variants, but limited them to seven, later ten and ultimately fourteen different strands of reading-traditions. These 'readings' were all declared to have been divinely revealed, i.e., to be of equal canonicity. While some of the reading variants are exegetically motivated, most of them have no discernible communal implication. The principle of such controlled pluralism, however, shaped the history of the qur'ānic text as it shaped Islamic exegesis and Islamic law. Just as there were fourteen different but equally canonical readings of the Qur'ān, there was more than one 'school of law', and there were many different ways of understanding a single qur'ānic verse: literal and metaphoric or allegoric, esoteric and exoteric. In a dialectical way, Islamic unity depended on a prudent dose of controlled pluralism.

It is scarcely surprising that political debates in early Muslim history were fought by referring to the qur'ānic text and that this led to differences of opinion about the text and its interpretation. The Qur'ān itself contains self-referential statements which can be called exegetical. Q 3:7 warns of people who show an unhealthy interest in ambiguous passages of the holy text: 'It is he who sent down upon you the book, wherein are verses clear that are the essence of the book, and others ambiguous. As for those in whose heart is swerving, they follow the ambiguous part, desiring dissension, and desiring its interpretation; and none knows its interpretation, save only God.'[1] The political dimension of exegetical disagreement and the resulting disunity of the Muslim community could hardly be more clearly asserted.

Probably the gravest political problem which beset the early Islamic community after the Prophet's death (11/632) was the question of who should be his successor. Deep dissensions in the community evolved well before the Qur'ān had reached its final canonical form. Those who claimed that the Prophet's cousin and son-in-law, ʿAlī b. Abī Ṭālib (d. 39/661), was the only legitimate candidate and should be his immediate successor were opposed by others with different agendas. The partisans of ʿAlī who came later to be called Shīʿīs accused their opponents – many of whom were later called Sunnīs – of having tampered with the holy text. They were said to have suppressed or changed qur'ānic verses that proved ʿAlī's special rank and supported his claim to be the Prophet's successor. According to some Muslim traditions, ʿAlī, who later became the fourth caliph, had himself written down the authentic Qur'ān as dictated to him by the Prophet. According to the same narrative, the opponents of ʿAlī had succeeded in replacing this version with another partly falsified or deficient one. While Shīʿī scholars today overwhelmingly accept the same qur'ānic text as the Sunnīs, they still insist that a number of verses have to be interpreted as sanctioning ʿAlī's claim. Moreover, the Shīʿīs (referring specifically to the Twelver-Shīʿīs or Imāmīs) never accepted either the legitimacy of the first three caliphs or the legitimacy of the caliphs following ʿAlī. In the eyes of the Shīʿīs, ʿAlī's legitimate successors were his sons and their offspring; ʿAlī and his descendants were called the Imāms. The last of these Imāms disappeared in 329/941; the Shīʿīs believe him to be concealed but still present in this world. The Imāms were, for the Shīʿīs, also the safeguards of legitimate exegesis. These differences between Shīʿīs and Sunnīs exist even today and are mirrored in their exegetical literature. As one of the principal differences between the two traditions of exegesis was the question of who was the legitimate Islamic ruler, the split between Shīʿī and Sunnī exegesis has always been, at least partly, a political one.

This seems to be the only relatively systematic and constant political split in pre-modern Islamic exegesis. Given the unparalleled dignity of the qur'ānic text, political claims to power were inevitably legitimised and supported by scattered references to qur'ānic verses. Anti-Umayyad writers liked to call the Umayyad dynasty 'the tree cursed in the Qur'ān' in a reference to Q 17:60. When the ʿAbbāsid caliph al-Ma'mūn (d. 217/833) imposed as state-doctrine that the Qur'ān was created and not eternal, he based his claim on Q 43:3, 'We have made it an Arabic Qur'ān.' Under al-Ma'mūn's successors this doctrine was reversed and the 'uncreatedness' of the Qur'ān was reinstated as dogma.

The standard format for exegetical works of the classical tradition was that of a running commentary that began with the first verse of the Qur'ān and concluded with its final one. Authors of such complete commentaries might have a definite leaning towards a mystical, a philological or a juridical interpretation, but their works were largely comprehensive and encyclopaedic in nature, if only because they proceeded verse by verse. This made them almost immune to systematic political exegesis – except for the Sunnī–Shīʿī cleft.

One of the most famous and most voluminous commentaries is that of al-Ṭabarī (d. 310/923), often considered the 'classical' model of Sunnī Muslim exegesis. It has recently been argued that a commentary by al-Thaʿlabī (d. 427/1035), which was printed for the first time as late as 2002, was even more influential.[2] Both collections were based on 'knowledge', i.e., on the learned exegetical traditions dating back to the Prophet or his contemporaries. Both commentaries list and preserve much material of which the authors do not necessarily approve. In many cases, contradictory interpretations are left open or left to the reader to decide.

Exegetical works of the classical period constitute a large but self-enclosed discipline. They rarely reflect influence from currents of thought outside the foundational 'religious sciences'. For example, in his writings the Aristotelian philosopher Ibn Rushd (Averroes, d. 595/1198) postulated a distinction between two kinds of interpretation of the qur'ānic text, one for the philosophical elite and another one for the masses of normal believers. Yet a systematic discussion of this highly charged political distinction did not appear in any of the contemporary or later exegetical works.

CONTEMPORARY POLITICAL EXEGESIS OF THE QUR'ĀN

Exegesis and the West

Much of modern Muslim exegesis of the Qur'ān is incomprehensible without an adequate understanding of the background of Western colonialism. At the beginning of the twentieth century, the majority of Muslims worldwide were under colonial rule: British, French, Dutch, etc. The Ottoman empire, the last multi-national Islamic state, had become the 'sick man of Europe'. The collapse of the empire after the First World War swept away the caliphate, the central symbol of Sunnī Islam, and brought large parts of the empire under European colonial rule. Islam was seen by many

Muslims as the only effective weapon against the overwhelming cultural, economic and military superiority of 'the West'. The interest of Western, non-Muslim scholars in Islam and particularly in the Qur'ān, was usually viewed as either based on Christian missionary projects or a strategy to undermine Muslim political resistance, to demoralise Muslims and to ensure Western colonial dominance. The consequences of the Orientalist discourse, analysed in Edward W. Said's *Orientalism*,[3] are felt until today. Muslim scholars who try to develop new approaches to the qur'ānic text face the standard reproach that they have succumbed to the political enemy. Many traditional Muslim scholars see such innovative work as simply heretical. The differentiation between religious belief and traditional religious knowledge on the one hand, and scholarly research on a particular religion or a particular religious text on the other hand, is very often understood as part of a conspiracy against Islam and the Qur'ān. From the nineteenth century until today, the relation of Muslim exegesis and Muslim exegetes with the colonising West and its scholarly methods has sparked unending discussions.

A sensitive point for many contemporary Muslim exegetes is whether a scholarly co-operation between Muslim and non-Muslim academic work on the subject of qur'ānic exegesis is desirable or indeed possible. In intra-Muslim polemics, the suspected alignment with 'the West' and the related reproach of dependence on non-Muslim 'Western' scholarship in explaining the Qur'ān are even now leitmotivs of a considerable part of Muslim exegetical production, especially in the Arab world. Muhammad Mustafa al-Aʿzami (b. *c.* 1932), an Indian-born scholar who is close to the Saudi establishment and to the Meccan-based Islamic World League, includes in his most recent book an extra chapter entitled, 'An Appraisal of Orientalism'. In this chapter he deals with 'The Orientalist and the Qur'ān'. His judgement is clear: on Islamic topics like the Qur'ān 'only the writings of a practising Muslim are worthy of our attention'. Indeed, the Orientalists 'must . . . see Muhammad as a deluded madman or a liar bearing false claims of prophethood . . . If they did not set out to prove Muhammad's dishonesty or the Qur'ān's fallacy, what would hinder them from accepting Islam?'[4] Al-Aʿzami can in no way claim to represent international Muslim scholarship, but he does stand for a widespread attitude, and one with a financially powerful support network. There are, of course, numerous Muslim scholars who collaborate with non-Muslim scholars in common projects dealing with the Qur'ān, one of the most recent examples being the *Encyclopaedia of the Qur'ān*.[5] On the other hand, many non-Muslim qur'ānic scholars remain unwilling to demythologise orthodox concepts of Islamic scripture – an idea advocated by Mohammed Arkoun (b. 1928).[6] In the shadow of the ill-fated anti-Islamic alliance between Western scholars, missionaries and colonialists in the nineteenth century they consider it inappropriate to enter an intra-Muslim debate.

Modern times have radically changed the form and content of Muslim exegesis. Sustaining continuity with the past, the traditional encyclopaedic verse-by-verse method remains alive. Such works may be revolutionary in content, but they follow the established exegetical form. There is, however, a growing number of works which follow a different model. They implicitly or explicitly reject the traditional comprehensive form and concentrate instead on only one aspect or one topic of the Qur'ān. Usually, hermeneutical discussions of the nature and meaning of the Qur'ān in modern times are eclectic and interpret only a limited number of verses or passages; they refuse to produce a complete verse-by-verse commentary. The most important qualities of this new kind of exegesis seem to be several. The first of these is a growing interest in hermeneutics and method. This emphasis often considers the Qur'ān in relation to its historical embeddedness and sees the text as well as its reception as, at least partly, historically mediated. From this perspective, there is no 'objectively attainable' interpretation of the text valid for all ages and all social settings. A plurality of non-traditional methods to understand the text is as admissible as a plurality of understandings.

Secondly, this development runs parallel to the emergence of a new class of exegetes who deal with contemporary issues, such as physicians, engineers, journalists, as well as academics trained in fields like literature, history or the social sciences. These new commentators are either ignorant of or uninterested in the classical transmission of exegetical knowledge. Some of them claim that the preoccupations of classical exegesis are too far removed from the needs of present-day society. By speaking the language of modernity, they reach a non-specialist Muslim public.

Finally, attention should be drawn to the growing importance of scholarship by non-Arab Muslims. This has begun to balance the traditional predominance of work produced by those writing in Arabic. While an excellent knowledge of Arabic is a precondition for any scholarly approach to qur'ānic exegesis, more and more Turkish, Iranian, Indian, Pakistani, Indonesian, Malaysian, South African, etc., scholars address their own communities in their own languages. There is also a growing number of Muslim academics teaching Islam and related subjects in non-Muslim societies in North America, Europe and elsewhere. Normally they can publish their work under far fewer restrictions than those faced by their colleagues in Muslim countries. They also address an increasing number of Muslims in the West. The

English language is rapidly becoming, in some ways, more important for a globalising Islam than Arabic.

Five voices can be considered fairly typical of an intentionally modernist approach. (1) Fazlur Rahman (d. 1988), a Pakistani by birth, who taught for decades in the United States, argues that contemporary Muslim scholarship on the Qur'ān faces two main problems: the lack of a genuine feel for the relevance of the Qur'ān today, which prevents presentation in terms adequate to the needs of contemporary society, and a fear that such a presentation might deviate on some points from traditionally received opinions.[7] (2) The Egyptian philosopher Ḥasan Ḥanafī (b. 1935) goes beyond criticism and identifies three important traits of what he considers to be modern exegesis, a genre which he calls 'thematic': (a) revelation is neither affirmed nor denied, exegesis begins with the text as given, without asking questions about its origin; (b) the Qur'ān is considered to be subject to the same rules of interpretation as any other text; (c) there is no true or false interpretation and the conflict over interpretation is a conflict of interest and, therefore, essentially a socio-political conflict, not a theoretical one.[8] (3) An even more radical example of political exegesis can be found in the work of the South African Muslim scholar Farid Esack. He bases his quest for a qur'ānic hermeneutic of liberation on the South African socio-political experience:

> Because every reader approaches the Qur'ān within a particular context it is impossible to speak of an interpretation of the Qur'ānic text applicable to the whole world . . . On this basis, I argue for the freedom to rethink the meanings and use of scripture in a racially divided, economically exploitative and patriarchal society and to forge hermeneutical keys that will enable us to read the text in such a way as to advance the liberation of all people.[9]

(4) The Iranian philosopher and scientist ʿAbd al-Karīm Sorūsh (b. 1945), who was for a time close to Imām Khomeini and the Islamic Revolution in Iran, distinguishes in his work between 'religion' and the 'science of religion' and concludes: 'While revelation is true and without inner contradictions, scientific investigation of revelation is not. Religion is divine, its interpretation is completely mundane and human.'[10] (5) And finally there is Mohammed Arkoun (professor emeritus at the Sorbonne), who opts for a rigorously multi-disciplinary approach, which involves the most advanced Western, particularly French, epistemological methods in order to deconstruct all types of orthodoxy. His revolutionary quest calls for structural anthropology, generative grammar, semiotics and many other approaches

to open up a new epistemology within which to read the Qur'ān.[11] His ideas are fiercely critical and universalist; sometimes they transcend the visionary and border on the utopian. Such modern and modernist positions, however, co-exist with a mainstream exegesis which largely ignores hermeneutical problems.

Major exegetical issues

Belief and knowledge

One of the first concerns of modern Muslim exegetes was their demand that the Qur'ān be read as a text relevant for modernity. A basic tenet in the nineteenth century was the assertion that the Qur'ān could not but be in accord with progress and modern science, especially the natural sciences. Sayyid Aḥmad Khān (d. 1898), an Indian reformist scholar, taught that nothing in the Qur'ān contradicted the laws of nature. Where Copernican astronomy seemed to be in conflict with a qur'ānic verse, the latter was not intended as an astronomical statement, but had to be taken metaphorically. One of his opponents, Muḥammad Qāsim Nānautvī (d. 1879), represented the diametrically opposed view, insisting that if human reason and scripture contradicted each other, reason should not be trusted.

One of the most influential commentaries of early modernity was the collective work of two pillars of reformist thought in Egypt, Muḥammad ʿAbduh (d. 1905) and Rashīd Riḍā (d. 1935), published initially in the prestigious Egyptian journal *al-Manār* (1927–35). Both authors agreed in theory that a complete commentary was unnecessary, because that work had already and often been done in an admirable manner. It was only necessary to explain certain verses. In practice, however, the *al-Manār* commentary did follow the 'verse-by-verse' model.

This *al-Manār* exegesis was characteristic of the reform movement in Egypt and also set out to prove to a colonised public that there was no contradiction between human reason and Western-dominated science, on the one hand, and the Islamic faith on the other. Wherever reason and the Qur'ān contradicted each other, reason should prevail. The commentary suggested, for example, that actions attributed in the Qur'ān to jinn might in reality be caused by microbes. Rationalist scientific thought combined with Islam would lead to social reform and progress. The *al-Manār* commentary may have been the first to invoke Q 13:11 in this sense: 'God will never change [the condition of] a people until they change what is in themselves.' In the nineteenth century, Muslim exegesis also found allusions to inventions such as the telegraph, telephone and steamships in qur'ānic verses. Some exegetes like the Indo-Pakistani Ghulām Aḥmad Parvez (b. 1903), who wrote a book on qur'ānic terminology, discovered Darwin's evolutionary theory in the Qur'ān. In the twentieth century, this list could be prolonged: nuclear power and AIDS were, according to some, also predicted in the holy text.

In the nineteenth and early twentieth centuries, most Muslim reformers deplored the fact that the rationalist Islam, which they propounded, was not the faith of most of their Muslim contemporaries. In the reformers' eyes most of these had lapsed into blind traditionalism. The genuine, but largely ignored, Islam was *the* religion of reason and it had to be re-established as the pure unadulterated Islam that existed at the time of the Prophet and of the four rightly guided caliphs. Many Muslim exegetes of quite different persuasions followed and follow this kind of retrogressive utopian idea.

The concentration on natural sciences produced a separate sub-class of commentaries, which formed the school of 'scientific exegesis' (*tafsīr 'ilmī*). This school flourished especially in Egypt in the late nineteenth and early twentieth centuries, and is still not completely extinct. Its aim was to prove that the Qur'ān already contained all natural discoveries and laws of nature, aspects of creation which European science had come to know only in the nineteenth century and later. The authors were often physicians or journalists, not scholars versed in the traditional religious sciences. The Egyptian writer Tanṭāwī Jawharī (d. 1940) wrote such a commentary in twenty-six volumes, illustrated with drawings and photographs. Whether the Qur'ān validated modern sciences, or the other way around, the subtext of these and many other like-minded exegetical works was political: Islamic culture was equal to 'Western' culture, and the Qur'ān did not block but encouraged scientific and cultural progress. A Shīʿī commentary such as that of Ayatollah Abū l-Qāsim al-Mūsawī al-Khū'ī (d. 1992), 'Prolegomena to the Qur'ān' (*al-Bayān fī tafsīr al-Qur'ān*), written by the greatest Shīʿī authority of its time, also lists some of these 'mysteries of creation'.[12] This type of exegesis was popular but far from generally admitted. Jawharī's commentary, for example, was banned in several Muslim countries.

In the case of the earlier-mentioned Sayyid Aḥmad Khān the political side of this kind of exegesis is particularly clear. After the Indian mutiny (1857), he devoted his life to a reconciliation between the British and the Indian Muslims. In his book on the 'roots of exegesis', written originally in Urdu, he developed, in advance of Muḥammad ʿAbduh, the idea that there could be no contradiction between religion and science. At the same time he showed a sceptical attitude towards miracles and supernatural phenomena. For many of his Muslim contemporaries in India, however, this kind of anti-traditional exegesis was Anglophile, pro-Western and tantamount to a pact with colonialism.

Islamic law and the state

One of the most influential modern works of radical exegesis is the voluminous 'In the Shadow of the Qur'ān' of the Egyptian Sayyid Quṭb (1906–66).[13] This has become a 'book-icon'[14] for most of the Islamist movements, doubly sacred because it was written in prison and because the author was executed – in part for the exegesis put forward in this book – and was therefore venerated as a martyr. As a verse-by-verse commentary, Sayyid Quṭb's work resembles the commentary of *al-Manār* but he takes its authors to task: he accuses Muḥammad ʿAbduh and Rashīd Riḍā of falling prey to the exegetical methods of the West, the methods of the Orientalists. Sayyid Quṭb's commentary is more than an example of an 'activist's exegesis'; it is directly anti-Western and anti-colonialist. For Quṭb, the Meccan part of the Qur'ān is a purely revolutionary message: there is one God and humans are his servants. The Medinan part of the Qur'ān is characterised by the experience of the emigration of the Prophet and his community from Mecca to Medina (*hijra*). The Muslim community in Mecca was in danger of succumbing to dissension and internal strife; therefore it had to leave Mecca. This *hijra* should be the model of all Muslim communities throughout history. A comprehensive Islamic state must be established – even by force – to give a home to the Muslim community. For Sayyid Quṭb, a key figure in the Egyptian Muslim Brothers, this Islamic state did not yet exist anywhere. All states, including existing Muslim-majority nations, lived in a condition of practical paganism regardless of whether Islam was the religion of state or not. The leaders of these so-called Muslim states had to be viewed as apostates; their rule, even if legitimated by corrupt Muslim scholars, was illegitimate. Quṭb's ideas were important for the Muslim Brothers both within Egypt and beyond, and inspired splinter groups like 'The community of declaring infidel and emigration' (*Jamāʿat al-takfīr wa-l-hijra*) and *al-Jihād*, which claimed responsibility for the assassination of the Egyptian president Anwar Sadat (1981).

Sayyid Quṭb's exegesis fights two major enemies: the powerful but spiritually bankrupt anti-Islamic West and the apostate Muslim societies and individuals, who are no better than pagan societies. In spite of his anti-Western rhetoric he does use Western concepts like 'revolution', 'democracy' and 'social justice'. His activist ideology was, and is, a source of inspiration for revolutionary Islamic movements fighting misrule and injustice in their societies. Officially banned in most Arab countries, these groups are active almost everywhere. Sayyid Quṭb's exegetical message was translated into Persian, Urdu, Turkish and English. It influenced the Iranian revolution (1979), the Shīʿī Hezbollah (*ḥizb Allāh*, 'party of God') in Lebanon and the

Ḥamās in the West Bank and the Gaza strip. His most famous political exegesis dealt with Q 5:44–7: 'If any do fail to judge by what God has revealed, they are unbelievers, . . . wrongdoers, . . . rebels.' Quṭb interpreted the Arabic word 'to judge' (*yaḥkum*) as 'to rule' and built on this interpretation a complete theory of Islamic government establishing the 'Islamic order' in one all-embracing Islamic state. All Muslims were called upon to wage jihād against Muslim leaders who failed to strive for this Islamic state. Its main characteristic was the adoption of comprehensive Islamic law (*sharīʿa*). One of the favourite slogans of the Muslim Brothers was: 'The Qur'ān is our constitution.'

Chirāgh ʿAlī (d. 1895), an associate of Aḥmad Khān, had held a completely different view on the sources of Muslim law: 'The Koran does not profess to teach a social and political law; all its precepts and preaching being aimed at a complete regeneration of the Arabian community. It was the object of the Koran . . . neither to give particular and detailed instructions in the Civil Law, nor to lay down general principles of jurisprudence.'[15] Chirāgh ʿAlī was an early proponent of one of the thorniest issues of modern exegesis, i.e., the question of if and how Islamic law (*sharīʿa*) should be adopted by the modern state. Whereas general legislation in most Muslim countries followed Western models, the Qur'ān-based *sharīʿa* laws of personal status and family law were generally applied for and by Muslims. Muslim activists like Sayyid Quṭb strove for a complete Islamisation of the body politic. And even more moderate Muslim scholars who did not insist that the whole *sharīʿa* should become the law of the state were extremely loath to admit the legitimacy of laws of personal status which openly conflicted with the letter of the Qur'ān.

A revolutionary exegetical approach designed to deal with the same problem was developed by the Sudanese engineer and member of a Ṣūfī brotherhood Maḥmūd Muḥammad Ṭāhā (d. 1985). He based himself upon a principle of classical Muslim exegesis: the distinction between abrogated verses and abrogating verses. Since the earliest periods of qur'ānic exegesis it had been generally accepted that some verses had later been repealed by divine intervention and other verses had been revealed to abrogate them. The qualified exegete was expected to know which verses had been abrogated by other verses. Ṭāhā expanded this theory and designed an exegetical model according to which the corpus of verses revealed in Mecca and the verses revealed in Medina were of a radically different character. The Meccan verses were the primary, timelessly valid revelation addressed to all humankind. As for the Medinan verses, they were revealed after the Prophet had established a political community in Medina; therefore these revelations had to compromise with existing socio-political circumstances and were not binding for all future societies. The point of this exegetical volte-face is that according to Ṭāhā the Meccan revelation taught the complete equality of sexes, the command to use exclusively peaceful means to spread the Muslim message, and the equality of all social groups, i.e., the abolishment of slavery and the freedom of physical punishment such as the amputation of hands. In Medinan verses, according to Ṭāhā, all of these principles had been diluted or abolished. But now the time had come to reinstate them. The subtext of this exegesis was the Universal Declaration of Human Rights of the United Nations promulgated in 1948. A number of states, in which Islam was the religion of state, had opposed this declaration because in some points it contradicted Islamic law, which was and is based among other things on certain Medinan verses of the Qur'ān. The radical revisionist approach of Ṭāhā would have left little room for the *sharīʿa*. He was convicted of apostasy and executed by a Sudanese court.

Another revisionist attempt is the work of a Syrian engineer, Muḥammad Shaḥrūr (b. 1938). His work 'The book and the Qur'ān: A contemporary reading'[16] was hailed – mostly by non-Muslim scholars – as a Copernican revolution in Muslim exegesis and drew massive criticism from more traditionally minded Muslim scholars. It is based on a radically new understanding of the core-vocabulary of the Qur'ān and tries to construct an unfamiliar modern Islamic discourse. For example, the 'Muslim' as mentioned in the Qur'ān is redefined and recharacterised as one who accepts God's existence, professes the creed 'There is no god but God,' accepts the day of judgement and does deeds of righteousness. The adherent of this religion is a Muslim, regardless of whether such an individual is a follower of Muḥammad, of Moses or of Jesus; or even a Zoroastrian, a Hindu or a Buddhist. Needless to say, according to Shaḥrūr's exegesis the greater part of the *sharīʿa* does not apply any more – except for strictly ritual questions like communal prayer, the pilgrimage (*ḥajj*), fasting, etc.

Literary exegesis

An important part of contemporary exegesis deals with the Qur'ān as a literary document, probably because the interrelation of the text with its linguistic and cultural setting is easy to show and is also, to some degree, operative in pre-modern Muslim exegesis. This approach started at the University of Cairo with the great liberal intellectual Ṭāhā Ḥusayn (d. 1973) for whom the Qur'ān was the first authentic document of Arabic literature. He created a scandal by calling the qur'ānic narrative about Abraham and Ishmael building the Kaʿba a 'myth'. He had to retract this statement and the issue of whether qur'ānic narratives had to be taken as historical truth remained unsolved.

His idea of a literary approach to the qur'ānic text was taken up by Amīn al-Khūlī (d. 1967), who taught at the same university and who called the Qur'ān the greatest book in the Arabic language and in Arabic literature. As such, he judged the use of literary methods to do research on the Qur'ān to be perfectly appropriate. The religious establishment at al-Azhar university in Cairo was shocked when a student of al-Khūlī, Muḥammad Aḥmad Khalafallāh (d. 1997), proceeded to write a thesis on the 'narrative genre' in the Qur'ān. The 'stories' in the Qur'ān, at the centre of which stood figures such as Noah, Solomon or Joseph, were, according to Khalafallāh, not primarily intended to relate a historical reality. Their aim was rather admonitory: artistic means were used to appeal to the emotions of the listener. In order to analyse the text correctly, the qur'ānic message had, therefore, to be seen in the psychological perspective of the contemporaries of the Prophet in Mecca and Medina. This hermeneutical principle scandalised his more traditional colleagues; his thesis was rejected and he was removed from his post at the university. Al-Khūlī's wife 'Ā'isha 'Abd al-Raḥmān (pen name, 'Bint al-Shāṭī", d. 1998) wrote several commentaries concentrating on the literary qualities of the qur'ānic language. As she steered clear of all dogmatic problems, her work did not come under any criticism from the side of al-Azhar. A later follower of al-Khūlī was Naṣr Ḥāmid Abū Zayd (b. 1940). He created the fiercest uproar in the recent history of Egyptian exegesis by publishing a book on 'The notion of the text: A study in qur'ānic sciences'.[17] The book interprets the Qur'ān as a 'message' in a communicative process. In this process a sender, a receiver and a code, in which the message is delivered, can be distinguished. Abū Zayd also insists on the importance of embedding the Qur'ān in its historical, social and mental environment of the first/seventh century. Moreover, he emphasises the dignity of the Qur'ān as a product of a process of revelation, not as a reified, miraculous object. According to Abū Zayd, it is incumbent on each generation of Muslims to decode the encoded message in and for its time. Further, he insists that the text itself is sometimes not as important as the 'direction of revelation'. By that Abū Zayd means the following: when the Qur'ān informed its listeners that a woman was entitled to a share of the inheritance, the 'direction of revelation' was to assure the woman's right to inherit, since she was, in pre-Islamic times, often deprived of any share. This 'direction of revelation' is more important than the rule that her share should be exactly half of what a man receives. In circumstances different from the social world of the first/seventh century on the Arabian peninsula, Abū Zayd argues, that share could be adjusted. The reaction of the majority of Egyptian scholars was extremely hostile. Naṣr Abū Zayd was ostracised as an apostate, and his marriage was dissolved by a court order invoking the rule that an apostate cannot be married to a Muslim woman. Faced with the possibility of being killed by a fanatic, he and his wife chose to emigrate into exile in Europe.

The case of Abū Zayd reveals the political side of all qur'ānic exegesis in countries in which Islam is the religion of state. Abū Zayd's text-linguistic approach to the Qur'ān has little direct political relevance. But the question of who is qualified to interpret the holy text is itself a political issue. Abū Zayd questioned the monopoly of the scholarly religious establishment which claims to be the sole competent source of religious knowledge. This was the core of the scandal.

Some contested exegetical issues

A widely debated, economically important aspect of political economy is whether the qur'ānic prohibition of interest must be upheld in modern times. It has often been argued that the Arabic word for 'interest' (*ribā*, e.g., Q 2:276) really meant 'usury'. The important consequence would be that only exorbitant interest rates are forbidden in a Muslim economy and normal banks can lawfully function. While some high-ranking Muslim scholars like Muḥammad Sayyid al-Ṭanṭāwī (today rector of al-Azhar) hold that 'harmless' forms of interest are in conformity with the Qur'ān, mainstream Islamic thought is strictly anti-interest.[18]

Another bone of contention is the question of polygamy, centred around Q 4:3: '. . . marry women of your choice, two, or three or four. But if you fear that you shall not be able to deal justly [with them], then [only] one.' Much modernist and feminist exegesis tends to interpret this verse in conjunction with Q 4:129, 'You are never able to do justice between wives (*al-nisā'*) even if it is your ardent desire . . .' as equivalent to a prohibition of polygamy. Muḥammad ʿAbduh did not consider these verses decisive proof for the imposition of monogamy, but held that in modern times polygamy was incompatible with the 'education of nations' and for that reason had to be severely restricted.[19]

When the al-Azhar scholar and judge ʿAlī ʿAbd al-Rāziq (d. 1966) published in 1925 his book 'Islam and the roots of authority: A study on the caliphate and government in Islam' in Cairo,[20] Mustafa Kemal Pasha and the Turkish National Assembly had a year earlier abolished the caliphate. ʿAbd al-Rāziq explained that the caliphate was not an originally Islamic institution and one of his arguments was that the Qur'ān did not mention it. In his view, Islam did not legitimise any particular kind of government. His thesis was furiously contested and he himself was ousted from his position as a judge in a religious court. But in the end, history was with him: the caliphate is today not an issue which is on the minds of many Muslim scholars.

CONCLUSION

When comparing the history of modern political exegesis in other monotheistic religions, there will be few issues without a parallel in Muslim exegesis. The main difference seems to be that Jewish and Christian exegeses have, by and large, been spared the need to develop a modern exegesis in the context of colonisation and foreign domination. The historical-critical method of text-analysis and the attempt to introduce new hermeneutical approaches still face an uphill battle among Muslim scholars. But also in this respect, problems of Muslim exegesis do not differ greatly from those of Jewish or Christian exegesis in the nineteenth or early twentieth century. Some forms of exegesis closely resemble the Catholic theology of liberation in Latin American countries. The radical politicisation of most modern exegesis explains why the attempt to find new hermeneutical methods is frequently a dangerous undertaking.

Notes

1. Cf. S. Wild, 'The self-referentiality of the Qur'ān: Sūra 3:7 as an exegetical challenge', in J. D. McAuliffe, B. D. Walfish and J. W. Goering (eds.), *With reverence for the word: Mediaeval scriptural exegesis in Judaism, Christianity and Islam* (Oxford: Oxford University Press, 2003), pp. 422–36; J. D. McAuliffe, 'Text and textuality: Q. 3:7 as a point of intersection', in I. Boullata (ed.), *Literary structures of religious meaning in the Qur'ān* (Richmond, Surrey: Curzon, 2000), pp. 56–76.
2. W. A. Saleh, *The formation of the classical* tafsīr *tradition: The Qur'ān commentary of al-Tha'labī (d. 427/1035)* (Leiden: Brill, 2004), passim.
3. E. Said, *Orientalism*, first ed. (New York: Pantheon Books, 1978).
4. M. M. al-Aʿzami, *The history of the qur'ānic text: From revelation to compilation: A comparative study with the Old and New Testaments* (Leicester: UK Islamic Academy, 2003), p. 341.
5. J. D. McAuliffe (ed.), *Encyclopaedia of the Qur'ān*, 5 vols. (Leiden: Brill, 2001–6).
6. M. Arkoun, *Lectures du Coran* (Paris: G.-P. Maisonneuve et Larose, 1982), and his 'Contemporary critical practices and the Qur'ān', in McAuliffe (ed.), *Encyclopaedia of the Qur'ān*, vol. I, pp. 412–31.
7. F. Rahman, *Major themes of the Qur'ān* (Minneapolis: Bibliotheca Islamica, 1980), ch. 12, passim.
8. H. Hanafi, 'Method of thematic interpretation of the Qur'ān', in Wild (ed.), *The Qur'ān as text*, pp. 195–211.

9. F. Esack, *Qur'ān, liberation and pluralism: An Islamic perspective of interreligious solidarity against oppression* (Oxford: Oneworld, 1997), pp. 12, 78.
10. Cf. K. Amirpur, *Die Entpolitisierung des Islam: Abdolkarim Sorushs Denken und Wirken in der Islamischen Republik Iran* (Würzburg: Ergon Verlag, 2003).
11. Cf. U. Günther, 'Mohammad Arkoun: Towards a radical rethinking of Islamic thought', in S. Taji-Farouki (ed.), *Modern Muslim intellectuals and the Qur'an* (Oxford: Oxford University Press, 2004), pp. 125–67; and also her *Mohammad Arkoun: Ein moderner Kritiker der islamischen Vernunft* (Würzburg: Ergon, 2004).
12. S. M. al-Khū'ī, *The prolegomena to the Qur'ān*, trans. and intro. A. A. Sachedina (New York: Oxford University Press, 1998), pp. 62ff.
13. S. Quṭb, *Fī ẓilāl al-Qur'ān*, 6 vols. (Cairo: Dār Iḥyā' al-Kutub al-ʿArabiyya, (1959)); Eng. trans. M. A. Salahi and A. A. Khamis, *In the shade of the Qur'ān* (London: MWH, 1979).
14. O. Carré, *Mystique et politique: Lecture révolutionnaire du Coran par Sayyid Qutb, Frère musulman radicale* (Paris: Les Editions du Cerf, 1984), p. 20.
15. A. Ahmad and G. E. von Grunebaum (eds.), *Muslim self-statement in India and Pakistan 1875–1968* (Wiesbaden: O. Harrassowitz, 1970), p. 48.
16. M. Shaḥrūr, *al-Kitāb wa-l-Qur'ān: Qirā'a muʿāṣira* (Damascus: al-Ahālī lil-Ṭabāʿ wa-l-Nashr wa-l-Tazīʿ, 1990).
17. N. Ḥ. Abū Zayd, *Mafhūm al-naṣṣ: Dirāsa fī ʿulūm al-Qur'ān* (Cairo: al-Hay'a al-Miṣriyya al-ʿĀmma lil-Kitāb, 1990).
18. T. Kuran, 'Interest', in J. Esposito (ed.), *Oxford encyclopedia of the modern Islamic world*, 4 vols. (New York: Oxford University Press, 1995), vol. II, pp. 205–7.
19. J. Jomier, *Le commentaire coranique du Manar: Tendances actuelles de l'exégèse coranique en Egypte* (Paris: G.-P. Maisonneuve, 1954), pp. 179ff.
20. ʿA. ʿAbd al-Rāziq, *al-Islām wa-uṣūl al-ḥukm* (Cairo: Maṭbaʿat al-Salafiyya, 1344/1925); Eng. trans. in Ch. C. Adams, *The modern reform movement in Egypt and the caliphate* (Chicago: University of Chicago, 1928), pp. 368–529.

Further reading

Akhavi, S., 'Quṭb, Sayyid', in J. Esposito (ed.), *The Oxford encyclopedia of the modern Islamic world*, 4 vols., New York: Oxford University Press, 1995, vol. III, pp. 400–4.

Ayoub, M., 'The speaking Qur'ān and the silent Qur'ān: A study of the principles and the development of Imāmī Shīʿī *tafsīr*', in A. Rippin (ed.), *Approaches to the history of the interpretation of the Qur'ān*, Oxford: Oxford University Press, 1988, pp. 177–98.

Baljon, J. M. S., *Modern Muslim Koran interpretation (1880–1960)*, Leiden: Brill, 1968.

Brunner, R., *Die Schia und die Koranfälschung*, Würzburg: Ergon, 2001.

Christmann, A., '"The form is permanent, but the content moves": The qur'ānic text and its interpretation(s) in Mohamad Shahrour's *al-Kitāb wa-l-Qur'ān*', *Welt des Islams* 43 (2003), 143–72.

Encyclopaedia of Islam, new ed., 11 vols., Leiden: Brill, 1979–2002.

Gilliot, Cl., 'Exegesis of the Qur'ān: Classical and medieval', in J. D. McAuliffe (ed.), *Encyclopaedia of the Qur'ān*, 5 vols., Leiden: Brill, 2001–6, vol. II, pp. 99–124.

Goldziher, I., *Die Richtungen der islamischen Koranauslegung,* second ed., Leiden: Brill, 1952.

Günther, U., *Mohammad Arkoun: Ein moderner Kritiker der islamischen Vernunft,* Würzburg: Ergon, 2004.

'Mohammad Arkoun: Towards a radical rethinking of Islamic thought', in S. Taji-Farouki (ed.), *Modern Muslim intellectuals and the Qur'an,* Oxford: Oxford University Press, 2004, pp. 125–67.

Jansen, J. J. G., *The interpretation of the Koran in modern Egypt,* Leiden: Brill, 1974.

Kermani, N., *Offenbarung als Kommunikation: Das Konzept* wahy *in Nasr Hamid Abu Zayds* Mafhum an-nass, Frankfurt/Main: Lang, 1996.

Quṭb, S., *In the shade of the Qur'ān,* trans. M. A. Salahi and A. A. Khamis, London: MWH, 1979.

Rahman, F., *Islam and modernity: Transformation of an intellectual tradition,* Chicago: University of Chicago Press, 1982.

Rippin, A., 'Tafsīr', in *Encyclopaedia of Islam,* new ed., 11 vols., Leiden: Brill, 1979–2002, vol. X, pp. 83–8.

Rudoph, E., 'Methodological approaches towards Orientalism in some recent Arabic texts', *Sharqiyyāt* 6 (1994), 71–81.

Sonn, T., 'Fazlur Rahman's Islamic methodology', *Muslim World* 81 (1991), 212–30.

Ṭāhā, M. M., *The second message of Islam,* trans. and intro. A. A. An-Na'im, Syracuse, NY: Syracuse University Press, 1987.

Troll, C. W., *Sayyid Ahmad Khan: A re-interpretation of Muslim theology,* New Delhi: Vikas Publ. House, 1978.

Wielandt, R., 'Exegesis of the Qur'ān: Early modern and contemporary', in J. D. McAuliffe (ed.), *Encyclopaedia of the Qur'ān,* 5 vols., Leiden: Brill, 2001–6, vol. II, pp. 124–42.

Wild, S. (ed.), *The Qur'ān as text,* Leiden: Brill, 1996.

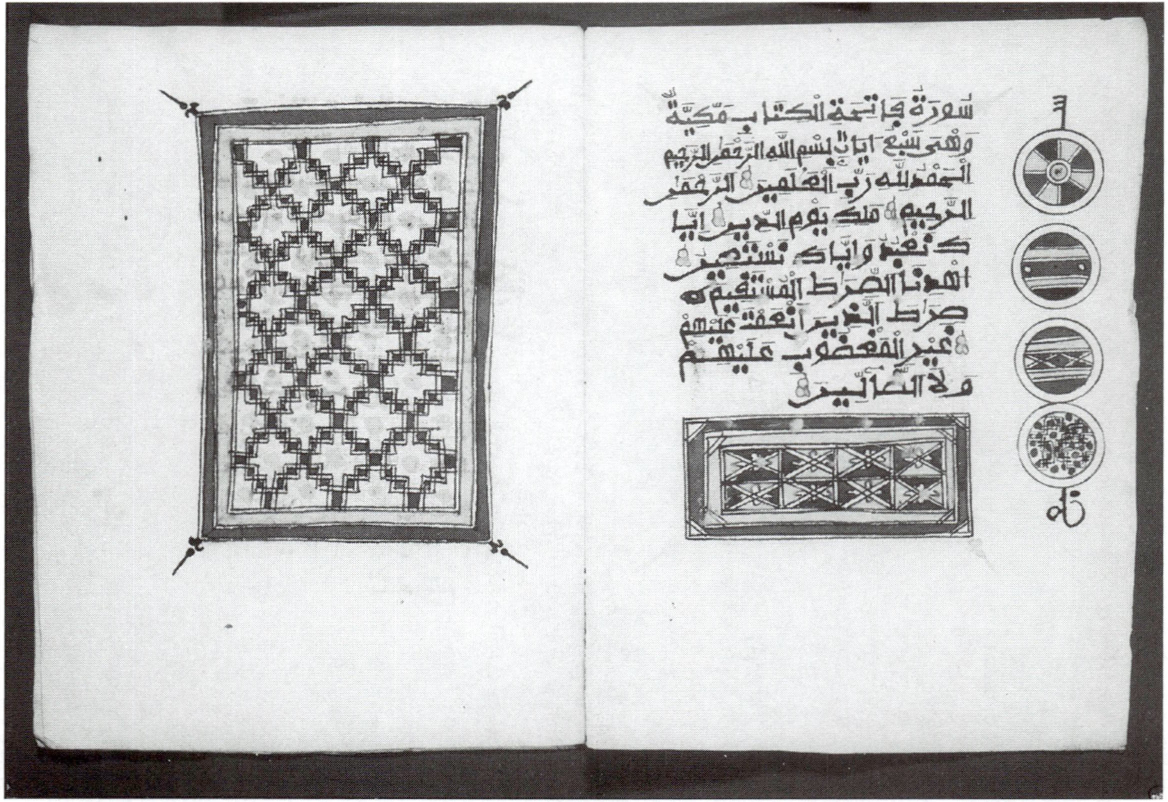

Fig. 14 Section from a nineteenth-century west African Qur'ān manuscript. Depicted here is the frontispiece and Q 1 (Sūrat al-Fātiḥa, 'The Opening') (CBL Is. 1601, fols. 1v–2r). Courtesy of the Trustees of the Chester Beatty Library, Dublin

14 The Qur'ān and other religions

ABDULAZIZ SACHEDINA

The role of religion in building bridges between communities is under greater scrutiny today than it was in the 1970s and 1980s. In the present period, religion has assumed a critical responsibility in defining the guidelines for life in a civil society in which a modern notion of inclusive citizenry is at odds with a community of the faithful defined as religiously exclusive. Monotheistic traditions like Judaism, Christianity and Islam are notoriously exclusivist in their theologies and discriminatory in their laws. In order to meet the challenge of all-encompassing secularisation, religious scholars are engaged in exploring the scriptural resources of their respective traditions to provide relevant textual references and their accompanying interpretations that can accommodate the demands of plurality in human religious commitments. This chapter undertakes to examine Islamic scriptural sources to demonstrate that the Qur'ān and its interpreters were fully aware of the need to provide principles that could guide co-existence among religious communities so that people could learn to live together in harmony and peace.

Taking pluralism to mean the acknowledgement and affirmation that various spiritual paths are capable of guiding and saving their adherents, the basic argument to be made about the relation between the Qur'ān and pluralism is that Muslim scriptures capture the real experience of the early community as it struggled to balance tolerance with exclusive truth claims that provided the nascent Muslim community with its unique identity among communities of the faithful. The guidelines that appeared for promoting religious tolerance in the classical age continue to foster the ongoing project of cultivating and furthering interfaith relations between Muslims and other religious groups. There are differing, and often conflicting, interpretations of those passages in the Qur'ān that address the questions of religious diversity and of disbelief and its negative, and even damaging, consequences for the spiritual and moral well-being of humanity. As with other commentary traditions, different periods of Muslim history have generated different interpretations of the Qur'ān in consonance with the social and political conditions that the community faced. During the political ascendancy of the Muslim empire some qur'ānic passages were used to ratify a tolerant attitude towards other faiths, and religious minorities enjoyed, relatively speaking, better treatment. By contrast, in the age of colonialism other passages of the holy book provided justifications for war against non-Muslim powers and their representatives. Certainly, the differences between traditional and modern perspectives on human nature, society and the world at large greatly influenced the way scriptural resources were retrieved and manipulated to authorise varying interpretations about the reality of religious diversity and its impact on interfaith relations in Muslim societies. A recognition of how history affects the hermeneutics of the Qur'ān often eludes both modernists and religiously oriented intellectuals. Furthermore, this lack of awareness leads to many misunderstandings and unjustified accusations about Muslims and their scriptures. Such misrepresentation about Islam and Muslims has, in turn, become the major source of fears and concerns that can easily be, and often are, transmuted into hatred and violence.

In the community of nations, the term 'pluralism' has become one of the watchwords of the new world order. It is being hailed as the reality of the world in which we live – the world that is composed of diverse cultures, systems of belief and different standards of morality, the world that can be destroyed if irreducible and irreconcilable claims to exclusive truth do not learn to co-exist. Evocation of pluralism of all sorts indicates the urgency with which the citizens of the world are exhorted to come to terms with the diversity that characterises human life on earth. The endless conflicts between Christians and Muslims, Hindus and Sikhs, Tamils and Buddhists, as well as the atrocities committed against innocent civilians, have rendered imperative the recognition of the dignity of the human being regardless of his or her religious, ethnic and cultural affiliations.

Perhaps what has triggered the need to understand the religious, cultural and moral outlooks of the 'other' today is the inescapable awareness of the plurality that the developments in international relations, transportation and communication technology have revealed. Until recently nations existed in relative isolation from each other, but today's ever-increasing forms of contact have irretrievably altered the relations between peoples and nations. These new encounters in diversity, however, have not always been friendly. In fact, as many conflicts around the world indicate, situations of diversity can become primary occasions for dehumanising the 'other'. Each tradition with its own system of comprehending religious truth, instead of learning to co-exist with other radically different positions, can become engaged in laying an exclusive claim to the same space in the salvific realm. Recognition of religious pluralism within a community of faithful promises to advance the practical principle of inclusiveness by which the existence of competing claims to religious truth need not precipitate conflict within religiously and culturally varied societies. Quite the contrary, such an inclusiveness should lead to a sense of multiple possibilities for enriching the human quest for spiritual and moral well-being in religious traditions other than one's own.

Is the promise of pluralistic religiosity one that is peculiar to the modern world of increasing interdependence, an interdependence brought about by the phenomenal technological advancements that have changed the way we think or learn about diverse faiths and cultures? Or, is it part of the human heritage preserved in classical religious discourse, which had to come to terms with comparable and competing claims of exclusive salvation both in relation to other faiths and within the community of the faithful?

As the youngest of the Abrahamic faiths, Islamic revelation had actually found expression in a world of religious pluralism, a world which it acknowledged and evaluated critically but never rejected as false. In fact, the spiritual space of the Qur'ān was shared by other monotheistic religions. The major task confronting the early Muslim community was that of securing an identity for its followers within the God-centred worldview on which different groups had claims. This involved seeking answers to some important questions. How could the community provide necessary instruments of integration and legitimisation without denying other religious groups their due share in a God-centred religious identity? Could it build its ideal public order through creating an inclusive theology to deal with the broad range of problems arising from the encounter of Muslims with other religions? And other human beings? Investigation of qur'ānic responses to these questions should provide resources by which contemporary Muslim societies could institutionalise pluralism without having to succumb to the pressure to secularise Islam.

HUMANITY AS ONE COMMUNITY

The message of the Qur'ān underscores both the universal and the particular dimensions of human societies. At the universal level the Qur'ān establishes the unity of human beings as members of a single community. At the particular level it conveys the specific identity of belonging to the community of the faithful that gathered under its founder, a prophet who came with a message from God to guide people to their total welfare in this and the next world. There is an oft-repeated reference to humankind being one community, and that God reserved the power to unite people into a single community, even after sending prophets to various communities separately: 'The people were one community (*umma*); then God sent forth the prophets, good tidings to bear and warning, and he sent down with them the book with the truth, that he might decide among the people touching their differences.' In this citation of Q 2:213, three facts emerge: the unity of humankind under one God;[1] the particularity of religions brought by the prophets; and the role of revelation, i.e., 'the book',[2] in resolving the differences that touch communities of faith. I regard all three of these declarations to be fundamental to the qur'ānic conception of religious pluralism. On the one hand, that conception does not deny the specificity of each religion and the contradictions that might exist among them in matters touching correct belief and practice. On the other, it emphasises the need to recognise the oneness of humanity in creation and to work towards better understanding among peoples of faith.

The major argument for religious pluralism in the Qur'ān is based on the relationship between private faith and its public projection in Islamic polity. While in matters of private faith the position of the Qur'ān is 'non-interventionist', asserting that human authority in any form must defer to individuals acting on their own internal convictions, in the public projection of that faith, the qur'ānic stance is based on the principle of co-existence, the willingness of a dominant community to recognise self-governing communities as free to run their internal affairs and co-exist with Muslims.

Islam, with its programme of organising its own public order, defined its goals in terms of a comprehensive religious and social-political system, requiring its adherents to devote themselves exclusively to the well-being of the community of the believers, on the one hand, and to defend its social system, on the other. Such intense loyalty to one's religion has been the reason for the survival of many nascent religious movements. Yet such loyalty has also been the source of intolerant behaviour towards those who do not share the particular tradition's exclusive claims and its concern for living right according to the true religion. The record of Islam, as a religion and a civilisation, reveals the tension between the qur'ānic recognition of pluralistic responses to divine guidance and the freedom of human conscience to negotiate its spiritual space, on the one hand; and the emerging new socio-political order constructed upon unquestionable and exclusive loyalty to the tradition, on the other. The immediate concern of the community was to alleviate this tension by limiting its jurisdiction only to the public projection of human faith, that is, to its commitment to build a just social order.

ISLAM AS A PUBLIC RELIGION

Of all the Abrahamic religions based on the biblical ethos of shaping public culture in accord with the divine will, it is Islam that was, from its inception, the most conscious of its earthly goal. In its commitment to founding an ethical public order, Islam has been accurately described as a faith in the public realm.[3] In comparison to the performance of religious-moral duties (*al-takālīf al-sharʿiyya*), which are laid down in minute detail in the *sharīʿa* (the sacred law of the community), official creed plays a secondary role in orienting the faithful to this goal. It is relevant to note that communal identity among Muslims is even today defined less in terms of a person's adherence to a particular school of theology, and more in terms of his or her loyalty to one of the officially recognised rites of the *sharīʿa*.[4] Personal faith is a private matter and, hence, inaccessible to the public for scrutiny. By contrast, the performance of the duties and rites, especially in the context of a congregation, makes one's private religious commitment objectively accessible to others in the community. The fundamental beliefs of religion form the private face of a person's religious expression and hence are subjective; the religious practices derived from one's belief, however, form the public face of a person's religious life, both individually and collectively, and hence are objective. Yet the full scope of Islamic adherence relates the private to the public in such a way that the private life is scrutinised from the perspective of its impact upon the public order.

For the *sharīʿa*, religious pluralism was not simply a matter of accommodating competing claims about religious truth in the private domain of an individual's faith. It was and remains inherently a matter of public policy in which a Muslim government must acknowledge and protect the divinely ordained right of each and every person to determine his or her spiritual destiny without coercion. The recognition of freedom of conscience in matters of faith is the cornerstone of the qur'ānic notion of religious pluralism, at the level of interreligious as well as intrareligious relations.[5]

The qur'ānic principle of freedom of conscience provided critical justification for the direction of interfaith relations in religiously plural societies. It required Muslims to acknowledge salvific value in other religions and to work towards peaceful co-existence. Consequently, contemporary Muslim historians judge the treatment of minorities within Islamic societies to have been more tolerant than that accorded non-Christians within Christian polities. They believe that without the qur'ānic endorsement of religious pluralism as a divinely ordained mystery, Muslim treatment of religious minorities throughout history would have been no different than what European history records as its treatment of the non-Christian 'other'. It is acknowledged, however, that the state policies of Muslim dynasties differed in their treatment of non-Muslim minorities. In most periods and places, the task of formulating these policies was given to the religious scholars who ordinarily allowed for maximum individual as well as group autonomy for those adhering to a particular religious tradition.

A number of instances reveal, however, that the political situation of Muslim societies had far-reaching consequences for the ways in which the qur'ānic teachings about pluralism were sometimes ignored in order to gain control over conquered peoples. The active employment by contemporary militant Muslim leaders of the violent precedents that were set at those dark moments of Muslim history points to the tension that exists between the qur'ānic principles of justice and fair treatment of non-Muslims and the demands of maintaining the political vision of an ever-expanding *dār al-islām* (the territory over which Muslims ruled). There is little doubt that in the Muslim world the struggle has been for the shape of the public culture, for the style of life that is visible in the public square. Respect for the dignity of all humans is a key element in the principle of co-existence among peoples of diverse faiths and cultures. Consequently, understanding the way the Qur'ān treats human dignity and freedom of religion is essential in evaluating the pluralistic, tolerant impulse of Islam in dealing with minorities that do not share the faith of the dominant Muslim majority.

ABRAHAMIC TRADITIONS IN QUR'ĀNIC PLURALISM

Chronologically, Islam had the advantage of being the youngest of the Abrahamic traditions and of learning from the experience of its predecessors lessons about their treatment of minorities. Since its inception in the seventh century, Islam's self-understanding has included a conscious awareness of religious pluralism as the context for its own genesis. Instead of denying the validity of human experiences of transcendence that occur outside Islam, it recognises and even confirms the salvific efficacy of such experience. This confirmation operates, of course, within the boundaries of monotheistic formulations of spirituality and morality: 'Surely they who believe, and the Jews, and the Christians, and the Sabaeans, whoever believes in God and the last day, and works righteousness – their wage awaits them with their lord, and no fear shall be on them, neither shall they sorrow' (Q 2:62). In the understanding of Muslim commentators, the Qur'ān clearly expresses itself as a critical link in the revelatory experience of humankind, a universal path intended for all. In particular, it shares the biblical ethos of Judaism and Christianity and expresses a remarkably inclusive attitude towards the 'Peoples of the Book', those communities with whom it is linked through the genesis of the first man and woman on earth. Muslims assert that the unique characteristic of Islam is its conviction that belief in the oneness of God unites them with all of humanity, because God is the creator of all humans, irrespective of their allegiance to different faith communities.

The verse about 'the people are one community' (Q 2:213) lays down the foundation of a theological pluralism that takes the equality and equal rights of human beings as a divinely ordained system. Q 2:213 also indicates that while this unity is theologically grounded within the activity of the divine, it is best demonstrated in the sphere of ethics as this functions to sustain relationships among peoples of faith. The ethical disposition is natural to human creation because it is with the help of this innate ability, the primordial nature (*fiṭra*) that God placed in all human beings, that humans acquire the capacity to deal with each other in fairness and equity. This moral orientation allows for the development of a common moral ground that can provide the basis for regulating interreligious relations among peoples of diverse spiritual commitment, enabling them to build a fundamental consensus of ethical values and goals.

THE IDEA OF EXCLUSIVE SALVATION AND RELIGIOUS PLURALISM

All monotheistic traditions attest to the belief that the salvation of individuals or of communities depends on living correctly according to the true faith. As all monotheistic traditions are also concerned with salvation, recognition of other religions implies, therefore, a recognition of their claims to impart salvation. Unfortunately, the question of whether Islam can recognise all religions as possessing equally valid ways to salvation has become obscured by the theological doctrine of 'supersession'.[6]

A literal reading of the text argues that the Qur'ān is silent on the question of whether the supersession of previous Abrahamic revelations is a necessary result of the emergence of Muḥammad. There is no statement in the Qur'ān, direct or indirect, to suggest that the Qur'ān saw itself as the abrogator of the previous scriptures. In fact, as I shall discuss below, even when repudiating the distortions introduced in the divine message by the followers of Moses and Jesus, the Qur'ān confirms the validity of these revelations and their central theme, namely, 'submission', as founded upon sincere profession of belief in God. In the classical exegetical literature, however, the discussion about the chronology of divine revelation and its applicability for subsequent communities created an important theological consequence.

The tension between the qur'ānic acceptance of the notion that other Abrahamic traditions are capable of offering salvation to their adherents and the post-qur'ānic exclusivist theology expounded by Muslim theologians is manifested in the fundamental assertion of supersession that confronts the community in its efforts to maintain healthy interfaith relations. This doctrinal stipulation derives from the question of whether the qur'ānic revelation supersedes or abrogates all other revelations. Closely related to this question is the affirmation that requires acceptance of the prophethood of Muḥammad as an inescapable requisite for salvation. Taken together these developed dogmas have led many Muslims to negate the salvific efficacy of other monotheistic traditions as taught by the Qur'ān.

Religious systems have regularly claimed devotion and salvation history exclusively for themselves. Such insistence on unique salvific authenticity has been regarded as a natural and necessary instrument for the self-identification and self-defence of a group against other absolute truth claims. Even within the Muslim community it was by no means always conceded that the direction taken by another school of thought, for instance, the Shīʿī or Sunnī, could lead to authentic salvation.[7] The salvific value of the 'other', if admitted at all, was considered to be limited, adequate only to bringing people somewhat closer to this goal by virtue of their pious and moral lives.

From the standpoint of political organisation, exclusivist claims were effective in providing a legitimating and integrative discourse that could furnish members of the community with a reliable means to assert their collective and political identity. In addition, the newly fostered socio-political identity provided an effective basis for aggression and for exploitation of those who did not share this sense of solidarity with the dominant community of believers. Rationalisation of the aggression, characterised in religious terms as a 'holy war' (*jihād*), made it possible for the more powerful community to impose its hegemony over the 'infidels' by use of force in the name of some sacred authority.

It is relevant to note that religious justifications for such hegemonic interests and methods were questionable. The Qur'ān, for instance, prohibits coercive conversion: 'There is no compulsion in religion' (*lā ikrāha fī l-dīni,*

Q 2:256). More importantly, the prohibitive social and legal structures built upon religious absolutism were totally against the spirit of those qur'ānic teachings concerning freedom of conscience. Religious justification for discriminatory politics had to be concocted through exegetical devices applied to selective scriptural references for the purpose of extrapolating from these references a convincing statement of exclusive claims to absolute truth. The use of exegetical extrapolation – and even interpolation – allowed jurists and political officials to subvert the plain meaning of the text. Additionally, spurious and politically motivated traditions (*aḥādīth*, sing. *ḥadīth*) attributed to the early community were used to defend the declaration that Islam is the only true faith, the only one that guaranteed salvation to its adherents. In this way, other religions were systematically excluded as being superseded and, consequently, their ability to lead their own followers to salvation was regarded as ineffective. In these various ways, some classical Muslim scholars of the Qur'ān attempted to separate the salvation history of the community from that of other Abrahamic faiths, insisting upon the supersessionist validity of the Islamic revelation over Judaism and Christianity.[8] In an attempt to secure unquestioning acceptance of the newer faith, these Muslim theologians had to devise terminological as well as methodological stratagems to circumscribe those verses of the Qur'ān which underscored its ecumenical thrust by extending salvific authenticity and adequacy to other monotheistic traditions.

One of the methods of circumscribing the terms of a qur'ānic verse that can be read to support toleration was to claim its abrogation (*naskh*) by another verse that spoke of combating disbelief. There are a number of classical treatises in which Muslim commentators discuss verses that are judged to have been abrogated. Modern scholarship, undertaken by some prominent Muslim jurists, however, has proven with incontrovertible documentation that not even one of the 137 verses commonly listed as abrogated has been abrogated.[9] The jurists do concede that a number of laws in the early days of the community were abrogated. But there is continuing disagreement about whether any qur'ānic ordinances were abrogated by other qur'ānic verses, as has sometimes been reported in the form of an authentic prophetic tradition (*ḥadīth*), or established by the agreement (*ijmāʿ*) of Muslim scholars, or simply deduced through reasoning. With respect to the first form of verification, all scholars agree that an argument for abrogation cannot be regarded as authentic if based on a weak tradition reported by a single authority. The reason for this is that transmission by a single authority, to the exclusion of others, is considered to be an indication of falsehood or error on the part of the narrator.

The principal problem that modern Muslim scholars face is deciding whether or not to accept the judgement of past scholars that qur'ānic verses which deal with interfaith relations have been abrogated.[10] Evidently, in resorting to the principle of abrogation, many earlier commentators and legal scholars have not paid attention to the apparent sense of the verses that have been regarded as abrogated and which they have assumed to be inconsistent with each other. As a result, they have felt free to maintain that the chronologically later verse, which speaks about initiating hostilities with the disbelievers, abrogates the tolerant ruling of the earlier one. In my estimation, this attitude is rooted either in poor judgement or in a loose application of the meaning of the term abrogation in its lexical sense. The lexical sense of this concept conveys the meaning of 'transformation', 'substitution' or 'elimination' of conditions that consequently require repeal of the earlier ruling. When this lexical sense assumes a technical signification, however, abrogation moves from text to religious tradition and becomes interpreted as 'supersession', thereby eliminating any claim by other Abrahamic traditions to salvific validity. Obviously, this interpretive move is unwarranted when one considers those verses of the Qur'ān that speak about other religions and affirm their saving capacity.

It suffices to note the evident sense of pluralism that is being conveyed by Q 2:213 which was cited earlier. Yet Muslim scholars have found it difficult to extract and accept the moral universalism that underlies this verse. This and other verses that command Muslims to build bridges of understanding and co-operation between the once united human community have been regarded as abrogated by those verses that require Muslims to fight the unbelievers (for instance, Q 9:5 and 9:29).

In speaking about humanity as one community, Q 2:213 introduces a universal message that relates all humankind to the unique and single divine authority. Furthermore, it relativises all competing claims to exclusive truth. This universal message is firmly founded upon the principle of divine unity. Humanity must acknowledge one God in order to focus on the ultimate reality, the source of all beings. This acknowledgement is the most basic statement of faith that a Muslim can make. Related to it is the correlative assertion of the Islamic creed that the unity of God underscores the unity of all who have been created as human beings by that God and endowed by the divine being with the ability to negotiate their spiritual destiny. The oneness of God, moreover, places God as the unique source of all divine revelation as communicated through the prophets. The prophets are therefore understood to be God's multiple messengers, representing in different forms the same revealed message, a message that embodies God's will for humankind at different times in history.

As Islam laid the foundation of its political order, however, Muslim leaders forged a particular kind of integrative discourse in order to furnish the believers with both a unique identity and a practical means of asserting that identity through the creation of an exclusive community based on the declaration of faith – the *shahāda* – in God and his prophet Muḥammad. It cannot be overemphasised that this political development marked a clear shift from the qur'ānic recognition of religious pluralism in the sense of a God-centred human religiosity (within each instance of historical revelation of the divine reality) and of the unity of humankind in the sphere of universal moral-spiritual advancement.

The establishment of the first Islamic society was an important phase in Muslim self-definition as a community endowed with specific salvific efficacy. Moreover, in the sectarian milieu of seventh-century Arabia early Muslims encountered competing claims to authentic religiosity as posed by other monotheists like the Christians and Jews. This encounter, which produced extended interreligious polemics, led to the notion of the independent status of Islam as a unique and perfect version of the original Abrahamic monotheism. The universally accepted understanding that emerged from these polemics was the doctrine that the qur'ānic revelation completed the previous revelations, which had had no more than a transitory and limited application. Such a notion also led to the doctrine of supersession among some Muslim theologians who argued that neither the Mosaic law intended for exclusively Jewish use, nor the Christian scripture directed towards the Children of Israel, had any claim to eternal validity.

The apparent contradiction between some passages of the Qur'ān that recognised other monotheistic communities as worthy vehicles of salvation for their adherents, and others declaring Islam to be the only source of salvation, had to be resolved in order to provide a viable system of peaceful co-existence with the competing communities. The promise of qur'ānic pluralism is expressed by offering the prospect of salvation to, at least, 'whoever believes in God and the last day' among 'those who are Jews, and the Christians, and the Sabaeans' (Q 2:62). In contrast, the Islamic absolutism of Q 3:85 asserts in no uncertain terms that 'whoever desires another religion than Islam, it shall not be accepted of him; in the next world he shall be among the losers'. Hence, the resolution of the non-pluralistic, absolute claim on the one hand, and the recognition of a pluralist principle of salvation, on the other, had enormous implications for the community's relations with other communities in general, and the 'People of the Book' in particular.

REVELATORY CHRONOLOGY AND SUPERSESSION

The principle of revelatory chronology provided theologians with the notion of supersession or abrogation which, in turn, predicated various stages of revelation throughout history. According to this principle, essentially the same revelation was delivered piecemeal, the later revelation completing and thereby abrogating the previous ones. What was overlooked in this exegetical analysis was the fact that the Qur'ān introduces the idea of abrogation in connection with *legal injunctions.* This is the context in which a legal requirement that has been revealed in an earlier verse may subsequently be altered or abrogated by a later one. Invoking abrogation in connection with Islam's attitude towards former Abrahamic traditions constitutes an illegitimate expansion of this original context. Even those classical exegetes like Muḥammad b. Jarīr al-Ṭabarī (d. 310/923), who had supported the principle of revelatory chronology to argue for the exclusive salvific efficacy of Islam and its role as the abrogator of the previous monotheistic traditions, could not fail to notice that the logical extension of this notion of 'abrogation' appears incompatible with the qur'ānic promise of rewarding those who believe in God and the last day, and work righteousness (Q 2:62). In fact, al-Ṭabarī regards such an extension as incompatible with the concept of divine justice.[11]

Nevertheless, those who accepted the concept of the supersession of pre-qur'ānic revelations depended on a ḥadīth reported in many early commentaries on Q 3:85 which, in effect, states that no religion other than Islam would be acceptable to God. This tradition purports to establish that Q 3:85, which was revealed after Q 2:62, actually nullified God's promise in Q 2:62 to those who acted righteously outside Islam. A later Sunnī commentator, Ismā'īl b. 'Umar b. Kathīr (d. 774/1373), had no hesitation in maintaining that based on Q 3:85 nothing other than Islam was acceptable to God after Muḥammad was sent. Although he does not appeal to the concept of abrogation as evidence, his conclusions obviously point to the idea of supersession when he makes a judgement about the salvific state of those who preceded Muḥammad's declaration of his mission. Ibn Kathīr maintains that the followers of previous divine guidance and their submission to a rightly guided life guaranteed their way to salvation *only before* the Islamic revelation emerged.[12]

Evidently, the notion of the abrogation of previous revelation was not universally maintained even by those exegetes who required, at least in theory, other monotheists to abide by the new *sharīʿa* of Muḥammad. While it is difficult to gauge the level of Christian influence on Muslim debates about the supersession of the previous revelation, it is not far-fetched to suggest that assertions about Islam superseding Christianity and Judaism, despite the explicit absence of any reference to these assertions in the Qur'ān, must have entered Muslim circles through Christian debates about Christianity having superseded Judaism. Christians, it was surely noted, claimed to be the legitimate heirs to the same Hebrew Bible that was the source of Jewish law. The Muslim community, with its independent source of ethical and religious prescriptions, the Arabic Qur'ān, and with its control over the power structure that defined its relationship with others, could equally afford to establish its sense of self-determination in relation to previous monotheistic traditions in a way that did not completely sever its theological connection with them.[13]

It is important to bear in mind that this qur'ānic spirit of ecumenism within the Abrahamic family, even when circumscribed through politically motivated hermeneutics, never lost its potential effectiveness in maintaining good relations with the Jewish and Christian communities. The commitment to pluralism was differently expounded, however, at various times in history as the Muslim community negotiated its relationship to the vicissitudes of power that dominated its destiny. Depending upon the social and political fortunes of the Muslim community, scholars recaptured the pluralistic thrust of the Qur'ān in varying degrees to foster or to oppose relations with the non-Muslim world. In addition, theological doctrines about the ultimate divine purpose in sending the last Prophet with a conclusive and perfect message played a significant role in shaping the rulings that determined the outcome of the community's relation to other faith communities.

Over time the Muslim community and its scholars have espoused essentially two theological positions regarding the moral and spiritual guidance that God provides to humanity in order for it to attain salvation. Those theologians who understood divine will as all-encompassing and all-omnipotent considered it necessary for humanity to be exposed to revealed guidance through the prophet Muḥammad for its ultimate prosperity. On the other hand, theologians who maintained freedom of human will endowed with the cognition necessary to exercise its volition considered the human intellect capable of attaining a godly life by choosing from among an array of prophets and their messages. It is for the most part the latter group, identified among the Sunnīs as the Muʿtazilīs, and the majority of the Shīʿīs, who conceded the continuing salvific efficacy of the other monotheistic faiths on the basis of both the revealed and the rational guidance to which the Christians and the Jews were exposed. They regarded the 'People of the Book' as responsible for acting upon their revelation whose substance has remained recognisable despite the neglect and alteration (*taḥrīf*) it has suffered. The former group of scholars, on the contrary, postulating a theory of sequential revelation, afforded efficacy to these religions as a source of divine guidance, only before the time of Muḥammad.[14]

The exigencies of modern living, which have allowed for multicultural and multifaith societies to live side by side, have inevitably made the Muʿtazilī theological position regarding the freedom of human agency to determine individual spiritual destiny a desirable theology for the cultivation of peaceful co-existence among peoples. The Muʿtazilīs maintain that human beings are endowed with adequate cognition and volition to pursue their spiritual destiny through the revealed message of God. Thus, Rashīd Riḍā (d. 1935), reflecting the Muʿtazilī attitude of his teacher, the prominent Muslim modernist Muḥammad ʿAbduh (d. 1905), maintained that human responsibility to God is proportionate to the level of a person's exposure to God's purpose through either revelation or reason. The purpose of revelation is to clarify and elucidate matters that are known through the human intellect. Basic beliefs like those about the existence of God and the last day are necessarily known through it. Prophets come to confirm what is already recognised by the human intellect. Accordingly, there is an essential unity in the beliefs of 'the people of divine religions' (*ahl al-adyān al-ilāhiyya*) who have been exposed to divine guidance and who, as well, are innately disposed to believe in God and the last day, and to do good works.[15] Moreover, God's promise applies to all who have this divine religion, regardless of formal religious affiliation, for God's justice does not allow favouring one group while ill-treating another. To all peoples who believe in a prophet and in the revelation he has brought to them God has promised that 'their wages await them with their lord, and no fear shall there be on them, neither shall they sorrow' (Q 2:62). Rashīd Riḍā does not stipulate belief in the prophethood of Muḥammad for Jews and Christians desiring to be saved, and, hence, implicitly maintains the salvific validity of both the Jewish and Christian revelations.[16]

Among the Shīʿī commentators, Muḥammad Ḥusayn Ṭabāṭabāʾī (d. 1982), following well-established Shīʿī opinion from the classical age, rejected the assertion that the divine promise in Q 2:62 had been abrogated.

In fact, he did not support the supersession of pre-qur'ānic revelations even when he deemed them distorted and corrupted by their followers. Nevertheless, he regarded the ordinances of the Qur'ān as abrogating the laws extracted from the two earlier scriptures. Evidently Ṭabāṭabā'ī confined abrogation to its juridical meaning where it signifies 'repeal' of an earlier ordinance by a fresh ruling because of the former's inapplicability in changed circumstances. In connection with those passages like Q 2:62 that supported the ecumenical thrust of the Qur'ān, he rebuffed the opinion held by some Muslims that God promises salvation to particular groups because they bear certain names. On the contrary, anyone who holds true belief and acts righteously is entitled to God's reward and protection from punishment, as promised in Q 5:9, 'God has promised those of them who believe and do good, forgiveness and a great reward.'[17]

Modern commentators like Rashīd Riḍā and Ṭabāṭabā'ī assert the qur'ānic spirit of humanity's God-centred identity in which the external form of religion is relegated to the inward witness of the divine that defies any exclusive and restrictive definition. In fact, religious pluralism is seen by the Qur'ān as fulfilling a divine purpose for humanity. That purpose is the creation of an ethical public order, for the attainment of which, before even sending the prophets and the revelation, God created an innate disposition in human beings (Q 91:8), a capacity of distinguishing good from evil. This divine gift requires humans, regardless of their affiliations to particular religious paths, to live with each other and work towards justice and peace in the world. The Qur'ān in the following verse admonishes humankind 'to compete with each other in good work': 'For every one of you [Jews, Christians, Muslims], we have appointed a path and a way. If God had willed, he would have made you but one community; but that [he has not done so in order that] he may try you in what has come to you. So compete with one another in good works' (Q 5:48).

CONCLUSION

It was critical for the Muslim tradition to work out the tension between the apparently pluralistic impulse of the Qur'ān founded upon the spiritual equality and moral ability of each and every person on earth, and the reality of Muslim political power intent on conquering and converting all humanity to its universal faith. The exegetical materials examined for this chapter reveal this tension in dealing with those verses that promise salvation to all peoples who believe in God and the final resurrection and who perform good acts, in contrast to those verses that require people to accept Islam as the only religion that can save. Within this theology, the verses that are inclusive limit this inclusiveness to other monotheists; the fate of non-monotheistic traditions, such as particular south Asian and east Asian religions, is not mentioned anywhere in the Qur'ān.

On the basis of the innate moral capacity that is given to all human beings 'to compete with one another in good works', it is even possible to argue that ultimate salvation, according to the Qur'ān, depends on good works. Good works, to be sure, have always been linked to faith, at least when the Qur'ān speaks about Muslims. But, in order to resolve the problem of hostility among the Abrahamic family, the qur'ānic prescription separates faith from action so as to preclude the interference of any human institutions in matters of religious faith and the commitment that is due to God as the creator and master of the final day of judgement. At the same time, it outlines a common framework founded upon ethical responsibility in which all humans share equal responsibility to uphold justice and equity on earth. In other words, the foundation of a pluralistic society is not dependent upon an inclusive theology. In reality, however, such unity is hard to realise because of the vested interests of each faith community in maintaining its unique identity. Yet the admonition to forge a common moral front to do good for everyone as members of human society can function as the most important principle to create unity of purpose for the betterment of human society. In this sense, I would argue that qur'ānic pluralism rests upon an inclusive, universal morality that works for the good of all humans as humans. Regardless of one's affiliation with a specific religious or cultural group, according to the Qur'ān, human beings endowed with moral cognition must work together to create a just society. Hence, the Abrahamic and non-Abrahamic traditions do not differ about the need to respect other religions while not abandoning one's own faith. This is the qur'ānic paradigm of religious pluralism in which each community retains its internal integrity while accepting the dignity of all humans as equal in creation and as equally endowed with the knowledge of and the will to do good.

Notes

1. Muslim commentators have argued about the period of time when humankind was one community. Was it the community that lived between Adam and Noah? Were they united during that time and subsequently became divided? Since there is no indication in the Qur'ān or the tradition of the time of the unity or of the time when the first discord occurred in that community, I read the passage as presenting a matter open for reflection and interpretation. For the views of different commentators in the classical as well as modern periods, see M. M.

Ayoub, *The Qur'ān and its interpreters*, 2 vols. (Albany: SUNY Press, 1984), vol. I, pp. 215–16.

2. A majority of the Muslim commentators believe that the introduction in the Qur'ān of the term 'the book' in singular form, in spite of the plurality of the prophets, suggests the generic nature of revelation which shares an essential unity and functions as a source of spiritual guidance and prescriptive conduct for organising communities in regulating their inter-communal affairs, i.e., 'touching their differences'. See ʿAbdallāh b. ʿUmar al-Bayḍāwī, *Anwār al-tanzīl* (Cairo: Aḥmad Najīb, 1887), p. 45; Muḥammad Ḥusayn Ṭabāṭabā'ī, *al-Mīzān fī tafsīr al-Qur'ān*, 20 vols. (Beirut: Mu'assasat al-Aʿlāmī, 1972), vol. II, pp. 128–9.
3. M. G. S. Hodgson, *The venture of Islam: Conscience and history in a world civilization*, 3 vols. (Chicago: University of Chicago Press, 1977), vol. I, p. 336.
4. The term 'rite' or 'legal school' is the translation of the Arabic word *madhhab* – a system of rules that cover all aspects of the human spiritual and moral obligations (*takālīf*, plural of *taklīf*) that a Muslim must carry out as a member of the community. Four *madhhab*s, Mālikī, Ḥanafī, Shāfiʿī and Ḥanbalī, were ultimately accepted as legitimate by the Sunnīs, while the Shīʿīs formulated and followed their own rite, known as Jaʿfarī.
5. I have treated the matter of freedom of conscience from the qur'ānic point of view in my earlier work: 'Liberty of conscience and religion in the Qur'ān', in A. Sachedina, D. Little and J. Kelsay (eds.), *Human rights and the conflict of cultures: Western and Islamic perspectives on religious liberty* (Columbia, SC: University of South Carolina Press, 1988), pp. 53–100; see also for further details of the concept, my *The Islamic roots of democratic pluralism* (New York: Oxford University Press, 2001).
6. The Arabic term *naskh* actually means 'abrogation' or 'repeal'. Although its usage is limited to legal matters, it has been extended to include 'abrogation' of the pre-qur'ānic revelations. For the full discussion of 'abrogation' as 'supersession' see J. D. McAuliffe, *Qur'ānic Christians: An analysis of classical and modern exegesis* (Cambridge: Cambridge University Press, 1991); see also her 'The abrogation of Judaism and Christianity in Islam: A Christian perspective', *Concilium* 3 (1994), 154–63.
7. Historically, Muslims, like other religious groups, have demonstrated a far stronger attitude of intolerance towards dissenters within their own ranks than to those outside the faith. Muslim history is replete with instances of intra-religious violence, not only between the majoritarian Sunnī and the minority Shīʿī communities, but also among the Sunnī adherents of different legal rites, such as the Ḥanafī and the Ḥanbalī schools. See B. Braude and B. Lewis (eds.), *Christians and Jews in the Ottoman empire: The functioning of a plural society* (New York: Holmes and Meier, 1982), pp. 1–34; G. R. Elton, 'Introduction', in W. J. Shields (ed.), *Persecution and toleration* (Oxford: Basil Blackwell, 1984), pp. xiii–xv.
8. McAuliffe, *Qur'ānic Christians*, has done extensive work on the qur'ānic verses dealing with Muslim perceptions of Christians through an analysis of the exegetical works produced by both Sunnī and Shīʿī commentators from the classical to the modern period. Her study concludes that belief in the prophethood of Muḥammad remained an important element in deciding whether to afford

non-qur'ānic 'Peoples of the Book' a share in salvation. Despite this predominantly exclusivist soteriology, however, there have been Muslim commentators, especially in the modern period of interfaith hermeneutics, who have regarded the promise in Q 2:62 as still important in constructing an inclusive theology founded upon belief in God, the hereafter and right action as the dominant criteria in attaining salvation.

9. al-Sayyid Abū l-Qāsim al-Mūsawī al-Khū'ī, *The prolegomena to the Qur'ān*, trans. with an introduction by A. Sachedina (New York: Oxford University Press, 1998), pp. 186–253; also, J. Burton, 'Introductory essay: "The meaning of naskh"', in J. Burton (ed. and com.), *Abū 'Ubayd al-Qāsim b. Sallām's K. al-Nāsikh wa-l-mansūkh* (Suffolk: St Edmundsbury Press, 1987), pp. 1–45.
10. For the classical exegetical formulations that support the intolerant and exclusivist attitude towards the 'Peoples of the Book' based on the notion of 'abrogation' of the tolerant Q 2:62 by Q 3:85, see their compilation in Abū Ja'far Muḥammad b. Jarīr al-Ṭabarī, *Jāmi' al-bayān*, 16 vols. (Cairo: Dār al-Ma'ārif, 1954), vol. II, pp. 155–6. Al-Ṭabarī cites the exclusivist opinions and then rejects the view that God will condemn those who had lived in faith and acted righteously because the commentator finds this incongruent with the divine promise; 'Imād al-Dīn Ismā'īl b. 'Umar b. Kathīr, *Tafsīr al-Qur'ān al-'aẓīm*, 8 vols. (Beirut: Dār al-Andalus, 1966), vol. I, p. 103, limits salvation to those 'People of the Book' who lived before the prophethood of Muḥammad; in his early twentieth-century commentary, Rashīd Riḍā, *Tafsīr al-Qur'ān al-ḥakīm al-shahīr bi-Tafsīr al-Manār*, 12 vols. (Beirut: Dār al-Ma'rifa, 1990), vol. VI, p. 479, grudgingly concedes the validity of salvation for the 'People of the Book'.
11. al-Ṭabarī, *Jāmi' al-bayān*, ad loc.
12. Ibn Kathīr, *Tafsīr*, vol. I, p. 103.
13. For the theological problems faced by early Christianity in declaring its originality and working out its relation to Judaism, see M. Simon, *Verus Israel: A study of the relations between Christians and Jews in the Roman empire (AD 135–425)* (New York: Oxford University Press, 1986), in particular ch. 3.
14. Ibn Kathīr, *Tafsīr*, vol. I, p. 180; vol. II, p. 67.
15. Riḍā, *Tafsīr al-Manār*, vol. I, p. 339.
16. Ibid., p. 336.
17. Ṭabāṭabā'ī, *al-Mīzān*, vol. I, p. 193.

Further reading

Ayoub, M. M., *The Qur'ān and its interpreters*, 2 vols., Albany: SUNY Press, 1984.

al-Bayḍāwī, 'Abdallāh b. 'Umar, *Anwār al-tanzīl*, Cairo: Aḥmad Najīb, 1305/1887.

Braude, B. and B. Lewis (eds.), *Christians and Jews in the Ottoman empire: The functioning of a plural society*, New York: Holmes and Meier, 1982.

Burton, J., 'Introductory essay: "The meaning of naskh"', in J. Burton (ed. and com.), *Abū 'Ubayd al-Qāsim b. Sallām's K. al-Nāsikh wa-l-mansūkh*, Suffolk: St Edmundsbury Press, 1987, pp. 1–45.

Elton, G. R., 'Introduction', in W. J. Shields (ed.), *Persecution and toleration*, Oxford: Basil Blackwell, 1984, pp. xiii–xv.

Hodgson, M. G. S., *The venture of Islam: Conscience and history in a world civilization*, 3 vols., Chicago: University of Chicago Press, 1977.

Ibn Kathīr, ʿImād al-Dīn Ismāʿīl b. ʿUmar, *Tafsīr al-Qur'ān al-ʿaẓīm*, 8 vols., Beirut: Dār al-Andalus, 1966.
al-Khūʾī, al-Sayyid Abū l-Qāsim al-Mūsawī, *The prolegomena to the Qur'ān*, trans. and intro. A. Sachedina, New York: Oxford University Press, 1998.
McAuliffe, J. D., 'The abrogation of Judaism and Christianity in Islam: A Christian perspective', *Concilium* 3 (1994), 154–63.
Qur'ānic Christians: An analysis of classical and modern exegesis, Cambridge: Cambridge University Press, 1991.
Rashīd Riḍā, *Tafsīr al-Qur'ān al-ḥakīm al-shahīr bi-Tafsīr al-Manār*, 12 vols., Beirut: Dār al-Maʿrifa, 1990.
Sachedina, A., *The Islamic roots of democratic pluralism*, New York: Oxford University Press, 2001.
'Liberty of conscience and religion in the Qur'ān', in A. Sachedina, D. Little and J. Kelsay (eds.), *Human rights and the conflict of cultures: Western and Islamic perspectives on religious liberty*, Columbia, SC: University of South Carolina Press, 1988, pp. 53–100.
Simon, M., *Verus Israel: A study of the relations between Christians and Jews in the Roman empire (AD 135–425)*, New York: Oxford University Press, 1986 (in particular ch. 3).
al-Ṭabarī, Abū Jaʿfar Muḥammad b. Jarīr, *Jāmiʿ al-bayān ʿan ta'wīl al-Qur'ān*, 16 vols., Cairo: Dār al-Maʿārif, 1954.
Ṭabāṭabāʾī, Muḥammad Ḥusayn, *al-Mīzān fī tafsīr al-Qur'ān*, 20 vols., Beirut: Mu'assasat al-Aʿlāmī, 1972.

Qur'ān citation index

General index

al-'Abbās b. 'Abd al-Muṭṭalib 181
'Abd al-Ḥamīd b. Yaḥyā 228
'Abd al-Jabbār al-Hamadhānī 154, 190
'Abd al-Malik 48, 163, 165, 212
'Abd al-Raḥmān, 'Ā. 285
'Abd al-Raḥmān b. Thābit 45
'Abd al-Rāziq, 'A. 286
'Abd al-Razzāq 48
'Abdallāh b. Abī Sarḥ 43
'Abdallāh b. Mas'ūd 45, 47, 48, 49, 50, 117, 145, 146, 148, 149, 181, 184
'Abdallāh b. Mu'āwiya 173
'Abdallāh b. Rawāḥa 127–8
'Abdallāh b. al-Zubayr 45
'Abdallāh Muḥammad b. Aḥmad b. Sālim al-Baṣrī 193
Abdel Haleem, M. S. 16
'Abduh, M. 190, 280, 281, 282, 286, 304
Abraham 27, 87, 106, 171, 262, 284
  Abrahamic faiths 293, 296, 297, 298, 299, 300, 301, 302, 303, 306
abrogation 43, 62, 184, 187–8, 195, 204n.27, 217–18, 273, 283
  intra-qur'ānic 187, 299–300, 304, 307n.6, 308n.10
  of previous scriptures *see* supersession
Abū 'Alā' al-Ma'arrī 228
Abū 'Amr b. al-'Alā' 48, 52, 149, 150, 151, 153, 213
Abū 'Amr al-Shaybānī 213
Abū Aswad al-Du'alī 48
Abū Bakr 31, 44, 45, 46, 62, 63
Abū Bakr Muḥammad b. 'Abdallāh al-Ma'āfirī; *see* Ibn al-'Arabī
Abū l-Dardā' 44
Abū l-Ḥārith al-Layth 51
Abū Ḥayyān al-Andalūsī [al-Gharnāṭī] 46, 215
Abū Ḥudhayfa 46
Abū Isḥāq al-Ṣābī 228
Abū Ja'far Yazīd b. al-Qa'qā' 51
Abū Jahl 181, 185, 204n.13
Abū Kurayb Muḥammad b. al-'Alā' 191–2
Abū Mūsā al-Ash'arī 47
Abū Muslim 173
Abū Nuwās 227
Abū l-Qāsim al-Balkhī 44
Abū Sa'īd 174, 175
Abū Ṣāliḥ 181
Abū Sufyān 29
Abū Ṭālib 24, 25, 26
Abū 'Ubayda 213
Abū Zahra, M. 126
Abū Zayd 44
Abū Zayd, N. Ḥ. 285–6
'Ād 106
Adam 82, 192, 211, 259, 260, 306n.1
Adonis 131, 227
adultery 216
Afghanistan 164, 167
Africa
  north 150, 173, 194
  north-west 150, 151, 152
  south 279
  west 150
Aḥmad b. Jubayr al-Kūfī 50
Aḥmad Yasawī shrine 171
Ahmad, S. B. 201
Ahmed, L. 258
aḥrūf 51, 117; *see also ḥurūf*; readings
'Ā'isha 27, 29, 30, 31, 218, 256
al-Akhfash al-Awsaṭ 49